# THEORIES OF ETHICS

A Study in Moral Obligation

TO LUCYLE

# THEORIES OF ETHICS

## A Study in Moral Obligation

### By W. H. WERKMEISTER

*Director*
*School of Philosophy*
*University of Southern California*

**JOHNSEN PUBLISHING COMPANY**

LINCOLN, NEBRASKA

# Table of Contents

# Introduction

Ethics, Henry Sidgwick wrote, is "the science or study of what ought to be, so far as this depends upon the voluntary action of individuals" (9:4); it "imparts or seeks the most perfect knowledge possible of the rightness or goodness of voluntary actions or their results" (9:4). These statements appear to be clear and to the point; actually, however, they are not unambiguous but require clarification in at least two respects.

First, it is important to distinguish between *practical morality* or the development of specific moral codes, and *theoretical ethics* or the analysis and interpretation of basic concepts. Important as the development of moral codes may be, it is not of primary concern to the philosopher. We may grant, of course, that the ultimate aim of all ethics is practical, for "we desire moral knowledge in order to act on it" (9:4; *10*:122); but the immediate and most fundamental concern of theoretical ethics is analytic and interpretative. The ethicist examines and seeks to elucidate the meanings of such key concepts as *good, right, ought,* and their respective opposites, derivatives, and interrelations, and he attempts to explicate the criteria underlying all moral judgments. This work has practical as well as theoretical priority because without it the development of moral codes must remain a blind and uncritical dogmatism which, in itself, is a hindrance to moral growth.

Secondly, the very meaning of Sidgwick's reference to "the rightness or goodness of voluntary actions or their results" requires clarification, for even a cursory examination of the statement discloses important ambiguities. For instance, are "rightness" and "goodness" synonymous terms? Do both pertain to "results" as well as to "actions"; or does "goodness" pertain to "results," whereas "rightness" pertains to "actions" only? Are both terms elementary and non-derivative; or does the "rightness" of an "action" follow from the "goodness" of the "results"? More basically still: Do "rightness" and "goodness" have cognitive meaning (in the sense in which "rectangularity" and "punctuality" have such meaning); or are they merely emotive expressions signifying nothing but states of feeling or attitudes of approval on the part of the speaker?—To ask these questions is to plunge at once into the complex and basic problems of theoretical ethics. Sidgwick's original statement is therefore not so much a definition of ethics as it is an initial step in the delimitation of ethical analysis; and we shall here regard it as such.

In the chapters which follow we shall leave aside all problems of applicability and moral codes and shall concern ourselves only with questions of analysis and, therefore, with theoretical ethics. We do not intend to prescribe concrete rules of conduct but hope, instead, to clarify the concepts and principles which are foundational to all such rules. Historically, the questions we have raised in the preceding paragraph (and questions which are related to them) have been answered in radically different ways; and so numerous are the answers that it will be impossible for us to consider them all.[1] However, certain approaches to the problems in question stand out as landmarks in the field of theoretical ethics. A careful analysis of these approaches will contribute much to our understanding of the crucial issues involved, and to a clarification of our own point of view. We shall therefore undertake such an analysis. And since our aim is posi-

---

[1] For general surveys see Tsanoff (11), and Hill (5).

tive and constructive rather than negative and critical only, the book as a whole has been so arranged that the discussions which follow may be regarded as steps in an over-all dialectic which, centering around the key concepts and criteria of moral conduct, is part of an effort to clear the ground for a new orientation with respect to morals. It is part of an introduction to a general theory of value.

Lest my reference to the outstanding landmarks in the field of theoretical ethics be misunderstood, I hasten to add that, in view of the multitude of interrelated questions which cut across the whole realm of ethics and which each theory must answer from its own perspective, an absolute distinction between various types of theories is impossible. Examination readily reveals that the respective perspectives overlap in manifold ways and that seemingly irreconcilable theories are in remarkable agreement in many respects. Let me illustrate this point.

In a recent article entitled "Moral Philosophy at Mid-Century," W. K. Frankena classifies the prevailing ethical theories as naturalism, intuitionism, and noncognitivism. He then suggests that we may state and compare these rival theories in a rough way by taking three metaethical statements as the basis for our comparison:

"(1) Ethical sentences are cognitive and true or false.
(2) Ethical terms do not name any unique or simple non-natural characteristics.
(3) Ethical sentences are nondescriptive" (3:45).

Examination will now show, according to Frankena, that "naturalism affirms (1) and (2) and denies (3)"; that "intuitionism affirms (2) and (3), denying (1)" (3:45). "Put otherwise, naturalism and intuitionism agree on (1) as against noncognitivism; intuitionism and noncognitivism agree on (3) as against naturalism; and naturalism and noncognitivism agree on (2) as against intuitionism" (3:45).

On the fact of it, all this seems clear and precise; [2] but the

_____
[2] For discussions of specific difficulties involved in Frankena's simple schema see 4 and 7.

precision vanishes when we realize that Frankena's schema of classification rests upon semantic considerations only, and that it completely disregards a variety of non-semantical questions which any ethicist may legitimately ask, and which, as a matter of historical fact, have been and are now being asked in the field of ethics. Browne, for instance, points out that at least four distinct types of questions are relevant to discussions in ethics (2:190), namely: (1) Questions of psychology, i.e., questions which deal either with human nature generally or with human motivation, and questions which deal with "the psychological processes by which the moral judgments of most people are, as a matter of fact, ordinarily formed." (2) Questions of semantics —questions, that is, which pertain to the meaning of such terms as "good," "right," and "duty." (3) Questions of logic and epistemology: "Is knowledge of objective truth in moral matters possible?" "How can I discover what I ought to do?" "What is the *valid* procedure to follow in moral judgments?" (4) Questions of ethics proper: "What ought I to do?" "What kinds of act are right?" "In what does my duty consist?"

It is possible, of course, that specific answers to some of these questions have the effect of eliminating all other questions from consideration. Thus, if, at the semantic level, we hold that ethical words are meaningless in a cognitive or descriptive sense, then "all questions of the logic and epistemology of ethics, as well as those of ethics proper, must be brushed aside" (2:190); for "there can be no question about what I ought to do, or how I can find this out, if the statement that I ought to do so-and-so has no significance" (2:190). Again, if, at the epistemological level, we maintain that "the rightness or wrongness of each particular act is known immediately by intuition" (2:190), then we have no longer any need for logic. By and large it will be found, however, that "an answer to one type of question involves no commitment with reference to the others" (2:191), and that therefore any two theories which differ fundamentally in their answers to one type of questions may yet be in perfect agreement in their answers to other types of questions. Sidgwick's intuitionist epistemology and Hume's approbative epistemology, for example, are both combined with an utilitarian answer to the ethical question (2:190); and, at the psychological level, any utilitarian may or may not explain the fact that most people are not utilitarians as being "the effect of the pernicious influence of their emotions, or of their cultural environment" (2:197).

If the distinction (given above) of various types of questions in the field of ethics hints at all at a correct interpretation of the complex interrelations of different theories—and I believe that it does—, then it is obvious that the customary classification of ethical theories as naturalism, intuitionism, rationalism, utilitarianism, approbationism, noncognitivism, self-realizationism, and so on, involves a confusion of levels of discourse. The classification does not rest upon one and only one principle of division, and the theories in question are therefore by no means incompatible alternatives.

The confusion can be avoided only if we keep the different types of questions clearly separated and proceed with our classification of theories with this separation in mind. It will then be obvious that a first division may be made at the semantic level. Do ethical words, such as "good," "right," and "duty," have cognitive (or descriptive) meaning? If the answer to this question is negative, ethical theories must be classified as *noncognitive;* if the answer is affirmative, the theories are *cognitive.* The noncognitive views include various forms of emotive and approbative theories, which differ one from another at the level of psychological interpretation, but for which epistemological considerations are essentially irrelevant. The cognitive theories, on the other hand, may be divided at the epistemological level into *empiricism, rationalism,* and *intuitionism;* but the ethical contents of these theories, i.e., the specific conceptions of good, right, and duty, may well overlap. However, at the level of ethics proper, each one of the epistemological positions may, in turn, be subdivided into *teleological* and *deontological* theories; and under each of these headings further distinctions may be made. A teleological theory, for example, may be *naturalistic* or *nonnaturalistic* depending on how the term "good" is defined;

and a deontological theory may emphasize either the *motive* for, or the *character* of, an act.

It may be argued, of course, that even this schema for the classification of ethical theories is inadequate; and there is truth in such an argument. However, at two levels at least the alternatives given are exhaustive as well as exclusive. Thus, ethical theories in general are either cognitive or noncognitive, and teleological theories are either naturalistic or nonnaturalistic. Contradictories allow no additional alternatives, and if any given theory wavers indecisively between the possible alternatives, such wavering merely indicates logical defects in the theory itself.

At the epistemological level ethical theories are no worse off than are theories of knowledge in any field of inquiry. Empiricism, rationalism, and intuitionism are rather well defined historical positions. The terms, therefore, serve well as classificatory categories when we deal with ethical theories of the past. That they indicate supplementary aspects of cognition rather than mutually exclusive alternatives merely shows that it is necessary to approach the problems of ethical theories with a new vision of cognitive possibilities.

A similar situation prevails at the level of ethics proper, where teleological and deontological theories are not necessarily mutually exclusive alternatives. Historically the facts are clear. As Ross puts it: "On the one hand there is a group of opinions involving the closely connected ideas of duty, of right and wrong, of moral law or laws, of imperatives. On the other hand, there are opinions involving the idea of goods or ends to be aimed at. In the one case the idea of human life is envisaged as obedience to laws; in the other as the progressive satisfaction of desire and attainment of ends" (*8*:3). Examination of the facts shows, however, that the conflict between deontological and teleological "opinions" is more apparent than real, that ethical thought and practice require both perspectives, and that each position, consistently developed, implies the other (*1*:765). From the vantage point of today, therefore, the conflict of deontological and teleological interpretations merely argues for some new integrative concept which includes the alternative views as supplementary aspects in a more comprehensive view of man's moral existence. This does not mean, however, that the terms "deontological" and "teleological" are useless as classificatory categories when we deal with historically given theories in ethics. Lastly, as far as theories are concerned which stress, respectively, the motive for, or the character of, an act, it is well to remember that, although the motive is basic, by itself it gives us no clue as to what is right; and, conversely, a right act is morally significant only if its motive is good. To make an imperative of the right out of a pure act of will is as great a confusion in ethics as is the confounding of a merely wrong action with an imagined evil impulse of the heart (6:471). The relevant facts demand that both the *motive for* and the *character of* an act be considered together, and that an integration be sought which does justice to them both as supplementary aspects of the same moral phenomena. Pending the development of such a synthesis, however, the categories in question indicate important differences between types of deontological theories and thus serve a useful function in our classificatory scheme.

In conformity with the classification of ethical theories here suggested, we shall deal, first, with noncognitive interpretations of moral phenomena and shall take up, next, various cognitive theories. In the case of the cognitive theories we shall examine, first, the teleological types, both naturalistic and nonnaturalistic, and, after that, shall consider the most representative deontological views. But throughout all these discussions we shall keep in mind that we are here engaged in preparing the ground for a new integration, and that what we are doing now is but a matter of preliminary orientation.

## REFERENCES

1. Ashby, W., "Teleology and Deontology in Ethics," *Journal of Philosophy*, XLVII (1950).
2. Browne, S. S. S., "Independent Questions in Ethical Theories," *Philosophical Review*, LXI (1952).
3. Frankena, W. K., "Moral Philosophy at Mid-Century," *Philosophical Review*, LX (1951).

4. Golightly, C. L., "Legerdemain in Ethics," *Philosophical Review,* LXI (1952).
5. Hill, T. E., *Contemporary Ethical Theories,* New York, 1950.
6. Margolius, H., "The Two Realms of Ethics," *Journal of Philosophy,* XLVII (1950).
7. Mothersill, Mary, "Moral Philosophy and Meta-Ethics," *Journal of Philosophy,* XLIX (1952).
8. Ross, W. D., *Foundations of Ethics,* Oxford, 1939.
9. Sidgwick, H., *The Methods of Ethics,* 2nd edition, London, 1877.
10. Ibid. 4. Stevenson, C. L., *Ethics and Language,* New Haven, 1944.
11. Tsanoff, R. A., *The Moral Ideals of Our Civilization,* New York, 1942.

PART **I**

*Non-Cognitive Theories*

# CHAPTER I

# The Emotive Theory of Ethics

Common sense and philosophical tradition regard ethical statements as normative assertions (2). This very fact, however, raises a problem; for analysis reveals that to prescribe a norm (i.e., to tell a person what to do or what to approve) is one thing, and to assert a fact (i.e., to tell him that such and such is the case) is quite another. How, then, is it possible that a statement both prescribe a norm and assert a fact? And if it is not possible, what is the correct interpretation of ethical statements?

Contemporary empiricists have answered these questions in various ways—some holding with Schlick (10) that, in the end, ethics is but a branch of the psychology of human motivation or of social psychology; others maintaining that, strictly speaking, ethical statements are not assertions at all but emotive utterances which have no cognitive significance. We shall here deal with the latter interpretation only, singling out for special attention the related views of Ayer (1) and Stevenson (11).

The simplest form of the non-cognitive emotive theory is Ayer's interpretation of ethical statements as "expressions and excitants of feeling which do not necessarily involve any assertions" (1:109; 10:108). We shall call this the *pure emotive theory*.

Underlying the pure emotive theory is the fact that language may, and usually does, have a logical and an emotive use, and that *evincing* specific feelings is not at all the same thing as asserting that one has them (*1*:109). In conformity with this fact the theory regards all ethical statements as consisting of a non-ethical assertion and an ethical word or phrase having the force of an exclamation. The primitive ethical utterance, however, would not even have the form of a statement. It would be an exclamation expressing a certain emotion. Thus, when I catch someone in the act of taking his wife's life, I may utter a horrified *Oh!*, or I may say with growing horror in my voice: *You are murdering her!* In either case the utterance is a mere exclamation expressive of my emotional response to the act in question. The pure emotive theory holds that when I say: *It is wrong to murder your wife,* I am (a) asserting that you are (or might be) taking her life, and (b) expressing my horror at the act; and what is ethically significant here is not the assertion but my expression of horror.

Since Ayer develops this theory of ethics within the framework of his general theory of knowledge, it will be necessary to view it in the same setting. We shall begin, therefore, with a few basic definitions.

Ayer stipulates (*1*:8) that "any form of words that is grammatically significant shall be held to constitute a sentence, and that every indicative sentence, whether it is literally meaningful or not, shall be regarded as expressing a statement." "Any two sentences which are mutually translatable will be said to express the same statement." The word "proposition" is reserved for "what is expressed by sentences which are literally meaningful." "A statement is held to be literally meaningful if and only if it is either analytic or empirically verifiable" (*1*:9). But what does "verifiable" here mean? Ayer holds that there is a *strong* and a *weak* sense of that term. He holds, for example, that "there is a class of empirical propositions of which it is permissible to say that they can be verified conclusively" (*1*:10). It is characteristic of these "basic propositions" or "observation-statements" that "they refer solely to the content of a single experience, and what may be said to verify them conclusively is the occurrence of the experience to which they uniquely refer" (*1*:10). The vast majority of propositions, however, are neither themselves basic statements, nor are they deducible from any finite set of basic statements. The principle of verification, therefore *as a criterion of meaning,* must be reinterpreted in such a way as to admit statements other than basic statements. As Ayer formulates the principle it reads: "A statement is directly verifiable [and therefore meaningful] if it is either itself an observation-statement, or is such that in conjunction with one or more observation-statements it entails at least one observation-statement which is not deducible from these other premises alone" (*1*:13). "A statement is indirectly verifiable [and therefore also meaningful] if it satisfies the following conditions: first, that in conjunction with certain other premises it entails one or more directly verifiable statements which are not deducible from these other premises alone; and secondly, that these other premises do not include any statement that is not either analytic, or directly verifiable, or capable of being independently established as indirectly verifiable" (*1*:13). Put briefly, *the principle of verification requires of a literally meaningful statement, which is not analytic, that it should be either directly or indirectly verifiable,* in the sense just defined. If one accepts this principle, then one must hold that any statement one may make does not have any other factual meaning than what is contained in at least some of the relevant empirical propositions; and one must hold also that if the statement is "so interpreted that no possible experience could go to verify it [either directly or indirectly, in the above sense], it does not have any factual meaning at all" (*1*:15).

Turning now to ethical judgments, Ayer finds that "what seems to be an ethical judgment is very often a factual classification of an action as belonging to some class of actions by which a certain moral attitude on the part of the speaker is habitually aroused" (*1*:21). Judgments of this kind are, of course, verifiable and, therefore, literally meaningful. There are, however, many statements in which an ethical term is used in a purely normative way; and it is statements of this kind which, according to Ayer, are neither true nor false but simply expressive of emotions (*1*:103).

As Ayer sees it, the basic question of theoretical ethics is not which term, within the framework of ethical terms, is to be taken as fundamental; not "whether 'good' can be defined in terms of 'right' or 'right' in terms of 'good', or both in terms of 'value' "; but whether or not the whole sphere of ethical terms can be reduced to non-ethical terms; whether or not "statements of ethical value can be translated into statements of empirical fact" (*1*:104). That the reduction is possible is, according to Ayer, the contention of the utilitarians and the subjectivists; "for the utilitarian defines the rightness of actions, and the goodness of ends, in terms of the pleasure, or happiness, or satisfaction, to which they give rise; the subjectivist, in terms of the feelings of approval which a person, or group of people, has towards them" (*1*:104). The utilitarian reduction makes moral judgments a sub-class of sociological judgments; the subjectivist reduction makes them a sub-class of psychological judgments. In either case they cease to be distinctively moral statements.

Ayer rejects the utilitarian thesis because "it is not self-contradictory to say that some pleasant things are not good, or that some bad things are desired" (*1*:105); and he rejects the subjectivist view because "it is not self-contradictory to assert that some actions which are generally approved of [or are approved of by me] are not right, or that some things which are generally approved of [or are approved of by me] are not good" (*1*:104). Recognizing the distinctive nature of moral statements, Ayer holds that "sentences which contain normative ethical symbols are not equivalent to sentences which express psychological propositions, or indeed propositions of any kind" (*1*:105).

We must be careful, however, in making the distinction just mentioned, for normative symbols and descriptive symbols are often signs of the same sensible form. "Thus a complex sign of the form 'x is wrong' may constitute a sentence which expresses a moral judgment concerning a certain type of conduct, or it may constitute a sentence which states that a certain type of

conduct is repugnant to the moral sense of a particular society"
(*1*:105). If the latter is the case, the symbol "wrong" has
descriptive meaning and the sentence in which it occurs expresses a proposition which belongs to the field of sociology;
but if the former is the case, then the symbol "wrong" is normative and, according to Ayer, the sentence in which it occurs does
not express an empirical proposition at all (*1*:106). Only normative symbols and statements containing them are of concern to
us here.

It is evident that with respect to normative statements Ayer
finds himself in a difficult position. In so far as he rejects all
naturalistic reductionism (subjectivism and utilitarianism), he
is in agreement with the absolutists or intuitionists who regard
normative terms as unanalyzable. But in so far as he maintains
that, in order to be literally meaningful, synthetic statements
must be verifiable, he is forced to concede that normative statements, being unanalyzable and unverifiable, are literally meaningless. Ayer's way out of this difficulty is the emotive theory of
ethics according to which ethical concepts are unanalyzable
because they are mere pseudo-concepts which add nothing to
the factual content of a proposition but merely show that the
statement of the proposition is "attended by certain feelings in
the speaker" (*1*:107-108). Earlier in the chapter we have called
this thesis the *pure emotive theory of ethics.*

It follows from Ayer's interpretation that another person may
disagree with me about the rightness or wrongness of an act,
in the sense that he may not have the same feelings with respect
to it that I have, but he cannot, strictly speaking, contradict me;
"for in saying that a certain type of action is right or wrong, I
am not making any factual statement, not even a statement about
my own state of mind. I am merely expressing certain moral
sentiments. And the man who is ostensibly contradicting me is
merely expressing his moral sentiments. So that there is plainly
no sense in asking which of us is in the right. For neither of us
is asserting a genuine proposition" (*1*:107-108).

It is Ayer's contention, however, that ethical terms serve not
only to *express* feeling but also to *arouse* feeling, that, in fact,

"some of them are used in such a way as to give the sentences in which they occur the effect of commands" (*1*:108). It is therefore possible to determine the significance of the various ethical words in terms both of the different feelings which they ordinarily express, and of the different responses which they are calculated to evoke. This is true especially when—as is the case for some words—the expressive function normally dominates over the evocative function, or when—as is the case for other words—the evocative function normally dominates over the expressive function. The essentially expressive significance of the word "good" may thus be distinguished from the essentially evocative significance of the word "ought." "We can now see," Ayer continues, "why it is impossible to find a criterion for determining the validity of ethical judgments." The reason is that sentences which simply express moral judgments do not say anything. "They are pure expressions of feeling and as such do not come under the category of truth and falsehood. They are unverifiable for the same reason a cry of pain or a word of command is unverifiable—because they do not express genuine propositions" (*1*:108-109).

In order to comprehend fully the significance of Ayer's argument, one must keep in mind that to express a feeling is by no means the same as to assert that one has this feeling. The assertion that one has a particular feeling is, in principle, empirically verifiable and is therefore a literally meaningful proposition; the expression of a feeling is not. The subjectivists, Ayer holds, confuse the issue by their failure to make the required distinction. To be sure, the situation is complicated by the fact that "the assertion that one has a certain feeling often accompanies the expression of that feeling, and is then, indeed, a factor in the expression of that feeling" (*1*:109). But—and this is the important point—"the expression of a feeling assuredly does not always involve the assertion that one has it" (*1*:109). Expression and assertion of a feeling are not one and the same thing. Therefore, if ethical statements are interpreted as expressions and excitants of feeling which do not necessarily involve any assertions, it is clear that the emotive theory of ethics is not simply another version of subjectivism, in Ayer's sense of that term.

Now, if ethical statements are merely expressions and excitants of feeling which, as such, can be neither true nor false, then it is impossible to argue about the truth or falsity of some particular ethical statements; yet, we seem to engage precisely in such arguments. But what appears to be the case is not necessarily what actually is the case. Analysis will show, Ayer maintains, that in all disputes of the kind here under consideration we are really not arguing about a question of value but one of fact. "When someone disagrees with us about the moral value of a certain action or type of action, we do admittedly resort to argument in order to win him over to our way of thinking. But we do not attempt to show by our arguments that he has the 'wrong' ethical feeling towards a situation whose nature he has correctly apprehended. What we attempt to show is that he is mistaken about the facts of the case" (1:110-111). Our hope is that if we can get our opponent to agree with us about the nature of the empirical facts, he will adopt the same moral attitude towards them as we do. If agreement in moral attitude cannot be achieved through arguments about the facts in the case, we have, in the end, recourse to "mere abuse" (1:111).

Argument on moral questions is possible only if some system of values is presupposed. That is to say, "if our opponent concurs with us in expressing moral disapproval of all actions of a given type t, then we may get him to condemn a particular action A, by bringing forward arguments to show that A is of type t. For the question whether A does or does not belong to that type is a plain question of fact" (1:111). What Ayer is saying here is that if a man accepts certain moral principles, then, in order to be consistent, he must react morally to certain things in a certain way. "What we do not and cannot argue about is the validity of these moral principles. We merely praise or condemn them in the light of our own feelings" (1:111-112).

## II

I have devoted so much space to an exposition of Ayer's emotive theory of ethics in order to make evident to the reader that this theory is by no means intrinsically simple. There are at least six interrelated but divergent aspects of the theory which require special attention: (i) the assertion that ethical statements are *expressions* of feelings; (ii) the assertion that ethical statements are *excitants* of feelings; (iii) the admission that there may be disagreement in moral attitude; (iv) the contention that a man's moral reactions must be consistent with the moral principles which he accepts; (v) the thesis that the moral principles cannot be proved or disproved, but only praised or condemned in the light of our own feelings; and (vi) the statement that our last resort in disputes over moral attitudes is mere abuse. We shall now consider these six aspects of the theory in the order in which they have been given here.

First, however, let us remind ourselves of a most important fact. When Ayer says that ethical statements are meaningless, he is not saying that they are insignificant, or that they do not make a difference in human behavior. He is saying that ethical symbols add nothing to the descriptive content of the statements in which they occur; that they are *descriptively* meaningless (*4*:11).

Even if this fact is clearly understood, there still remains an ambiguity in Ayer's basic doctrine, for at times he likens ethical statements to "a cry of pain," whereas at other times he likens them to "a word of command." Ethical symbols, in other words, serve two functions; and these functions are sufficiently different to require specific analyses. Ayer's presentation of the emotive theory tends to obscure this fact. We shall here discuss each function separately.

(1) *Ethical Statements are Expressions of Feelings.*—Ayer holds that the fundamental ethical concepts are unanalyzable because they are mere pseudo-concepts. Hence, "in saying that a certain type of action is right or wrong, I am not making any factual statement, not even a statement about my own state

of mind. I am merely expressing certain moral sentiments" (*1*:107). The presence of such ethical symbols as "right" and "wrong" in a proposition adds nothing to its factual content. Like a cry of pain or a certain tone of voice, the utterance of an ethical word merely expresses a feeling, an emotion, or a moral sentiment; and to express an emotion is to ejaculate it, not to say that one has it.

If we accept this pure emotive theory of ethics, then, as has been noted before, the primitive ethical utterance does not even have the form of a statement but is a mere ejaculation—like *Ouch!* or *Ah!* And an utterance which has the form of a statement is ethical only insofar as it contains at least one ethical, i.e., ejaculatory, symbol. Let us see what this means in a concrete situation.

When I catch someone in the act of taking money from my safe, I may utter a shocked *Oh!* or an angry *Thief!;* or I may say with increasing emotion in my voice: *You are stealing my money!;* or I may say: *Taking money which does not belong to you is wrong.* This last statement has the form of an assertion and is representative of a large class of moral judgments. According to the emotive theory, however, its moral character, too, lies in its expressive rather than its descriptive function. What is meant here will become clear when we analyze the statement in conformity with Ayer's principles of interpretation.

The statement, *Taking money which does not belong to you is wrong,* as made in the concrete situation described above, can be reformulated without change in meaning and can be shown to consist of two parts: (a) *You are taking money which does not belong to you.* (b) *To do this is wrong.* There can be no argument about the meaning of (a). It is a purely descriptive statement which, under the stipulated conditions, is verifiable and thus literally meaningful even in Ayer's sense of that term. The difficulties arise in connection with (b).

If we assume for a moment that (b) is a descriptive assertion, then it may be interpreted either (i) as ascribing to the action in question the inherent but unanalyzable quality "wrong"; or (ii) as asserting disapproval of the action; or (iii) as relating this particular action to a class of disapproved actions. As far as Ayer is concerned, the first of these interpretations (bi) is impossible because there is no unanalyzable quality "wrong" which is demonstrably present in the action itself. If statement (b) is taken as referring to such a quality, then, on Ayer's principles, it is in a strict sense meaningless.

If (b) is interpreted as an assertion of disapproval (bii)— either on the part of the speaker or on behalf of society—then it is verifiable and literally meaningful, but it is a proposition of psychology or sociology, respectively, and not of ethics. It is descriptive and factual rather than normative. If (b) is taken to be a statement asserting that the action described in (a) belongs to a class of disapproved actions (biii), then it is again verifiable and meaningful, but not normative. The problem of the norm has merely been transposed and now arises in conection with the basic statement, *All actions of a certain type are wrong*. This means, of course, that the crucial question of ethics has been evaded rather than answered.

It is Ayer's contention that (b) has no descriptive meaning whatever, and that the correct transcription of the original ethical statement, *Taking money which does not belong to you is wrong*, would be something like *You are taking money which does not belong to you; bah!!*, where the exclamation adds nothing to the factual content of the statement but expresses a feeling of contempt aroused in the speaker by the action described. But let us be clear on one point: the use of the exclamatory *bah!!* (or its emotive equivalent) is either a deliberate attempt on the part of the speaker to let the hearer know that he (the speaker) feels a certain emotion, or it is an involuntary symptom of the emotion, "as bursting into tears of grief" (2:9) or saying *Ouch!* when one accidentally hits one's thumb with a hammer are such symptoms. If it is a deliberate attempt to convey to the hearer the information that the speaker has a certain feeling, then the emotive expression is really an elliptical assertion of a psychological fact, and the so-called emotive theory is but the old subjectivism in disguise. Ethical statements are in that case simply propositions of psychology. But if the exclamatory expression is regarded as an involuntary symptom of the felt emotion, then, surely, difficulties of interpretation arise whenever ethical statements are made with full deliberation; and since most ethical statements are so made, the ejaculatory theory seems to be a distortion rather than adequate account of ethical statements.

The difficulties of the theory become even more apparent when we consider ethical statements which do not pertain to an immediately present concrete situation. Let us examine, for example, a father's long-range advice to his son: *You ought never to take money which does not belong to you.* If we translate this statement into an assertion plus an exclamation, we obtain either (i) *Some people obtain money which does not belong to them; you ought not to do it;* or (ii) *Some people take money which does not belong to them; to do so is wrong.* In either case the nonethical assertion does not pertain to a specific action which is in process of execution here and now, but to a class of past and, possibly, future actions; and this fact has a decisive bearing on the meaning of the ethical part of the statement, for it is now impossible to argue that the statements, *You ought not to do it* and *to do so is wrong,* are purely ejaculatory utterances which have merely the significance of involuntary symptoms of an emotional reaction to an observed action. The most plausible interpretation would be to say that these utterances are intentional statements of disapproval of the kind of action described. But such an interpretation is hardly reconcilable with the basic assumption of the pure emotive theory. It presupposes a subjectivistic assertive theory which reduces the statements in question to propositions descriptive of psychological facts. *You ought not to do it* and *to do so is wrong* would then simply mean: *I do not approve of it;* and this is a verifiable and therefore meaningful proposition. It is not simply the expression of an emotion.

The difficulties which beset the pure emotive theory of ethics may be viewed from a still different angle. We may ask, for example, does the emotive theory really give us an adequate analysis of linguistic usage (7:110)? Let us consider a simple case.

In conformity with the basic principles of the theory here under discussion, *X is good* must be taken to be the linguistic equivalent of *X; ah!,* said in a certain tone of voice. In ordinary usage, however, *X is good* may be uttered in a variety of situations and in each situation the word "good" seems to have a descriptive meaning which is not completely reducible to a purely expressive function. Thus, *X is good* may be the equivalent of *X is pleasant,* as when we say *This is a good flavor.* Or it may be the equivalent of *X is aesthetically successful,* as when we say *This is a good poem.* But *X is good* may also be equivalent to *X is useful,* as when we say *This is a good knife.* It may mean *X contributes to my health* (or to my welfare or happiness), as when I say *Exercise is good for me.* In a different situation, *X is good* may mean *X possesses great skill,* as when we say *Mr. Blank is a good pianist;* or it may mean *X possesses certain character qualities,* as when we say *Mr. Doubleblank is a good man.* Now, surely, we do not come to understand the ethical meaning or function of the word "good" by looking for the common emotional denominator in the variety of usages just indicated, for most of these usages are ethically irrelevant, and at least one specifically ethical use of the word "good" is not even included in the list. *X is good* may also mean *X is a morally good act,* as when we say *To love one's neighbor is good.* And statements of this type, rather than of any other, are under consideration when we try to ascertain the ethical meaning or the ethical function of the word "good." The very fact, however, that we can make all the distinctions in usage indicated above implies that in various concrete situations the word "good" has descriptive meanings which are sufficiently well understood to enable us to distinguish the different uses, and that "good" expresses an ethically significant emotion only under certain specifiable conditions which fall within a specific range of relevancy of the word. This raises the question, however, as to what is an ethically significant emotion; and to this question we shall return in a moment.

In the meantime let us consider once again the thesis that the use of ethical symbols is purely ejaculatory; that ethical words simply express an emotion. If this thesis is true, and if *X is good* is taken to be the equivalent of *X; ah!,* spoken in a certain tone of voice, then *X is exquisitely beautiful* ought also to be the equivalent of *X; ah!,* spoken in some particular tone of voice. But if both statements are thus but expressions of feelings, then why is ethics so sharply distinguished from aesthetics (6:130-131)? To argue that in the one case we express a moral feeling whereas in the other we express an aesthetic one is hardly more than to argue in a circle; and in any case the conception of feelings or emotions involved requires clarification. In addition, why is the word "good" intimately bound up with such other words as "ought," "right," and "duty," whereas the word "beautiful" has no such connections? Is this because ethical symbols are excitants as well as expressions of emotions?

(2) *Ethical Statements as Excitants of Feelings.*—The second thesis of the pure emotive theory of ethics is that ethical words are excitants as much as expressions of feelings; that these words "possess a dispositional property of affecting substantially the emotions and attitudes of people, which is not dependent upon any alterations the expressions introduce into the cognitive field" (3:308); or, more briefly, that these words have the power to arouse emotion independently of what they describe or name (8:79). The question is, Is this thesis tenable?

It may readily be granted that ethical words do have power to arouse feelings. Such an admission, however, is not strictly speaking the equivalent of the basic assertion of the pure emotive theory of ethics. The word "good," for example, may be said to arouse a certain emotion of approval, not directly, but indirectly through evoking the thought of the attribute goodness, whose name it is (8:81)—in which case it actually is the attribute goodness, not the word "good," that evokes the emotion. Thus, following Kant, Sir David Ross holds that the word "good" cannot evoke an emotion of approval apart from evoking the idea of goodness because "it is impossible to approve of anything without thinking it *worthy* of approval—without thinking that it has a goodness of its own which makes it fit to be approved" (9:261). And when the question is what we actually mean, in common speech, by the words "right" and "good" and "beautiful," then, as far as their descriptive function is concerned, Ross may here have given us the clearest statement of the true answer (8:84). The pure emotive theory of ethics, however, is not a commonsense doctrine. We must therefore examine more closely the claim that, independent of any descriptive meaning, ethical words are excitants of feelings. But let it be understood that what is in question here is not the fact that words are used to evoke emotional responses, for they are so used; it is the manner in which they (presumably) arouse ethical feelings.

Let us assume for a moment that the pure emotive theory of ethics is true. Let us assume, in other words, that ethical symbols have no descriptive meaning whatever. And let us assume also for a moment that, when uttered, ethical words express (but do not assert) an emotion felt by the speaker. Let us assume, in other words, that ethical symbols function as exclamatory or ejaculatory utterances. The question is, Do ethical words arouse or evoke ethical feelings within the framework of these assumptions? The pure emotive theory must assert that they do; the facts of experience, however, lead to a different conclusion.

In order to clarify the issue let us consider a case in which no moral problem is directly involved (5:133-134). Thus, as I attempt to drive a nail into the wall I may hit my thumb with the hammer and say *Ouch!* in a certain tone of voice. The word "ouch," of course, has no descriptive meaning; but in saying *Ouch!* under the circumstances described I am expressing a feeling of pain. Let us now assume that there is another person in the room and that this person hears my ejaculatory *"Ouch!."* What will be his response to my linguistic utterance? It is difficult to give a specific answer to this question because many factors are involved in the concrete situation; but a very common response is a question—*What happened? What did you do?*—and not an emotion or feeling. If there is an emotional response at all—be it one of sympathy or one of malicious joy—it is most probably a response to the total situation *as descriptively understood,* not to the ejaculatory utterance as such; and this fact is worth noting.

But let us consider another example. When a speaker says in a matter-of-fact manner *Professor Blank believes that public utilities should be publicly owned,* I understand him to refer to a particular person and to assert that this person holds such and such views. However, when the speaker, raising his voice, says *Professor Blank is a red!,* I understand him to refer to the same person as before but, in addition, I also infer that the speaker disapproves of Blank (or at least of the views Blank holds) and that he wants me to disapprove likewise. Thus, the situation here described seems to be the sort of situation in which the evocative aspect of the pure emotive theory of ethics is in evidence. But what are the facts in the case?

Let us grant for the sake of argument that the utterance, *Professor Blank is a red!,* expresses (but does not assert) the speaker's feeling of disapproval of Blank. Such an admission, however, does not warrant the conclusion that some peculiar emotional power of the linguistic symbols themselves directly arouses a similar emotion in the hearer (5:132). In fact, it may well be the case that, in the situation described above, the use of the words "is a red" leads the hearer to a disapproval of the speaker rather than of Professor Blank; and this possibility is hardly reconcilable with the pure emotive theory.

The problem which arises here has prompted Robinson to attempt an explanation of the evocative power of ethical words. As he puts it, a most important fact about our use of the word "goodness" is that "no one is willing to call a thing 'good' if he disapproves it and wishes to prevent it." This is so, Robinson goes on, "because we are all aware that the word 'good' has a certain practical force, which we can no more alter by our definitions than most of us can alter the economic system of our country"—a "practical force," that is, which "comes to nearly every one of us as an inexorable necessity to which he must conform." "The nature of this inevitable practical force is that, each time we declare to another man that x is good, we are doing something that tends to make him approve x or evaluate it favorably"; and "each time another man declares to us that x is good, he not being ironical or mad or irreconcilably hostile, he influences us to value x favorably, though the influence is often extremely slight and comes to nothing." Nevertheless, this practical force of the word "good" is "something human and contingent." "It belongs not to the mere noise 'good,' nor to the mere letters on paper, but to these forms as habitually functioning in the minds of men. And they might have functioned in some other way in our minds, or not at all" (8:89-90).

Now if—as Robinson contends—the practical force of the word "good" (and therefore of any ethical word) belongs not to the mere noise or the mere letters on paper but to "these forms *as habitually functioning in the minds of men*," then three and only three alternative interpretations of this habitual functioning of ethical words are possible. Either (1) the words in question have descriptive meanings and any reference to their habitual functioning is but a reference to the conventionalized fixation of this meaning; or (2) the words have no descriptive meaning (or no descriptive meaning which is ethically relevant) but merely express and/or excite an emotion, in which case any reference to their habitual functioning can mean only that they are cues of stimuli in a socially acquired stimulus-response pattern of behavior in the same sense in which nonsense syllables or flashing lights may serve as cues for stimuli; or (3) the words in question have prescriptive meaning and their habitual functioning is that of rationally significant imperatives. The first of these alternatives is irreconcilable with the basic thesis of the pure emotive theory of ethics; but it also fails to explain the imperative character of ethical statements. The second alternative is irreconcilable with the facts of rational human living. The crucial error of the advocates of a pure emotive theory (Ayer among them) has been to regard (1) and (2) as exhaustive alternatives. The third alternative they have ruled out by insisting on confirmability in principle as the sole criterion of meaning. But let us examine the third alternative—(3) above—more carefully.

It will be helpful to view the problem of prescriptive meaning in its widest possible context and, at first, without specific relation to ethics. Consider, therefore, the following case. On a certain container we read: *Apply powder freely several times daily. Superficial wounds and minor burns may be covered with a dry bandage.* This statement, obviously, tells us *what to do* rather than *what is the case.* It is a prescription, not a statement of (presumed) fact. But as a prescription the statement is not confirmable, either actually or in principle, and is therefore outside the area of true and false. This does not mean, however, that it is meaningless or purely emotive. No one will seriously argue, I am sure, that the statement, as printed on the container, is simply an expression of an emotion felt by its author; nor can anyone plausibly hold that the function of the statement is to evoke an emotion in the reader. On the contrary, the function of the statement is to serve as a rational guide for action; and this function is inseparable from its intelligibility or meaning. The meaning involved here consists of directives for action and is *pre*scriptive rather than *de*scriptive. It is evident from this one example that prescriptive meanings are so genuinely a part of human experience that their denial must be adjudged a complete distortion of fact. People do understand directives and follow them, and their following them is proof that they understand them; and they understand them despite the fact that the imperatival character of prescriptive statements cannot be translated into purely descriptive propositions.

But if prescriptive statements are meaningful guides for action, then it is at least plausible to hold that ethical utterances are a form of prescriptive statements and therefore intelligible and meaningful despite their imperatival character (5:140). To escape this consequence one would have to argue that, whereas the verbs of ordinary prescriptive statements (when taken in their indicative mood) have descriptive meaning, the moral *ought* is at all times descriptively meaningless. But such an argument encounters at once serious difficulties because moral imperatives do not necessarily contain words other than those found in nonmoral prescriptive statements; nor are the verbs of moral imperatives, when taken in the indicative mood, necessarily without descriptive meaning. For instance, the moral imperative, *Do not take money which does not belong to you,* is related to the descriptive statement, *You are taking money which does not belong to you,* in exactly the same way in which the nonmoral imperative, *Do not skate on thin ice,* is related to the descriptive statement, *You are skating on thin ice;* and in neither case is the imperatival statement without intelligible meaning. What must be noted, however, is the fact that the moral or non-moral character of an utterance lies not in its imperatival form but in its justification or ground. Let me illustrate my point.

Suppose that, in a specific situation, A says to B, *Take the high road.* This statement is a directive for action. It is intelligible in the sense that B understands what he is to do. However, the experiential context within which the statement is made and understood contains at least one (suppressed) premise which has direct bearing on the significance of the statement, and this premise varies with the situation. For example, if A were an army officer and B a soldier, A's statement might be a *command* backed up by the established authority of A's rank. But if B had invited A for a Sunday afternoon drive in the country and had given him a choice between alternative roads, A's statement might be the expression of a *wish.* Again, if B were a stranger asking about the most scenic drive between X and Y, A's statement might be merely a *suggestion.* That such a suggestion may be made with varying degrees of persuasiveness is obvious but unimportant. What is significant is that, as far as their justification or ground is concerned, nonmoral directives can be classified under at least three headings—commands, wishes, and suggestions—and that it is the ground or justification which makes all the difference in the world. In the case of commands, no justification is given. Blind obedience is expected on the basis of established authority and/or an implied threat. In the case of wishes, the justification of the imperatival statement is the desire of the speaker, weighted as this desire may be by prestige or authority. In the case of suggestions, however, the justification is neither an established authority nor a personal desire on the part of the speaker; it is, in principle at least, an appeal to relevant facts and to logical arguments.

The question now is, How are we to classify moral imperatives? It is evident, I believe, that they are not wishes, for the difference between *wishing* to do so and so and *regarding it as one's duty* to do so and so is experientially obvious to all who have had the experience. It is true, of course, that at times one may wish to do what one feels to be also one's duty; but what one regards as one's duty is often opposed to what one wishes to do, and this opposition eliminates the possibility of interpreting the *moral ought* as a mere wish. But neither is the *moral ought* simply a command. It cannot be plausibly argued that an act becomes a *moral* act simply because someone placed in a position of authority has given the command to perform it. The crimes of Dachau and Maideneck cannot be redeemed by a command theory of ethics. And the Ten Commandments, though essentially commands, derive their *moral* significance from the implied assumption that God is good and that he therefore commands only what is good.

If moral imperatives are neither wishes nor commands, are they suggestions? Before we can answer this question we must examine more fully what is involved here (2:16; 18). Let us consider the case, mentioned above, of the stranger, B, who inquires about the most scenic drive between X and Y. A replies to the inquiries by saying, *Take the high road*. A's imperatival statement here finds its justification within the situational context; and with respect to this context the full statement is: *Since you desire to go from X to Y by the most scenic road you ought to take the high road*. This statement contains (a) the *suggestion* that B take the high road, and (b) the *justification* of this suggestion in terms of (i) an explicit reference to B's desire and (ii) an implied reference to the fact that of all the alternatives available the "high road" is the most scenic drive between X and Y. Any argument between A and B can pertain only to some aspect of (b), and any persuasiveness of A is centered primarily in (bii).

But suppose now that, in a different context, A says to B, *Pay your grocer*. It is possible, of course, to treat this imperatival statement as either a command or a wish; but we are interested here in an analysis paralleling that of suggestions. If the parallelism holds in any degree, then A's statement must find its justification within the situational context; and with respect to this context the full statement may well be, *You ought to pay your grocer, since you promised you would*. This statement consists of (a) a suggestion for action and (b) a justification of this suggestion. But there is an urgency and earnestness in the suggestion here which was absent in the earlier example. The justification contains (i) an explicit reference to a promise made, and (ii) an implied reference to B's desire to live up to his promise. What argument there may be between A and B can arise again only with respect to (b) and will probably center on (bii). Apparently the parallelism is complete. Actually, however, such is not the case.

In the first example the desire of B is taken for granted and the arguments center around the facts in the case. In the second example the facts are taken for granted (the promise made), and the arguments center around the desire or attitude of B, culminating in an attempt on A's part to persuade B that he *ought to keep his promise*. This difference between the two examples is crucial, for it means that situations involving a nonmoral ought may be essentially self-contained, whereas situations involving a moral ought are essentially not self-contained but refer to at least one other *ought* which is or is not accepted as ultimate. In principle, therefore, any particular moral ought can be justified only by appeal to a universal ought. And the question is, How can such an ultimate ought, the first premise of all morality, be itself justified? This question brings us back to the emotive theory of ethics, for it is the contention of this theory that an ultimate ought is accepted only on the basis of an emotive persuasion.

(3) *Moral Attitudes.*—We shall examine the nature of disagreement in attitude more fully in the next chapter, when we deal with Stevenson's version of the emotive theory. For the present we shall attempt merely to come to a better understanding of what a reference to moral attitude may mean.

An attitude, it seems, is not a mere feeling nor a simple desire. It may involve both; but, in addition, it also includes elements of cognition and of will. Feelings are purely subjective states; attitudes are responses to apprehended situations. The apprehension includes an understanding of the desirability as well as of the facts in the case. "One wills a particular line of conduct relatively to an apprehended situation" (6:126). This does not preclude the possibility that attitudes become habitual or that the apprehension in any given case may be faulty. It does mean, however, that an attitude is taken on the basis of past experiences and with respect to a concrete situation *as that situation is apprehended*. If this is so, then the word "attitude" rather than the word "feeling" or "emotion" expresses what is significant in the moral situation. But the crux of the matter is the apprehension of what is desirable or of what *ought to be*—which is the cognitive element in all attitudes that are morally significant; and this apprehension the emotivists cannot admit. Hence, when the adherents of the emotive theory speak about attitudes, they cannot mean what we have taken the word "attitude" to imply; but what they do mean is not clear from their evasive statements and their avoidance of a precise definition. Says Stevenson: the term "attitude" "must for the most part be understood from its current usage and from the usage of the many terms ('desire,' 'wish,' 'disapproval,' etc.) which name specific attitudes" (*11*:60). Current usage, however, is itself vague in the extreme and stands badly in need of clarification (5:136). To say, for example, that I approve of something may mean that I have a certain feeling (or disposition) towards it; but it may also mean —and, etymologically, this is its basic meaning—that I believe or judge it to be good. But to approve something, in the sense of judging it to be good, obviously involves a cognitive act; and this, as we have seen, the emotivists cannot accept. We are thus forced to conclude that what they do mean are specifically moral emotions of approval and disapproval. But now the question is, What are specifically moral emotions? And to this question we find no satisfactory answer in the writings of Ayer and his followers. However, as here used, the word "moral" either has no specific and definable meaning, or it has such a meaning. If it does not have a specific meaning, then the whole reference to specifically moral emotions is essentially meaningless. But if it has such a meaning, then this meaning cannot be defined in terms of emotions only, for the range of emotions—even of emotions of approval—transcends that of specifically *moral* emotions. It would seem, then, that the adherents of the emotive theory fail to give us an adequate interpretation even of their own key concepts—such as "attitude," "specifically moral emotion," "emotional approval"; and introspection is of no avail.

(4) *A Man's Moral Reactions Must be Consistent.*—Nowhere, to my knowledge, does Ayer commit himself to a demand for consistency in moral reactions. Stevenson, on the other hand, seems to assume that, somehow, men aim at some sort of harmonious or systematic satisfaction of their contingent desires. This assumption is especially evident in an article in which he discusses a man engaged in ethical reflection (*12*:291-304). So long as this man is ethically undecided, Stevenson tells us, "his attitudes are in a psychological state of *conflict*. . . . Only when he has resolved his conflict, making his attitudes, at least in greater degree, speak with one voice, will he have made his decision." Moreover, in resolving that conflict the man "makes up his mind about 'what he *really* approves of.' " Stevenson here admits that "part of what we are doing in ethical thinking is finding what types of action are agreeable to our relatively permanent ethical attitude or conviction" (*2*:316; *7*:121). "When a man has conflicting attitudes," we are told (*12*:292), "he is virtually forced to think—to recall to mind whatever he knows about the alternatives before him, and to learn as much more about them as he can"; for "a change in his thoughts is likely to *bring about* a change in his attitude and, in particular, is likely to end or minimize his conflict by strengthening, weakening, or redirecting one of the attitudes involved." The harmony of attitudes which is thus to be achieved may appear to be purely a matter of psychological adjustment; yet, as Stevenson points out, in resolving his conflict the man will also be "establishing, cognitively, the varied beliefs that may *help* him to resolve it." Reasoning, "by serving as an intermediary" in the resolution of the conflict of attitudes, thus "fulfills an ethical function." "With-

out such reasoning, each attitude would be compartmentalized from the others; and the net result would not even be conflict; it would be psychological chaos" (12:293).

It is evidently Stevenson's belief that a harmonious pattern of attitudes is to be preferred to attitudes in conflict and, especially, to a psychological chaos. And if this is a demand of "practical reason" (12:293)—of "ordinary reasoning made practical by its psychological context"—, then a new rationale has been added to the purely emotive aspect of the emotive theory, and the pure emotive theory has been found wanting in an essential respect.

Suppose I say with reference to a specific act, *A is right,* and, shortly after, I say with reference to this same act, *A is wrong.* In ordinary usage this means that, for one reason or another, I have changed my mind about A. But it also means that I now believe that I was in error when I made the first statement. However, if we accept the emotive theory, then the words "right" and "wrong" have no cognitive significance but are merely expressive of emotions, and the change from *A is right* to *A is wrong* signifies merely a shift in my emotional response to A—a shift from approval to disapproval. The question is, Is the ethically significant approval or disapproval simply the passing emotion at the moment of its occurrence, or is it a dispositional response and therefore of more than passing interest? If the emotivists mean the former—i.e., if they mean that *A is wrong* is adequately interpreted by *I now, at this moment, feel an emotion of disapproval of A*—, then the compartmentalization of attitudinal responses is complete, and conflict and chaos are inevitable. But if they mean that dispositional responses are of special significance, then (in the words already quoted) "part of what we are doing in ethical thinking is finding what types of action are agreeable to our relatively permanent ethical attitudes or convictions" (2:316), and in solving our conflicts we are making up our mind about what we *really* approve of. In this case patterns of responses emerge, and reason and understanding augment our emotional attitudes. We have transcended the limitations of the pure emotive theory.

(5) *Moral Principles Cannot be Proved or Disproved.*— Philosophers have pointed out often that ultimate principles— even the principles of ethics—are not susceptible of proof, if by proof we mean logical demonstration or derivation. These same philosophers may have argued at great length about which principles are ultimate, but they have been in agreement that in a specific sense all first principles are contingent only. And yet, when the adherents of the emotive theory maintain that moral approval or disapproval is merely contingent, that it can be understood causally but cannot be accounted for in terms of principles, they speak of a contingency in a much more immediate sense than do the philosophers of the past.

For the emotivists moral approval or disapproval is an affective-conative attitude, not a judgment claiming truth. Perhaps it is not amiss to transcribe their interpretation of "I approve" as "I happen to like"; and liking something is notoriously contingent. But, as Paton points out, " 'I approve morally' is fundamentally opposed to 'I happen to like' "; and "when I say that an action is morally good I am at least attempting to rise above my contingent personal likes and dislikes" (7:120). However, to rise above contingent personal likes and dislikes means to appeal to principles which claim some degree of generality. And when the emotivists admit—as Robinson does (8:102)—that the objective language *(A is wrong)* has "greater authority" than has the subjective language *(I happen to dislike A),* they admit, in principle, an appeal from purely contingent to the less contingent; and if they do not admit this, they destroy the effectiveness of the objective language itself by depriving it of all transpersonal authority. Robinson, however, is quite clear on this point. "I say," he writes, "that there are such things as moral obligations." But, being an adherent of the emotive theory, he adds: "In saying that, I am uttering a general approval of the habits of making moral demands and acknowledging them. . . . I am doing the same sort of thing as when at my marriage I promised to cherish my wife." "I am not also trying to describe the world" (8:96).

Let us note, first, Robinson's admission that "there are such things as moral obligations"—even if these obligations are, presumably, but "habits of making moral demands and acknowledging them." In the light of such an admission, statements made in the objective language obviously derive their greater authority not from any momentary emotional response to a given situation but from their implied reference to the moral obligations which, as matters of habit, have been acknowledged by the individual concerned. This, however, is merely another way of saying that broad principles provide the objective basis for our most significant moral responses.

But if objective principles are essential to moral action, then arbitrary definitions of words like "meaningful," "true," and "good" should not induce us to abandon them. On the contrary, the pragmatic requirements of moral living should furnish part of the criterion of the meaningful, the true, and the good. Ordinary usage, I am sure, supports such a view. As Paton puts it, "the ordinary man takes it for granted that it is possible to judge in accordance with objective ethical principles and to act in accordance with these principles" (7:109).

However, in having made this point we have by no means settled the question of the ultimate principles themselves. Here the fundamental difficulty of the emotive theorists arises from the fact that they delimit meaning to sense-experience and that, in so doing, they deny the cognitive meaning of ethical terms and, thus, the possibility of rational insight in moral matters. If we insist that verification is possible only in terms of sense data (private experience though these may be), then, of course, moral judgments (A is right, A is better than B) must remain unverifiable. But if moral judgments can be evaluated in terms of broad principles (as I think they can), then, if these principles are meaningful and if there are reasonable grounds for accepting them, moral judgments as such find a rational and, therefore, an objective justification which places them beyond mere emotive responses. Thus, the sole question which need concern us now is, Are there reasonable grounds for accepting the broad principles of ethics?

(6) *Our Last Resort in Moral Disputes is "Mere Abuse."*—

Robinson, so we have seen, holds that, in acknowledging that there are moral obligations, I am merely "uttering a general approval of the habits of making moral demands." But this statement is obviously ambiguous, for the phrase "general approval" may mean either a considered judgment of evaluation or a merely emotive response. Ordinary usage distinctly favors the first of these two meanings; the emotivists, however, insist upon the second. But the plausibility of their argument, it seems to me, depends upon the ambiguity of the statement involved.

The broad principles of the natural sciences—the principle of the conservation of matter-energy, the principle of entropy, the principle of causality, to mention but a few—also transcend sense data and are, in a strict sense, beyond proof. They are "habits" of making certain "demands" pertaining to the formulation of laws and the construction of theories in the physical sciences. The practical success in the integration of experience achieved by the laws and theories formulated in the light of these demands provides the rational grounds for accepting the principles themselves. A continued process of re-appraisal and progressive refinement in definition is characteristic of the whole history of these principles. We accept them as "ultimate" because of their effectiveness in the interpretation of experience. Is it unreasonable to suppose that we accept broad principles of morality because of their effectiveness as guides for action, always keeping in mind that a continued process of re-appraisal and progressive refinement in definition will lead to ever broader and ever better understood "first" principles? The alternative is to abandon all moral issues to the quicksands of fluctuating emotions and thus to undermine morality itself.

The adherents of the emotive theory, I am sure, do not intend to discredit morality. But it is certain beyond all question that acceptance of their thesis cuts the ground from under all objectivistic conception of morality (7:119-120) and that, in doing this, it "plays into the hands of the demonic types who have brought the world to its present pass" (7:122), and whose contingent approvals and disapprovals threaten our very existence; for if we cannot appeal to principles which we believe to hold for all men and which bid us to respect the dignity of man as a human being, then we have no answer to the horrors of Maideneck and Dachau and to the bullying tactics of would-be tyrants big and small except the emotive response *I don't like it*. And, surely, so long as we maintain that we cannot argue about the validity of moral principles but can "merely praise or condemn them in the light of our own feelings" (*1*:112); so long as our final resort is "mere abuse"; we cannot hope for the spread of "moral" action in the world nor even for the continuation of "moral habits" anywhere. In fact, the break-down in the personal and public morals of our time is largely the result of a far-reaching repudiation of "moral habits" and objective principles of morality. And there can be no doubt: the emotive theory, although it is but the by-product of an arbitrarily narrow doctrine of meaning, contributes—though unintentionally—to that break-down.

## III

In his second book, *Philosophical Essays* (1954), Alfred J. Ayer attempts to develop a more adequate emotive theory of ethics, and to meet some of the criticisms directed against his first formulations. He still holds that, strictly speaking, ethical judgments are not "statements" and, therefore, are neither true nor false, and that there are no specifically "ethical facts" (A:231-232); but he admits that we can give reasons for our moral judgments—although such reasons do not support the judgments "logically" (A:236), i.e., by way of implication or entailment. "Reasons are merely expressive or influential" (B:271).

It must be granted, of course, that in everyday discourse we often use arguments which are a mixture of deductive and inductive reasoning. Even in our sciences the "mixed" arguments predominate. But the question is, Where do "reasons" which are "merely expressive" fit into the scheme—if they fit at all? Ayer himself speaks of "recommending a new way of speaking" (A:232). But, since we do give reasons for our moral judgments, we must at least be able to state these reasons. That is to say, we must be able to use descriptive language. It is also a fact, moreover, that we must make decisions in nonmoral situations. Even the construction of a scientific theory, for example, involves such decisions. We may therefore conclude (with A. P. Brogan) that "trustworthy thinking involves more than Mr. Ayer recognizes when he says [that] moral judgments are not to be considered true or false because they do not fit into his incomplete disjunction of deductive *versus* scientific" (B:273).

Nor is the situation altered in Ayer's favor when he now argues that moral judgments are "directives" which "determine attitudes" (A:237). I have already dealt with this problem in Section II, but, because of Ayer's reiteration of his thesis, it may be necessary to consider it further. After all, he now rejects his earlier assertion that moral judgments are "merely expressive of certain feelings, feelings of approval or disapproval" (A:238). But the alternatives which Ayer here stipulates of moral judgments being either expressions of emotions or attempts to modify attitudes (of oneself or of others) is not exhaustive. As Professor Brogan has pointed out, moral judgments may also "involve reference to some system of rules, principles, criteria, or standards by which moral judgments may be justified" (B:274). And Ayer's interpretation gives us not even a clue as to what a systematic ethical theory might be. In fact, his own "theory" eliminates in principle the possibility of constructing an ethical theory because it eliminates the kind of rational decisions required in the justification, the vindication, or the validation of those presuppositions and procedures requisite to the construction of a system (B:277-279). In the sciences such justification or validation is accomplished by the cognitive validity of the system as a whole. In the realm of ethics, the conditions are, admittedly, different, because here no verification through sense-perception is possible. But, as I shall attempt to show in Chapter X, even in ethics the case is not hopeless once we discard Ayer's emotivism as inadequate. And that we have ample ground for discarding the latter I believe to have shown throughout this chapter.

Ayer, it will be remembered, does not deny that, in the moral realm in general, there may occur disputes. What he does deny, however, is that such disputes can correctly be described as disputes on *moral* questions. The arguments in such disputes, Ayer holds, will never be concerned with "ultimate right and wrong and intrinsic good and evil." "Instead they will turn out to be disagreements concerning questions of fact (or of logic)" (D:484); and what in such disputes cannot be settled by a recourse of facts and/or logic, can be settled only by "emotive persuasion," or, ultimately, by abuse (*1*:111). A close examination of our moral existence reveals, however, that such is not the case.

The relations in which we stand to our fellowmen are in objective fact grounds of real obligations, for they are shot through and through with explicit and implicit commitments on our part; and each such commitment entails an obligation. In another book I shall develop this thesis fully. It is sufficient for the present to have referred to it in passing. And if it be argued that in a more subtle sense our obligations depend upon our beliefs, then this can readily be admitted, for beliefs include valuations, and it is only because of our respective valuations that we make the commitments we do make. Again, however, I must postpone until later a full discussion of the thesis here briefly indicated.

Sir W. David Ross points up a still further difficulty encountered by an emotivist interpretation of ethics. It is this: If we are to do justice to the meaning of "right" or "wrong," we must take account also of cases "where the judgment of obligation has reference either to a third person, not the person addressed [he ought to do so-and-so], or to the past [you ought to have done so-and-so], or to an unfulfilled past condition [had circumstances A occurred, we ought to have done so-and-so], or to a future treated as merely possible [if such-and-such should come about, then he ought to do so-and-so], or to the speaker himself [I ought to do so-and-so]" (*9*:33). In not one of these cases is it plausible to hold that the obligation is a command or simply the expression of an emotion. And there is even a difference between "You ought to do so-and-so" and "Do so-and-so!"; for the former implies that there are reasons which justify the *ought;* the latter is a command simple and, in itself, requires no justification. It is also true that not all commands are of a moral nature. "Squad right!," for instance, has in itself no moral character. However, the soldier's duty to obey that command has a moral basis—and a basis which is not grounded in emotive expression. It is grounded, rather, in a more inclusive commitment which, as commitment, entails the obligation.

And with this reference I rest my case against Ayer and his emotivism.

## REFERENCES

1. Ayer, Alfred Jules, *Language, Truth and Logic,* 2nd edition, London, 1946, Chapter VI.
2. Barnes, Winson H. F., "Ethics Without Presuppositions," *Logical Positivism and Ethics,* Aristotelian Society, Supplementary Volume XXII, London, 1948.
3. Brandt, Richard B., "The Emotive Theory of Ethics," *Philosophical Review,* LIX (1950).
4. Cavell, S., and Sesonske, A., "Logical Empiricism and Pragmatism in Ethics," *Journal of Philosophy,* XLVIII (1951).
5. Cross, R. C., "The Emotive Theory of Ethics," *Logical Positivism and Ethics, op. cit.*
6. Joad, C. E. M., *A Critique of Logical Positivism,* Chicago, 1950.
7. Paton, H. J., "The Emotive Theory of Ethics," *Logical Positivism and Ethics, op. cit.*
8. Robinson, Richard, "The Emotive Theory of Ethics," *Logical Positivism and Ethics, op. cit.*
9. Ross, W. David, *Foundations of Ethics,* Oxford, 1939.
10. Schlick, Moritz, *Problems of Ethics,* New York, 1939.
11. Stevenson, Charles L., *Ethics and Language,* New Haven, 1944.
12. Stevenson, Charles L., "The Emotive Conception of Ethics and Its Cognitive Implications," *Philosophical Review,* LIX (1950).
    (A) Ayer, Alfred J., *Philosophical Essays,* New York, 1954, Chapter IX.
    (B) Brogan, A. P., "A Criticism of Mr. A. J. Ayer's Revised Account of Moral Judgments," *Journal of Philosophy,* LVI (1959).
    (C) Hodges, Donald Clark, "Human Conduct and Philosophical Ethics," *Journal of Philosophy,* LII (1955).
    (D) Johnson, Oliver A., "On Moral Disagreement," *Mind,* LXVIII (1959).

(E) Meyerhoff, Hans, "Emotive and Existentialist Theories of Ethics," *Journal of Philosophy,* XLVIII (1951).
(F) Moore, Asher, "Emotivism: Theory and Practice," *Journal of Philosophy,* LV (1958).
(G) Olson, Robert G., "Emotivism and Moral Skepticism," *Journal of Philosophy,* LVI (1959).

# CHAPTER II

# Emotive Theory and Disagreement

# in Attitude

I

Underlying our discussions in the preceding chapter is the conviction that moral judgments mean something and can be significantly contradicted (9:411), and that there are rational grounds for accepting certain broad principles as guides for moral action. After all, a moral obligation—to respect, for example, the human dignity of another person—does not vary with our emotive responses, and to say that, in doing his duty, an individual acted morally—even though such a statement may be accompanied by a feeling of approbation—is not to express a feeling but to judge an act in the light of an obligation. The emotive theory is in basic conflict with such a view. However, let us not prejudge the case. On the contrary, with Hume and Stevenson let us "glean up our experiments in this science from a cautious observation of human life, and take them as they appear in the common course of the world, by men's behavior in company, in affairs, and in their pleasures" (19:vii).

Stevenson regards it as his first task to clarify the meaning of the ethical terms—the meaning of such terms as "good," "right," "just," and "ought"; and he regards it as his second task "to characterize the general methods by which ethical judgments can be proved or supported" (*19*:1). His starting point is the question, "What is the nature of ethical agreement and disagreement? Is it parallel to that found in the natural sciences, differing only with regard to the relevant subject matter; or is it of some broadly different sort" (*19*:2)? This seemingly peripheral question proves, in the end, to be of central importance for Stevenson's whole position.

Stevenson distinguishes initially between two broad kinds of disagreement: (i) "the disagreements that occur in science, history, biography, and their counterparts in everyday life"—that is to say, "disagreements in belief"; and (ii) the disagreements involving "an opposition, sometimes tentative and gentle, sometimes strong, which is not of beliefs, but rather af attitudes—that is to say, an opposition of purposes, aspirations, wants, preferences, desires, and so on" (*19*:2). "The two kinds of disagreement differ mainly in this respect: the former is concerned with how matters are truthfully to be described and explained; the latter is concerned with how they are to be favored or disfavored, and hence with how they are to be shaped by human efforts" (*19*:4).[1] However, "it is by no means the case that every argument represents one sort of disagreement to the exclusion of the other. There is often disagreement of both sorts"; for "our attitudes . . . often affect our beliefs" and "our beliefs often affect our attitudes" (*19*:5). In some cases, therefore, the existence of one type of disagreement may wholly depend on the existence of the other. But this is by no means always the case. "The beliefs which attend opposed attitudes need not be incompatible." In fact, "A and B may both believe that X has Q . . . and have divergent attitudes to X *on that very account*" (*19*:6). It is Stevenson's basic contention that *when ethical issues become controversial, they involve disagreement that is of a dual nature. There is almost inevitably disagreement in belief, which requires detailed, sensitive attention; but there*

---

[1] "A parallel distinction holds for the positive term, 'agreement,' which may designate either convergent beliefs or convergent attitudes" (*19*:5).

*is also disagreement in attitude. An analysis which seeks a full picture of ethics, in touch with practice, must be careful to recognize both factors"* and must *"show in detail how beliefs and attitudes are related" (19:11).*

As Stevenson sees it, the beliefs that are in question in normative ethics are "preparatory to guiding or redirecting attitudes," and "moral judgments are concerned with *recommending* something for approval or disapproval" (19:13). In moral disputes, therefore, the disagreement in attitude is crucial. "It determines what beliefs will relevantly be discussed or tested; for only those beliefs which are likely to have a bearing on either party's attitudes will be *a propos";* and "it determines when the argument will terminate" (19:14).

Within the framework of these general ideas Stevenson now turns to an interpretation of ethical terms, using for his purpose specifically defined working models. Thus he tells us:

"(1) 'This is wrong' means *I disapprove of this; do so as well.*

(2) 'He ought to do this' means *I disapprove of his leaving this undone; do so as well.*

(3) 'This is good' means *I approve of this; do so as well"* (19:21).

In each case the definiens has two parts: "first a declarative statement, 'I approve' or 'I disapprove,' which describes the attitude of the speaker, and secondly an imperative statement, 'do so as well,' which is addressed to changing or intensifying the attitudes of the hearer." Stevenson adds: "These components, acting together, readily provide for agreement or disagreement in attitude" (19:22). The models, however, show something else, too. Let us note that "the model for 'This is good' consists of the conjunction of (a) 'I approve of this,' and (b) 'Do so as well' "; and that "if a proof is possible for (a) and (b) taken separately, then and only then will it be possible for their conjunction" (19:26). Now, obviously, sentence (a) offers no trouble. Since it makes an assertion about the speaker's state of mind, it is open to empirical confirmation or disconfirmation. "Sentence (b), however, raises a question. Since it is an imperative, it is not open to proof at all" (19:26). Proof in ethics is therefore not like proof in science. The question is, Is there "some 'substitute for a proof' in ethics, some support or reasoned argument which, although different from a proof in science, will be equally serviceable in removing the hesitations that usually prompt people to ask for a proof" (19:27)?

Although imperatives cannot be proved in any strict sense of the term "prove," they may yet be supported by some reason. This supporting reason may be a description of the situation which the imperative seeks to alter, or of the new situation which the imperative seeks to bring about; and if the description discloses that the new situation will satisfy a preponderance of the hearer's desires, he may thereby be induced to change his attitude. In other words, "reasons support imperatives by altering such beliefs as may in turn alter an unwillingness to obey" (19:27).

Having thus indicated in broad outlines the perspective of his approach to ethical problems, Stevenson now returns to his working model in a somewhat critical mood. The first inadequacy of the model to which he calls attention is this: "The imperative component, included to preserve the hortatory aspects of ethical judgments, and stressed as useful in indicating agreement or disagreement, is really too blunt an instrument to perform its expected task" (19:32). One may wonder, however, if the assertive component of the model is not also in need of revision.

In the preceding chapter I have already called attention to the fact that to say *I approve of this* may mean (i) to state the result of an evaluative judgment or (ii) to express a purely emotive response comparable to a spontaneous feeling of liking something. From Stevenson's model alone it is not clear which of these alternatives is meant. The general orientation of Stevenson's argument implies, however, that the emotive response rather than the result of an evaluative judgment is intended. But even then it is not the expression of a feeling but the assertion that I have this feeling of approbation (or disapprobation). If this is indeed what is meant, then the statement asserts a psychological fact and is confirmable or disconfirmable; and to this extent Stevenson's first model is not representative of an emotive theory of ethics. It is directly opposed, for example, to Ayer's point of view, and is subjectivism in the very sense repudiated by Ayer (7:111-112).

Moreover, it may well be doubted that the cognitively significant meaning of "This is good" can be adequately rendered as *I approve of this,* when nothing more is intended than the assertion *I have a feeling of approbation with respect to this* or, less ambiguously, *I happen to like it.* The claim to objectivity which, in ordinary usage, characterizes the statement "This is good" is totally lacking in the transcription.

## II

But let us return to Stevenson's augmentation of his original working model.

Imperatives, he tells us, are often used to exert a unilateral influence, and only this usage is brought out in the model. The first model, therefore, may give the distorted impression that "a moralist is obsessed by a desire to make others over into his own pattern—that he wishes only to propagate his preconceived aims, without reconsidering them" (19:32). In addition, the working model may also misrepresent the manner in which moral influence is exerted. Both deficiencies, Stevenson believes, will be eliminated when we take into consideration the emotive meaning of words—the power, that is, which a word acquires, "on account of its history in emotional situations, to evoke or directly express attitudes, as distinct from describing or designating them" (19:33). Because of this power of words, "ethical judgments alter attitudes, not by an appeal to self-conscious efforts (as is the case with imperatives), but by the more flexible mechanism of *suggestion.* Emotive terms present the subject of which they are predicated in a bright or dim light, so to speak, and thereby *lead* people, rather than command them, to alter their attitudes" (19:33). This emotive meaning of words, however, requires further analysis.

There is nothing magical about words themselves, and their power to express or evoke feelings is not unrelated to their cognitive meanings. It is conceivable that in a few isolated instances certain linguistic expressions may serve as specific stimuli setting off conditioned emotive responses, as the sound of a bell may make saliva flow in the mouth of a dog; but it seems truer to human experience to hold, as does Brandt, that "emotional and attitudinal effects arise only from perception, belief, and understanding, perhaps often involving entities only vaguely outlined or hinted at," and that "at least *most* of the influence of discourse on feelings or attitudes derives from *what* is said, or from the hearer's impression of the type, intensity, and determination of the attitudes of the speaker," not from any particular "power" of the word itself (*8*:306-307).

Stevenson, however, holds that ethical terms cannot be taken as fully comparable to scientific terms, for "they have a quasi-imperative function which . . . must be explained with careful attention to emotive meaning; and they have a descriptive function which is attended by ambiguity and vagueness" (*19*:36). It is the "emotive meaning" of ethical terms which is now under consideration.

A sign, Stevenson argues, has "a disposition to produce responses in people" (*19*:56), and this disposition, "if it has been caused by . . . an elaborate process of conditioning which has attended the sign's use in communication," is the "meaning" of the sign (*19*:57). "Emotive meaning" is thus that "meaning" of a sign "in which the response (from the hearer's point of view) or the stimulus (from the speaker's point of view) is a range of emotions" (*19*:59). That is to say, "the distinction between descriptive and emotive meaning depends largely on the kind of psychological disposition that a sign . . . is disposed to evoke" (*19*:67). A sign may, of course, have both kinds of meaning; "it may at once have a disposition to affect feelings or attitudes and a disposition to affect cognition" (*19*:71). In fact, "in their origin and practical operation," emotive and descriptive meaning "stand in extremely close relationship" (*19*:76).

Stevenson here holds an "essentially causal view of meaning" (*19*:79). His justification for accepting this point of view is that "a sign's meaning can be constant even though its psychological effects vary," and that "the effect of a sign on feelings and attitudes, in virtue of emotive meaning, can be much more powerful than any 'additive' effect of its passing associations" (*19*:79).

The substance of Stevenson's causal theory of meaning is that "the 'descriptive meaning' of a sign is its disposition to affect cognition," whereas the "emotive meaning" of a sign is its "disposition to affect feelings and attitudes" (*19*:70-71). In either case, however, the meaning of a sign is assumed to lie entirely in its functioning as a causal factor. One may well doubt that this is an adequate interpretation of meaning in any sense, for it restricts meaning entirely to pragmatics, neglecting the semantic and syntactical aspects of language. If the causal interpretation is taken to be the whole story, then there seems little sense in holding that the cognitive meaning of a word is a concept, or that the cognitive meaning of a declarative sentence is a proposition and that a proposition is either true or false (*1*:317). It is Stevenson's "identification of cognitive or descriptive meaning as such with the pragmatic aspect of cognitive meaning that renders plausible his generic causal theory of meaning which embraces the dispositions of a sign to affect both cognition and conation" (*1*:317). But if the significance of the semantic and syntactical aspects of cognitive meaning is well understood and kept in mind, then it is only confusing, to say the least, to speak of emotive meaning when nothing more is intended than some specific aspect of the pragmatics of language. Furthermore, the significance of semantics and syntactics in relation to cognitive meaning has far-reaching consequences for philosophical analysis in the field of morals; for analysis can now no longer aim at persuading people through recourse to emotive meanings or persuasive definitions but must attempt "to render language both (1) a more efficient cognitive tool by clarifying and modifying it so that it may better serve the purpose of conveying information and (2) a more intelligent practical instrument by making the affecting of attitudes a function of the information conveyed rather than of a causal disposition of the words as such" (*1*:319).

If the causal theory of meaning is as deficient as has been indicated, then the question arises, On what grounds does Stevenson defend his theory of emotive meaning? His principal argument seems to be that the distinction between emotive and descriptive meaning is of great use in studying human situations in which a change in cognitive meaning may not be followed by a change in emotive response, or in which a change in emotive response occurs which is not dependent upon a prior change in cognitive meaning (*19*:72). As Robinson admits, the best way of demonstrating the occurrence of emotive meaning would be "to find a pair of words which name the same thing but arouse different feelings towards it; for, if there is such a pair, the power of at least one of the pair to arouse emotion must be at least partly independent of its power to arouse the thought of that thing" (*18*:79). As examples of pairs which fulfill this condition Robinson mentions "to ape—to imitate," "liberty-license," "murder—slaughter—liquidate—kill—execute." But do these pairs of terms really have the same meaning? Consider, more specifically, the pair "liberty-license." Surely, only an arbitrary stipulation contrary to ordinary usage can ascribe identical cognitive meanings to these two terms; for "license" means *excess of liberty, of freedom; abuse,* and not just *liberty.* The case is similar for all other pairs. Neither Robinson nor Stevenson have yet produced a single pair of terms "with different emotive effects which clearly have the same meaning" (*8*:307; *10*:131-132).

But not only have Stevenson and Robinson failed to demonstrate the occurrence of emotive meanings by the argument just considered, the argument itself points up additional difficulties for their theory. If we assume for a moment that a word—the word "right," let us say—has an emotive meaning which is independent of its cognitive meaning, i.e., if the emotive power adheres simply to the sound or visual form of the word, then it seems to follow that this word "would carry the same emotive power through all of its various senses, so that, if we are emotionally affected by 'Be sure to do the *right* thing,' then, given similar intonations and gestures, we should be equally stimulated by 'Be sure to take the *right* fork' " (*8*:307-308). But, obviously, our emotive response varies here with the cognitive meaning of the term "right," and the question is, How can such a variation be accounted for in terms of the emotive theory which ascribes the emotive effect to a power or disposition of the word itself? An adherent of the cognitive theory can fully explain what happens by pointing out that, of course, we respond emotionally to the situation as described and cognitively understood. Recourse to the magic power of words is in this case unnecessary.

R. C. Cross has called attention to still another difficulty which arises for the emotive theory. "When [a] speaker says 'negro,' " Cross writes, "I understand him to be indicating a certain sort of human being with certain specific characteristics. When the speaker says 'nigger' I understand him to be indicating as before, but I also infer something about his feelings, namely that *he* dislikes the object named. The word 'nigger,' however, does not function in the way of arousing *in me* a different emotion towards the object from that which the word 'negro' does. So far as emotions are concerned, the only change that perhaps occurs is that I feel an emotion of dislike for the man who uses the word 'nigger' instead of the word 'negro' " (*10*:132). The point is that the listener may not only remain uninfluenced by the so-called emotive meaning of a word, but that the emotive use of words may lead him to re-appraise the character of the speaker and to react emotionally to the result of this cognitive re-appraisal. In no sense, therefore, have Stevenson and Robinson demonstrated the occurrence of independent emotive meanings.

### III

But let us return to Stevenson's working model and let us consider in what sense and with what success he attempts to dispense with the overt imperative that was used in the first model (*19*:81). To be sure, Stevenson's argument depends throughout upon the assumption that there are independent emotive meanings and that the causal theory of meaning is sound. We shall therefore have to bracket our objections to this thesis for the present.

Because the term "good," Stevenson tells us, has a specific emotive meaning, it is indefinable, for it has *no* exact emotive equivalent. "The term is indefinable for the same reason that 'hurrah' is indefinable" (*19*:82). Two points must now be noted: (1) "Since the emotive meaning of a term is of a dispositional nature, its psychological effects will vary with the attendant circumstances" (*19*:82); and (2) " a term which has an emotive meaning is not always used for purposes of exhortation" (*19*:83). More important still, however, is Stevenson's thesis that, "for the contexts that are most typical of normative ethics, the ethical terms have a function that is *both* emotive and descripive" (*19*:84). Consider, for example, the following two cases. (1) "If Mrs. Smith tells her daughter that Jones is a 'good' suitor, we may, knowing Mrs. Smith of old, be reasonably well assured that Jones is wealthy." (2) "A respected friend tells us that Brown has 'good' intentions, and we conclude that Brown habitually tries to be considerate and altruistic." "Now," Stevenson asks, "does 'X is good' actually *mean,* in part and on occasion, what it thus leads us to conclude, or does it merely *suggest* these conclusions?" And he answers that "perhaps it merely suggests them, for the inferences depend so largely upon our knowledge of the speaker's psychological habits" (*19*:85). But the crucial point here is not *that* we use our psychological knowledge of the speaker, but *how* we use it. "Do we use it to determine *what sense* of 'good' the speaker was using? . . . Or do we presume that 'good' refers, so far as its descriptive meaning is concerned, only to the speaker's approval" (*19*:85)? "In point of fact," Stevenson argues, " 'good' had *no* precise sense; it was used vaguely. The distinction which the question presupposes, that between what 'good' *means* and what it *suggests,* is often beyond the precision of ordinary language" (*19*:86). We may therefore maintain that the conclusions in the examples were simply suggested by "X is good"; or we may maintain that they were analytically implied by it. Either position involves the stipulation of "rules for the use of 'good' "

(*19*:86). "We must remain sensitive," however, "to the fact that ethical terms are not predestined to abide by any one set of rules, and that analysis cannot 'discover' the 'real' sense" (*19*:87).

At this point let us stop for a moment to reconsider Stevenson's argument, for it seems to me that this argument is faulty in several respects. The fact that "analysis cannot 'discover' the 'real' sense" of the term "good" need not disturb us too much, for to expect such a discovery assumes that words have a " 'real' sense" which is simply *there* to be discovered; and such an assumption is obviously unjustifiable, for the sense or meaning of terms depends on intention, and no sense or meaning exists outside a context of intentions. But let us examine the two examples given above. In each case "we" take "good" to have some specific cognitive meaning. In the first case "we" take it to mean "Jones is wealthy." In the second case "we" take it to mean "Brown habitually tries to be considerate and altruistic." With respect to these cognitive interpretations Stevenson asks, Does "good" actually *mean* them, or does it merely *suggest* them? The question, however, is not clear, and the answer which Stevenson gives is misleading.

From the context within which Stevenson raises the question it is evident that he takes "mean" to be the linguistic equivalent of "analytically implied by." If this strict sense of "mean" is assumed, then the inferences in the two examples are justified only if we know already the specific meaning which the term "good" has for "Mrs. Smith" and for our "respected friend" *in the particular combinations* of "good suitor" and "good intentions," respectively. However, ordinary discourse, as a rule, is not carried on within so rigid a framework of antecedent knowledge. On the contrary, in ordinary discourse we must infer the intended meaning of words from the situational context which includes our knowledge of the speaker's beliefs and valuations. It is this fact which apparently supports Stevenson's position that our inferences (in the two examples given above) are not what the term "good" *means* but what it *suggests*. Actually, however, the word "good" does not suggest our inferences;

it is the situational context which leads us in each case to a comprehension of the specific meaning of the word "good" in that situation. We do indeed determine *what sense* of 'good' the speaker was using." The alternative which Stevenson proposes—that "we presume that 'good' refers, so far as its descriptive meaning is concerned, only to the speaker's approval"—is untenable; for, if such were our presumption in the two examples, we could not infer in any sense whatsoever either that "Jones is wealthy" or that "Brown habitually tries to be considerate and altruistic" (the wealth of Jones and the specific habits of Brown not being part of the speaker's emotional response of approval).

## IV

So far we have used only the word "good" to illustrate Stevenson's thesis. We are told, however, that the term "right" functions essentially in the same sense as does the term "good," except for "slight emotive differences, and different ranges of ambiguity" (*19*:97), the word "right" being used to indicate more specifically our approval of actions. "The terms 'duty,' 'obligation,' and 'ought,' like the term 'right,' usually occur in judgments that are overtly about actions" (*19*:99), although they cannot be equated with "right." Thus, "duty" and "obligation" *"blame* for *omission,"* whereas "right," having a less coercive effect, *"praises* for *commission"* (*19*:99). "The shade of menace that often attends "duty" and "ought" is the emotive, quasi-imperative counterpart of their use in indicating strong disapproval of omission. We usually do not bother to tell a person that he *ought* to do something unless we suspect that the free run of his impulses will otherwise lead him to neglect it" (*19*:100). But now a new problem arises.

Obviously, "when 'good' is assigned no other descriptive reference than that of the speaker's approval, the statement 'Whatever I approve of is good' appears to have all the certainty of an analytic statement" (*19*:102). It also appears to be an expression of unadulterated egotism. Stevenson, however, now insists that the "I" in "I approve this" "refers to *any* speaker, and so favors no one person's attitude over those of any other" (*19*:103); and, despite his protestations to the contrary, such an interpretation leads to moral chaos unless the approval intended is not a mere emotive response but the result of a cognitively significant evaluation. Stevenson himself admits that " 'This is good' is more nearly approximated, in its full meaning, by 'This is worthy of approval' than by 'I approve of this' " (*19*:107); but his reason for admitting this—namely, that " 'worthy' has an emotive strength which 'approves' lacks"— is far from adequate. It is not the emotive strength of the word— this imaginary power of a sound or visual impression—which is decisive, but the fact that "worthy of approval" implies a cognitive judgment of evaluation even more definitely than does "I approve."

## V

Let us turn next to a consideration of Stevenson's doctrine of disagreement in attitudes.

Two persons, A and B, may disagree in their attitudes towards a given object, situation, or action—A maintaining that *X is good,* B maintaining that *X is bad.* In the language of the emotive theory this is equivalent to A saying *I approve of X,* and B saying *I disapprove of X.* Both A and B may give reasons for their respective attitudes, and now there may be an argument about these reasons.

It is Stevenson's contention that the reasons which support or attack an ethical judgment are, with few exceptions, related to the judgment psychologically rather than logically. "They do not strictly imply the judgment in the way that axioms imply theorems; nor are they related to the judgment inductively, as statements describing observations are related to scientific laws. Rather, . . . they serve to intensify and render more permanent the influence upon attitudes which emotive meaning can often do no more than begin" (*19*:113). Hence, in ethical disputes, "*any* statement about *any* matter of fact which *any* speaker considers likely to alter attitudes may be adduced as a reason for or against an ethical judgment" (*19*:114). Since the primary aim is to alter attitudes, the reasons need only be psychologically related to the ethical judgment. Their effectiveness lies in their power to persuade.

The reasons advanced may "call into question the descriptive *truth* of the initial judgment, so long as the judgment describes . . . merely the speaker's present attitudes"; or they may "represent efforts to change attitudes, or to strengthen them, by means of altering beliefs" (*19*:118). Again, the reasons may concern "attendant motives" (*19*:121); they may be appeals to authority (*19*:125), or they may constitute more or less skilful disguises of the real points at issue (*19*:129). Also, "there are times when a person is faced not with the need of convincing others, or deliberating with them, but rather with a problem of convincing himself" (*19*:130); and it is not always a simple matter to settle problems in one's own mind. "The individual's attitudes do *not* speak with one voice, but urge him both this way and that, with the net result of leaving him in a painful and inactive state of irresolution" (*19*:130). In resolving this paralyzing conflict "he is making up his mind about 'what he *really* approves of,'" and he does this "by strengthening, weakening, or redirecting one of the attitudes involved" (*20*:292; *19*:131).

Under one condition, Stevenson holds, rational methods alone will be sufficient to bring about agreement in attitude—under the condition, namely, that all disagreement in attitude is rooted in disagreement in belief, and that rational methods alone are sufficient to bring about agreement in belief (*19*:136). On the other hand, "if any ethical dispute is *not* rooted in disagreement in belief, then no *reasoned* solution of any sort is possible" (*19*:138). As a matter of fact, "attitudes are the outcome of many determining factors, and beliefs figure as but one set of factors among others" (*19*:139). It follows that both rational and nonrational methods may be effective in bringing about ethical agreement; but it is clear that, in Stevenson's opinion, the nonrational or persuasive methods [which depend on "the sheer, direct emotional impact of words—on emotive meaning, rhetorical cadence, apt metaphor, stentorian, stimulating, or pleading tones of voice, dramatic gestures, care in establishing *rapport* with the hearer or audience, and so on" (*19*:139)] are by far the more important in altering attitudes, although *"purely* persuasive methods are seldom found" (*19*:141). All self-persuasion, incidentally, depends upon the same methods (*19*:149).

Following Stevenson, we shall now distinguish between "intrinsically good"—which is "roughly synonymous with 'good for its own sake, as an end' "—and "extrinsically good"—which is roughly synonymous with "good as a means to something else" (*19*:174); and, again following Stevenson, we shall say that "X is intrinsically *good"* asserts that the speaker approves of X, disregarding all of its consequences upon other objects of his attitudes, and that he "acts emotively to make the hearer or hearers likewise approve of it" in this way (*19*:177-178).[2] It is, of course, possible that something is good *both* intrinsically *and* extrinsically; as it is also possible that X is good intrinsically but bad extrinsically, or vice versa (*19*:178).

If the distinction between "intrinsically good" and "extrinsically good" be granted, then "four 'basic types' of agreement in attitude" are possible: (1) "A and B both approve of X intrinsically." (2) "A and B may agree on the intrinsic value of Y, and thus, if both believe that X leads to Y, may agree that X is good extrinsically, being a means to their common end." (3) "A may approve of X as an end, and B, although indifferent to it as an end, may approve of it because he believes it is a means to Y." (4) "A may approve of Y intrinsically but be indifferent to Z, and B may approve of Z intrinsically but be indifferent to Y. If they believe respectively that X leads to Y and to Z, then, so long as no other factors enter, they will agree that X is good—good as a means to their divergent ends" (*19*:180-181). It is now obvious that if all ethical agreements were of types (1) and (2), then every sort of ethical agreement would either be, or would presuppose, an agreement on ends. It is equally obvious, however, that agreements of types (3) and (4) involve no agreement on ends. As Stevenson puts it,

---

[2] And "so, *mutatis mutandis,* for 'extrinsically good,' 'intrinsically bad,' and 'extrinsically bad' " (*19*:178).

"although no one person can approve of anything as a means without approving of something else as an end, it remains possible for people to *agree* in approving of something without *agreeing* on ends" (*19*:183). The peculiarly evaluative aspects of ethics are thus not exhausted by an effort to establish common ends (*19*:185), and judgments about ends are not indispensable to all other ethical agreement (*19*:186). However, "intrinsic desires" may be "reinforced by extrinsic ones," and "extrinsic desires will reinforce each other whenever an object is a means to several ends." "Accordingly, much of ethical agreement, wherever it is possible, will be complex; and no theory of ethics can be acceptable which leaves complex agreement out of account" (*19*:191).

Still, "for a *direct* alteration of intrinsic attitudes, only one procedure is available—and that is the exclusive use of persuasion, whether overt or concealed, clear or confused" (*19*:200). In the first pattern the attempt at persuasion is a blunt and explicit reference to the speaker's attitude (see the working model); in the second pattern the same attitude is suggested by the presence of emotive meaning, i.e., by persuasive definition (*19*:207). That is to say, in the second pattern "the definition is used, consciously or unconsciously, in an effort to secure, by this interplay between emotive and descriptive meaning a re-direction of people's attitudes" (*19*:210). It is, of course, "possible to use reasons to support persuasive *definitions,* just as it is possible to use them to support first-pattern *judgments*" (*19*:218). The second pattern, thus, "differs from the first in its external aspects alone. The old factors have only to be recognized in their new form" (*19*:223). The persuasive elements are now contained in the definition itself, and "persuasion is effected by a combination of emotive and descriptive meaning, the latter giving direction to the former" (*19*:229). But "the persuasive support of a second-pattern definition will be no different from that of a first-pattern judgment" (*19*:229), and it still remains true that rational methods can resolve ethical disagreement if and only if it is rooted in disagreement in belief.

The contention that ethical judgments are neither true nor

false, Stevenson holds, is wholly misleading. "It is more accurate and illuminating to say that an ethical judgment *can* be true or false, but to point out that its descriptive truth may be insufficient to support its emotive repercussions" (*19*:267). Stevenson, in other words, although expressing sympathy with the views of Carnap and Ayer (finding much more to defend than to attack in the analyses of these men), attempts to dissociate himself from the extremes of the pure emotive theory. He seeks to qualify that extreme view and to free it from "any seeming cynicism" by emphasizing the complex descriptive meaning which ethical judgments may have "in addition to their emotive meaning" (*19*:267).

## VI

We turn now to a critical re-examination of Stevenson's thesis concerning disagreement in attitude. Our task is simplified by the fact that, as we have just seen, the second pattern of analysis differs from the first in its external aspects alone, and that the persuasive support of a second-pattern definition will be no different from that of a first-pattern judgment. In fact, all that Stevenson says about the second pattern follows from what he has said about the first, for "once we assert that judgments of goodness are emotive, then to define 'good' by reference to any describable qualities can only be to direct emotion to these qualities," and the definition must be persuasive in Stevenson's sense. "To choose a definition of this kind is merely 'to plead a cause'" (*17*:116). The second-pattern analysis, therefore, stands or falls with the first.

It must be granted that Stevenson has effectively called attention to disagreement in attitudes as distinguished from disagreement in beliefs; and it must be admitted also that an emotional conflict is, in a sense, more serious than a logical contradiction, for our emotionally charged attitudes are practical, active, militant (*18*:100). But is it true, as Stevenson says, that disagreements in belief require only brief attention? Is it not rather true, as Vincent Tomas has pointed out, that if a difference of opinion is to be an occasion for dispute, it must also be a difference of appraisals of opinion and thus of attitudes (*23*:209)? After all, if A and B hold contradictory opinions concerning X, they have no reason for argument unless they also disapprove of each other's opinions. Once this is admitted, it will be seen that disagreements in belief, like Stevenson's ethical disagreements, are of two kinds (*23*:210-213): (1) There are those disagreements in which the parties who disagree both regard the same sort of reasons as good reasons for believing or disbelieving something; and (2) there are those disagreements in which the parties who disagree are not in agreement as to what constitutes good reasons for believing or disbelieving something. Disagreements of type (1) are essentially disagreements in belief only and can be settled on rational grounds alone. Most disagreements in the exact sciences are of this type, for the methods employed in these fields include far-reaching agreement on what constitutes good reasons for believing or disbelieving something. Corresponding to this agreement on methods in the realm of the sciences, we find in the realm of ethics fairly general agreements on basic values; and to the extent to which this is the case, ethical disputes, arising within the framework of a given agreement on values, can also be settled by rational methods alone. Stevenson's theory is, therefore, at once too sweeping and not sweeping enough. It is too sweeping "because, when a disagreement in attitude arises between people who implicitly acknowledge the same standards of values, discussion and inquiry can in principle at least disclose whose attitude, if either's, is correct, as defined by the mutually accepted standards of correctness"; and it is not sweeping enough "because, when a disagreement in belief arises between people who do not ultimately abide by the same rules for acquiring and rectifying beliefs, rhetoric, and not logic, will settle their disagreement, if it is to be settled by discussion at all" (*23*:213). In disputes of this kind, the accusation, *You are unscientific,* is as emotive as is the statement, *You are immoral,* in an ethical context.

Stevenson, I am sure, might admit all of this and, if pressed, might retreat to the position that the disagreements with which he is primarily concerned are the disagreements on basic values —disagreements on the value of science and scientific method included. With respect to these ultimate matters and all intrinsic values he might still hold that only persuasive arguments can achieve agreement. Let us therefore restrict our examination for the moment to this assertion. But let us keep in mind at the same time that there is a crucial difference between a *reason for* belief and a *cause of* belief, just as there is a difference between a rational man (whose beliefs are the result of reasoned analyses) and an irrational man (whose beliefs are determined, not by a consideration of reasons, but by other causes) (*23*:- 214). And let us keep in mind, furthermore, that there is an equally crucial distinction between the psychological question, Why does a man hold the beliefs which he does hold?, and the epistemic question, Are moral judgments essentially emotive expressions?

It is true, of course, that there are irrational men, and that in all probability all men hold some beliefs not because of considerations of reason but because of some other cause. But this fact is in itself no reason why moral judgments should be regarded as essentially emotive rather than cognitive. Stevenson's whole thesis, however, has been built around the psychological question, Why does a man hold the beliefs which he does hold? It is this question which he attempts to answer in his detailed analyses of disagreements in attitude.

It must be remembered also that underlying the idea of Stevenson's working model and patterns of analysis is the assumption that ethical sentences, like imperatives, are "used more for encouraging, altering, or redirecting people's aims and conduct than for simply describing them" (*19*:21), and that ethical reasoning—even when it is supported by the systematic presentation of a whole body of beliefs—is selective in the sense that it emphasizes those beliefs which will exert the greatest psychological pressure on the attitudes that are to be guided (*19*:129). Except for a few special cases, the relation of beliefs to attitudes, Stevenson tells us, remains "a psychological one, involving the *resultant* effect on attitudes of a great number of beliefs" (*19*:130). In fact, so we are told, "reasons and reasoning processes become 'practical' or 'ethical' only by virtue of their psychological effect upon attitudes" (*19*:133). Unfortunately, this thesis of a psychological relation between attitudes and beliefs is by no means unambiguous or clear. And what, precisely, is meant by "persuasion"? Is an attitude taken because of an insight or an understanding still an attitude determined by persuasion? If it is, must not every instance of such *rational persuasion* be carefully distinguished from those instances in which insight and understanding play no decisive part? But, as Levy has pointed out, "if one admits [as I think one must] that there is such a thing as rational persuasion . . . , then Stevenson's thesis reduces to the trivial contention that some people are not so persuaded" (*15*:182).

Let us assume for a moment that the psychological influences which determine attitudes have all the significance which Stevenson attributes to them. Then it must be the case that two persons who disagree in their attitudes towards X either are aware of these influences or they are not aware of them. If they are not aware of them and if, therefore, the influences blindly determine their attitudes, then these attitudes can in no sense be called rational. On the other hand, if the two men are aware of the influences and, recognizing them for what they are, still continue in their disagreement in attitude, then we must conclude that the disputants are irrational men who willfully permit irrational influences to go on uncorrected (*15*:181). But such a situation, although often encountered in human experience, is not decisive for the fundamental questions of ethics. The point is not that some men submit blindly to psychological influences or are irrational in their attitudes; the point is that some men can and do decide moral issues on rational grounds and that *not all men are nonrational*. This point, however, Stevenson seems to neglect; and he must neglect it so long as he adheres to the causal theory of meaning and fails to distinguish clearly between *attitudes of will* and *mere emotions*.

It is perfectly true, of course, that emotions are essentially nonrational, that we have to understand them in the light of their cause, that when we speak of the reason for them we mean only the causes of which they are the psychological effects, and that we do not regard them as following from rational principles consciously understood and deliberately adopted (17:112-113). Stevenson holds, however, that all this is true of our attitudes of will also. Let us examine the facts in the case.

An attitude of the will, I believe, is epitomized in decisions, and decisions depend on evidence. Even Stevenson admits this. The point at issue, therefore, is the nature of the relation between evidence and decision, Stevenson holding that this relation cannot be logical and must therefore be causal (20:302). Lest we lose ourselves in a squabble over words, let us grant at once that, as an act of will and, thus, as a mental event, a decision is not a logical implicate of descriptive propositions. If this were all that Stevenson claims, there would be no issue. But a decision culminates in a judgment, a resolve, or an imperative; and that is a different matter. Stevenson admits that "the reasons [read: evidence] do make a difference: they help to determine whether the man will continue to make his judgment, or qualify it, or replace it" (20:302). And Stevenson admits also that, unless a man is rather less than a rational animal, he will not make a decision or render a judgment without stopping to think, to consider the reasons (20:301); he admits, in other words, that some knowledge at least is relevant to a decision. The question is, In what sense is it relevant?

If, with Kadish, we take "logically relevant" to mean that the truth or falsity of certain propositions affects in a determinate way the value of the decision (14:230), that, in fact, it is decisive for the decision, then we can assert, I believe, that knowledge is logically rather than causally relevant to a decision. This assertion finds support in the fact that wherever men seek to deal with human problems responsibly, they try to reach warranted conclusions based upon verifiable knowledge (14:232).

Within every situation that requires a choice on our part there exist factual and value conditions which our choice must satisfy, and these conditions are cognitively ascertainable. Our choice itself depends largely upon our understanding of, and insight into, these conditions and their entailments—which is but another way of saying that the conditions are logically relevant to our choice. Stevenson, however, bids us to consider the following: "Suppose that one man, contemplating the nature and consequences of S, finds that his approval 'wins in competition with other desires,' and that another man, contemplating the same factors, finds that his disapproval wins. And suppose that this divergence continues, no matter how much agreement there is about the factual content of S. Would not the same body of potential data, in that case, be taken by the one man as confirming evidence for the judgment 'X is good' and by the other man as disconfirming evidence? And would not the discrepancy be irreconcilable" (*21*:387-388)? It is Stevenson's contention that in view of such basic disagreements we cannot maintain that our choice is determined by logically relevant conditions. Examination of Stevenson's argument reveals, however, that he refers to "the factual content of S" without characterizing further what he means. I assume from the general orientation of his thesis that "factual" is here intended to exclude any reference to values and valuations. But such a restrictive meaning of "factual" is utterly inadequate as descriptive of all the conditions present in a given choice-situation; for whenever I am called upon to make a choice, I am myself part of the choice-situation. My valuations no less than the facts simple are discernible elements in the situation and are logically relevant to my choice. Only when we think of choice-situations as value free and as abstracted from our valuations, and when we think of the person who must make the choice as disengaged and as separated from the situation, can we hold that no set of propositions descriptive of the situation is ever adequate as evidential basis for a decision. But when we see a choice-situation for what it is: a human being engaged in a factual-evaluative context demanding resolution of inner tensions or conflicts, then the problem of justifying a decision reduces without remainder to the problem of applying complete knowledge of the situation as a whole to the problem of action.

## VII

It may now be argued that in the preceding argument we have evaded rather than met the crucial issue—the issue, namely, which arises when two persons, A and B, responding to a given situation in radically different ways, A approving and B disapproving, come to contradictory decisions. The answer to this argument is, of course, that A and B do not respond to identically the same situation since both, together with their respective valuations, are part of the situation in which they are engaged. The fact, therefore, that they disagree in their decisions does not affect the truth-value of our thesis.

In another sense, however, we have evaded the issue. Let us assume that, with respect to a given situation, A and B have reached contradictory decisions. A believes that B has made his choice because he did not understand fully the facts and values involved in the situation. But in discussing the matter with B, A discovers that B is aware of all the facts and values, that, moreover, he completely agrees on all points with A. B, nevertheless, adheres to his decision, arguing that neither the facts nor the values of the situation are logically relevant to his choice. What can A do? He can do nothing but write B off as an utterly irrational person, and turn to other matters. Admittedly, the case we have described is an extreme and, if it is encountered at all in actual life, is found only under borderline conditions of compulsive neuroses. But the very fact that it is a pathological extreme shows the relevancy, under ordinary circumstances, of a total description of the choice-situation to the choice itself.

If it now be argued that statements containing value terms are expressive and/or evocative rather than descriptive and that therefore we never can obtain that complete description of a situation which, as sufficient evidence, would justify our choice, two points may be made in reply. First, statements of the form "X is good," when "X" designates an actual object or situation, cannot be analyzed into statements of the form "I approve of X" or "I approve of X; do so as well," without a distorting shift from the objective to the subjective mode of speech. And the shift is not merely a matter of linguistics. Statements of the form "X is good" can more reasonably be translated into statements asserting that X has certain qualities, *a, b, c,* by virtue of which it deserves approval. Such an interpretation of "X is good" enables us to understand that at times we may be mistaken in our evaluation of X—namely, when X does not possess the qualities ascribed to it; and it enables us also to correct our attitude towards X, in so far as that attitude depends on qualities mistakenly imputed to X. More to the point, however, is the fact that when we adopt the interpretation here suggested, we see clearly the difference between judging X to be worthy of approval or recommendation and actually to approve or recommend it; and this distinction is more significant in choice-situations than is the purely expressive or evocative use of language. It allows for a rational connection of our decisions with the evidence upon which these decisions are based.

The second point to be made is that the emotive theory does not provide a criterion of relevance when we are dealing with evidence supporting a moral judgment (8:313). Consider two examples: (1) If A disapproves of X merely because B, whom A regards as a person of great prestige, disapproves of it, then, according to the emotive theory, A has been motivated by an ethically relevant consideration. (2) If A approves of X merely because to disapprove would be frowned upon by the social group of which A wishes to be a member, then, according to the emotive theory, A has again been motivated by an ethically relevant consideration. It is possible, of course, to hold this view. It seems to me, however—and moral tradition supports my contention—that in a very strict sense the considerations which moved A in the two cases, although persuasive, are *ethically* irrelevant for A's decisions—although they provide relevant factual evidence for our (negative) evaluation of A as a moral being. The emotive theory here distorts rather than clarifies the meaning of ethical situations and of morally significant decisions. This does not mean that men are not persuaded by considerations of the type suggested above; for they certainly are. It does mean, however, that a distinction can be drawn between what is and what is not morally relevant, and that this distinction is fatal to any attempt at interpreting the very essence of moral decisions in terms of emotive considerations only.

A test of relevance, I am sure, can be agreed upon once we accept a cognitive theory of ethics. The following formula may at least serve as a starting point: A factual statement, S, may be said to be logically relevant to an ethical statement about an action, A, when from a set of premises including S something can be inferred, at least with probability, about the moral character of A which is different from what would have been inferred if the set of premises had included non-S rather than S. If this criterion is accepted, then various relationships between factual and ethical statements can be shown to be forms of logical relevance (*8*:310; *25*:125-129).

(1) The meaning of the predicate of a factual statement may be identical with the meaning of an ethical predicate. Thus, if "good" is taken to mean "conducive to the greatest happiness of the greatest number," then the factual statement *A is conducive to the greatest happiness of the greatest number* entails that *A is good* and is therefore logically relevant to the ethical statement. (Brandt's *"analytic* relevance.")

(2) Some self-evident or inductively established general principle may connect the predicate of a factual statement with an ethical predicate. Thus, if we would accept as established the general proposition *All actions conducive to the greatest happiness of the greatest number of people are good,* then, from the factual statement that *A will be conducive to the greatest happiness of the greatest number of people,* we could infer that *A is good.* Here again the factual statement would be logically relevant to the ethical statement. (Brandt's *"synthetic* relevance.")

(3) From S, in conjunction with other empirical premises, the factual statement S′ can be inferred (at least with probability), and from S′ an ethical statement can be inferred either analytically or synthetically as above. Thus, the factual statement, S, *This action would make World War III inevitable,* in conjunction with the general premise that *World War III will not be conducive to the greatest happiness of the greatest number*

*of people,* allows the factual inference S′ that *This action will not be conducive to the greatest happiness of the greatest number of people* and, in the manner of either (1) or (2) above, the further inference that *This action is not good.* (Brandt's *"secondary* relevance.") [3]

It follows from the nature of our criterion of relevance that when factual statements are not logically relevant in one of the senses indicated, they are ethically irrelevant. The demarcation line is clear and precise. Mr. Stevenson's contention that most cognitive theories must omit as ethically relevant many factual considerations which are in fact relevant is no argument against the proposed criterion nor against every cognitive approach to ethics. It is an argument only against inadequately conceived theories and one-sided interpretations.

## VIII

It is Stevenson's contention that ethical opinions or judgments can be fully accounted for in causal terms if we assume that they are attitudes rather than beliefs. The crux of the matter is, not that ethical opinions, being essentially cognitive, also involve attitudes—a view which would be generally acceptable—, but that in their very essence they *are* attitudes and nothing else. Only this sweeping assumption is a repudiation of all cognitive approaches to the problem. It alone justifies the contention that ethical disagreement is, in the end, always a disagreement in attitudes. Such a view, however, is plausible at all only if we assume at the outset that we are motivated exclusively by emotions, not by reason, and that our emotions are not subject to rational control (22:76). These assumptions and contentions now require special examination. The question is: What precisely is the place and function of reason in ethics?

According to all advocates of an emotive theory of ethics the essential purpose of moral discourse is to influence conduct, to redirect attitudes, to affect beliefs; and there is some truth in

---

[3] "Secondary relevance," it seems to me, is adequate to deal with situations such as those suggested by Henry Aiken (5:347).

this thesis. Difficulties arise, however, as soon as we ask precisely what is meant by "influencing conduct," "redirecting attitudes," "affecting beliefs," and so on; for the terms in question are notoriously ambiguous, designating activities which range from providing information to making insinuations, from giving advice to persuading by fair means or foul. Also, it is not necessarily true that the distinctive function of moral discourse is to bring about changes in a person's behavior. We must not confuse questions concerning the purpose of making a statement with questions concerning its truth-value. Lying, for example, involves the purpose or intention of deceiving as well as the making of a false statement; and questions concerning the former differ radically from questions concerning the latter. To persuade or convince one need not say what is true; and "to know that what is said is true is not the same as knowing that the saying of it is either morally good or bad" (13:310).

Normally, when we express an opinion or make a statement of any kind, we do so for a reason—even if that reason merely is to amuse. But if in connection with a public utterance we are asked, "Why do you say that?," this question may mean either, "What is your purpose in saying that?" or, "What are your grounds for believing what you say?" (13:314). It is in connection with the latter question in particular that the problem of the place and function of reason in ethics raises. That this is so becomes especially obvious when we consider the case where a person comes to a conclusion or resolves a problem in the privacy of his own first-person experience, for in that case no public utterance is involved and the first form of the question is essentially irrelevant.

But even in the case of public utterances the problem of the place and function of reason in ethics arises. It is perfectly true that public utterances may serve no purpose other than to express or evoke an emotion or to change an attitude; but not all discourse is of this type. There is a vast difference between telling someone to do (or not to do) something, and telling him that such and such is (or is not) the case (13:315). There is a vast difference, for example, between (a) telling a man not to break a promise and (b) telling him what consequences breaking a promise might entail, although in either case his actions may be affected. The difference lies in the fact that in case (a) it is our purpose to persuade, to advise, to command, whereas in case (b) it is our purpose to give information, to clarify a situation, to express an opinion. It is because the emotivists take all public utterances in the realm of ethics to be essentially of type (a) that they minimize the function of reason to the point of upholding for all practical purposes an irrationalist thesis; and this is at least a one-sided interpretation.

## IX

In the discussion which follows we shall consider the problem of reason in ethics in connection with the question, "What are your grounds for believing as you do and for resolving your problem as you do?" We shall neglect the question, "What is your purpose in saying what you say?" Moreover, if we accept the usual distinction between means and ends, or between instrumental and intrinsic, then, as we have seen already, all judgments and evaluations pertaining to means and instrumental values can be justified on rational grounds (see *synthetic* and *secondary* relevance). The crucial problem arises in connection with ultimate ends and/or intrinsic values (25:12); and in connection with this problem let us remind ourselves of the fact that even in an integrated logical system, such as any system of geometry, the postulates, while providing the logical foundation of the system as a whole, are not themselves demonstrable within the system and must therefore be accepted on grounds other than the system itself. The problem of ultimate ends and intrinsic values thus has an analogy in the problem of first premises of any integrated deductive system.

Let us now consider the statement *X is good,* and let "good" mean "intrinsically good." Let us assume also that the statement is a synthetic proposition rather than a definition, that it is the kind of statement, in other words, which may serve as ultimate premise of a deductive system but which cannot itself be derived within that system (*25*:128). The question is, On what grounds, if any, can we justify acceptance of *X is good* (*12*:320)? Our answer to this question will depend on whether we believe that *psychological* persuasion alone is possible—meaning by this that we are moved exclusively by irrational emotive influences (*7*:181); or whether we are willing to admit that *rational* persuasion is also possible—that, being rational, we can and do act because of insights into (factual and/or logical) relations.

The problem arises in the sciences no less than in ethics. Thus, in describing the spatial interrelations of things in the world around us, we must select one out of several possible geometries. That is to say, we must select certain first premises in conformity with which we then interpret the relations in question. On what grounds do we choose or justify our premises? Are we psychologically or rationally persuaded to accept one set rather than another? Being rational and reasonable beings, we select that set of premises which will yield a complete and consistent account of all the relevant facts. If this means that we must abandon habits of long standing (such as thinking in terms of Euclidean geometry), then we willingly do so, persuaded—if that term be permitted—by the demands of reason.

The selection of ultimate principles may be more complicated in the realm of morals than it is in the sciences, but, basically, it is of the same type, for we do not cease to be rational beings when we make moral decisions. Being rational, we are concerned about our life as a whole and about the future no less than the present; and a rational concern of this type may well override psychological persuasions of the moment. The fact that, in principle at least, we are rational beings is one of the brute givens of human experience and requires no justification. Its importance is not diminished by the further fact that not all men are rational at all times. The advocates of the emotive theory confuse the analytically true proposition, *There can be no rational grounds for ejaculations,* and the factually true proposition, *In specific situations there may be no rational grounds for moral judgments.* If the distinction is maintained—as I believe that it must—, then the emotive theory collapses. In fact, it is self-defeating; for if we refuse to interpret moral judgment as nothing but ejaculatory or evocative utterances, the emotivist, adhering strictly to his thesis, can produce no reason why we should accept his rather than our own first principle. All he can do, as Toulmin has pointed out, is to evince disapproval of our attitude, and urge us to change it. "If, instead, he retorts, 'very well; but nothing else will get you anywhere,' that is a challenge worth accepting" (24:60).

In the sciences no proposition is accepted merely because someone approves of it or finds it credible; nor is any argument valid merely because someone finds it plausible. The proposition itself must be *worthy of* credence, and the argument must be *worthy of* acceptance. Similarly, it seems to me, a course of action is right not because we approve of it but because we find it *worthy of* approval (24:71). And in each case we must ultimately have recourse to the broad principles which determine the meaning of "worthy of."

In their over-all empiricistic orientation, the advocates of the emotive theory stand committed to a confirmability theory of meaning and a correspondence theory of truth. That these theories themselves are ambiguous, defective in many ways, and ultimately untenable (26:40-44; 136-141) need here be mentioned only in passing; for even if they were sound, they would prove only that moral judgments are not purely descriptive. They would not prove that moral judgments are nothing but emotive (ejaculatory and/or evocative) utterances (24:78). It will generally be admitted, I am sure, that in certain situations moral judgments may serve an essentially emotive function; but to take moral judgments made in special circumstances as being typical of all moral judgments is as misleading as would be the acceptance of immediate perceptual judgments as representative of all scientific statements. In the one case as in the other the fully developed judgment transcends the immediacy of first-person experience and finds justification in a broader and rationally coherent context. Within that context the fully developed judgment—be it scientific or moral—may also be corrected (24:124); and the correction may be made on rational grounds.

On a previous occasion (*26*:210-221; 343) I have indicated the role which the ideal of an integrated and closed system plays in the development of science. A brief reminder of what happened in physics will therefore be sufficient at this time. Galileo's discovery of the law of falling bodies brought a vast number of observable phenomena under one integrative formula. So did Kepler's discovery of the three laws of planetary motions. Newton's law of gravitation integrated Galileo's and Kepler's discoveries. But the laws of electrodynamics, as formulated by Maxwell, were independent of the laws of Newtonian mechanics. When both sets of laws were applied to the same phenomenon, light, they were found to involve a contradiction. This contradiction Einstein eliminated in his theory of relativity. The whole historical process was one of integration, expansion, and correction; and each step in the process was justified on rational grounds. At each step also the ultimate premises of the emerging system were found *worthy of* acceptance because of the effectiveness of the system as a whole in dealing with the facts of observation.

The history of ethics, of course, shows no such cumulative and integrative development. A certain parallelism can, nevertheless, be found. Ethical maxims correspond, in a sense, to the laws of science; and, just as in the case of the laws of science, not all maxims are of the same scope. Nor are they equally well established or are all integral parts of an ill-encompassing system. Moreover, just as in factual situations several laws of science are ordinarily involved, so in moral situations several maxims must usually be taken into consideration. Any reference to a single law or a single maxim is but a partial interpretation of the situation as a whole.

For reasons which will soon become obvious, let us now consider an oversimplified moral situation in which only one maxim is deemed relevant. Suppose that I say, *I feel that I ought to write the letter of recommendation for Smith,* thus describing my state of mind. You may now ask the specifically ethical question, *But ought you to do so?* To this challenge I may reply, *I ought to, because I promised Smith that I would;* and let this be the only relevant consideration in our oversimplified case. If you press further, I answer, *I ought to, because everyone ought to keep whatever promise he makes;* and, beyond this, I answer, *Keeping one's promise is part of the accepted moral code of the society of which I am a member* (24:146). Let us rest the case here for a moment; for we have now subsumed a concrete situation in a straightforward and direct manner under a general maxim which is accepted as part of the code of conduct by a given society; and, in a very real sense, this ends our problem. The *specific* ought has been justified on *rational* grounds.

A new problem arises, however, when the accepted code itself is challenged—as it may well be by an outsider (i.e., by a member of some other society which adheres to a different code) or by a philosophically minded member of the society itself, who raises the question, *Why should this maxim be accepted?* To reply merely that the maxim should be accepted because it is part of the accepted code is a dogmatic evasion of the issue. But two types of answers—both legitimate—may now be given. The first type is in essence a matter of logical analysis and consists in showing that the maxim is either a logical implicate of the basic presuppositions which, integratively, determine what, for the lack of a better term, we shall call *our way of life,* or it is itself one of these presuppositions. In either case, however, it is obvious that the matter cannot rest here; for our way of life itself may be challenged.

The second type of answer involves an attempt to justify that way of life. And such justification requires considerations other than mere logical analysis.

The analogy to the sciences is again clear. Thus, in connection with any given set of material bodies we may ask, *Are the spatial interrelations of these bodies Euclidean in character?* We may reply that they are because the Euclidicity of space is part of the Newtonian system of mechanics. If this answer is challenged, we may attempt to show that the Euclidicity of the spatial interrelations of material bodies follows from the (implicit) Newtonian assumption that rigid bodies exist (Euclidean geometry being the geometry of rigid bodies). But now it may be asked, *Why should we accept the Newtonian system?* An answer to this question requires considerations other than mere logical analysis—such as recourse to a wider range of observations and a more meticulous epistemological analysis; for the presuppositions of the system itself have now become problematic.

We began by asking the question, *Ought I to write the letter of recommendation for Smith?* Our first level of justification was (a) the assertion, *I ought to, because I promised him that I would,* and (b) the subsumption of this specific case under the general maxim, *Everyone ought to keep the promise he makes.* If now our general maxim is challenged, we must advance to the second level of justification, which is essentially a matter of logical analysis, showing that the maxim is indeed an integral part (either a logical implicate or an indispensable presupposition) of our way of life. If our way of life itself is challenged, we must advance to a third level of justification. And it is at this level that the ultimate questions of ethics arise.

### X

So far, however, we have considered only an oversimplified case, for we have stipulated at the beginning that at the first level of justification only the subsumption of the case under a general maxim was to be relevant. This restrictive stipulation points up one essential aspect of every moral situation. In concrete situations, however, the crux of the matter is never as simple as that, for the same act is subsumable under different maxims, and the maxims are not always in harmony. Thus, in the case of the letter of recommendation for Smith, a side of Smith's character may have come to my attention of which I was ignorant when I made the promise but which substantially alters my opinion of Smith. Ought I still to write the letter or ought I to tell Smith that I can no longer recommend him? But let us suppose that Smith has a sick wife and needs the position for which he is applying and for which he is otherwise well qualified; and let us assume also that my letter of recommendation would bring about his appointment, provided I did not mention the newly discovered flaw in Smith's character. The case is now subsumable under at least three general maxims— namely, (i) the maxim of promise-keeping, (ii) the maxim of truth-telling, and (iii) the maxim of helping a person in need— all of which are part of the accepted code of the society of which I am a member. But, obviously, it is impossible to subsume the case under all three maxims at the same time; for a combination of (i) and (ii) will not help Smith in getting the position; and a combination of (i) and (iii) is irreconcilable with (ii) because of the conflict of (ii) and (iii). It is evident, therefore, that justification by subsumption under general maxims must give way to other considerations at the first level of justification. And thus we find that under ordinary circumstances of human existence all three levels of justification may be involved and that the problem of justification of an act is by no means as simple as it appeared to be under the restrictive condition first imposed upon the example used above.

It must be noted that the maxims just referred to as (i), (ii), and (iii) are neither self-contradictory nor mutually inconsistent when taken simply as general maxims. It is therefore possible, at least in principle, to develop an integrated system of such maxims, which, as system, would be the accepted code of a given society. Difficulties arise only when the maxims are applied to situations in which the *facts* of the situation, when subsumed under the maxims, lead to irreconcilable conflicts. These difficulties can be resolved, however—or so it seems to me—when we adopt a new approach to moral problems—one based upon a comprehensive theory of values. But this is not the place to develop such a theory. A blue-print for it I have given elsewhere (*27; 28*). More of it will be presented in the chapters which follow. But a full and systematic development I intend to present in a separate volume.

The comprehensive theory of values here referred to has the additional advantage of combining as supplementary aspects of our moral experience the equivalent of utilitarian considerations with the imperatival demands of Kant and the deontologists, the value of Toulmin's "consideration of consequences" with the ought-equivalent of C. I. Lewis's "dictum of justice" (*16*:482). The hope may therefore be justified that this theory will also contribute to the problem of justification at the third level; that it will provide a broad framework of values within which maxims, in the only morally significant sense of universal prescriptions, can be derived when certain premises pertaining to values are taken in conjunction with a basic reasonableness of man.

It is true, of course, that people are not always reasonable. But it is also true that we need not produce a reasoned argument capable of convincing the wholly unreasonable; for to attempt to do so would involve us in a contradiction (*24*:165).

## XI

The emotive theory derives what plausibility it possesses from the fact that (a) the function of moral judgments is not exclusively, or even primarily, informative and predictive, and that (b) the normative or practical sense of such judgments cannot be explicated in terms of their descriptive meanings alone (*4*:173). But the emotive theory breaks down in its claim that the nondescriptive remainder is purely emotive, for the prescriptive force of *This ought not to be done* involves an element of objectivity which the basic schema of the emotivists, *I disapprove of this; do so as well,* does not express (*6*:517). Stevenson would argue, I am sure, that much, if indeed not all, of the objective force of moral judgments can be preserved if we interpret them as *We disapprove of this; do so as well,* or as *They disapprove of this; do so as well.* Yet I am equally sure that even in this form moral judgments will not long retain their prescriptive significance, if the person addressed is not convinced that what "we" or "they" disapprove *deserves* disapproval, that it is inimical to the highest values to which he himself stands committed.

What any theory must account for is not only the fact that moral judgments are not purely descriptive, but the further fact that they are also not mere expressions of personal approval, that, on the contrary, they imply a claim to impartiality, impersonality, and interpersonal authority which is independent of individual preferences (*3*:498; *11*:6). This claim can be justified only by an appeal to general rules of conduct and, ultimately, to a universal *ought*. What is required, therefore, is an interpretation of the ultimate *ought* as the first premise of *any* moral code. Such an interpretation, I believe, can be given in terms of the reasonableness of man. If a man's actions were completely determined by the facts and values given in a concrete situation, any reference to an *ought* would be meaningless, and moral judgments could have no normative significance. Man would be a mere automaton, responding tropistically to given stimuli. The emotive theory reduces man essentially to this position. But what raises man above this level of automatic responses is not simply his reason—his ability to think and to think clearly and logically; it is, rather, his reasonableness—his willingness and ability, that is, to act in conformity with his thinking and his insights; his willingness and ability to act in conformity with principles and in harmony with understood value relations. If this is so, then the imperative of reasonableness, embodying, as it does, the ultimate *ought,* can be formulated simply as follows: Act so that your actions tend at all times to realize the highest possible value. In terms of this imperative, taken in conjunction with the facts and values given in any concrete situation, every specific moral judgment pertaining to that situation can, in principle, be evaluated, can be justified or rejected on rational grounds.

But the rational justification (or rejection) of moral judgments here indicated does not preclude the presence of emotional elements in moral experience. In our mature experience the rational and emotional elements are inseparably interwoven (*11*:7). Admiration, love, respect, indignation, scorn, shame—these are but indicative of the wide range of emotions which are relevant to moral experience. And on many occasions our emotions rather than our rationally grounded judgments determine our course of action. By calling this fact most forcefully to our attention, the advocates of the emotive theory have rendered us a service. Their error lies in their denial of the efficacy of reason in moral decisions and in the modification of attitudes. But, surely, reliance on reason, on insight and rational argument, is a sign of maturity in moral matters no less than in science.

There may be a time in our life when our actions are essentially nothing but emotive responses—just as there is a time when our knowledge of things is purely perceptual. And there unquestionably is a time when our notions of morality stem from the persuasive influence of parents, teachers, and "persons of authority"—just as in science and history we derive most of what we know from others (*11*:11). But just as, in the realms of knowledge, we discover (as we mature intellectually) that consistency and comprehensiveness are criteria of the truth and progress of science, so, in our moral experience, we find that the very same criteria are significantly relevant to our moral judgments (*11*:17). As C. I. Lewis puts it with respect to one of these criteria: "If it were not that present valuing and doing may later be a matter of regret, then there would be no point and no imperative to consistency of any kind. No act would then be affected by relation to any principle, and no thinking by any consideration of validity. Life in general would be free of any concern; and there would be no distinction of what is rational from what is perverse or silly" (*16*:481). This imperative to be consistent in thought and action and valuation requires no proof, no justification in reason, for, "being itself the expression of that which is the root of all reason," it is also "that in the absence of which there could be no reason of any sort or for anything" (*16*:481).

The criterion of comprehensiveness emerges when the imperative of consistency is conjoined with the totality of (actual and possible) human experience; for consistency itself cannot be assured until the whole of experience is subsumed under all-comprehensive principles.

## XII

One final point is of importance. Moral judgments, as traditionally understood, are of two types. They are (a) judgments of evaluation: *X is good;* and they are (b) judgments of obligation: *I ought to do A.* But unless the evaluative judgments can be interpreted as being essentially descriptive, the emotivists may find in them disconcertingly strong support for their position. On the other hand, if evaluative judgments are in fact bona fide empirical judgments, the normative function of moral judgments remains inexplicable in terms of the evaluative judgments alone (2:16).

This difficulty can be solved, I am convinced, by a value-theoretical approach to ethics; for such an approach recognizes the descriptive character of judgments of evaluation (as grounded in value experience) and the independent normative function of imperatives (as grounded in the reasonableness of man). Traditional theories, in so far as they have tended to obliterate this distinction, have fallen victim to a mistaken ideal of unity. Believing that systemic unity requires an ultimate commitment to but one principle, the traditional ethicists have sacrificed the essential distinction between moral evaluation and the moral ought (attempting to derive the one from the other), and have to that extent falsified their interpretation of moral experience. We know, however, that systemic unity does not require reduction to one principle; that, as a matter of fact, the systemic integrations of experience which we call science all rest upon several first premises, the basic requirements being that the premises are not contradictory, and that they are as comprehensive as possible. The first of these requirements springs from the demands of reason alone, the second from the demand for a unified interpretation of all relevant facts of experience. There is no apparent reason why the requirements in ethics should not be the same. And if they are the same, then the value-theoretical approach already referred to completely satisfies (in principle, at least) the demands for a systemic interpretation which will do justice to the full richness, the inexhaustible manifoldness, of moral experience.

## REFERENCES

1. Adams, E. M., "Word-Magic and Logical Analysis in the Field of Ethics," *Journal of Philosophy,* XLVII (1950).
2. Aiken, H. D., "Evaluation and Obligation: Two Functions of Judgments in the Language of Conduct," *Journal of Philosophy,* XLVII (1950).
3. Aiken, H. D., "A Pluralistic Analysis of the Ethical 'Ought,' " *Journal of Philosophy,* XLVII (1951).
4. Aiken, H. D., "The Role of Conventions in Ethics," *Journal of Philosophy,* XLIX (1952).
5. Aiken, H. D., "Definitions, Factual Premises, and Ethical Conclusions," *Philosophical Review,* LXI (1952).
6. Aiken, H. D., "The Authority of Moral Judgments," *Philosophy and Phenomenological Research,* XII (1952).
7. Ayer, A. J., *Language, Truth and Logic,* rev. ed., London, 1948.
8. Brandt, R. B., "The Emotive Theory of Ethics," *Philosophical Review,* LIX (1950).
9. Carritt, E. F., "Moral Positivism and Moral Aestheticism," *Readings in Ethical Theory,* W. Sellars and J. Hospers, editors, New York, 1952.
10. Cross, R. C., "The Emotive Theory of Ethics," *Aristotelian Society,* Supplementary Volume XXII (1948).
11. Field, G. C., "The Nature of Ethical Thinking," *Aristotelian Society,* Supplementary Volume XXIV (1951).
12. Garvin, Lucius, "The New Rationalism in Ethics," *Journal of Philosophy,* XLVIII (1951).
13. Gilman, Eric, "The Distinctive Purpose of Moral Judgments," *Mind,* LXI (1952).
14. Kadish, M. R., "Evidence and Decision," *Journal of Philosophy,* XLVIII (1951).
15. Levy, S. E., "On the Tautologous Nature of Stevenson's Distinction between Disagreement in Belief and Disagreement in Attitude," *Journal of Philosophy,* XLIX (1952).
16. Lewis, C. I., *An Analysis of Knowledge and Valuation,* La Salle, 1946.
17. Paton, H. J., "The Emotive Theory of Ethics," *Aristotelian Society,* Supplementary Volume XXII (1948).
18. Robinson, R., "The Emotive Theory of Ethics," *Aristotelian Society,* Supplementary Volume XXII (1948).
19. Stevenson, C. L., *Ethics and Language,* New Haven, 1944.
20. Stevenson, C. L., "The Emotive Conception of Ethics and Its Cognitive Implications," *Philosophical Review,* LIX (1950).

21. Stevenson, C. L., Review of Ray Lepley's *Verifiability of Value, Journal of Philosophy,* XLI (1944).
22. Stroll, Avrum, *The Emotive Theory of Ethics,* University of California Publications in Philosophy, Berkeley–Los Angeles, 1954.
23. Tomas, V., "Ethical Disagreements and the Emotive Theory of Values, *Mind* LX (1951).
24. Toulmin, Stephen, *The Place of Reason in Ethics,* Cambridge, 1950.
25. Werkmeister, W. H., "Normative Propositions and the Ideal of an Integrated and Closed System," *Philosophy of Science,* XVIII (1951).
26. Werkmeister, W. H., *The Basis and Structure of Knowledge,* New York, 1948.
27. Werkmeister, W. H., "Prolegomena to Value Theory," *Philosophy and Phenomenological Research,* XIV (1954).
28. Werkmeister, W. H. "Ethics and Value Theory," *Proceedings of the XIth International Congress of Philosophy,* Brussells, 1953, Volume X, 119-123.
29. Frankel, Charles, "Empiricism and Moral Imperatives," *Journal of Philosophy,* L (1953).
30. Sesonske, Alexander, "On the Skepticism of *Ethics and Language,*" *Journal of Philosophy,* L (1953).

*Cognitive Interpretations*

*of Moral Phenomena*

SECTION ONE

TELEOLOGICAL

THEORIES

# INTRODUCTION TO
## PART II, SECTION ONE

In a paper significantly entitled "The Absolute Truth of Hedonism," W. H. Sheldon wrote: "Hedonism is true, so far as man is concerned absolutely true, true without qualification, everywhere and always, never denied in any degree. Pleasure—experience of things, events, objects which are desired—that is the only good, the only value in and for itself, known to man or animal. Everything else which we call good is good just so far as it tends toward pleasure, leads to happiness" (2:292). And again: "For conscious beings . . . all good, be it moral, esthetic, ontological, or whatever, . . . is what pleases when experienced" (2:286). "The goodness of the good is the pleasantness of it, pleasantness explicit at the moment or implicit for the future" (2:286). Hedonism is true, Sheldon adds, because it is a tautology, "and it is a waste of time to try to refute tautologies" (2:286).

Tautologies, of course, are irrefutable; but from Sheldon's own statements of the hedonistic thesis it is not altogether clear which of the formulations he regards as tautological. In one context he says that good is "what pleases *when experienced";* whereas in another context he says, more narrowly, that pleasure—"the only good, the only value in and for itself"—is the "experience of things, events, objects *which are desired."* The difference between the two statements is important; for the first formulation allows the pleasurable experience to occur independently of any antecedent desire, whereas the second specifically identifies it with the experience of a thing (event, object) desired. If we assume the ordinary meaning of the terms involved, the second formulation is hardly a tautology; for the actual experience of a thing desired may be distinctly unpleasant—as when the taste

91

of the red berry which we desire turns out to be bitter as gall. And to insist, in the face of such possibilities, upon the identity of pleasure with the experience of a thing desired is to distort the facts of human experience.

But let us assume for the sake of argument that Sheldon's basic thesis is correct, and that pleasure is the hedonist's moral good (2:285). We now face difficulties and problems which are bound up with the meaning of the term "pleasure" itself. To begin with, we are told that, "naturally, pleasure is not to be understood as sensual pleasure only" (2:286). Yet a qualitative distinction between pleasures is also not to be allowed. Pleasure, happiness, joy, bliss, satisfaction—the common element in all of them is pleasure. "The blissfulness of bliss, the satisfactoriness of satisfaction, and so on, is precisely the pleasantness of pleasure" (2:289). Higher quality, Sheldon points out, merely means greater intensity of pleasantness or a greater number or variety of pleasant objects (i.e., greater extensity of pleasantness)—or both (2:288). According to the hedonists, therefore, quantity elucidates quality in respect of good: "If something is good, more of it is better, and the maximum the best" (2:288). For the hedonist, "the *summum bonum* for morality is maximum intensity and extensity of pleasure," and "Socrates dissatisfied is better than a pig because Socrates has or could have a thousandfold more pleasures—those intrinsic to intelligent humanity—than a pig can have" (2:288). One wonders, however, whether the term "better," as used in the last statement, has a distinctive meaning. If it has no meaning other than "more, and more intensive, pleasure," then the statement as a whole is a vicious *petitio*. It is a *petitio* because it merely asserts that Socrates, even when dissatisfied, has (or could have) more pleasures than a pig because he has (or could have) a thousandfold more pleasures. It is vicious because, in the context of Sheldon's statement, the term "better" normally suggests, if it does not imply, an evaluation of Socrates himself rather than of the intensity and extensity of the pleasures he may have. But if the term "better," as used above, has a meaning which saves the statement in question from becoming a vicious *petitio;* if it refers, for example, to "a sense of dignity, which all human beings possess in one form or another" (as John Stuart Mill put it) (*1*:9), does not this fact alone re-introduce a qualitative evaluation which contradicts the hedonistic thesis?

In any case, as Sheldon admits, pleasure is clearly an individual matter, for one directly enjoys his own pleasures only (*2*:285). Hedonism has therefore been accused of being inevitably selfish. Sheldon maintains, however, that hedonism does not necessarily contradict altruism. Herbert Spencer, for example, has pointed out that the egotist can enjoy the fullest and deepest happiness only by coming to delight in the happiness of all creatures, and actively working therefore (*2*:293). But Sheldon admits that this argument reduces the moral problem to a question of prudence only, and that the egotist "will not make the tremendous effort required to realize that his happiness does depend on the happiness of all men, still less on the happiness of animals" (*2*:293). Although the egotist, seeking at all times his own pleasure, will perhaps work for the good of the limited circle on whom his prosperity obviously depends, but his conduct will be guided by rules of prudence rather than by laws of an altruistic morality. The problem, therefore, is: Can hedonism satisfy the demand for an imperative, an ought, a moral law?

Sheldon contends that it is not the pleasure-motive as such which is wrong, but the radical evil of our nature which induces us to take that motive "in the exclusive sense of a search for one's own pleasure or the pleasure of one's group, regardless of others" (*2*:293). Egotism, in other words, is no implicate of hedonism itself. Hedonism, according to Sheldon, simply means that "the good of every wish lies in the joy of fulfillment of his natural wants"; and the means of this fulfillment "constitute the moral law" (*2*:294). But if this is so, then, Sheldon argues, "hedonism is intrinsically, inevitably universal": "When you come to understand that my happiness ought to be, *because* it is wanted by me, you have seen a universal truth: whatever is wanted (other things not interfering) should come to be, and no matter who brings it about" (*2*:294).

The force of this argument depends on the identification of

that which *ought to be* with that which is *wished for,* or, as Sheldon himself puts it most forcefully, "it all turns on the absolute identity of goodness or oughtness with wantedness" (2:294). And the question arises: Is this identification justified? It is possible, of course, to stipulate definitionally that "oughtness" means "wantedness" and nothing else; but such procedure does not solve the problem at issue. Ordinary usage clearly distinguishes "ought to be" and "is wanted," so that it is meaningful to say with respect to specific ends: *What is wanted ought not to be,* or: *What ought to be is not wanted;* and ordinary usage here makes sense. But if "oughtness" means "wantedness," and nothing else, then the statements in question can by tautological substitutions be shown to be inherently contradictory: *What is wanted is not wanted.* The complete identification of "oughtness" with "wantedness" is impossible because, in any given context, "is wanted" implies, explicitly or implicitly, a subject (individual or group) who *wants,* whereas "ought to be" implies instead a reference to criteria which transcend any particular want under consideration.

Let us examine another aspect of Sheldon's argument. Let us grant for the moment that, in the tautological sense intended by Sheldon, "my happiness ought to be, *because* it is wanted by me" (2:294). Does this concession redeem hedonism from its inherent egotism? Sheldon maintains that, having understood the proposition, we have come to see a universal truth—the truth, namely, that "whatever is wanted (other things not interfering) should come to be, and no matter who brings it about" (2:294). This argument, obviously, depends on an ambiguity; for it is one thing to say that, from *my* point of view, my happiness ought to be because it is wanted by me, and it is an entirely different thing to say that, from *anybody's* point of view, my happiness ought to be because it is wanted by me (3:650). The first statement does not in itself entail the second. That which, *from my point of view,* ought to be because I want it as something which gives *me* pleasure, is always something which, *from your point of view,* ought to be because you want it as something which gives you pleasure. In this tautological sense, therefore, if you want my happiness, you want it only because it *pleases you* to see me happy, not because *I want* to be happy. The essential egotism of the initial position has therefore not been overcome.

I have discussed Sheldon's article at such length because, in my opinion, it is a most forceful summary of the hedonistic theory of morals. It contains elements of psychological hedonism, egotistic hedonism, and universalistic hedonism; and its arguments are beset by the problems and difficulties which beset all hedonism. In the chapters which follow I shall discuss more fully the problems and difficulties which they encounter. My aim is an over-all evaluation of the whole hedonistic approach to morals.

## REFERENCES

1. Mill, J. S., "Utilitarianism," in *Utilitarianism, Liberty, and Representative Government,* Everyman's Library.
2. Sheldon, W. H., "The Absolute Truth of Hedonism," *Journal of Philosophy,* XLVII (1950).
3. Williams, G., "Hedonism, Conflict, and Cruelty," *Journal of Philosophy,* XLVIII (1950).

# CHAPTER III

# Psychological Hedonism

Hedonism, Sidgwick wrote, "aims at pleasure as pleasure and nothing else" (7:82); and psychological hedonism, in particular, holds that it is "a given fact of human . . . behavior that pleasure is the sole end pursued"; that "each organism [human or animal] does and can act only to the end of its own pleasure" (2:6). In these statements the emphasis lies upon the phrases, "a given fact," and, "does and can act only." In other words, psychological hedonism maintains that, *as a matter of fact,* of all alternatives present to an organism, that (and only that) response to a stimulus occurs which, "at the moment of inception, is associated with the greatest pleasantness" (2:13).

This hedonism, Sheldon holds, is not only "the instinctive view of the natural man" but is verified constantly in everyday life; for "men *do* seek things that bring pleasure, avoid those that give pain." And, Sheldon adds, "it is in practice impossible for [man] to avoid the search for pleasure and removal of pain." "Whenever we want something, be it duty for duty's sake, or knowledge for itself alone, or just a tasty morsel, we want the joy of getting it; whenever we dislike anything we hope for the joy of its absence" (6:290).

Pleasure, however, according to the psychological hedonists, is not always our *conscious* motive. We do not always *think* of

96

the pleasure we may obtain. Nevertheless, so we are assured, "the lure of pleasure is the power behind the throne." "Hedonism does not say that every man is conscious of his hedonism; only that he acts it" (*6*:291). "All objections to hedonism, therefore, which are based on what allegedly is or is not in the organism's 'consciousness' are irrelevant" (*2*:21).

Two crucial questions now arise: (1) Does psychological hedonism, as here defined, give us an accurate and complete description of motivated human behavior? (2) Does it provide an adequate basis for moral evaluations and the moral *ought?*

In our search for an answer to these questions, we shall begin with an examination of the traditional formulations of psychological hedonism—with an examination of formulations, that is, which are given in terms of pleasure and pain. Then, after having evaluated these, we shall try to determine whether or not a restatement of hedonism in terms of pleasantness and unpleasantness (as suggested by Hilliard) makes a significant difference in the basic position.

## I

To begin with, let us note that, in psychological hedonism, *feeling*—a feeling, namely, of "relative affectivity" (*2*:38)—is the necessary condition determining all actions; that, in Bentham's words, pleasure and pain are the "two sovereign masters," which alone "determine what we shall do" (*1*:1); and that, according to Hilliard, "relative pleasantness and unpleasantness occurring prior to or simultaneously with the response to a stimulus determines the actualization of one alternative and the rejection of all others" (*2*:36, 25). Volition, in other words, is always determined by the greatest pleasure (or absence of pain) in prospect (*7*:35).

Two important facts stand out in the quotations just given. One is the *determinism* inherent in psychological hedonism. The other is the emphasis upon *feeling* or affectivity. These facts are, of course, interrelated; and both deserve consideration.

If it is true that volition is always determined by the greatest pleasure in prospect or by the greatest positive affectivity, then, it seems, the efficacy of reason has been denied altogether and there is no basis for a moral *ought*. If no one can help pursuing at all times the greatest pleasure in prospect, then the *ought* is meaningless; for an *ought* can have meaning only if there is a choice between alternative courses of action.

Hilliard admits that in our own first-person experience we "perceive that the predicates 'being chosen' and 'being pleasantest' are logically distinct." He admits, in other words, that "I may in various circumstances feel one alternative object to be pleasantest without actually choosing any." But he hastens to add that whenever I have chosen an alternative, it is invariably the one which, at the moment of inception, appeared pleasantest to me among all its competitors (2:16). Conversely, "if an alternative is not felt as pleasantest, then it is not chosen" (2:17). This argument, however, hardly does justice to the meaning of choice. It freely concedes that only the pleasantest course of action is followed in all cases—thus confirming the basic determinism. But *not* to act (in the sense of pursuing a particular object) is also a course of action and is, in the behavioral sense, an additional alternative. Hence, if in certain circumstances I feel one alternative object to be pleasantest without actively pursuing it, then, on the basis of the hedonism here under consideration, this can be the case only because I experience my inactivity as still more pleasant. And, be it noted, there is no contradiction in saying that I feel one alternative *object* to be the pleasantest and yet feel at the same time that my *state* of inactivity is still more pleasant. The alternative *object* and *my state* belong to different realms of experience. Hilliard's argument, therefore, does not alter the basic determinism inherent in psychological hedonism. It does, however, make the term "choice" meaningless.

Sheldon holds that "the hedonist is right when he says that we always follow the stronger lure." But, he adds, the determinist "forgets that often, too often, we ourselves make it the stronger by choosing to dwell on it" (6:291). In reply to this argument one need only point out that to dwell on something is also a mode of action. Hence, if *all* our actions are determined by the stronger lure, then our dwelling on an object (or on an action) can be no exception to the law but must itself be determined by the object's (or the action's) being the stronger lure. We have in this case no freedom of attention.[1] On the other hand, if we have freedom of attention, i.e., if we can choose to dwell on something which is not already the stronger lure, then, obviously, we do not always follow the stronger lure. And if we do not follow the stronger lure in one type of action, then it is at least possible that we need not follow it in others. Sheldon's argument, therefore, if consistently followed through, either implies a denial of freedom and, therefore, of a moral *ought,* or it admits a motivation other than the greater lure of pleasure, of positive affectivity.

In order to save the moral *ought,* Sheldon goes on to argue that we always seek pleasure in our voluntary acts; that, "did we but realize it, deep in our hearts we want maximum pleasure, lasting and manifold" (6:291). He finds, however, that we seldom realize with sufficient force and clearness what our deepest wishes are, and that, for this reason, we often choose pleasures which work against them (6:291). Here, Sheldon maintains, "enters the truth and the import of ethical hedonism": "We *ought* to choose the most fruitful pleasures" (6:291). But—and this is the crucial point—"the oughtness of the ought," according to Sheldon, is "only the fact that ever the motive is at work within us, the subconscious drive toward maximum happiness— if only we would let it succeed" (6:291)! "Hedonism is but man the wisher coming to self-consciousness" (6:292).

In this argument two points require comment. The first is Sheldon's explicit reference to choice: We often choose pleasures which work against our subconscious drive toward maximum happiness. Sheldon admits that this happens only because we seldom realize with sufficient force and clearness what our deepest wishes are; but, still, he maintains that we *choose.* Would it not be more in keeping with the basic thesis of psychological

---

[1] Cf. "Freedom of will, at least in morals, is freedom of attention" (6:291).

hedonism to omit any reference to choice and to say instead that, at times, the stronger lure of certain objects determines our actions in such a way as to lead our deepest wishes astray? This would at least be consistent doctrine; but, being thoroughgoing determinism, it would also eliminate the moral *ought*.

The second point to be noted is Sheldon's identification of "the oughtness of the ought" with "the subconscious drive toward maximum happiness." If this identification were an adequate interpretation of the moral *ought*, it would imply that we act from a moral *ought* whenever our subconscious drive has full sway in determining what we do. Obviously, however, this is not what we mean when we speak of an *ought*. We mean, rather, a rational control and guidance of our actions and drives. And I am sure that Sheldon himself would agree with us; for he says: "We *ought* to choose the most fruitful pleasures, *even if for the present that means choosing* the painful" (6:291). The restraint, in the interest of future happiness, of our desire for present pleasures is possible only on the basis of a rational control of our actions. And in this control, rather than in any subconscious drive, lies the crux of the moral *ought*.

The basic difficulties of psychological hedonism arise from the fact that, on the one hand, in order to give any meaning whatever to the moral *ought*, it is forced to speak of choice and choosing, and that, on the other hand, it denies the efficacy of reason and thus makes effective choice impossible. These difficulties even Hilliard does not escape. To be sure, he speaks of the "persuasive powers of reason" (2:39) when we deal with mere means to an end. "A man," he says, "can be persuaded to approve, and so to choose a particular means by the demonstration that it *is* a means to something which is agreeable to him" (2:38); but he also holds, as we have seen, that of all alternatives present to an organism, that (and only that) response to a stimulus occurs which, at the moment of inception, is associated with the greatest pleasantness. And such determinism precludes genuine choice. The persuasive powers of reason can here function only in an emotive sense. That is to say, rational insight is here effective, not because it is rational, nor because it is insight, but solely because it is *persuasive,* i.e., because it adds to the positive affectivity which determines our every response. But to be persuasive in this sense is hardly the meaning of the moral *ought.* On the other hand, if rational insight is effective simply because it is rational and because it is insight, irrespective of its persuasive affectivity, then there is no reason whatsoever for restricting its efficacy to means only. In fact, a broadened interpretation would be more adequate to human experience than is the hedonist's denial of the efficacy of reason. After all, man is a rational and a reasonable being. He is *rational* in so far as he can and does think clearly and with logical coherence; he is *reasonable* in so far as he is guided by his reasoning. And insight is not *felt effectivity;* it is not a matter of *feeling.*

If the hedonists now argue that man's desire to avoid pain and to obtain pleasure is the true basis of the moral law and that the denial of the efficacy of reason does therefore not affect the significance of the *ought,* we hold, with Sidgwick and Kant, that such an argument misses the point; for "it is manifestly possible that our prospect of pleasure resulting from any course of conduct may largely depend on our conception of it as right or otherwise: and in fact this must be normally the case with the conduct of conscientious persons" (7:35) if psychological hedonism itself is true. In order even to imagine that a man is "tormented with mortification by the consciousness of his transgressions" of the moral law or that he is "delighted by the consciousness of doing dutiful acts," we must presuppose that this man is "at least to a degree morally good." This means, as Kant well knew, that "the concept of morality and duty [i.e., the concept of the *ought*] must precede all reference to the satisfaction and cannot be derived from it" (3:150).

## II

John Stuart Mill held that "desiring a thing and finding it pleasant . . . are . . . in the strictness of language, two different modes of naming the same psychological fact: that to think of an object as desirable . . . and to think of it as pleasant, are one and the same thing; and that to desire anything, except in proportion as the idea of it is pleasant, is a physical and metaphysical impossibility" (*4*:36). In a similar vein, Sheldon writes: "It is senseless to say that we desire a thing *because* it is good; it is just as senseless to say a thing is good because we desire it. Good and desire, for us human beings, . . . are the two sides or phases of one and the same event or state or entity" (*6*:299). "The very goodness of the pleasure lies in the fact that we want the object while we have it," and "an anticipated or hoped-for pleasure belongs to an object which we wish to gain" (*6*:286). Pleasure, in other words, "*means* the luring object gained," and *lure* is but "the promise of pleasure in the object" (*6*:287).

In these passages desire and pleasure (or good) are referred to as two aspects of one and the same psychological fact. The statements, however, are not as clear and precise as they appear to be at first glance, and the support they give to hedonism can easily be overrated.

Consider, for example, the first part of Mill's statement. If, "in the strictness of language," "desiring a thing" and "finding it pleasant" are but different ways of *naming* the same fact, then the two phrases are synonyms. And if this is the case, then to say that we always desire what is pleasant is a tautological assertion, not a psychological truth. On the other hand, if we follow ordinary usage—i.e., if we take "pleasure" to mean an *agreeable feeling* and take "desiring" to mean *longing for,* then the statement that we always desire pleasure is not tautological; but neither is it necessarily true.

Sidgwick, I believe, has seen clearer than have the psychological hedonists that "throughout the whole scale of our impulses, sensual, emotional, and intellectual alike, we can distinguish desires of which the object, what we are consciously moved to realize, is something other than our own pleasure." Hunger, for example, "is a direct impulse to eat food. Its indulgence is no doubt commonly attended with an agreeable feeling of more or less intensity: but it cannot . . . be strictly said that this agreeable feeling is the object of hunger, and that it is the representation of this pleasure which stimulates the will of the hungry man. Of course hunger is frequently and naturally accompanied with anticipation of the pleasure of eating: but careful introspection seems to show that the two are by no means inseparable: and that even when they occur together the pleasure is the object not of the primary appetite, but of a secondary desire which is to be distinguished from the former" (7:38; 39).

Moreover, it is a psychological fact—we may speak of it as the fundamental paradox of hedonism—that the impulse towards pleasure, if too predominant, defeats its own aim. This may not be so clear in the case of our passive sensual pleasures, "but of our active enjoyments generally, whether the activities on which they attend are classed as 'bodily' or as 'intellectual' . . . , it may certainly be said that we cannot attain them, at least in their best form, so long as we concentrate our aim on them" (7:41). The "pleasures of thought and study," for example, can really be enjoyed only by persons "who have an ardor of curiosity which carries the mind temporarily away from self and its sensations" (7:42). "And there are many pleasures of the merely animal life which can only be obtained on condition of not being directly sought, no less than the satisfactions of a good conscience" (7:43). We conclude therefore, with Sidgwick, that "a man's predominant desire is . . . most commonly not a conscious impulse towards pleasure" (7:44).

Hilliard admits that our conclusion may be true. He admits, in other words, that "what all men are conscious of pursuing are the myriad concrete goals of actual life—wealth, health, wisdom, food, shelter, friendship, and so on." He maintains, however, that although the fact is true, the objection is irrelevant; that "what men are *conscious* of, what they have in attention or awareness, has nothing to do with the case" (2:7). "Men's ends are to be determined from their behavior, not by what allegedly they did or did not have 'in mind' just prior to acting"; and, "as modern psychology agrees, most conduct is unconsciously motivated" (2:7).

Two comments are in order. First, to admit that all men are

conscious of pursuing concrete goals rather than pleasure, and yet to maintain (as Hilliard does) that what they are conscious of "has nothing to do with the case," is to deny the efficacy of consciousness in all our actions and thus to distort human experience beyond recognition. Even modern psychology does not go that far; for to hold that *most* conduct is unconsciously motivated is by no means the same as to assert that *all* conduct must be so motivated. But if some conduct is not unconsciously motivated, then what men are conscious of when they pursue the concrete goals of life may very well have something to do with the case.

Secondly, even if we were to admit for the sake of argument that all human behavior is completely determined by unconscious motives, it would not follow from this admission alone that psychological hedonism is true; for it would still be possible to assume unconscious motives of various kinds—such as a power drive, a death instinct, or instinctive parental love. If it be argued that all of these drives reduce to an unconscious desire for pleasure, one might well reply that such a reductive interpretation assumes rather than proves the basic contention of psychological hedonism, and that the argument, therefore, is a *petitio;* for if it is true—as Hilliard admits that it is—that men in their various activities are conscious of pursuing the concrete goals of life, then the contention that all this does not count and that the *real* motive in all human activities is an unconscious, i.e., an unknown or unrecognized, desire for pleasure is not an inference from *facts* but from a *hedonistic prejudice.* It is a reductionistic construction for the sake of a theory.

## III

It is Hilliard's contention that affectivity provides the experiential basis for all values; that, in fact, *value* is but "affectivity occurring in the relational contexture determined by the reaction of an organism to a stimulus object" (2:42). To be sure, value is not simply the equivalent of affectivity; but "the reaction of an organism to an object is the necessary and sufficient condition of the occurrence of value," and "value occurs or is capable of occurring in every case where an organism is able to respond (directly or indirectly) to an object" (2:43). Proponents of an empirically oriented value theory may be in far-reaching agreement with these contentions. They may agree, furthermore, that ethics is in some way related to the values disclosed in experience. A confusion arises, however, when an empirically grounded descriptive theory of values is, by itself, taken to be a theory of ethics. A good many naturalists in ethics, I fear, have become victims of this confusion.

The issue involved here can perhaps be best understood if we keep in mind two distinctive theses: (1) The thesis that values are disclosed in human experience and that laws may be discovered which govern the interrelations of these values and which "state regularities between the occurrences of value experiences and certain psychological, biological, and sociological factors" (5:518). (2) The thesis (of the ethical naturalists) that "the meaning of any ethical statement is the same as a statement reporting the occurrence of that set of 'natural' conditions which regularly accompany the value experience reported by the statement" (5:518). The confusion referred to arises from the fact (which Popkin has noted) that many naturalists have acted as if the evidence for (1) somehow constitutes evidence for (2), and as if an attack on this asserted connection between (1) and (2), through the disclosure of the naturalistic fallacy, were an attack upon (1). In the shuffle the real relation between ethics and value theory has been obscured (8:119-123).

That the evidence in support of (1) is overwhelming is, in my opinion, beyond all question. An empirically oriented descriptive theory of value and value interrelations is definitely within the realm of possibilities (9). The factual support for (1), however, is not at the same time also factual support for (2), for ethical statements are normative and not descriptive. Hence, to defend ethical naturalism by defending an empirically oriented value theory is not to defend the former at all.

In the preceding argument I have referred three times to Popkin's paper, "Ethical Naturalism and Hedonics," for there is a similarity in his argument and mine. This similarity, however, is more apparent than real, for we argue from different points of view based upon different interpretations of the facts. Popkin holds that "the ethical naturalist's philosophical thesis is something of the following sort: (1) all statements in which terms like 'good,' 'bad,' 'beautiful,' and 'ugly' occur, are equivalent in meaning to statements containing no value terms, but only natural ones like 'stimulus,' 'nervous tension,' 'conditioning,' etc., and (2) all statements in which terms like 'ought' occur are equivalent in meaning to disjunctive propositions containing only natural terms, of the form 'Either——happens, or such-and-such other events will occur' " (5:520-521). In support of this thesis, which Popkin himself is willing to accept, he argues, first, that such a thesis is not logically self-contradictory, and that his own intuitive experience confirms it. As he puts it: "I find that I can not intuitively discover any distinction or difference in what I mean by statements like 'x is good' and certain natural ones. Also I find that I know of no human value situation which can not be treated as if the identification between the value experience and the natural one were the case" (5:521).

Now, obviously, the equivalence in meaning of such terms as "good," "bad," "beautiful," and "ugly," on the one hand, and of "stimulus," "nervous tension," and "conditioning," on the other, can be established by definitional fiat. In that case, however, the terms in question no longer adequately describe the facts of value experience. A felt satisfaction, for example, which, surely, may be called *good,* is by no means the same as a nervous tension or a conditioning. *My* intuitive experience discloses here not an equivalence but an irreducible distinction; and the experience of the race, as reflected in the development of distinctive vocabularies for the description of value experience and of facts, confirms my observation. But if such terms as "good," "bad," "beautiful," and "ugly" pertain in some way to distinctive value experiences and are thus value terms, then the statements containing them cannot be equivalent in meaning to statements which contain no value terms. The first thesis of ethical naturalism, as stated by Popkin, is in that case inherently contradictory and therefore not tenable.

But the second thesis, too, is impaired. So long as the disjunctive proposition merely states that, *as a matter of fact,* "Either ——happens, or such-and-such other events will occur," what actually does happen remains a matter of complete indifference. But no statements in which the term "ought" occurs is equivalent in meaning to statements of such factual indifference. What makes the second thesis of ethical naturalism plausible at all is the implicit assumption that the disjunction has a specific reference to values. This value reference, however, is an illicit intrusion since, by stipulation, the disjunctive proposition is to contain only natural terms. We therefore find that the second thesis either does not justify the *ought* at all or that it, too, is inherently contradictory and therefore untenable.

As a matter of fact, even a reference to values and value alternatives does not in itself establish an *ought.* The sole justification of the *ought* lies, I believe, in the reasonableness of man. Why, for example, *ought* I to choose the higher of two values? I *ought* to do it because I am a reasonable being, and it would be unreasonable to do otherwise. The values involved may, of course, be pleasures and satisfactions—I do not deny that pleasures and satisfactions are values. But whatever the values are, the *ought* is in no way derivable from values alone. Whatever truth there may be in psychological hedonism may well find its place within a general value theory; but even a value theory does not in itself explain or justify an *ought.*

## IV

In conclusion let us consider whether or not Hilliard's change in terminology from "pleasure" and "pain" to "pleasantness" and "unpleasantness" alters the situation materially in favor of psychological hedonism.

To speak of "pleasure" and "pain" as opposites, Hilliard maintains, is an egregious error. It is in fact "the commonest and most venerable error associated with hedonism" (2:20); but it is an error just the same, for unpleasantness is not the same as pain (2:19). There are two reasons, Hilliard points out, for making the distinction: (1) Whereas pain is always correlated with the excitation of specific receptors in the nervous system, no such physiological correlates to pleasantness and unpleasantness have as yet been found. (2) "Unpleasantness, though usually, is not necessarily associated with pain. Mild pains are often indifferent and sometimes pleasant" (2:20-21).

Let us grant that Hilliard has established his case with respect to the difference between pain and unpleasantness. Let us grant, in other words, that a consistent hedonist can be concerned only with "affectivity" or "hedonic tone"—with a class of experiential elements the sole members of which are "pleasantness, indifference, and unpleasantness" (2:14); and, for the sake of clarity, let us restrict our discussion to "pleasantness" or "positive affectivity."

"Pleasantness," as Hilliard understands the term, denotes an element of experience which is definable only ostensively or by periphrasis (2:14). It does not denote bodily pleasures (2:19) but refers instead to "that quality attaching to experienced events in virtue of which they are reacted to as pleasant" (2:14). Also, the quality of pleasantness must not be confused with the ways in which pleasantness is experienced; for pleasantness "may be attained in countless ways . . . , but the thing attained is the same, save in degree" (2:20).

Two considerations will show, I believe, that even this modification of the doctrine does not save psychological hedonism.

(1) The terminological clarification which Hilliard has achieved does not mitigate the determinism inherent in psychological hedonism. As a matter of fact, Hilliard himself re-emphasizes that determinism. "Relative pleasantness and unpleasantness," he says, "occurring prior to or simultaneously with the response to a stimulus *determines* the actualization of one alternative and the rejection of all others" (2:36; 13). But this determinism, whether interpreted in terms of pleasure and pain or in terms of pleasantness and unpleasantness, completely destroys all meaning of choice and therefore of the *ought*.

(2) By recognizing pleasantness and unpleasantness as distinctive and irreducible elements of experience, Hilliard has repudiated the naturalistic reductionism attempted by Popkin (and others). In doing so he has pointed out facts relevant to any empirically oriented value theory—although the facts referred to may not be all the facts which must be taken into consideration. However, we are here concerned with ethics rather than with value theory. The difference is crucial. Propositions of value theory are descriptive in character. Propositions of ethics, on the other hand, are normative. And normative propositions cannot be derived from descriptive propositions, be the latter descriptive of facts or of values. Moreover, it does not matter whether values are interpreted in terms of pleasure and pain or in terms of pleasantness and unpleasantness. In either case the propositions of value theory are descriptive, whereas the propositions of ethics are and remain normative.

Hilliard's modification of psychological hedonism, although it may clarify issues of value theory, does not solve the basic problem of ethics.

## REFERENCES

1. Bentham, J., *An Introduction to the Principles of Morals and Legislation,* Hafner Library of Classics, 1948 edition.
2. Hilliard, A. L., *The Forms of Value: The Extension of a Hedonistic Axiology,* New York, 1950.
3. Kant, I., *Critique of Practical Reason,* L. W. Beck translation, Chicago, 1949.
4. Mill, J. S., "Utilitarianism," in *Utilitarianism, Liberty, and Representative Government,* Everyman's Library.
5. Popkin, R. H., "Ethical Naturalism and Hedonics," *Journal of Philosophy,* XLVIII (1951).
6. Sheldon, W. H., "The Absolute Truth of Hedonism," *Journal of Philosophy,* XLVII (1950).
7. Sidgwick, H., *The Methods of Ethics,* 2nd ed., London, 1877.
8. Werkmeister, W. H., "Ethics and Value Theory," *Proceedings of the Eleventh International Congress of Philosophy,* Brussells, 1953, X.
9. Werkmeister, W. H., "Problems of Value Theory," *Philosophy and Phenomenological Research,* XII (1950).
10. Werkmeister, W. H., "Prolegomena to Value Theory," *Philosophy and Phenomenological Research,* XIV (1954).

# CHAPTER IV

# Egoistic Hedonism

## I

In the preceding chapter I have maintained (a) that references to an *ought* are meaningless if all our actions are completely determined by affectivity or by feelings of pleasure and pain; and (b) that an *ought* cannot be derived from, or justified in terms of, purely descriptive propositions—be they descriptive of facts or of values. The determinism I have rejected because it denies the efficacy of reason which, being but an expression of the reasonableness of man, is deeply grounded in human nature. I shall assume now that man, as a reasonable being, can and does act in conformity with his rational insights. The non-descriptive nature of the *ought,* however, though obvious to all who consider the relevant facts, may require further consideration.

No one denies, as Sidgwick has pointed out, that "the proposition 'I (or you) ought to do A' is in form legitimate" (*12*:25), i.e., no one denies that it is of the form of propositions generally. But, as Sidgwick also noted, "the common meaning of such propositions is by some writers implicitly rejected" (*12*:25). Two lines of reasoning lead to this rejection. (1) It is argued that "the [normative] proposition really states no more than the

110

existence of a particular emotion in the mind of the person who utters it: that when I say 'Truth ought to be spoken' or 'Truth-speaking is right,' I mean no more than that the idea of truth-speaking excites in my mind a feeling of approbation" (*12*:25).[1] (2) It is argued that "when we say that a man 'ought' to do anything, we mean that he is bound under penalties to do it" (*12*:27).

In answer to the first line of argument Sidgwick admits—and I think rightly—that probably some degree of an approbative emotion always or ordinarily accompanies an ethical judgment. It is absurd, however, to think that such an admission implies that "a mere statement of my approbation of truthspeaking is properly given in the proposition 'Truth ought to be spoken' " (*12*:25). After all, as ordinarily understood, "Truth ought to be spoken" and "Truth ought not to be spoken" are mutually contradictory statements; but if the former expresses merely A's approbation of truthspeaking under certain conditions, whereas the latter expresses no more than B's disapprobation of truthspeaking under the same conditions, then the facts in the case are not contradictory. Two coexisting facts are stated in two mutually contradictory propositions—and this is at the very least a violation of good usage.

If thesis (1) is altered to read that "the existence of the emotion is all that there is any *ground* for stating, or perhaps that it is all that any reasonable person is prepared on reflection to affirm [when he speaks of an ought]," then, Sidgwick admits, there is indeed a class of common statements, in form resembling statements of objective fact, in justification of which ordinarily no reason is given save an appeal to our feelings. Thus, "if I say that 'the air is sweet,' or 'the food disagreeable,' it would not be exactly true to say that I mean no more than that I like the one or dislike the other: but if my statement is challenged, I shall probably content myself with affirming the existence of such feelings in my own mind" (*12*:25-26). But—and Sidgwick was well aware of this fact—there is a fundamental difference

---

[1] Here, in all essentials, is the formulation of the emotive theory which anticipates the work of Carnap, Ayer, and Stevenson.

between this case and that of "moral feelings"; for "the emotion of moral approbation is inseparably bound up with the conviction, implicit or explicit, that the conduct approved is 'right' or 'ought to be done'" (*12*:26). Mere liking, in other words, is not the equivalent of moral approbation. I approve because it is "right"; but it isn't "right" merely because I like it.

In answer to the second line of argument—(2) above—it may be admitted that this interpretation of the *ought* has some plausibility because of an analogy between moral and legal obligation. Analysis shows, however, that the meaning of the moral *ought* is not equivalent to the meaning of "you will be punished if you don't"; for "there are many things which we judge men 'ought' to do, while perfectly aware that they will incur no . . . penalties for omitting them" (*12*:28). The *ought* is again bound up with the idea of rightness. Something *ought* to be done because it is right, not because its omission will be punished. The threat of punishment establishes no moral obligation. If it did, then all threatened people would be under moral obligation to whatever men threaten them, and would be under the greatest moral obligation to those who threaten them the most; might would indeed make right. But the whole history of man's moral development belies such an interpretation.

It is true, of course, that rightness, too, requires an explanation, for the term "right" is ambiguous. If, in Ross's terminology (*10*:146-191), "an act's rightness is its suitabilty to the situation," is it its suitability to the objective situation, or to the subjective, i.e., to the agent's opinion about the objective situation? "In one sense it is right for me to do what I think it right to do: but again, my thought may be wrong, so that what in another sense is right for me to do, may be really something different" (*12*:30). Sidgwick maintains that, unless the contrary is expressly indicated, moral judgments predicate objective rightness. They state what in a certain respect is right and what must be judged right "by all rational beings who judge truly of the matter," irrespective of whether or not a particular agent thinks it right. In other words, Sidgwick holds that the cognition of objective rightness is the cognition of a dictate or precept of reason (*12*:30); and I think that Sidgwick's view here is correct.

Of course, some people may deny that they can find in their consciousness any such absolute imperative as is implied in the idea of objective rightness. But if such a denial is truly the final result of self-examination, then (I believe with Sidgwick) there is no more to be said; for there is no way of imparting the notion of moral obligation to any one who is entirely devoid of it or who dogmatically adheres to a basic unreasonableness. I am sure, however, (as was Sidgwick) that in many cases in which the notion of moral obligation does not appear to be explicit, it will be found to be implied in some other conception of common use (*12*:31); for the *ought,* I hold, is deeply grounded in man's rational and reasonable nature.

But let us consider for a moment some of the views according to which the *ought* is latent and implicit rather than explicit, and the moral ideal is presented as attractive rather than imperative (*12*:94). The Greeks, for example, generally took this view. Virtue or right action was for them only a species of the *good* or the *desirable,* and their basic problem was how to determine the relation of this species of good to the rest of the genus (*12*:95). The problem, however, is two-fold. First, the term "good" itself must be defined; then, when this has been accomplished, "a standard for estimating the relative values of different 'goods' has still to be sought" (*12*:96). After all, the idea of an *ought* implies an authoritative prescription to do (or to refrain from doing) a certain act; but "when we have judged conduct to be good, it is not yet clear that we ought to prefer this kind of good to all other good things" (*12*:96).

From the earliest times some thinkers have maintained that by calling anything "good" we mean no more than that it is *pleasant,* either directly or indirectly, so that "the comparison of different modes of conduct with each other, and with other things in respect of goodness, is really a comparison of them as sources of pleasure" (*12*:97). Epicurus thus held that "we recognize pleasure as the first good innate in us, and [that] from pleasure we begin every act of choice and avoidance, and to pleasure we return again, using the feeling as the standard by which we judge every good" (*3*:31-32). This position, however, must not be confused with psychological hedonism; for the view is not that pleasure or pain always *determines* a man's action, but that pleasure is the only thing which men call *desirable* or *good*. We shall speak of this position as *moral* hedonism.

## II

Let us repeat: Moral hedonism asserts that pleasure is the only thing which men call *desirable* or *good*. Pleasure, in other words, is said to be good, not in the sense of being actually *desired* (although, of course, it may be desired), but in the quite different sense of being *desirable*. The question is, How can one justify the identification of pleasure with what is desirable, and thus with the good? Such an identification, to be sure, can be established by definitional fiat (*4*:471); but definitional fiat, amounting to no more than an arbitrary stipulation, is not in itself a justification.

The classic attempt to *justify* the identification of pleasure with the desirable is John Stuart Mill's much misunderstood argument: "The only proof capable of being given that a thing is visible, is that people actually see it. The only proof that a sound is audible, is that people hear it: and so of the other sources of our experience. In like manner, I apprehend, the sole evidence it is possible to produce that anything is desirable, is that people do actually desire it. If the end which the [hedonistic] doctrine proposes to itself were not, in theory and practice, acknowledged to be an end, nothing could ever convince any person that it was so. No reason can be given why . . . happiness is desirable, except that each person, so far as he believes it to be attainable, desires his own happiness. This, however, being a fact, we have not only all the proof which the case admits of, but all which it is possible to require, that happiness is a good" (*8*:32-33).

Mill's argument has been analyzed at considerable length by Bradley (*2*:113-124) and G. E. Moore (*9*:64-74), who find it fallacious in an obvious and most elementary sense. Says

Moore: "Mill has made as naive and artless a use of the naturalistic fallacy as anybody could desire. 'Good,' he tells us, means 'desirable,' and you can only find out what is desirable by seeking to find out what is actually desired" (9:66). "The fact is," Moore continues, "that 'desirable' does not mean 'able to be desired' as 'visible' means 'able to be seen.' The desirable means simply what *ought* to be desired or *deserves* to be desired; just as the detestable means not what can be but what ought to be detested and the damnable what deserves to be damned. Mill has, then, smuggled in, under cover of the word 'desirable,' the very notion about which he ought to be quite clear. 'Desirable' does indeed mean 'what it is good to desire'; but when this is understood, it is no longer plausible to say that our only test of *that* is what is actually desired" (9:67). Mill, in other words, —so Moore maintains—"has attempted to establish the identity of the good with the desired, by confusing the proper sense of 'desirable,' in which it denotes that which it is good to desire, with the sense which it would bear, if it were analogous to such words as 'visible.' If 'desirable' is to be identical with 'good,' then it must bear one sense; and if it is to be identical with 'desired,' then it must bear quite another sense. And yet to Mill's contention that the desired is necessarily good, it is quite essential that these two senses of 'desirable' should be the same" (9:67-68). As Moore sees it, Mill's argument is a syllogism in *Barbara:*

> The desirable is the good.
> The desired is the desirable.
> Therefore, the desired is good.

And in this syllogism the middle term shifts in meaning. The fallacy, Moore says, is "so obvious, that it is quite wonderful how Mill failed to see it" (9:67).

I have quoted Moore at such length because his analysis of Mill's argument is the prototype of all similar criticisms. I believe, however, [with Hall (6:1-18)] that Moore misunderstood Mill's intention and, therefore, the nature of his proof as well.

Moral hedonists have often pointed out that it is impossible to prove a first principle; and they are right about this, if by proof is meant a deduction of the first principles from given premises; for in such proof the given premises, and not the inference drawn from them, would be the real first principles. Mill himself has specifically recognized this fact and has said that "questions of ultimate ends do not admit of proof, in the ordinary acceptation of the term"; that "to be incapable of proof by [deductive] reasoning is common to all first principles" (8:32); and, again, that "questions of ultimate ends are not amenable to direct proof" (8:4). But if this is so, then—Mill also tells us—the basic principle of moral hedonism cannot be proved "in the ordinary and popular meaning of the term" (8:4). Mill's concern, therefore, is with such proof as a first principle is "susceptible of" (8:4). That is to say, his concern is with an extra-systemic or meta-systemic proof, not with a proof within a given system. The question is, Is there such a proof? And if there is, what is its nature?

It is Mill's contention that proof is not restricted to deductive inferences from given premises; that, on the contrary, "there is a larger meaning of the word proof," for "considerations may be presented capable of determining the intellect either to give or withhold its assent to the doctrine; and this is equivalent to proof" (8:4). And it is Mill's declared intention to "examine . . . of what nature are these considerations; in what manner they apply to the case [at hand], and what rational grounds, therefore, can be given for . . . assenting to the [hedonistic] standard" (8:4-5). What Mill is concerned with, in other words, is persuasive meta-systemic arguments, not logical proof.[2]

If we now re-read Mill's proof (quoted above), certain phrases in the statement of that proof take on special significance. Thus, Mill says: "The *sole evidence* it is possible to produce that anything is desirable, is that people do actually desire it." What Mill is saying here is, not that "desirable" means no more than "actually desired," but that we can determine what is desirable

---

2 Please note the anticipation of Stevenson's thesis of "persuasion."

only by finding out what people actually do desire. Or, to adhere more closely to Mill's own formulation, "if the end which the [hedonistic] doctrine proposes to itself *were not . . . [actually] acknowledged to be an end,* nothing could ever convince any person that it was so." As I read these passages, Mill is saying that if no one ever appealed to pleasure or happiness to justify moral judgments or, finding pleasure desirable, ever desired it, no considerations capable of persuading people to accept the basic principle of moral hedonism could ever be found.[3] The choice of the basic principle would in that case be restricted to analytically self-evident propositions or would remain a matter of arbitrary stipulation. Either alternative might result in an ethical theory which is purely academic and unrealistic. Mill at least has attempted to preserve the empirical orientation of hedonism by pointing out the only *persuasive* proof available— the fact, namely, that people acknowledge pleasure or happiness to be an end which they do desire. And this, Mill maintains, is "all the proof which the case admits of."

When we turn to Bentham, we encounter a similar line of reasoning. We are told specifically that "that which is used to prove everything else, cannot itself be proved" (*1*:4). But, Bentham continues, if there be a person who "thinks the settling of his opinion on such a subject [as the basic principle of hedonism] worth the trouble," let him consider "whether the principle he thinks he has found is really any separate intelligible principle." "If he is inclined to think that his own approbation or disapprobation, annexed to the idea of an act, without any regard to its consequences, is a sufficient foundation for him to judge and act upon," then "let him ask himself whether his principle is not despotical" or, if it is not, whether it provides a standard at all (*1*:6-7). If he considers all these matters— and others which Bentham mentions—then "at length, perhaps, *he may come to reconcile himself*" (*1*:6) to the principle of hedonism. The italicized phrase in this statement is, obviously, meaningful only on the assumption that the basic principle of

---

[3] In a similar manner, no one could ever be persuaded that there are visible or audible things, if no one had ever seen or heard anything.

hedonism is made acceptable by *persuasive arguments,* not by logical proof.

The leading hedonists thus recognize clearly that no *proof* in the deductive sense of the term can be given for their basic principle, and that acceptance or rejection of the principle depends on *persuasive arguments* and meta-systemic considerations only. There are, however, good ways and bad ways of persuading people. The attempted persuasion may be an appeal to revelation, or to authority, or to personal sentiments—and history is full of such persuasions. But history also reveals their inadequacies. Bentham and Mill, on the other hand, appeal to empirical facts and to rational considerations based on these facts. Therein lies their strength. And we cannot accuse them of committing elementary errors in reasoning. It does not follow, however, that, in view of the inherent difficulties of hedonism, their persuasive arguments are sufficiently impressive to make the principle of hedonism generally acceptable.

### III

But let us now accept, for the sake of argument, the thesis of moral hedonism that pleasure is the only thing which men call *good,* the only thing which they regard as *desirable.* It will then be seen that this acceptance does not in itself solve the problem of the moral standard. In fact, the problem is now twofold.

(1) Epicurus said: "When we maintain that pleasure is the end, we do not mean the pleasures of profligates and those that consist in sensuality, . . . but freedom from pain in the body and from trouble in the mind. For it is not continuous drinking and revelings, nor the satisfaction of lusts, nor the enjoyment of fish or other luxuries of the wealthy table, which produce a pleasant life, but sober reasoning" and prudence; "for from prudence are sprung all other virtues" (*3*:32), and it is they that give "health of the body and the soul's freedom from disturbance." And these latter alone, according to Epicurus, are "the aim of the life of blessedness" (*3*:31). Epicurus thus clearly distinguishes between pleasures of the senses and pleasures of a

sound body and a tranquil mind, regarding the latter alone as desirable, as *really* good. Epicurus, in other words, adheres to a qualitative distinction of pleasures. His criterion is prudence. In so far, however, as an appeal to prudence is an appeal to man's rationality, Epicurus's criterion is not grounded in the basic principle of hedonism alone; in fact, the highest or really good pleasures are but the result of prudential living.

Much clearer on this point—but also much more clearly a departure from the basic principle of hedonism—are John Stuart Mill's frank statements that "some *kinds* of pleasure are more desirable and more valuable than others"; and that "it would be absurd that . . . the estimation of pleasures should be supposed to depend on quantity alone" (8:7). "The comparison of the Epicurean life," Mill points out, "to that of beasts is felt as degrading, precisely because a beast's pleasures do not satisfy a human being's conceptions of happiness. Human beings have faculties more elevated than the animal appetites, and when once made conscious of them, do not regard anything as happiness which does not include their gratification" (8:7). Hence, according to Mill, "it is better to be a human being dissatisfied than a pig satisfied; better to be Socrates dissatisfied than a fool satisfied" (8:9). "Few human creatures would consent to be changed into any of the lower animals, for a promise of the fullest allowance of a beast's pleasures" (8:8); for there is "a *sense of dignity,* which all human beings possess in one form or another, and in some, though by no means in exact, proportion to their higher faculties, and which is so essential a part of the happiness of those in whom it is strong, that nothing which conflicts with it could be, otherwise than momentarily, an object of desire to them" (8:9).

Now, the *sense of dignity* to which Mill here refers, obviously is the ultimate standard of all valuations which Mill applies even to the pleasures. That there is such a sense of dignity need not be questioned; but that a reference to it as to the ultimate criterion of what pleasures are *really* desirable or good, is a violation of the basic principle of hedonism seems clear. A consistent hedonism can admit only such value differentiations as are derivable from the notion of pleasure itself. It will then be found that the only legitimate differentiations of pleasure are those in terms of duration and intensity [as Hilliard holds (7:87)], or those in intensity and extensity [as Sheldon holds (11:285-304)]—or, possibly, those which result from a combination of duration, intensity, and extensity. Sheldon, in particular, is emphatic on this point. "Higher quality," he says, "means greater intensity of pleasantness or greater extensity of pleasantness—greater number or variety of pleasant objects—or both. Obviously Socrates dissatisfied is better than a pig satisfied because Socrates has or could have a thousandfold more pleasures —those intrinsic to intelligent humanity—than the pig can have. That is the hedonistic doctrine: the *summum bonum* for morality is maximum intensity and extensity of pleasure. Maximum, because if something is good, more of it is better, and the maximum the best. Quantity elucidates quality in respect of good" (11: 288). But is Sheldon's argument convincing?

To begin with, does the term "better," as employed here by Sheldon, have a distinctive meaning? If it has no meaning other than "more, and more intensive, pleasure," then the crucial part of Sheldon's argument is a vicious *petitio*. It is a *petitio* because it merely asserts that Socrates, even when dissatisfied, has (or could have) more pleasures than a pig because he has (or could have) "a thousandfold more pleasures." It is vicious because, in the context of Sheldon's statement, the term "better" normally suggests, if it does not imply, an evaluation of Socrates himself rather than of the intensity and extensity of the pleasures he may have. But if the term "better," as used in this crucial part of Sheldon's argument, has a meaning which saves the statement in question from becoming a vicious *petitio;* if it refers, for example, to something akin to what Mill meant by the sense of human dignity and what Sheldon himself may hint at when he speaks of "intelligent humanity"; then this fact alone reintroduces a qualitative evaluation which contradicts the hedonistic thesis.

Moreover, it may well be doubted that Sheldon's thesis is felicitous to human experience. For one thing, the evidence of history is definitely against it. As John Stuart Mill puts it: "There is no known Epicurean theory of life [until we come to our own times] which does not assign to the pleasures of the intellect, of the feelings and imagination, and of the moral sentiments, a much higher value as pleasures than to those of mere sensation" (8:61). For another thing, the sense of human dignity or the conception of intelligent humanity—call it what you wish—is, I believe, more important in our evaluation of pleasures than are the intensity and extensity of the pleasures themselves. Introspective analysis, it seems to me, bears this out; for, as William Godwin could show, our sensual pleasures, if reduced to their "true nakedness," would be "generally despised" (5:76)—not because they are less intense than the pleasures of the mind, or because there are fewer of them; but because they are *sensual* pleasures.

Finally, the pleasures of perverted sensibilities and of warped minds—especially in their greatest intensity and consuming extensity—can hardly be called desirable or good. Sheldon's argument, it seems to me, rests upon the implicit assumption of a normal human nature; and to the extent to which this is true, a criterion other than that of pleasure and its degrees of intensity underlies his whole position. What plausibility his hedonism has stems from the fact that it is not a pure or consistent hedonism.

(2) We said earlier that the problem of the moral standard, as encountered in hedonism, is twofold. We have so far discussed only the question of a qualitative differentiation of pleasures and have found that any reference to qualitative distinctions implies a standard other than that of pleasure itself. Let us now assume, again for the sake of argument, that all differentiations of pleasures are purely quantitative and are describable in terms of duration, intensity, and extensity. Does this settle the question of the ultimate standard of moral evaluation?

First, let us remind ourselves once more of the basic principle of hedonism—of the principle, that is, that pleasure is the only thing which is desirable or good. Now, unless we fall back into psychological hedonism and completely identify the desirable with the desired, i.e., unless we maintain that "desirable" does not mean "what *ought* to be desired," we must realize that some desires are bad in so far as they "prompt to actions for the consequences of which, when they arrive, we feel, on the whole, aversion more intense than the former desire" (*12*:32). It follows, on hedonistic principles, that, although the satisfaction of *any* desire may be to a certain extent good, each desire must be evaluated in the light of all our experiences, future as well as present. Regard for my "good on the whole" is therefore an essential characteristic of rational experience, and my "good on the whole" is what I actually should seek or aim at (*12*:32).

But if this is what the hedonists mean—and I am sure that it is—then new difficulties arise. For example, when do I know that I have acted for my "good on the whole"? In a strict sense, only the experience of my whole lifetime can provide an answer to this question; but even this is not certain. Interests shift and desires are modified by the very conduct which they initiate. Hence, even if in later life one should never "feel for the consequences of an action aversion strong enough to cause one to regret it," this alone would be no proof that one has acted for one's "good on the whole" (*12*:33). It may merely mean that one has become insensitive to the pain or the unpleasantness of those consequences.

Moreover, the very conception of one's "good on the whole" is vague and undefinable in terms of pleasure; for we do not know today what will give us pleasure tomorrow, or a year or ten years hence. Nor can we foresee all the consequences of our present actions. "Shall we say then that a man's 'true good' is what he would desire on the whole if all the consequences of the different lines of conduct open to him were actually exercising on him an impulsive force proportional to the desires or aversions which they would excite if actually experienced" (*12*:33)? But such a conception is an unrealizable and empty ideal rather than a specific and dependable guide for action. And if it is what the hedonists mean by the ultimate standard of evaluation, then they have given us but little help in our quest for a moral *ought*.

In addition, if, as Sheldon contends, the only legitimate distinction between pleasures are distinctions in intensity and extensity, then the proper balancing, for the sake of one's "good on the whole," of intensity with extensity creates also a problem; for it may be the case that, in a given situation, the intensity of a single sensual pleasure is irreconcilable with, but outweighs by far, all the intellectual pleasures realizable in that situation. And if this is so, then it is at least conceivable that, in the intensity of its pleasures, a pig satisfied is "better" than a Socrates who, in the extensity of his pleasures remains dissatisfied. Sheldon can settle the argument in favor of Socrates only on the implicit assumption that even a frustrated extensity of intellectual pleasures is still a greater "good on the whole" than is the pig's realized intensity. And such an assumption is not part of the basic principle of hedonism. If the hedonists reply that the decisive difference between Socrates and the pig lies in their respective *capacities for enjoyment* (rather than in the intensity or extensity of pleasures actually enjoyed), then the ultimate standard of evaluation is not the quantitative difference in pleasures but a valuative distinction between human nature and pig nature; and this distinction is not derivable from considerations of the intensity and extensity of pleasures alone.

The difficulties of hedonism are intensified further by the fact (which Sidgwick has noted) that, no matter how "closely connected the judgment that a thing is good may be with the consciousness that we derive pleasure from it," the pleasure actually derived may vary to an indefinite extent while our judgment that the thing is good remains constant (*12*:97). We may thus "derive pleasure from a thing to-day, and pronounce it 'good'; then if to-morrow it no longer gives us pleasure, we do not therefore say that it has become less good: we consider the fault to lie in our temporary incapacity to apprehend its goodness" (*12*:97). But does not this fact of a discrepancy between our capacity to enjoy and our judgment of valuation introduce a value standard which is not reducible to mere duration, intensity, and extensity of pleasure?

Let us consider this problem in its full meaning, as it affects not only our own fluctuating capacities for enjoyment but the varying capacities of different individuals as well.

It is an indisputable fact that the capacity of deriving pleasure from different kinds of good things is possessed by different persons in different degrees (*12*:97-98). It follows therefore, in a strict interpretation of hedonism, that each individual is, and must be, the final judge of his own pleasure; that there is, and can be, no appeal from his decision. Yet, in moral matters, such complete subjectivism is equivalent to the abolition of all moral standards. And not only in moral matters is this so; for it is a fact (as Sidgwick well knew) that it is not "always the person of best taste who derives the greatest enjoyment from any kind of good and pleasant thing." On the contrary, a person possessing "freshness and fulness of feeling" rather than good taste may "derive more pleasure from inferior objects than another from the best" (*12*:98).

## IV

The hedonists may, of course, argue that in the preceding sections we have not done full justice to their position. Let us therefore examine that position from a still different perspective. But let us also keep in mind that we deal here exclusively with moral hedonism in its egoistic form.

For our purposes Sidgwick's definition of egoistic hedonism is as good as any. Egoistic hedonism, Sidgwick wrote, is "a system that fixes as the reasonable ultimate end of each individual's action his own greatest possible Happiness: and by 'greatest Happiness,' again, we must definitely understand the greatest possible sum of pleasures; or more strictly, as pains have to be balanced against pleasures, the greatest possible surplus of pleasure over pain" (*12*:109). It is implied in this definition that "pleasures must be sought in proportion to their pleasantness: and [that] therefore the less pleasant consciousness must not be preferred to the more pleasant, on the ground of any other qualities that it may possess" (*12*:109). All distinctions of quality, in so far as they cannot be resolved into distinctions of quantity of pleasures, are irrelevant.

The basic assumption upon which this whole interpretation rests, and which alone gives significance to the idea of Greatest Happiness as an end of action, is the commensurability of pleasures and pains—the assumption, that is, that all pleasures and pains have quantitative relations to each other; that "they can all be arranged in a certain scale as greater or less in some finite degree"; for "otherwise they cannot be conceived as possible elements of a total of which we are to seek the maximum" (*12*:111).

It must be admitted that at times we actually do compare pleasures and pains in respect of their intensity. Such comparisons, however, are made but occasionally and are at best only rough estimates. They lack the precision and scope requisite for the development of a dependable calculus of pleasures. Moreover, these quantitative comparisons are vitiated by subjective illusions the precise amount of which we can never determine but the existence of which we cannot deny.

In view of these facts, the hedonists may hold that in estimating pleasure there is no conceivable appeal from the immediate decision of consciousness. But such a stipulation—for stipulation it would be—is at best only a partial solution of the problem, for it implies that our evaluative judgments are restricted to phenomena of the immediate present. Even Gardner Williams, who maintains that each and every one should pursue happiness only *from his own point of view* (*13*:656), admits that such is not the case, and holds that the ultimate principle of right is the principle of *long-range* individual satisfaction. Actually, of course, in estimating the intensity of a present state, we must necessarily compare it with some other state; and this other state is either a remembered or an anticipated feeling, not an actual one. That is to say, in estimating the value of different pleasures, we are never restricted to the immediate present but project ourselves into the future and imagine what such and such a pleasure will amount to under hypothetical circumstances (*12*: 120). This imaginative projection is chiefly determined by our experience of past pleasures, but not entirely so; for our state of mind at the time, which makes us more susceptible to some pleasures than to others, also has a bearing on the matter. Moreover, we are influenced by the experience of others; and "here again we sometimes definitely refer to particular experiences which have been communicated to us by individuals, and sometimes to the traditional generalizations which are thought to represent the common experience of mankind" (*12*:120). But if all of these factors enter into the complicated process of comparing pleasures, then it is not likely that the result is always free from error. On the contrary, it is a well-known fact that man's forecast of pleasure is conspicuously erroneous.

The hedonist may admit all this, but he may counter with the argument that we must substitute a more scientific process of reasoning for the instinctive, implicit inference; that we must deduce "the probable degree of our future pleasure or pain under any circumstances from inductive generalizations based on a sufficient number of careful observations of our own and others' experience" (*12*:121). But the question now is, How can such a scientific form of hedonism be established? Several problems are here involved.

To begin with, How far can anyone evaluate correctly his own past pleasures and pains? Any attempt at such an evaluation will readily show that our judgments, even when they pertain to feelings of the same kind (such as the agreeableness of taste, or the joys of creative enterprise), are by no means unwavering and precise. The uncertainty increases when different kinds of feelings must be compared. Moreover, our judgments are influenced at all times by our current susceptibilities. They differ, therefore, from time to time as we assess and re-assess our value estimates. But this variation in judgment casts doubt upon the validity of any given evaluation. As Sidgwick puts it: "Past hardships, toils, and anxieties often appear pleasurable when we look back upon them, after some interval: for the excitement, the heightened sense of life that accompanied the painful struggle, would have been pleasurable if taken by itself: and it is this that we recall rather than the pain" (*12*:123).

Again, in the state of satiety we cannot estimate adequately the gratifications of appetite, and we are apt to exaggerate them in the state of desire. "We cannot represent to ourselves as very intense a pleasure of a kind that at the time of representing it we are incapable of experiencing: as (e.g.) the pleasures of intellectual or bodily exercise at the close of a wearying day: or any emotional pleasure when our susceptibility to the special emotion is temporarily exhausted" (12:124). Nor can we appreciate adequately in a state of perfect tranquility the "many pleasures which require precedent desire, and even enthusiasm and highly wrought excitement, in order to be experienced in their full intensity" (12:124).

But if it is so difficult to estimate correctly the value of one's own pleasures, how far can one derive help from the experience of others? Any such transfer of experience presupposes an essential similarity among human beings. That in some respects there exists a basic similarity cannot be denied; for without it we could not even classify the individuals as human beings. But neither can it be denied that there are striking differences between the feelings produced in different men by similar causes (12:126). The delights of a sensualist, for example, may be but the cause of great anguish to a saintly man. Hence, if, in the evaluation of our own pleasures, we are to be guided by the experience of some other person, we must be convinced not only of his accuracy in evaluating his own pleasures, but also of the similarity of his susceptibilities and our own. We must be convinced, in other words, that the causes which produce his pleasures will produce similar effects in us (12:127). And this conviction cannot be definite proof. It rests at best upon considerations of probabilities based upon earlier comparisons.

But let us assume now, for the sake of argument, that the correct evaluation of past pleasures is possible, and also that the experience of other persons is comparable to our own. Does this enable us to forecast our future pleasures? By no means; for our capacity for particular pleasures may have changed. In Sidgwick's words, "we may have reached the point of satiety in respect of some of our past pleasures, or otherwise lost our susceptibility to them, owing to latent changes in our constitution: or we may have increased our susceptibility to pains inevitably connected with them: or altered conditions of life may have generated in us new desires and aversions, and given relative importance to new sources of happiness. Or any or all of these changes may be expected to occur, before the completion of the course of conduct upon which we are now deciding" (*12*:128).

The problem is still further complicated by the fact that we can change ourselves. We can develop a taste for the arts, for study, for physical exercise, for society, or can harden us against "certain sources of pain, such as toil, or anxiety, or abstinence from luxuries"; and our self-development or self-discipline may profoundly modify our susceptibilities (*12*:128). In what sense, then, can it be said that our desire for pleasure is a dependable guide to the realization of our "good on the whole"?

One additional point deserves consideration. Since the hedonism here under discussion is *egoistic* hedonism—since it is the view, in other words, that each person ought to realize his own greatest happiness—one may well wonder how our extra-regarding activities (our devotion to causes and other persons, our self-sacrifice) can be reconciled with our self-love. The answer is simple, Gardner Williams contends. "A man's duty . . . to help his fellows is . . . based upon his own need and his own love, in strict accordance with hedonic individual relativism. Helping those he loves pleases him because he loves them. . . . And the help he gets in return from them pleases him because he needs it. Ultimately, he should, from his own point of view, help others because to do so will be most deeply satisfactory to him in the long run" (*13*:652).

Now, the help a man gets may indeed please him because he needs it; but this fact is irrelevant here. It may also be granted that a man derives satisfaction from helping persons he loves; but does he help them because of the expected satisfactions for himself or because he loves the other persons? If the motive is his desire for personal satisfaction, then love has nothing to do with the case. But if the motive is love of the other persons, then he

EGOISTIC HEDONISM / 129

helps them because of his concern for *their* well-being, not because of his own pleasure. Any other interpretation makes a travesty of self-sacrificing love; for self-sacrifice is irreconcilable with self-love. Moreover, if, because of his love, a man "desires and tries to further the welfare of the object of his affection" (*13*:654), is not love or affection a motive force other than the hedonist's desire for his own pleasure? Surely, the desire for pleasure is neither the motive nor the existential ground for love.

But let us follow Williams' argument to its inevitable conclusion. "Each and every person," we are told, "should be satisfied . . . *from his own point of view*." Hence, "if a sadist could be satisfied most deeply in the long run only by torturing people, then, from his point of view, he ought to torture them. . . . And if the normal citizens can be most deeply satisfied only by preventing the sadist from attaining his highest good, then, from their points of view, they should prevent him. This would be a simple case of the ultimate conflict of duties. . . . The decent people then should gang up on the sadist and by force make their right *prevail*" (*13*:656).

In this argument, the references to normal citizens and decent people imply value standards other than pleasure. They are inconsistent with Williams' fundamental thesis; for all that Williams can legitimately assert is that some people obtain the maximum pleasure in one way, and others obtain it in some other way, and that from his own point of view each individual is right and *ought* to pursue the pleasures which appeal to him. When the desires of various individuals conflict, only brute force can decide which course of action is to prevail. Egoistic hedonism thus again leads to the maxim that *might makes right;* and this maxim, we have seen, does not establish a *moral ought* or a *moral right*. On the contrary, it signifies the complete collapse of egoistic hedonism as a moral doctrine.

V

We have said earlier that, in determining what course of action will yield the greatest amount of pleasure, we are guided in part by the traditional generalizations which are the combined experience of mankind. The combined experience, it may be argued, is of particular significance because, in it, "the divergencies due to the limitations of each individual's experience, and the differently tinged moods in which different estimates have been taken, have balanced and neutralized each other and so disappeared" (*12*:136).

It may readily be granted that many persons are guided more by tradition than by independent reasoning; but the hedonist can derive only small pleasure from this fact. In the first place, the tradition itself does by no means prove that pleasure is the only thing which has ever been regarded as desirable or good; for part of our cultural tradition is the denial of, and opposition to, all forms of hedonism. Hence, before the hedonist can appeal to tradition, he must distort it to suit himself; or, if "distort" is too harsh a word, he must selectively appraise the tradition, ascribing to errors in reasoning all deviations from the hedonistic thesis developed by the great moralists of the past—by Jesus and Buddha, by Aristotle and Kant, and by others too numerous to mention. The appeal to tradition, therefore, is not an appeal to tradition as it is, but as it is readjusted to suit the hedonist's purpose. An appeal to a readjusted tradition in support of hedonism is, however, a simple case of begging the question.

Let us grant, nevertheless—at least for the sake of argument —that guidance in our pursuit of pleasures can be obtained from the combined experience of mankind. It still remains true that such experience, because it balances and neutralizes individual differences and "differently tinged moods," can give us at best only an estimate true for a standardized or average person; and from this average person each individual differs in some respects. The individual, therefore, cannot accept uncritically the standard provided by the generalizations which are the result of the combined experience of mankind. On the contrary, he must reevaluate and correct those generalizations in the light of his own susceptibilities and of the particular conditions of his existence. Tradition, in other words, can at best provide suggestions which, for any given individual, may or may not lead to the realization of maximum pleasure.

Moreover, the generalizations which are the result of the combined experience of mankind vary not only from age to age and from country to country, they are far from being clear and consistent even in our own country and age. "Are we to be guided by the preferences which men avow, or by those which their actions would lead us to infer" (*12*:138)? Do not the high estimates set upon pleasures of the mind—intellectual and aesthetic—express the real experience of only small minorities (*12*:142)? And if they do, can they be said to represent truly the combined experience of mankind?

The difficulties increase with every question we thus raise. We must guard, however, against overstating our case; for it is true that the experience of the race does culminate in general rules suggestive of lines of conduct, and that any person who must decide upon a course of action will be well advised not to neglect completely those rules. He should at least take account of them even if, in the end, he finds them inapplicable to his own situation. Our chief criticism of hedonism here is, not that the hedonist appeals to rules expressive of mankind's common experience, but that he restricts his appeal to one type of rules only; that he neglects all rules which are in conflict with his basic assumption.

## REFERENCES

1. Bentham, J., *An Introduction to the Principles of Morals and Legislation,* Hafner Library of Classics, New York, 1948.
2. Bradley, F. H., *Ethical Studies,* 2nd edition, Oxford, 1927.
3. Epicurus's "Letter to Menoeceus," in Oates, W. J., *The Stoic and Epicurean Philosophers, The Complete Extant Writings of Epicurus, Epictetus, Lucretius, Marcus Aurelius,* New York, 1940.
4. Frankena, W. K., "The Naturalistic Fallacy," *Mind,* XLVIII (1939).
5. Godwin, W., *Enquiry Concerning Political Justice and Its Influence on Morals and Happiness,* 3rd edition, London, 1798, I.
6. Hall, Everett W., "The 'Proof' of Utility in Bentham and Mill," *Ethics,* LX (1949).

7. Hilliard, A. L., *The Forms of Value,* New York, 1950.
8. Mill, J. S., "Utilitarianism," in *Utilitarianism, Liberty, and Representative Government,* Everyman's Library.
9. Moore, G. E., *Principia Ethica,* Cambridge, 1903.
9a. Nielsen, Kai, "Egoism in Ethics," *Philosophy and Phenomenological Research,* XIX (1959).
10. Ross, W. David, *Foundations of Ethics,* Oxford, 1939.
11. Sheldon, W. H., "The Absolute Truth of Hedonism," *Journal of Philosophy,* XLVII (1950).
12. Sidgwick, Henry, *The Methods of Ethics,* 2nd edition, London, 1877.
13. Williams, Gardner, "Hedonism, Conflict, and Cruelty," *Journal of Philosophy,* XLVII (1950).
14. Williams, Gardner, "Hedonic Individual Ethical Relativism," *Journal of Philosophy,* LV (1958).

# CHAPTER V

# Universalistic Hedonism

Moral hedonism maintains that pleasure, and pleasure alone, is desirable or good. This thesis, however, occurs in two forms. The first form, interpreting pleasure or happiness as the sole aim of an individual, we have called egoistic hedonism. We have dealt with it in the preceding chapter. The second form, interpreting the ultimate goal of action as the realization of the greatest happiness for the greatest number, we shall call universalistic hedonism. We shall discuss and evaluate it in the present chapter.

In Bentham's words the basic principle of universalistic hedonism asserts that "the greatest happiness of all those whose interest is in question" is "the right and proper, and [the] only right and proper and universally desirable, end of human action" (*1*:1n).[1] In its broadest interpretation this principle encompasses all sentient beings—all beings, that is, who are capable of experiencing pleasure and pain and whose feelings are affected by our conduct (*21*:382). Bentham and Mill intended it in this

---

[1] Let it be noted that Bentham, although accepting psychological hedonism as a proven fact, does not confuse it with moral hedonism. Pleasure and pain, he admits, "determine what we shall do"; but they also "point out what we ought to do." "On the one hand the standard of right and wrong, on the other the chain of causes and effects, are fastened to their throne (*1*:1)." This distinction permeates the whole of Bentham's discussion of the principles of legislation.

broad sense. In actual application, however, both writers have concerned themselves almost exclusively with problems of *human* happiness; and, for the sake of simplicity, we shall here adopt this restriction.

Even so, certain questions arise at once. For instance, "How far are we to consider the interests of posterity when they seem to conflict with those of existing human beings" (*21*:383)? This question becomes particularly pertinent when we realize (a) that we can to some extent determine the number of future human beings, and (b) that we can largely condition their desires and interests (*24*). Again, to what extent must the question of an equitable distribution of happiness be taken into consideration? With respect to this last question Bentham at least is quite specific. Everybody, he says, should "count for one, and nobody for more than one" (*1*:1). And this principle seems reasonable and simple. Arguments have been advanced, however, to the effect that, because human beings are unequal in their capacities to enjoy the higher pleasures, individuals capable of the greatest enjoyment of the highest pleasures should be given preferential status.

But let us accept here Bentham's principle, for it is basic to the whole discussion; and let us accept also, for the sake of argument, Bentham's further contention that the interest of the community is nothing but the sum of the interests of the several members who compose it; that any action is good to the extent to which it tends to augment rather than to diminish the happiness of the community, and that, being good, such an action is right and *ought* therefore to be done (*1*:3-4).

John Stuart Mill agrees with and supplements Bentham on all of these points. "Each person's happiness," he says, "is a good to that person, and the general happiness, therefore, a good to the aggregate of all persons" (*16*:33). "By happiness is intended pleasure, and the absence of pain; by unhappiness, pain and the privation of pleasure" (*16*:6). Happiness, as here defined (Mill holds with Bentham), is the only thing desirable as an end. All other desirable things are "desirable either for the pleasure inherent in themselves, or as means to the promotion of pleasure and the prevention of pain" (*16*:6, 32, 35-36). "Actions [therefore] are right in proportion as they tend to promote happiness, wrong as they tend to produce the reverse of happiness" (*16*:6). And the ultimate goal of all morality is the greatest happiness for the greatest number of people.

Bentham and Mill, taken together, thus define the position of universalistic hedonism which is here under discussion.

## I

Many of the arguments advanced in the preceding chapter against egoistic hedonism apply directly, or with minor changes, to universalistic hedonism as well; we shall not repeat them here. A new problem arises, however, in connection with the very universalism which, in many respects, marks an advance beyond the egoism of the earlier position. What I, as an individual, ought to aim at is not my personal and private happiness, but the happiness of the greatest number of people—even if such action may radically limit my own happiness. The question is, How can such an expansion of the hedonistic principle be justified?

Bentham admits that a principle which is used to prove everything else, cannot itself be proved (*1*:4); and he is right about that. He believes, however, that "by the natural constitution of the human frame, on most occasions of their lives men in general embrace this principle"; and that they do so "without thinking of it" (*1*:4). But the truth of this belief may well be doubted. The numerous attempts made by the hedonists to establish or prove in some way their universalistic principle are in themselves evidence of the insufficiency of Bentham's declaration of faith. Beyond this, however, it is a fact that "although many people may readily agree that it is reasonable to seek one's own happiness, few (if any) would admit as self-evident one's obligation to aim at happiness universally" (*21*:386).

Mill, who (with Bentham) holds that questions of ultimate ends are not amenable to direct proof, maintains, nevertheless, that we must not infer from this admission that the acceptance or rejection of the universalistic principle depends on blind impulse or arbitrary choice (*16*:4). He is convinced, on the contrary, that "considerations may be presented capable of de-termining the intellect either to give or withhold its assent to the doctrine; and [that] this is equivalent to proof" (*16*:4). The considerations in question, so we have seen in the preceding chapter, are essentially persuasive arguments; and we admit here (as we did before) that persuasive arguments may indeed serve the purpose which Mill assigns to them. The difficulty, therefore, arises not because Mill, in his attempt to get the basic principle of universalistic hedonism accepted, resorts to persuasive argu-ment, but because his argument is not persuasive.

Consider once again Mill's own statement of his proof. "No reason," he says, "can be given why the general happiness is desirable, except that each person, so far as he believes it to be attainable, desires his own happiness. This, however, being a fact, we have not only all the proof which the case admits of, but all which it is possible to require, that happiness is a good: that each person's happiness is a good to that person, and the general happiness, therefore, a good to the aggregate of all persons" (*16*:32-33).

From this statement it is evident, as I have pointed out in the preceding chapter, that Mill does not intend his argument to be a formal proof but merely "all the [persuasive] proof the case admits of." And the persuasiveness of the argument—if it has any—lies in three distinct steps: (a) "happiness is a good"; (b) "each person's happiness is a good to that person"; and (c) "the general happiness [is] a good to the aggregate of all persons."

The first two of these steps, when taken together, constitute egotistic hedonism. The third step indicates the crucial advance to universal hedonism. And this third step, Bradley points out, is ambiguous: "Either Mill meant to argue, '*Because* everybody desires his own pleasure, *therefore* everybody desires his own pleasure'; or '*Because* everybody desires his own pleasure, *there-fore* everybody desires the pleasure of everybody else'" (*3*:113-114n).

It is Hall's contention that Bradley was mistaken in playing up this ambiguity, and that Mill did not mean to argue that, because everybody desires his own pleasure, therefore everybody desires the pleasure of everybody else. Or, as Hall himself puts it, "Mill cannot and does not argue that each seeks the general happiness," but only that, "since the pleasure of each is a good, the sum of these must be a good" (8:9). In support of his interpretation Hall quotes from one of Mill's letters: "I merely meant this sentence [step (c) above] to argue that, since A's happiness is a good, B's a good, C's a good, &c., the sum of all these goods must be a good" (6:116). It is Hall's contention, in other words, that Mill is actually not trying to prove anything; that "he is attempting simply to present the general-happiness principle in a way that will make it seem acceptable as an ethical first principle to people who, rejecting self-evidence in this matter, still wish to be intelligent" (8:9-10).

Much as I sympathize with Hall's efforts to rescue Mill from undeserved attacks, and much as I believe that Mill meant to present here, not logical proof, but a persuasive argument in support of the basic principle of universalistic hedonism, I am unable to accept the persuasiveness of the argument. My difficulties arise in two respects: (1) It seems to me that the sum of individual goods is not necessarily also a good. And (2) even if it were, this fact alone would not justify the concern for the welfare of others which is inherent in universalistic hedonism.

Let us assume for the moment (with Gardner Williams) that "it is self-evident that a man's pleasure or happiness is a good *for him, to him and from his point of view*" (25:649). It is then reasonable to maintain (as Williams does) that, *from his own point of view,* but not necessarily from anybody else's, each and every individual should try to obtain the maximum pleasure for himself. This means, however, that the greatest happiness of the greatest number is no good to an individual unless it satisfies him. Hence, "if a sadist could be satisfied most deeply in the long run only by torturing people, then, from his point of view, he ought to torture them"; and "if the normal citizens can be most deeply satisfied only by preventing the sadist from attaining his highest good, then, from their points of view, they should prevent him" (25:656). But since Williams admits no standard other than personal self-interest—the evaluation, that is, from one's own point of view—we have here the sort of conflict (Williams himself calls it "a simple case of the ultimate conflict of duties") which makes a mere summation of individual goods impossible, and which, when interpreted exclusively in terms of self-interest, leads to the principle that might makes right, and that the only pleasure which counts is the pleasure of those individuals who, by force, can make their own pleasures prevail. Williams accepts this conclusion and remains a consistent egoist. This is not the doctrine, however, which the universalistic hedonists seek to maintain. It is their view that the happiness of all men is to be the concern of each.

When developing his calculus of pleasures, Bentham specifically admonishes us to "take an account of the *number* of persons whose interests appear to be concerned" (*1*:31); and John Stuart Mill regards it as "noble to be capable of resigning entirely one's own portion of happiness" for the happiness of others (*16*:15). He applauds the self-renunciation which is "devotion to the happiness . . . of others; either of mankind collectively, or of individuals within the limits imposed by the collective interests of mankind"; and he specifically says that "the happiness which forms the . . . standard of what is right in conduct, is not the agent's own happiness, but that of all concerned" (*16*:16). Even Sheldon, maintaining as he does that "the sadist, delighting in another's pain, breaks [the] hedonist rule" (*20*:295), makes regard for the interests of others central to the hedonistic doctrine.

My point is that this regard for others, this "devotion to the happiness of others," which is the very core of universalistic hedonism, finds no support whatever in Mill's persuasive argument. On the contrary, if the sum of individual goods were in itself always also a good, i.e., if the aggregate of all pleasures involving the most diversified individual interests were of necessity always a good, then a pre-established harmony of pleasures would make unnecessary Williams' appeal to force as well as Mill's appeal to a "devotion to the happiness of others." If each individual's egoistic pursuit of his own pleasures automatically results in the greatest happiness for the greatest number of people, why should anyone ever take the happiness of others into consideration when deciding upon his own course of action?

## II

Mill, of course, has recourse to an additional argument. There is, he says, a "powerful natural sentiment"—the desire, namely, "to be in unity with our fellow creatures." Mill, in other words, now makes the "social feelings of mankind" the "firm foundation" of universalistic hedonism (*16*:29). So long as men co-operate, he argues, their individual ends are identified with those of other individuals, and "there is at least a temporary feeling that the interests of others are their own interests" (*16*:30). In time, each individual comes to identify his own feelings more and more with the good of others, and thus comes to be "conscious of himself as a being who *of course* pays regard to others. The good of others becomes to him a thing naturally and necessarily to be attended to, like any of the physical conditions of our existence" (*16*:30).

With this argument Mill seems to concede that on purely egoistic grounds a genuine concern for the happiness of others cannot be justified; for he now regards social feelings as of paramount importance and sees in them the real basis for altruistic actions. However, the argument is ambiguous. On the one hand, there is the suggestion that the concern for the good of others is acquired through co-operation. Just what is intended? An answer to this question may be obtained when we view the argument in a broader setting.

Jeremy Bentham, despite the emphasis he placed on "the greatest happiness of all those whose interest is in question," remained in all essentials an egoistic hedonist. To be sure, he distinguished between self-regarding and extra-regarding prudence (*2*),[2] but he also maintained that "the sympathetic affections are not, cannot be, as strong as the self-regarding affections," and that therefore "the good produced by effective benevolence is small in proportion to that produced by the personal motives" (*2a*: 176). In fact, Bentham argued, "to a great extent, the dictates of prudence prescribe the laws of effective benevolence"

---

[2] It is well known, of course, that John Stuart Mill regretted very much the publication of the *Deonotology*. However, his criticism of Bentham confirms the thesis here set forth.

(*2a*:177, 175). "A man is prompted by ill-will to aim a blow at another. His ill-will may be restrained by the apprehension that the blow will be returned by the person at whom it is aimed, or by a third party who is a looker-on; or . . . he may be restrained by the apprehension of legal punishment" (*2a*:167). Refraining from inflicting pain upon another person is thus motivated by purely selfish considerations. To be sure, Bentham admits that "popular and social sanctions" may also become effective in restraining a man from inflicting pain upon others; for "by some social link, more or less efficient, almost every man is bound to the great body of the public" (*2a*:167). But the sole source of the sympathy, the extra-regarding, the benevolence here involved is the dependence of man upon his fellow men. As Bentham puts it, "of man's pleasure, a great proportion is dependent on the will of others, and can only be possessed by him with their concurrence and co-operation. There is no possibility of disregarding the happiness of others without, at the same time, risking happiness of our own." Each individual is thus "linked to his race by a tie, of all ties the strongest, the tie of self-regard" (*28*:133). Putting it bluntly, Bentham warns: "Dream not that men will move their little finger to serve you, unless their advantage in so doing is obvious to them. Men never did so, and never will. . . . But they will desire to serve you, when by so doing they can serve themselves" (*2b*:133).

That Bentham's argument here carries us back to egoistic hedonism is obvious. But that Mill disagrees with Bentham's interpretation is also clear. "Man," Mill says (*17*:384-385), "is never recognized by [Bentham] as a being capable of pursuing spiritual perfection as an end; of desiring, for its own sake, the conformity of his own character to his standard of excellence." "Nor is it only the moral part of man's nature, in the strict sense of the term—the desire of perfection, or the feeling of an approving or of an accusing conscience—that he overlooks: he but faintly recognizes, as a fact in human nature, the pursuit of any other ideal end for its own sake." "Man, that most complex being, is a very simple one in [Bentham's] eyes. . . . If he thought at all of any of the deeper feelings of human nature, it was but an idiosyncrasy of taste, with which the moralist no more than the legislator had any concern, further than to prohibit such as were mischievous among the actions to which they might chance to lead." In Bentham's theory there thus "remained, as a motive by which mankind are influenced, and by which they are guided to their good, only personal interest" (*17*:387). A system so founded, Mill continues, "will do nothing for the conduct of the individual, beyond prescribing some of the more obvious dictates of wordly prudence, and outward probity and beneficence"; it "does not pretend to aid individuals in the formation of their own character"; and it "recognizes no such wish as that of self-culture, we may even say, no such power, as existing in human nature" (*17*:388). "Morality," as Mill here sees it, "consists of two parts. One of these is self-education—the training, by the human being himself, of his affections and will. That department is a blank in Bentham's system. The other and co-equal part, the regulation of his outward actions, must be altogether halting and imperfect without the first" (*17*:388). In Mill's judgment, Bentham's theory "will enable a society which has attained a certain state of spiritual development, and the maintenance of which in that state is otherwise provided for, to prescribe the rules by which it may protect its material interests. It will do nothing (except sometimes as an instrument in the hands of a higher doctrine) for the spiritual interests of society; nor does it suffice of itself even for the material interests. That which alone causes any material interests to exist, which alone enables any body of human beings to exist as a society, is national character: *that* it is which causes one nation to succeed in what it attempts, another to fail; one nation to understand and aspire to elevated things, another to grovel in mean ones; which makes the greatness of one nation lasting, and dooms another to early and rapid decay" (*17*:390-391). Bentham's theory, in other words, "can teach the means of organizing and regulating the merely *business* part of the social arrangement. Whatever can be understood, or whatever done, without reference to moral influences, his philosophy is equal to: where those influences require to be taken into account, it is at fault. [Bentham] committed the mistake of supposing that the business part of human affairs was the whole of them" (*17*:391).

I have quoted Mill at such length not merely because, in my opinion, his criticism of Bentham is unanswerable, but also—and primarily—because the arguments here set forth should caution us against interpreting Mill's own position in terms of egoistic hedonism. Mill, unfortunately, was not always clear or consistent in stating his theory. But in view of his criticism of Bentham, it seems safe to assume that the references to a "powerful natural sentiment" and to the "social feelings of mankind" as the "firm foundation" of universalistic hedonism are the very essence of his doctrine; and that in these references he departed, and meant to depart, from egoistic hedonism. In so far as this is not the case, Mill's arguments against Bentham must be directed against Mill himself. In so far, however, as Mill did mean to distinguish his own position from egoistic hedonism, the phrases "powerful natural sentiment" and "social feelings of mankind" require further clarification.

In one interpretation—and there are passages in Mill's writings which strongly support it (*16*:31-32)—the phrases just quoted may imply no more than a reference to that sympathy of which Bentham spoke, and which he regarded as "a restraint against the giving pain." "Perhaps there never existed a human being," Bentham said, "who had reached full age without the experience of pleasure at another's pleasure, of uneasiness at another's pain. . . . Community interest, similarity of opinion, are sources whence it springs" (*2a*:169-170). But even Bentham realized that this sympathy "may be narrowed to a domestic circle, and [that] that circle may be as it were at war with mankind" (*2a*:169). Bentham realized, in other words, that sympathy may misdirect our actions or lead to acts pernicious on the whole to the well-being of society (*2a*:173; *21*:461-464). But if sympathy may thus fail us as a dependable guide to the greatest happiness for the greatest number of people, then, obviously, the basic principle of universalistic hedonism cannot be justified in terms of sympathy.

In a different interpretation—and this also finds support in Mill's writings (*16*:31-32)—Mill's key phrases (quoted above) are strongly reminiscent of Joseph Butler's thesis that "there are a real and the same kind of Indications in Humane Nature, that we were made for society and to do good to our Fellow-creatures, as that we were intended to take Care of our own Life and Health and private Good" (5:5-6). Or, as Butler puts it more explicitly, "there is a natural Principle of *Benevolence* in Man, which is in some Degree to *Society* what *Self-Love* is to the *Individual*"(5:6). "It is as manifest," according to Butler, "that *we were made for Society, and to promote the Happiness of it, as that we were intended to take Care of our own Life, and Health, and private Good*" (5:16). If this is what Mill really means to assert, then, I believe, he is on psychologically sound ground; for the contrary thesis, dating back to Hobbes—the thesis, namely, that man is incapable of an unselfish act—is disproved again and again by man's noblest deeds—his acts of generosity, his unswerving devotion to duty, his self-sacrifice for a loved one, for a cause, for his country. In Butler's theory, however, this "natural Principle of Benevolence in Man" is inextricably interwoven with a conception of human nature which, in motives and valuations, far transcends the pleasure principle of hedonism—even that of universalistic hedonism; and there is reason for believing that on this point, too, Mill is in substantial agreement with Butler. His references to "a sense of dignity, which all human beings possess" (*16*:9), to "self-education" and "the formation of [one's] own character" as basic to morality (*17*:388), and to "national character" as that "which makes the greatness of [a] nation lasting" (*17*:391), are hardly logical implicates of hedonism as such.

We are forced to conclude, therefore, that if Mill's key concepts (powerful natural sentiment, social feelings of mankind) are interpreted in terms of sympathy, they are insufficient as a foundation of universalistic hedonism; but if they are interpreted in terms of a "natural Principle of Benevolence in Man," they transcend the basic assumption of hedonism that pleasure, and pleasure alone, is the sole motive for action, the only desirable end in life. From the horns of this dilemma Mill has found no escape.

### III

Francis Hutcheson also maintained that "an *ultimate Desire* of the Happiness of others" is "as certainly implanted in the human Breast, though perhaps not so strong as *Self-Love*" (*12*:xi). This "*Public Sense*," as Hutcheson calls it, is "our Determination to be pleased with the *Happiness* of others, and to be uneasy at their *Misery*" (*12*:5); it is our "desire of communicating happiness, an ultimate good-will, not referred to any private interest and often operating without such reference" (*13*:77). But Hutcheson, too, realized that private interest and public sense may conflict; and, in order to deal with such inconsistencies, he found it necessary to ascribe to man a *moral sense* which, "with that commanding power which it is naturally destined to exercise," "makes the generous determination to public happiness the supreme one in the soul" (*13*:77). This recourse to a moral sense, however, is hardly consistent with the basic principle of hedonism; and Hutcheson, to be sure, was not, and did not intend to be, a hedonist.

It is somewhat different, I believe, in the case of Hume. Hume "endeavoured to prove, *first,* that reason alone can never be a motive to any action of the will; and, *secondly,* that it can never oppose passion in the direction of the will" (*10*; *11*: 23). That he failed in this endeavor—as I think he did (*19*:48-71)—need not concern us for the moment. But if we assume, for the sake of argument, that he did prove his case, it then follows that the rules of morality are not conclusions of our reason (*11*:33). And if they are not conclusions of reason, then the question arises, What are they? Wherein are they grounded? It is Hume's contention that they are grounded in "some impression or sentiment" which actions occasion in us; that the distinguishing impressions by which moral good or evil is known are nothing but *particular* pains or pleasures. "An action, or sentiment, or character, is virtuous or vicious," Hume argues, "because its view causes a pleasure or uneasiness of a particular kind" (*11*:44)—the pleasure, namely, which implies approbation, and the uneasiness which implies disapprobation. In other words, "virtue is distinguished by the pleasure, and vice by the pain, that any action, sentiment, or character, gives us by the mere view and contemplation [of it]" (*11*:48).

Since we have dealt with Hume's approbative theory elsewhere, we need consider here only the hedonism inherent in his basic position; for if hedonism is defined as the theory that there is a reciprocal connection between goodness and pleasure (*4*:89), then, obviously, Hume is a hedonist. Let it be noted, however, that Hume's is a particular kind of hedonism; for, according to Hume, not every "sentiment of pleasure or pain" (even if it arises from "characters and actions") is morally significant. On the contrary, "it is only when a character is considered in general, without reference to our particular interest, that it causes such a feeling or sentiment as denominates it morally good or evil" (*10*:45). Hume admits that the sentiments from interest and morals are apt to be confounded; he maintains, however, that such confounding does not disprove the fact that the sentiments are in themselves distinct (*10*:45). A thing or action may please us because it satisfies a desire we have; but the pleasure which implies moral approbation springs from sympathy (*11*:134) rather than from self-love. It is *sympathy,* Hume says—the "social sympathy in human nature" (*11*:216) —"which takes us so far out of ourselves as to give us the same pleasure or uneasiness in the character of others, as if they had a tendency to our own advantage or loss" (*10*:135, 144, 167, 168). Because of this sympathy we respond, without selfish bias, to the qualities and actions of others. We may even admire the qualities of an enemy which are hurtful to us. And because of this sympathy, too, "every quality of mind is denominated virtuous which gives pleasure by the mere survey, as every quality which produces pain is called vicious" (*11*:144-145). But lest Hume's position be misunderstood at this point, let us add at once that he did not mean that we "*infer* a character to be virtuous because it pleases," but, rather, that "in feeling that it pleases after such a particular manner [involving praise or admiration] we in effect *feel* that it is virtuous" (*11*:44). The morally relevant pleasures, in other words, are immediately felt as *ap-*

*probative pleasures.* Or, as Hume puts it, "our approbation is implied in the immediate pleasure" (*11*:44).

This interpretation of morals Hume (like Hutcheson) bases upon an analogy with aesthetic experience. As he himself says, "the case is the same as in our judgments concerning all kinds of beauty, and tastes, and sensations" (*11*:44). "The same principle produces in many instances our sentiments of morals as well as those of beauty" (*11*:133). It is important to note, however, that Hume's aesthetic analogy is restricted to judgments of goodness and badness, of virtue and vice, and that it does not apply to the meaning of moral obligation. Obligations, Hume holds, arise from a convention entered into by all members of the society—from a convention, that is, which, although inspired by selfishness, induces all members of a given society to regulate their conduct by certain rules (*11*:59). Hume, in other words, has seen clearly that even the aesthetic analogy provides no basis for an *ought;* and on this point he is right. This does not mean, however, that Hume has solved the problem of the *ought.* On the contrary, his doctrine of moral obligation, it seems to me, is untenable. But this is not the place to argue the case; for here we are concerned only with Hume's aesthetic analogy and the hedonism which it entails.

What Hume is saying on this score is essentially this: When someone says, *X is beautiful* or *X is morally good,* he means (a) that X has certain characteristics which cause a feeling of a certain kind in him or would cause such a feeling in most spectators (*19*:78),[3] and (b) that his statement expresses this feeling. In the case of a specifically moral feeling, the characteristics ascribed to X, Hume holds, may be "generosity, humanity, compassion, gratitude, friendship, fidelity, zeal, disinterestedness, liberality, and all those other qualities which form the character of good and benevolent" (*11*:155). And the feelings which these qualities arouse in us, or in most spectators, are pleasures implying approval, respect, or admiration. In fact, the qualities mentioned are judged good only because they are immediately

---

[3] It must be noted, however, that there is a significant difference between Raphael's interpretation and my own.

felt to be good in and through the pleasures which they cause.

It must be admitted, of course, that most men feel towards a morally good person—towards a person, that is, who possesses all or some of the characteristics Hume mentions—a specific emotion which may be called approval, respect, or admiration; and that towards a morally bad person they feel opposite emotions. But the feeling of approval or disapproval springs in each case from an (actual or implied) judgment as to the goodness or badness of the qualities in question; the judgment is not rooted in the feeling. That is to say, we respond with an emotion of approval to generosity, humanity, compassion, gratitude, and so on, because we judge these qualities to be good. We do not call them good because they occasion in us a certain kind of pleasure.

Hume himself saw a difficulty at this point and tried to deal with it. "When any quality or character has a tendency to the good of mankind," he argued, "we are pleased with it and approve of it because it presents a lively idea of pleasure; which idea affects us by sympathy, and is itself a kind of pleasure. But as this sympathy is very variable, it may be thought that our sentiments of morals must admit of all the same variations. We sympathize more with persons contiguous to us than with persons remote from us; with our acquaintance, than with strangers; with our countrymen, than with foreigners. But notwithstanding this variation of our sympathy, we give the same approbation to the same moral qualities in China as in England" (*11*:136). How is this possible?

Hume, admitting that I cannot feel "the same lively pleasure from the virtues of a person who lived in Greece two thousand years ago that I feel from the virtues of a familiar friend and acquaintance," realized, of course, that we should find ourselves continually involved in contradictions with other people were each of us to consider characters and persons only as they appear from his peculiar point of view (*11*:137). In order to escape these contradictions and to "arrive at a more *stable* judgment of things," Hume goes on, "we fix on some *steady* and *general* points of view, and always, in our thoughts, place ourselves in them, whatever may be our present situation" (*11*:137). In our general decisions we thus disregard the present disposition of our mind as well as the variations in our situation of nearness or remoteness with regard to the person blamed or praised. "Experience," Hume adds, "soon teaches us this method of correcting our sentiments, or at least of correcting our language, where the sentiments are more stubborn and unalterable. . . . Such corrections are common with regard to all the senses; and, indeed, it were impossible we could ever make use of language or communicate our sentiments to one another, did we not correct the momentary appearances of things and overlook our present situation" (*11*:138).

The crux of this argument is again the aesthetic analogy. "A beautiful countenance," Hume tells us, "cannot give so much pleasure when seen at a distance of twenty paces as when it is brought nearer us. We say not, however, that it appears to us less beautiful; because we know what effect it will have in such a position, and by that reflection we correct its momentary appearance" (*11*:137). In a similar way, "our servant, if diligent and faithful, may excite stronger sentiments of love and kindness than Marcus Brutus, as represented in history; but we say not upon that account that the former character is more laudable than the latter"; for "we know that, were we to approach equally near to that renowned patriarch, we would command a much higher degree of affection and admiration" (*11*:138). In other words, Hume, although still maintaining that "the approbation of moral qualities most certainly is not derived from reason . . . but proceeds entirely . . . from certain sentiments of pleasure or disgust which arise upon the contemplation and view of particular qualities or characters" (*11*:137), now says in effect that, in moral valuation, we transport ourselves in imagination to distant ages and countries, and consider the emotions which we should have felt had we been contemporaries or friends of the persons whom we appraise.

By way of criticism of this Humean argument it is only necessary, I believe, to quote Hume himself when he says: "It is but a weak subterfuge . . . to say that we transport ourselves by the force of imagination to distant ages and countries and consider the advantage which we should have reaped from these characters, had we been contemporaries and had any commerce with the persons. It is not conceivable how a *real* sentiment or passion can ever arise from a known *imaginary* interest, especially when our *real* interest is still kept in view and is often acknowledged to be entirely distinct from the imaginary, and even sometimes opposite to it" (*11*:211). To be sure, the context in which this passage occurs shows that Hume is here arguing against the thesis that "all our sentiments of virtue" have a selfish origin; that we always consider the advantage which we should have reaped. But a simple substitution in the argument of *emotion* for *advantage,* and of *felt* for *reaped,* is sufficient to make it serve our purpose. The substitution, I am sure, is justiable within the framework of Hume's general theory; but it plays havoc with the thesis that "an action, or sentiment, or character, is virtuous or vicious . . . because its view causes a pleasure or uneasiness" in us (*11*:44).

## IV

Let us now continue our consideration of the various attempts to justify universalistic hedonism; and let us examine, first, Sheldon's argument.

"When you come to understand," Sheldon says, "that my happiness ought to be, *because* it is wanted by me, you have seen a universal truth: whatever is wanted (other things not interfering) should come to be, and no matter who brings it about. . . . It all turns on the absolute identity of goodness or oughtness with wantedness. The minute we realize that something is good and ought to be, do we to the degree of our appreciation of its goodness wish it to exist"; and "thus do you come to wish for my happiness" (*20*:294).

This argument, plausible as it may seem, breaks down because, as Williams has pointed out (*25*:650), a universal truth about a particular value does not make that value itself universal. It may be perfectly true, for example, that, *from my point of view,* my happiness ought to be, because it is wanted by me; and this may even be true universally in the sense that it is true every time anybody refers to his own happiness. But to argue from such a premise that what ought to be *from my point of view* ought to be *from your point of view* and therefore *from the point of view of everybody else,* is to abandon logic in favor of wishful thinking. Given the egoistic starting point of Sheldon's position, the happiness of A can be of interest to B only in so far as it contributes to the happiness of B. But the fact that it is A's happiness does not logically imply that it is, or contributes to, B's happiness also. On the contrary, it may well be the case that the happiness which, *from A's point of view,* ought to be, is such that, *from B's point of view,* ought not to be. Sheldon's argument justifying the transition from self-interest to an unselfish regard for others is thus, clearly, not sufficient.

Let us consider next Sidgwick's solution of the problem.

Having rejected all attempts to provide either a logical or an empirical proof for the basic principle of universalistic hedonism, Sidgwick takes his cue from the sciences. "If we find," he says, "that in other departments of our supposed knowledge propositions are commonly taken to be true, which yet seem to rest on no other grounds than that we have a strong disposition to accept them, and that they are indispensable to the systematic coherence of our beliefs; it will be difficult to reject a similarly supported assumption in ethics, without opening the door to universal scepticism. If on the other hand it appears that the edifice of physical science is really constructed of conclusions logically inferred from premises intuitively known, it will be reasonable to demand that our practical judgments should either be based on an equally firm foundation or should abandon all claim to philosophic certainty" (*21*:469). Sidgwick is arguing, in other words, that the basic premises in every field of knowledge are either (arbitrary) stipulations accepted because they are indispensable to the systematic coherence of our beliefs, or they are intuitively known to be true. But if, in the field of ethics, we accept the first of these alternatives, then we open wide the door to universal scepticism even in the field of our most exact sciences. On the other hand, if we accept basic intuitions as the foundation of the sciences, then there is no reason why we should not do the same in ethics.

Confronted with these alternatives and being unfamiliar with modern postulational procedures, Sidgwick accepts unhesitatingly the intuitionist's view. "I find," he says, "that I undoubtedly seem to perceive, as clearly and certainly as I see any axiom in Arithmetic or Geometry, that it is 'right' and 'reasonable,' for me to treat others as I should think that I myself ought to be treated under similar conditions, and to do what I believe to be ultimately conducive to universal Good or Happiness" (*21*: 467). "As rational beings," we are told, "we are manifestly bound to aim at good generally," and to "regard the good of any other individual as much as [our] own, except in so far as it is less, or less certainly, knowable or attainable" (*21*:355). With Kant, Sidgwick holds it to be "evident *a priori* that each rational agent is bound to aim at the happiness of all other rational beings no less than its own," and that it is "a *duty* for me to seek my own happiness [only] in so far as I consider it a part of Universal Happiness" (*21*:360). This fundamental maxim Sidgwick holds to be a synthetic rather than an analytic proposition.

Sidgwick's position, as thus defined, has at least the advantage over other forms of hedonism that it does not confuse the desire to enjoy pleasure with the desire to produce it. Moreover, Sidgwick does not deny the efficacy of reason as far as ultimate ends are concerned, nor does he reduce morality to desires and feelings. On the contrary, he holds that happiness—universal happiness—ought to be pursued because reason pronounces it desirable or good (*21*:8). Nevertheless, even this position encounters serious difficulties.

The first of these difficulties arises from the conflict between egoistic and universalistic hedonism. The *egoistic* hedonist holds that there is my pleasure or happiness, and there is your pleasure or happiness. My duty is to maximize my happiness, and your duty is to maximize your happiness. But my happiness and your happiness may not be reconcilable, for they are not parts of a total happiness the maximization of which is my duty as well as yours. The *universalistic* hedonist, on the other hand, holds that there is a universal happiness, and that it is my duty and yours to aim at maximizing it—even if such maximization can be achieved only through the partial or total sacrifice of our personal happiness. The two principles—the egoistic and the universalistic—are obviously irreconcilable.

Now, Sidgwick holds that it seems reasonable to seek one's own happiness, and that, to Common Sense, it undoubtedly seems paradoxical to ask for a reason why one should seek one's own happiness (*21*:386-387). He admits, in other words, that the egoistic principle is widely accepted as self-evident, and nowhere does he show that it is in itself contradictory. Sidgwick maintains, however, that the universalistic principle is at least equally clear (*21*:467). Does this mean that there are two basic principles of hedonism—both self-consistent and axiomatic—which, when taken together, are mutually inconsistent? Sidgwick provides no answer to this question.

The second difficulty arises from the fact that, for Sidgwick, the basic principle of universal hedonism is an *a priori* synthetic proposition and a self-evident truth. This means that the whole controversy over propositions of this kind is pertinent to an evaluation of Sidgwick's position. Unless a specific criterion of self-evidence can be agreed upon, all so-called self-evident truths are in a precarious position; "too many of them have been shown to be false" (*23*:131-136). But Sidgwick gives us no criterion of self-evidence. He merely says that "I undoubtedly seem to perceive" the basic principle of universalistic hedonism "as clearly and certainly as I see any axiom in Arithmetic or Geometry"; and this analogy, obviously, does not help us. The axioms of arithmetic and geometry are assumptions or postulates. They are stipulations explicitly made with a specific deductive system in mind, and are thus subject to revision whenever we find it necessary or convenient to modify the system (*23*:235-247).

Then, too, recent trends in logic and epistemology reveal a good deal of scepticism concerning synthetic *a priori* truths;

and Sidgwick's principle seems as vulnerable as any other. This is not the place to determine whether all so-called synthetic *a priori* propositions are ultimately analytic [as Lewis believes (*15*:158-163)], or whether there is some special sense in which it is still meaningful to speak of certain propositions as synthetic and *a priori*. Suffice it to say that at present the whole problem is in flux (*18*:349-367). To be sure, various attempts to rescue the synthetic *a priori* have been made. It has been argued, for example, that *a priori* synthetic propositions are but stipulations or postulates whose apriority is purely systemic in the sense that all deductions within the postulational system depend upon them. Again, it has been argued that *a priori* synthetic propositions are commitments to which we intend to adhere regardless of consequences. In neither case, however, are the propositions in question necessarily unchallengeable truths; and nowhere does Sidgwick show that, in this respect, his own principle of universalistic hedonism constitutes an exception.

The third difficulty arises from Sidgwick's attempt to specify more fully what it means to contribute to universal happiness.

When Bentham faced a similar problem, he sought a way out by developing his famous *calculus of pleasures*. We ought to consider, he said, the "intensity" and "duration," the "certainty" and "propinquity," the "fecundity" and "purity," and the "extent" of any given pleasure; and by *extent* he meant "the number of persons . . . who are affected by it" (*1*:30). That, strictly speaking, intensity and duration alone are qualities of pleasure itself need here be mentioned only in passing; for we are now not concerned with a detailed analysis of Bentham's position. The whole calculus, however, rests upon the assumption that quantitative values can somehow be assigned to the various factors which Bentham enumerates; and if this assumption is granted, then the functioning of the calculus is simple indeed—*in principle*. For each individual concerned, Bentham tells us, "sum up all the values of all the *pleasures* on the one side, and those of all the pains on the other. The balance, if it be on the side of pleasure, will give the *good* tendency of the act upon the whole, with respect to the interests of that *indivi-*

*dual* person; if on the side of pain, the *bad* tendency of it upon the whole." Then, "take an account of the *number* of persons whose interests appear to be concerned. . . . *Sum up* the numbers expressive of the degrees of *good* tendency, which the act has, with respect to each individual, in regard to whom the tendency of it is *good* upon the whole: do this again with respect to each individual, in regard to whom the tendency of it is *bad* upon the whole. Take the *balance;* which, if on the side of *pleasure* will give the general *good tendency* of the act, with respect to the total number or community of individuals concerned; if on the side of pain, the general *evil tendency*, with respect to the same community" (*1*:31).

Bentham realized, of course, that it is not to be expected that this process of balancing pleasures and pains should be strictly pursued prior to every moral judgment. He believed, however, that "in all this there is nothing but what the practice of mankind, wheresoever they have a clear view of their own interest, is perfectly conformable to" (*1*:32). Still, the *practical* difficulties of such a calculus of pleasures have been pointed out often. They all center around the question of whether or not approximately accurate estimates can be made of the relative balance of pleasure and pain in alternative future possible states of affairs (*4*:238; *7*:417-419). Sidgwick, however, indicates an additional difficulty; for, he maintains, even if we pass over the uncertainties involved in hedonistic comparison generally and assume that "the *quantum* of happiness" which will result from any type of behavior can be ascertained with sufficient exactness for practical purposes—even then it has to be asked, "What is the nature of the human being for whom we are to construct this hypothetical scheme of conduct? For humanity is not something that exhibits the same properties always and everywhere" (*21*:431). As a matter of fact, individual differences—be they of intellect, or emotion, or physical condition and circumstances —are so great that it is absurd to attempt, on hedonistic premises, to formulate specific rules of conduct for all men. The difficulty is not diminished, as Sidgwick well knows, even when we restrict the attempt at formulating such a set of rules to man as we know him, in our age and country; for the difficulty lies in this, that (a) any man we know is more or less definitely committed to a certain moral code, and that (b) this commitment cannot be included in our conception of him as a being for whom a moral code is yet to be constructed *de novo*. But if we take an actual man and abstract his moral beliefs and commitments, then there remains only "an entity so purely hypothetical that it is not clear what practical purpose can be served by constructing a system of moral rules for a community of such beings" (*21*:432). How, then, does Sidgwick solve the difficulty which confronts his own system no less than it does Bentham's?

Let us keep firmly in mind at this point that Sidgwick is a hedonist—a universalistic hedonist—who is intuitively certain that one ought to do always what is ultimately conducive to universal happiness, and who is convinced, furthermore, that in view of our conflicting duties even a hedonist must formulate specific principles of right conduct. "It will not suffice to say," he tells us—and rightly—"that the extent and comparative force of [the] different obligations vary according to circumstances and must be determined as occasion arises: since we still require to know generally what kinds of circumstances have weight and how much" (*21*:215).

Now, Sidgwick, in conformity with this basic point of view, holds that there are certain absolute practical principles which, although too abstract or universal in scope for immediate application, will yet indicate in broad outline the nature of right conduct, and "the truth of which, when they are explicitly stated, is manifest" (*21*:352).

One such principle states that "whatever action any of us judges to be right for himself, he implicitly judges to be right for all similar persons in similar circumstances" (*21*:353).[4] Another principle is that "it cannot be right for *A* to treat *B*

---

[4] Or, as Sidgwick himself reformulated it, "if a kind of conduct that is right (or wrong) for me is not right (or wrong) for some one else, it must be on the ground of some difference between the two cases, other than the fact that I and he are different persons" (*21*:353).

in a manner in which it would be wrong for *B* to treat *A*, unless we can find some difference between the nature or circumstances of the two which we can state as a reasonable ground for difference of treatment" (*21*:353).[5] Still another principle demands impartiality in the application of general rules (*21*:354).[6]

Sidgwick himself admits (see footnotes 5 and 6) that these principles, although self-evident and necessary, are insufficient for complete guidance of moral conduct. They are insufficient mainly because they do not specify in any way what differences in the natures or circumstances of numerically distinct persons do constitute a reasonable ground for difference of treatment. They are, as Broad has observed, much like the Principle of Indifference in probability theory: "Two alternatives are equally possible if there be no relevant dissimilarities between them; but what kinds of dissimilarity are relevant and what are not" (*4*:224)?

Another principle, which Sidgwick accepts, states that "the mere difference of priority and posteriority in time is not a reasonable ground for having more regard to the consciousness of one moment than that of another." That is to say, "a smaller present good is not to be preferred to a greater future good" (*21*:354). But even Sidgwick admits that this principle "need not be restricted to a hedonistic application: it is equally applicable to any other interpretation of 'one's own good' . . . of which the integrant parts are realized in different parts or moments of a lifetime" (*21*:355).

A still different principle, which Sidgwick regards as self-evident, states that "the good of any one individual is of no more importance, as a part of universal good, than the good of any other; unless, that is, there are special grounds for believing that more good is likely to be realized in one case than in the other" (*21*:355). To this he adds the further "self-evident truth"

---

[5] This principle, Sidgwick adds, "manifestly does not give complete guidance; but its truth, as far as it goes, is self-evident; and Common Sense has amply recognized its practical importance."

[6] Sidgwick adds, "there ultimately appeared to be no other element [of justice] which could be intuitively known with perfect clearness and certainty. [But] here again it must be plain that this precept of impartiality is insufficient for the complete determination of just conduct, as it does not help us to decide what kind of rules should be thus impartially applied."

that, "as rational beings, we are manifestly bound to aim at good generally, not merely at this or that part of it" (*21*:355).[7] And these last two principles lead Sidgwick to assert the abstract principle of the duty of Benevolence, so far as it is cognizable by direct intuition—the principle, namely, that "one is morally bound to regard the good of any other individual as much as one's own, except in so far as it is less, or less certainly knowable or attainable" (*21*:355).

Summing up his discussion of these principles, Sidgwick concludes: "I regard the apprehension, with more or less distinctness, of these abstract truths, as the permanent basis of the common conviction that the fundamental precepts of morality are essentially reasonable" (*21*:356). And in this appeal to reason Sidgwick finds himself in complete agreement with Kant.

We need not be concerned here with the question whether or not Sidgwick's principles actually are self-evident (as he believes), or whether or not they are true at all. For our purposes it is sufficient to observe (1) that the principles are not derivable from the basic principle of hedonism but are (for Sidgwick himself) distinct and independent intuitions; and (2) that, in turn, the principles do not imply hedonism but are reconcilable with nonhedonistic interpretations of the good. The first of these observations implies that Sidgwick, although a hedonist in his interpretation of the good as pleasure, is a deontologist in his recourse to intuited principles. The second observation implies the possibility of developing even within Sidgwick's framework of principles various teleological ethical theories which are alternatives to hedonism. The two observations together thus open up new perspectives for theoretical ethics and carry us beyond hedonism proper.

## V

As we have seen, Sidgwick clearly recognizes the fact that, for the guidance of our conduct, we require to know generally what

---

[7] Sidgwick adds: "We can only evade the conviction of this obligation by denying that there is any such universal good."

kinds of circumstances have weight and how much; but we have seen also that the basic principles which Sidgwick accepts as self-evident truths do not give us the required knowledge, for they are purely formal demands of reason. The question is, can the necessary information be obtained from the hedonistic principle that pleasure or happiness is the ultimate goal of moral conduct?

It is implicit in egoistic hedonism that each individual ought to sacrifice any amount of happiness in others if by so doing he can increase his own pleasure even to the slightest degree more than he can by following any other course of action. But it is implicit in universalistic hedonism that each individual ought to sacrifice his own happiness if by so doing the total net amount of happiness in the world is increased more than it would be if he did not make the sacrifice. What alone counts here is the *total net amount* or *positive balance* of happiness *in the world.*

It is obvious, however, that this total net amount might be increased in various ways. It might be increased, for example, by increasing the number of people affected—even though the happiness of each individual would have to be reduced. Or, given a fixed number of individuals—say, A, B, and C—an increase in the total net amount of happiness might be achieved by an intensification of the happiness of A—even though this affects adversely the happiness of B and C, or, perchance, intensifies the misery of C. In other words, an unequal distribution of happiness might actually yield a positive balance of happiness greater than that obtainable from an equal distribution. But if this is so, then it is also possible that unequal distributions involving different combinations of individuals may yield identical increases in happiness over the net total obtainable from an equal distribution. The question, therefore, arises, On what grounds would the hedonist decide which combination he ought to favor? Obviously, his choice is either completely arbitrary or it is determined by some factor (or factors) other than the idea of a total net balance of happiness (4:250-251). To the extent, however, to which the decision is not arbitrary, the course of action is not guided exclusively by the universalistic conception of hedonism. On the contrary, principles comparable to Sidgwick's self-evident truths play once more a crucial rôle in ethics, and the difficulties previously pointed out in connection with such principles again confront the hedonist. Thus, when Hilliard, on hedonistic grounds, defines *justice* as "the character manifested in individual or social behavior patterns such that they tend to the resolution, in the direction of enhancement or maintenance of the general happiness, of value imbalances arising within the social environment" (9:264), it is clear, I believe, that this definition either remains ambiguous as to the precise nature of value imbalances and leaves justice at the mercy of arbitrary decisions, or it assumes implicitly a principle (or set of principles) comparable to Sidgwick's self-evident truths which govern the *distribution* of happiness. In either case, however, the idea of justice or just conduct is not derived from the basic principle of hedonism itself.

Nor is the position of hedonism improved at this point by a recurrent reference to a qualitative distinction of pleasures. Mill's appeal to a sense of dignity, which all human beings possess, we have discussed in the preceding chapter. Here we need remind ourselves only of the fact that such an appeal introduces a standard of judgment not derivable from the pleasure principle, and that it therefore transcends hedonism. But Sheldon's reformulation of hedonism, too, breaks down at this point. "We sense," he says with special reference to Kant's apostrophe to duty, "a deeper-going joy in the austere beauty of the stern daughter of the voice of God than in the pleasant graces of the sirens of this world" (20:296). Such deeper-going joy, however, (as Kant well knew) presupposes rather than establishes a moral *ought*. When Sheldon argues that "the torture . . . of a conscience that knows its guilt" is greater than the "pains that follow the righteous course" (20:290), Kant replies—and rightly: "One must already value the importance of what we call duty, the respect for the moral law, and the immediate worth which a person obtains in his own eyes through obedience to it, in order to feel satisfaction in the consciousness of his conformity to law or bitter remorse which accompanies his awareness that he has transgressed it. Therefore, this satisfaction or spiritual unrest cannot be felt prior to the knowledge of obligation, nor can it be made the basis of the latter" (14:150). We are brought back, in other words, to principles which cannot be derived from the basic conceptions of hedonism itself.

Beyond all of these considerations, however, still further difficulties arise for every form of hedonism which regards pleasure as a simple experiential fact and the sole basis of morality; for such a conception of pleasure neglects the significance of context in human experience. Let us suppose, for example, that I feel pleasure when I perceive or think of the undeserved misfortune of another man (4:233). Even a hedonist—a universalistic hedonist—I am sure, regards this *malicious joy* as a morally undesirable state of mind. But malicious joy is not undesirable or bad merely because it is pleasure (for pleasure, the hedonist holds, is desirable and good); nor is it undesirable or bad merely because it pertains to the undeserved misfortune of another man (for an attitude of compassion with respect to the same misfortune may well be morally good). The badness of malicious joy—I believe with Broad—depends on the *combination* of being pleasant with having this particular kind of object. What is important for the ethicist, therefore, is not pleasure as such, but pleasure in context; and it may well be the case, as Broad points out, that the goodness or badness of an act or attitude depends, not on a single simple characteristic, but on the combination of certain characteristics in the same experience. In any case, "the hedonist can neither produce nor conceive an instance of an experience which was just pleasant or painful and nothing more" (4:234-235). He can therefore not determine by direct inspection that hedonic quality alone is sufficient to determine moral value. At the most he can show that it is necessary.

## VI

One final point deserves consideration. As Stace puts it, "the difficulty of the problem of the basis of moral obligation is precisely the difficulty of seeing why I ought to do something which I do not desire to do" (22:123). The universalistic hedonists have tried to cope with this problem in various ways. Their efforts, however, (as we have seen) have not been successful. We must now examine Stace's own attempt to deal with the difficulty to which he refers.

To begin with, Stace holds (and no one will contradict him) that "we certainly do experience states of consciousness which we call joy, happiness, delight" (22:126), and that "everyone knows in his own experience the difference between being happy and being unhappy" (21:128). Everyone knows, for example, "whether he is happy or not now at this moment. He knows whether he is happy or unhappy in his relations with his wife. He knows that in some periods of his life he was happier than in other periods" (22:128). That is to say, everyone knows immediately and directly when he is happy and when he is not happy. The term "happiness," therefore, requires no formal definition. Stace maintains, however—and this is the crux of his doctrine—that happiness is not composed of pleasure, and that any interpretation of happiness as an aggregate of pleasure is false (22:129, 140). It is the crucial mistake of hedonists to identify happiness and pleasure. As Stace points out, the volume of happiness is not necessarily proportional to the volume of the satisfactions or pleasures (22:145); for "one man may be happy although he has very few pleasures or satisfactions; while another whose life is replete with pleasures and satisfactions may be relatively unhappy" (22:140). And to increase pleasures or satisfactions is not the same as to increase happiness.

"Happiness is not proportional to satisfactions," Stace holds, "because, although satisfactions are among the conditions of happiness, they are not its only conditions. Satisfactions are what come to a man from the outside, and they do in part determine happiness. But what is within the secret chambers of the man's own soul determines it too." *"The intensity of a satisfaction* [therefore] *has nothing whatever to do with the quantity of happiness which results from it."* For Stace, "the essential point is that it is upon the specific character of our satisfactions that the greatness of our happiness depends, and *not upon their intensity"* (*22*:146-147).

If we grant Stace's distinction between pleasures and satisfactions on the one hand, and happiness on the other—as I think we must—and if we also admit that the specific character of our satisfactions, rather than their intensity, determines the greatness of our happiness, then it follows that we now have a standard in the light of which we can speak of lower and higher pleasures. As Stace formulates it: *"Those satisfactions are higher which are found in experience to contribute more to happiness. Those satisfactions are lower which are found in experience to contribute less to happiness"* (*22*:156). This standard, to be sure, transcends all forms of hedonism which identify pleasure and happiness, but it is at least basically related to the hedonistic conception of value.

Applying his standard to man's cultural history, Stace finds that "the impressive array of warnings uttered by all the great moralists against over-indulgence in bodily pleasures means, in effect, that the universal experience of men—finding its utterance in these men of genius—is that bodily satisfactions, however intense, however great their own 'size' or 'volume,' add extremely little to the 'size' or 'volume' of the happiness into which they enter" (*22*:148). Stace admits, of course, that no desires, no satisfactions are in themselves bad or immoral, and that, therefore, the desires of the flesh are perfectly legitimate (*22*:151). He holds, however, that "the satisfactions of the mind and spirit, in art, in science, in philosophy, in religion, are higher and nobler than the satisfactions of the flesh" (*22*:152); for the satisfactions of the body do not yield true happiness, whereas "the things of the mind and the spirit are the only possible bases of a happy life" (*22*:157, 159). Support for this view Stace finds in the whole history of human experience.

Stace is convinced, however, that not every happiness-producing action possesses *ipso facto* any positive moral value (*22*: 162). He holds, in fact, that "there are two other characters, besides the character of producing happiness, which an action must have if it is to be morally good. These are the characters of *unselfishness* and *justice"*—neither of which can be reduced by analysis to happiness-production (22:161, 166, 174, 181, 182), although it is Stace's view that justice may be reduced to un-selfishness (22:185). What is important here is that, according to Stace, only those actions possess positive moral value which aim at increasing the happiness of others (22:162). And this brings us back to our initial question. Why should I increase the happiness of other people? Why should I be unselfish and just? Why should I do something which I do not desire to do?

Stace is right in maintaining that the ideas of duty and obli-gation arise only where there is at least a possibility of a clash between what I want to do and what I ought to do. "To render the idea of obligation meaningful at all it must at least be *possible* that inclination should be opposed to duty" (22:163). In actuality, Stace holds, "there is but one moral evil—selfish-ness. And there is but one moral duty—unselfishness" (22:186, 179, 203-206, 244-248). This interpretation, I believe, over-simplifies the case. Let us accept it, however, because it points up most clearly the crucial problem. Our question then is, Why ought I to be unselfish rather than selfish? Why ought I, why ought any man, to be moral? And to this question Stace replies that it is "the only way to reach *my own* happiness" (22:254). In other words, " 'You ought to be moral' means that *if* you wish to be happy yourself, the only means to adopt is to be moral." And, Stace adds, "all men are so constituted that this is true of them. Therefore one and the same moral obligation falls upon all men. All men ought to be unselfish because all men wish to be happy and because for all men unselfishness is the only way of attaining that end" (22:255, 275).

But even Stace realizes that the principle just stated must be qualified in order to bring it into closer harmony with the facts of human existence. He grants, therefore, that unselfishness is not necessarily the *sole* condition of happiness; it is only an indispensable condition (22:258, 274). "It is not necessary," Stace says, "that we should be able to give an absolute guarantee that if a man is moral, this *alone* will ensure his happiness. . . . In addition to morality a man requires for his happiness absence of physical pain, some external goods, some 'pleasures,' and so on" (22:258, 276). We cannot expect him to be absolutely altruistic, to deny himself everything, but must grant that he is entitled to be just to himself as well as to others. Stace insists, however, that "without morality it is impossible that I should be happy" (22:258, 266, 273, 279).

Two comments are in order. (1) If we accept the thesis that unselfishness is an indispensable condition for happiness, but maintain—as Stace does—that a man should not deny himself everything, then we find that this doctrine fails to provide a specific criterion for the degree of selfishness which we may tolerate in ourselves. It will not do to say that our happiness is proportional to our unselfishness; for it is conceivable that a person may be very happy although his unselfish acts are limited in scope and number, and Stace himself admits that absolute altruism, far from giving us perfect happiness, is inimical to our happiness. Stace's doctrine thus yields no clear-cut principle which might guide us in setting bounds to our selfishness or in determining when we are just to ourselves as well as to others. Without such a principle, however, the whole doctrine loses all practical significance.

(2) The thesis that I ought to be moral, *if* I wish to be happy, is, for Stace, a statement of empirical fact. He specifically says that all men are so constituted that it is true of them. But a universal proposition of this kind can hardly be proved. It is, and remains, an empirical generalization which may or may not be true. Stace certainly has not demonstrated its universal truth. He merely asserts his belief in it (22:274). But since Stace also admits that the sources of human happiness are many, that they include the satisfactions of art, or religion, of intellectual exercise, of bodily function, besides the specific sources of satisfaction, sociality and disinterested altruistic feeling, on which morality is founded, it is difficult to see how it can ever be shown that unselfishness is an indispensable condition of happiness. But if Stace cannot show this, then his whole thesis collapses; and with it collapses the last attempt to salvage whatever truth there may be in a modified hedonism.

## VII

T. H. Green has argued that, irrespective of all the flaws in hedonism, the doctrine has at least the advantage that "the theory of an ideal good, consisting in the greatest happiness of the greatest number, as the end by reference to which the claim of all laws and powers and rules of action on our obedience is to be tested, has tended to improve human conduct and character" (7:399). This may be granted. It must not be forgotten, however, that any other theory of morals which projects an ideal good may serve as well—provided only that the goal itself has sufficient appeal to be generally accepted. Moreover—and Green himself recognizes this fact—utilitarianism "has not given men a more lively sense of their duty to others," for no theory can do that (7:400); but "it has led those in whom that sense has already been awakened to be less partial in judging who the 'others' are, to consider all men as the 'others,' and, on the ground of the claim of all men to an equal chance of 'happiness,' to secure their political and promote their social equality" (7:400). By insisting that the happiness of the greatest number alone counts, utilitarianism "has given a wider and more impartial range to public spirit" (7:400), and has thus been of inestimable value. It has tended to rationalize our social and political life (7:402) and has inspired humanitarian reforms in modern society. Also, it seems to entail a frank recognition of the principle of universal suffrage, which is the core of our democracy.

These considerations seem to be strong arguments in support of utilitarianism; but they are not conclusive. Their force is broken by the fact that alternative theories might well serve the same purpose; that it is at least not contradictory to think of alternatives which serve the same practical ends—and serve them even better. There is, for example, the ideal of a Christian brotherhood of all men, or Kant's "kingdom of ends," or Royce's "beloved community." And it must also be admitted that inherent in utilitarianism is the tendency toward pleasure-seeking egalitarianism which, in all ages and climes, has been a first sign of cultural decay and of a deterioration of the entire social structure. *Panem et circensum*—this slogan expresses perhaps a distortion of the loftiest meaning of utilitarianism; and yet, it seems to be the inevitable result of the pursuit of "happiness" in terms of "pleasure for everyone"; for when the pursuit of pleasure is made a goal, only the lowest common denominator is ultimately important.

But what is most significant for our purposes here is the fact that the utilitarians have failed to establish (except by definition) that an act's being productive of pleasure (or happiness) is always a sufficient ground for its being right or morally obligatory. As Herbert Schneider points out, distinguishing the "prudential" from the "moral" ought: "If I wish to run an automobile, I am *physically* obliged to put oil in the engine, and I am *prudentially* obliged to keep the oil at a proper level. . . . But no one *obliges* us to seek happiness" (*19b*:312). "Utilitarianism is a body of technical advice by specialists in prudence" (*19b*:312); but the *moral* "ought" is a different matter (*19b*:313). On this point Ross most heartily agrees with Schneider (*19a*:69-70). And Ross adds one further point: For a utilitarian it should be morally indifferent whether a certain act produces x units of pleasure for A and inflicts y units of pain on B, or confers x-y units of pleasure on either A or B, because in each case the net result will be x-y units of pleasure contributed to the whole (*19a*:75). But who is to measure the increments of pain and pleasure? Is it to be A or B, or is it to be C, who is the cause of either? Or is there some other agent or agency which determines the units of pain and of pleasure? Must the moral ought remain on such shaky, ambiguous, and irrational grounds?

## REFERENCES

1. Bentham, J., *The Principles of Morals and Legislation,* Hafner Library of Classics, New York, 1948.
2. Bentham, J., *Deontology: Or, The Science of Morality,* arranged and edited from the manuscript of Jeremy Bentham by J. Bowring, London, 1834.
2a. *Ibid.,* Volume I, chpts. XI and XII.
2b. *Ibid.,* Volume II, chpts. II and III.

3. Bradley, F. H., *Ethical Studies,* 2nd ed., Oxford, 1927.
4. Broad, C. D., *Five Types of Ethical Theory,* London, 1934.
5. Butler, J., *Fifteen Sermons Preached at the Rolls Chapel,* London, 1726.
5a. Clark, George A., "Mill's 'Notorious Analogy,' " *Journal of Philosophy,* LVI (1959).
6. Elliot, H. S. R., *The Letters of John Stuart Mill,* 1910, II.
7. Green, T. H., *Prolegomena to Ethics,* 5th ed., Oxford, 1906.
8. Hall, E. W., "The 'Proof' of Utility in Bentham and Mill," *Ethics,* LX (1949).
9. Hilliard, A. L., *The Forms of Value,* New York, 1950.
10. Hume, D., *A Treatise of Human Nature,* 1739, Book II, Part III, Section 3; Book III, Part I, Section L.
11. Hume, D., *Moral and Political Philosophy* (Henry D. Aiken, editor), Hafner Library of Classics, New York, 1948.
12. Hutcheson, F., *Essay on the Nature and Conduct of the Passions and Affections. With Illustrations on the Moral Sense,* 3rd edition, London, 1742.
13. Hutcheson, F., *A System of Moral Philosophy,* London, 1755, I.
14. Kant, I., *Critique of Practical Reason,* Beck translation, Chicago, 1949.
15. Lewis, C. I., *An Analysis of Knowledge and Valuation,* La Salle, 1946.
16. Mill, J. S., "Utilitarianism," *Utilitarianism, Liberty, and Representative Government,* Everyman's Library.
17. Mill, J. S., *Dissertations and Discussions,* Boston, 1864, I. The essay entitled "Bentham" was first published in the *London and Westminster Review,* August 1838.
17a. Moore, G. E., *Principia Ethica,* Cambridge, 1903.
18. Peach, B., "A Nondescriptive Theory of the Analytic," *Philosophical Review,* LXI (1952).
19. Raphael, D. D., *The Moral Sense,* London, 1947.
19a. Ross, W. D., *Foundations of Ethics,* Oxford, 1939.
19b. Schneider, Herbert W., "Obligations and the Pursuit of Happiness," *Philosophical Review,* LXI (1952).
20. Sheldon, W. H., "The Absolute Truth of Hedonism," *Journal of Philosophy,* XLVII (1950).
21. Sidgwick, H., *The Methods of Ethics,* 2nd ed., London, 1877.
22. Stace, W. T., *The Concept of Morals,* New York, 1937.
23. Werkmeister, W. H., *The Basis and Structure of Knowledge,* New York, 1948.
24. Werkmeister, W. H., "Value in an Age of Crisis," *Tully Cleon Knoles Lectures in Philosophy,* College of the Pacific, 1950, (unpublished), Second Lecture.
25. Williams, G., "Hedonism, Conflict, and Cruelty," *Journal of Philosophy,* XLVII (1950).

CHAPTER  **VI**

# Nietzsche's Transvaluation

# of Values

Nietzsche's "transvaluation of values" is in every respect antithetic to hedonism—as it is antithetic to Kant's formalism. Hedonism, in Nietzsche's judgment, is a "signpost to Nihilism" (XIV:29),[1] and Kant's critical philosophy is but "the craftiest of subterfuges" (XIV:210)—"a sign of decadence—a symptom of *degenerating* life" (XVI:23;138). Nietzsche objects not only to Kant's "transcendentalism" and "Christian" values, but to his formalism as well. "A virtue," he believes, "must be *our* invention, *our* most personal defense and need: in every other sense it is merely a danger. That which does not support our life, *harms* it. . . . The 'Virtue,' the 'Duty,' the 'Good in itself,' [i.e.] the

---

[1] All quotations are my own translations from the German text of *Nietzsche's Werke*, Taschen-Ausgabe, edited by Elisabeth Förster-Nietzsche, Leipzig 1906. However, for the convenience of readers who desire to check the context, all references (by volume and page) are to *The Complete Works of Friedrich Nietzsche*, authorized translation, edited by Dr. Oscar Levy, London: G. Allen & Unwin, Ltd., 18 vols., 1923-24 reprint. The volumes specifically referred to in the text are: VI, *Human, All-Too-Human I*, tr. Helen Zimmern; VII, *Human, All-Too-Human II*, tr. Paul V. Cohn; VIII, *The Case of Wagner* and *Nietzsche Contra Wagner*, tr. Anthony M. Ludovici; IX, *The Dawn of Day*, tr. J. M. Kennedy; X, *The Joyful Wisdom*, tr. Thomas Common; XI, *Thus Spake Zarathustra*, tr. Thomas Common; XII, *Beyond Good and Evil*, tr. Helen Zimmern; XIII, *The Genealogy of Morals*, tr. Horace B. Samuel; XIV-XV, *The Will to Power I* and *II*, tr. Anthony M. Ludovici; XVI, *The Twilight of the Idols* and *The Antichrist*, tr. Anthony M. Ludovici; XVII, *Ecce Homo*, tr. Anthony M. Ludovici.

168

Good stamped with the character of impersonality and universal validity—these are mere delusions in which the decline, the ultimate enfeeblement of life . . . express themselves. The most fundamental laws of preservation and growth demand precisely the reverse, namely, that each individual invent *his own* virtue, *his own* categorical imperative" (XVI:136-137). In Nietzsche's opinion, "nothing is more profoundly, more inwardly ruinous than is an 'impersonal' duty, a sacrifice to the Moloch of Abstraction" (XVI:137). It is strange, therefore, Nietzsche finds, that "no one has ever felt Kant's Categorical Imperative to be dangerous to life" (XVI:137).

But Nietzsche is opposed also to any "philosophy [which] itself is criticism and critical science—and nothing else whatever" (XII:151). Critics, he holds (and I agree with him), are "tools of the philosopher," and are "far from being philosophers themselves" (XII:151). As Nietzsche sees it, *"all* the sciences have now to prepare the way for the future task of the philosopher"— this task being: to "solve the *problem of value,"* to "determine the *order of rank of values"* (XIII:58). "The real philosophers [therefore] are commanders and law-givers; they say, 'Thus *shall* it be!' They determine the Whither and the Why of man and, in doing so, dispose of the preparatory labors of all philosophical workers, of all subjugators of the past. With creative hand they reach out toward the future, and whatever is or was becomes for them a means, a tool, a hammer. Their 'cognition' is a *creating,* their creating is a law-giving, their will to truth is— *will to power"* (XII:152). "It may be necessary for the education of the real philosopher," Nietzsche concedes, "that he himself should once have stood upon all those steps upon which his servants, the scientific workers in philosophy, remain standing —and *must* remain standing. He himself must perhaps have been critic and sceptic and dogmatist and historian and, beyond this, poet and collector and traveler and riddle-solver and moralist and seer and 'free spirit' and almost everything in order to traverse the whole range of human values and value feelings and *to be able* to see from the height into every distance, from the depth up to every height, from a nook into every expanse—and to do so with a variety of eyes and of consciences. But all of these are only preliminary conditions for his task; this task itself demands something else—it demands that he *create values"* (XII:151-152), that he "determine the *order of rank of values"* (XIII:58).

It is only natural that the *real* philosopher, as Nietzsche thinks of him—though *"indispensable* for tomorrow and the day after tomorrow"—"has at all times found himself, and *has been compelled* to find himself, in contradiction with his own day," whereas "his enemy has always been the ideal of the day" (XII: 153); for the task—"the hard, unwanted, inescapable task"—of the real philosophers has always been "to be the bad conscience of their time" (XII:153). "In putting the vivisector's knife to the breast of the very *virtues of their age,"* these real philosophers "betrayed what was their own secret, namely, that they knew of a *new* greatness of man, of a new and untrodden path to his aggrandizement. They always disclosed how much hypocrisy, indolence, self-indulgence and self-neglect, how much falsehood was concealed under the most honored types of their contemporaneous morality, how much virtue was *outlived"* (XII:153).

It is in this spirit of a "real philosopher" that Nietzsche approaches his own task and conceives his work. It will be well to remember this fact, together with Nietzsche's deep earnestness and profound concern for the future of man, when, later on, we discover that his antagonisms and enthusiasms carry him at times to intolerable extremes. At no time, however, does Nietzsche ask us to accept his philosophy as "final truth." On the contrary, he explicitly states that "one requites a teacher badly if one remains always merely the pupil" (XI: 90); and: "I bid you to lose me and to find yourselves" (XI:90).

# I

Nietzsche's book, *The Dawn of Day,* written in 1881, represents in a distinctive sense the dawn of Nietzsche's own philosophy.[2]

---

[2] For a critical analysis of "The Nietzsche Legend" and of "Nietzsche's Life as a Background of his Thought" see Kaufmann, *op. cit.,* 3-51. Special notice

It is possible, of course, to find traces of Nietzsche's approach and ultimate point of view in such earlier works as *The Birth of Tragedy* and *Human, All-Too-Human,* I and II; but these traces are scattered and are clearly discernible only in retrospect and from the vantage-point of the later works. In *The Dawn of Day,* however, Nietzsche tells us at once that "in this book we find a 'subterrestrial one' at work, one who bores from within, who digs, who undermines" (IX:1); one who has "gone to the depths" and has "tunnelled to the bottom," who has "started to investigate and to unearth an old *faith* upon which, for thousands of years, we philosophers used to build as upon the safest foundation— upon which we used to build again and again, although every structure so far has crumbled." He tells us, in other words, that with this book he himself "began to undermine our *faith in morality*" (IX:2).

Nietzsche's later works—beginning with *The Joyful Wisdom,* but especially (in the order given): *Thus Spake Zarathustra, Beyond Good and Evil, The Genealogy of Morals, The Case of Wagner, The Twilight of the Idols, The Antichrist, Ecce Homo,* and *Nietzsche Contra Wagner*—carry out in varying degrees of intensity this program of undermining an old faith and of re-valuing all values in the light of a new ideal.

It is important to stress this unity and organic growth of Nietzsche's world-view, for the shifting emphases and his aphorismic style tend to leave an impression of incoherence. That Nietzsche himself regarded his world-view as a coherent whole is certain beyond all doubt, even though he denounced all "systems." He says, for example, in *The Genealogy of Morals,* that the thoughts expressed in this book "are older" even than "their first frugal and provisional expression" in *Human, All-Too-Human,* and that they have "held together even closer," have "intertwined and grown into one another" (XIII:2). The fact that he still adheres to them gives him "the joyous confidence that,

---

should be taken of Kaufmann's judicious evaluation of the scribbles and notes which were collected and arranged under the editorship of Nietzsche's sister, Elisabeth Förster-Nietzsche, and were published after Nietzsche's death as *The Will to Power.*

from the beginning, these thoughts originated within [him] not individually, not haphazardly, not sporadically, but from a common root, from a *basic will* of cognition which reigns in the depth [of his soul], which speaks ever more precisely, which always demands that which is more determinate" (XIII:2). *Ecce Homo* traces the interrelations of Nietzsche's ideas in some detail.

It must not be inferred, however, that the outlines of Nietzsche's "system" are always apparent or clear, or that there are no contradictions in his writings. On the contrary, at one level of understanding it can even be said that self-contradiction is the basic character of Nietzsche's thinking, and statements can be found in his books to support almost any point of view. But if such statements are viewed, not in isolation, but within the context of the whole, the contradictions, as a rule, give way to more adequate formulations or can be shown to be illuminating disclosures of startling paradoxes of human existence. An attempt will be made here to avoid the paradoxical and to bring out the over-all unity of Nietzsche's thought; and in the foreground of our discussions will always be the problem of values.

## II

"These are my demands upon you," says Nietzsche, "even though they sound bad in your ears: that you subject moral valuations themselves to criticism; that you stop your moral impulse—which demands submission and not criticism—with the question: 'Why submission?'; that you regard this request for a 'Why?,' for a critique of morals, as your *present* form of morality itself, as the most sublime kind of morality, which will bring honor to yourselves and to your age" (XIV:320).

What, then, is the "morality," this "greatest mistress of seduction" (IX:3;4), which is to be subjected to criticism? According to Nietzsche, it is "nothing other (and therefore especially *nothing more!*) than obedience to custom" (IX:14). "Customs, however, are *traditional* ways of acting and valuing. [Hence,] in matters in which no tradition commands, there is no morality;

and the less life is determined by tradition, the smaller is the circle of morality" (IX:14).

Tradition itself, Nietzsche holds, is "a higher authority which is obeyed not because it commands *what is useful* to us, but because it *commands*" (IX:15). The "feeling for tradition" which makes us obey is thus but "the fear of a higher intelligence which commands, [the fear, that is,] of an incomprehensible, indefinite power, of something more than personal—[and] there is superstition in this fear" (IX:15).

From the point of view of tradition, Nietzsche argues, he is "the most moral man" who either "most frequently obeys the law" (IX:15) or "obeys [it] in the most difficult cases" (IX:16). From the point of view of tradition, therefore, "the most moral man is he who *sacrifices* most to custom" (IX:16); whereas the immoral man is the "free man," "because it is his *will* to depend in everything upon himself and not upon a tradition" (IX:14).

Where tradition dominates, "every individualistic action, every individualistic mode of thinking causes dread. It is impossible to compute how much the more uncommon, the more select, the more original minds must have suffered in the course of history from always being considered as the evil and dangerous ones—*yes, from considering themselves to be such.* Under the dominance of the morality of custom, originality of every kind has acquired a bad conscience" (IX:17).

To be sure, custom "represents the experience of earlier men with respect to what presumably is useful and what harmful; but *the feeling for custom* ([which is] morality) pertains not to that experience as such, but to the age, the sacredness, the unquestioned authority of the custom. This feeling, therefore, acts against our acquiring new experience, against our correcting the custom—which is to say that morality [as the feeling for custom] acts against the formation of new and better customs; that it stupefies" (IX:27).

Understanding morality in the sense just indicated, Nietzsche now voices his demand for a critique of moral values: *"the value of these values is itself to be called in question"* (XIII:9). Hitherto, Nietzsche maintains, "the *value* of these 'values' has been taken for granted, has been accepted as a matter of fact, as being beyond all question. Hitherto, no one has in the least doubted or hesitated in judging the 'good man' to be of higher value than the 'evil man'—higher in the sense of furtherance utility, prosperity with respect to *man* in general (including the future of man). But what, if the reverse should be true? What, if there should lurk in the 'good man' a symptom of retrogression, or a danger, a temptation, a poison, a narcotic, by means of which the present lives *at the expense of the future?* . . . What, if morality itself [as feeling for custom] should have to bear the responsibility if *the highest power and splendor,* although in themselves possible, could never be attained by the human species; if morality itself [this feeling for custom] were the real danger of dangers?" (XIII:9).

### III

Preparatory to his critique of morality and his own "transvaluation of values," Nietzsche examines "the conditions and circumstances out of which [the customary standards and values] grew, and under which they evolved and were transformed" (XIII:9). This examination leads him, first, to a brief discussion of epistemological problems.

Philosophy, Nietzsche holds, has hitherto proceeded from a "faulty starting-point"; for it has proceeded "as if there were 'facts of consciousness'—but no *phenomenalism* in *introspection*" (XV:6). Actually, Nietzsche argues (in substantial agreement with modern depth psychology), "everything of which we become conscious is first thoroughly adjusted, simplified, schematized, interpreted—the *real* process of inner 'perception,' the *causal connection* between thoughts, feelings, desires, between subject and object is absolutely concealed from us—and is perhaps purely imaginary" (XV:7). But if this is so, then it follows (1) that "everything which becomes conscious is [an] end-result, a conclusion—and causes nothing"; and (2) that "all succession in consciousness is perfectly atomistic" (XV:9). The basic error of philosophy has been to neglect these facts and to attempt to understand the world "from the *opposite* point of view—as if nothing were effective and real except thinking, feeling, willing" (XV:9).

Once we assume (with Nietzsche) the fundamental importance of the unconscious, certain conclusions follow—conclusions which facilitate greatly our understanding of crucial aspects of Nietzsche's philosophy. We can understand, for example, Nietzsche's contention that "consciousness exists only to the extent to which it is useful" (XV:24), and that truth may be a "kind of error" (XV:20). But let us examine more fully the problems which are here involved.

Nietzsche holds that, at the level of consciousness, any species of life, in order to "maintain itself" and to "grow in its power," "must comprehend in its conception of reality enough that is calculable and constant to make it possible, upon the basis of [such knowledge], to construct a schema of its conduct" (XV: 12). "The *utility of preservation*—not some abstractly theoretical desire not to be deceived—[thus] stands as the motive behind the development of the organs of cognition; [these organs] evolve in such a way that their observations suffice for our preservation" (XV:12). Upon this "utilitarian" ground Nietzsche takes his stand at all times.

Against the positivists, who consider "only phenomena" and who say that "only facts exist," Nietzsche argues that "facts are precisely what does not exist," and that "only *interpretations*" exist. "We cannot establish a fact 'in itself'; [and] perhaps it is nonsense to desire to do such a thing" (XV:12). Hence, "in so far as the word 'cognition' has any meaning at all," it may be admitted that "the world is knowable" (XV:13). But there is not simply "one sense" of the world. There are "countless senses," and they depend upon our "instincts" and our impulses "for or against" the given. "It is our needs," in other words, "which *interpret the world*" (XV:13). "Every instinct is a sort of thirst for power; each has its perspective which it desires to impose upon all other instincts as their norms" (XV:13), and in the light of which it tends to interpret the world. It is in this sense that Nietzsche says, "we can *comprehend* only a world which we ourselves have *made*" (XV:21).

But if our "instincts" and "desires" impose the perspectives from which we interpret the "world," then "the value of *life* is ultimately decisive" (XV:20), and truth is but a relative matter. In fact, "a belief can be a condition necessary to life, and nevertheless be *false*" (XV:14). Truth, in other words, may be but "that *kind of error* without which a particular species of living beings could not exist" (XV:20); and even "the most strongly believed a priori 'truths' are . . . [only] *assumptions for the time being*" (XV:21).

This "relativity of truth" does not mean, however, that reason and judgment play no part in our adjustment to the world, or that "feelings" are primary. In Nietzsche's opinion, "feelings are nothing final, nothing original." On the contrary, behind them "there are judgments and evaluations" (IX:41). In fact, "the inspiration which stems from a feeling is the grandchild of a judgment—often of an erroneous judgment!—and certainly not of one's own judgment! To trust one's feelings—this simply means to obey one's grandfather and grandmother and their grandparents more than the gods *within ourselves:* one's own reason and one's own experience" (IX:41).

However, our task of re-evaluating tradition, of breaking away from the past is made especially difficult by the fact that the very language we employ to express our thoughts carries with it the whole metaphysics of tradition (XVI:21). "Wherever ancient men placed a word," Nietzsche points out, "there they believed to have made a discovery" (IX:53). "But how different the situation really was!—they had come upon a problem and, while they thought they had *solved* it, they had actually created an obstacle to its solution.—In every act of cognition we must now stumble over petrified and mummified words, and are bound to break a leg rather than a word in the process" (IX:53).

But even if we were not thus restricted by the past, Nietzsche maintains, our knowledge would still be limited and relative. "My eye, no matter how keen or weak it may be, can see only a certain distance, and within this space I live and move; this horizon is my immediate fate, great or small, from which I cannot escape. A concentric circle is drawn in this manner around every living being, having a center which is peculiar to it. Similarly, our ear encloses us in a small space, and so likewise does our touch. It is in accordance with these horizons, within which, as within prison walls, our senses enclose each of us, that we *measure* the world; that we call this near and that far, this great and that small, this hard and that soft; and this measuring we call sensation—all of this is error *per se!*" (IX:122). "We measure our life," Nietzsche continues, "—as short or long, poor or rich, full or empty—by the number of events and emotions which it is possible for us, on an average, to experience at a given moment; and we measure the life of all other creatures by the average human life—and all of this is error *per se!*" (IX:122-123). "If we had eyes a hundred times keener for what is near us, a human being would appear to us to be enormously tall; we can even imagine organs through which he would be experienced as immeasurable. On the other hand, organs could be so constructed that whole solar systems would be experienced and reduced and contracted like a single cell; and to beings of a contrary order, one cell of the human body might present itself in its motion, structure, and harmony as if it were a solar system. The habits of our senses have enmeshed us in the lies and deceptions of sensations; and these, in turn, are the foundation of all our judgments and 'cognitions,'—there is no possibility of escape, no hidden or secret paths which lead to the *real world!* Like spiders we sit in our own webs and, regardless of what we catch in them, we can catch nothing but that which can be caught in *our* webs" (IX:123).

The question now is, What are the implications of Nietzsche's basic contention? What is the true nature of our experiences? And to this question Nietzsche replies: Our experiences are "rather more what we put into them than what is given in them. Or must we even say that, in themselves, they contain nothing? that experience is a fabrication?" (IX:128).

As Nietzsche elaborates this idea, we learn that, for him, "the essence of a thing is only an *opinion* concerning the 'thing,' " and that "the real meaning of *'it is'* " actually is: *"it is effectual"* (XV:65). The "coming into being of 'things' " is therefore "the work of those who imagine, who think, who will, and who feel" (XV:65). It is their *interpretation* of experience which converts the flux of experiential data into "things." But, according to Nietzsche, "even 'the subject' is a creation of this kind, a 'thing' like all others: a simplification for the purpose of designating the *power* which posits, invents, and thinks, in distinction from all particular positing, inventing, and thinking as such" (XV:65). All cognition thus becomes an "interpretation"—"the putting of meaning into things"—*not* an "explanation" (XV:102-103); and, in the end, "man finds in things nothing except what he himself has put into them" (XV:103). "The process of finding again," Nietzsche says, "calls itself science." The process of "placing meaning into things" is "art, religion, love, pride"; and with this latter process Nietzsche himself is concerned (XV:103).

If the premises here stated are accepted—or are accepted at least for the purpose of understanding Nietzsche—then it follows that the world with which we as living and active human beings are concerned is, in a very specific sense, *false;* that "it is not a matter of fact, but an imaginative interpretation and completion based on a meager sum of observations"; that "it is 'in flux,' a something which *becomes,* an ever changing falsehood which never gets closer to the truth; for there is no 'truth' " (XV:107). It follows, furthermore, that the whole "value of the world" lies in our interpretations; that "perhaps still other interpretations besides the merely human are possible"; that "the interpretations made hitherto are perspective valuations by means of which we maintain our existence"; that "every *elevation of man* entails the overcoming of a narrower interpretation"; and that "every strengthening and expansion of power which has been attained opens up new perspectives and commands a belief in new horizons" (XV:106-107). An infinite number of interpretations of "the world" may thus be possible; and "every interpretation is a symptom either of growth or of decay" (XV:101).

## IV

Now, of all the interpretations of the world hitherto attempted, the mechanistic interpretation, Nietzsche holds, is today the most prominent. "Apparently," he says, "it has a clean conscience on its side; for no science believes inwardly in progress and success unless it be [achieved] with the help of mechanical procedures" (XV:109). But, Nietzsche points out, a mechanistic interpretation, reducing process to an interplay of stresses and thrusts, explains nothing; for "stress and thrust themselves cannot be 'explained' " (XV:110). In fact, "the mechanical concept of 'movement' is already a translation of the original process into the *language of symbols of the eye and of touch*" (XV:112). In order to be able to "compute," we must have "unities" and "constant causes"; and "since we find no constant causes in reality, we *invent* them for ourselves" (XV:112). The concept "atom," for example, "the distinction between the 'seat of a motive force and the force itself,' " belongs to "a language of symbols derived from our logical and psychical world" (XV: 112). It would be a grave error to assume that "atoms" "actually *exist*" (XV:118-119). And similarly, according to Nietzsche, "it is an illusion to maintain that something is *known,* when all we have is a mathematical formula of what has happened" (XV:114). At best, such formulae "only characterize or describe"; they do not explain (XV:114). Mechanism, as exemplified in our most advanced sciences, is but *"the reduction* of all phenomena to a level of men with senses and with mathematics" (XV:123). It is "based upon a *sense-prejudice* and a *psychological prejudice*" (XV:119).

But if "all presuppositions of a mechanistic world view—matter, atom, gravity, pressure, and thrust—are not 'facts in themselves,' but interpretations arrived at with the help of mental fictions," then one may well ask: "Is mechanism only a language of signs for the concealed fact of a world of fighting and conquering quanta of will-power?" (XV:164). And to this question Nietzsche gives an affirmative answer.

However, before we consider this answer in detail, let us return once more to the problem of truth.

The "essence of 'truth,' " Nietzsche tells us, is "the *valuation*, 'I believe that this and that is *so*' " (XV:26). In all "valuations" of this kind, however, "the conditions of preservation and of growth find expression" (XV:26). But this means, according to Nietzsche, that "all our organs of cognition and our senses have been developed only in view of certain conditions of preservation and growth," and that our "trust in reason and its categories, in dialectic—and thus our valuation of logic—proves only the *usefulness* of the latter for our existence . . . , *not* their 'truth' " (XV:26). Life, he points out, presupposes "a large amount of *faith*"; it presupposes that "something must be *regarded as* true—*not* that it *is* true" (XV:26).

However, in order to flourish, "we must be stable in belief"; and in order to become stable, we must transform the "changing" and "evolving" world into "the 'true' world" of "Being" (XV:26; 27). Actually, of course, (so Nietzsche maintains) this transformation of a "world of Becoming" into a "world of Being" is a "falsification" of reality (XV:107; 28; 29; 33; 37), and through it all values are distorted; for now "illusion is what confers value" (XV:107).

From such premises it follows that the same relativism which permeates our knowledge of the world permeates also our knowledge of values; and, as Nietzsche points out, the history of philosophy shows only too clearly that "the basic belief of the metaphysicians is the belief in the antithesis of values" (XII:6-7). Yet—and this is the important point— "it never occurred even to the most cautious among [the metaphysicians] to begin doubting here at the threshold, where doubting would have been most necessary" (XII:7). They accepted "the popular valuations and value contrasts" and pressed upon them their "seal of approval." It will be Nietzsche's task to carry the philosophical doubt to its limit, and to challenge the very foundations of morality.

Only one principle is to guide us—the principle, namely, that *"the criterion of 'truth' lies in the enhancement of the feeling of* power" (XV:49). The crucial question, therefore, will at all times be: "How far is a given judgment life-furthering, life-preserving, species-preserving, perhaps even species-rearing?" (XII:8-9). And it may well be the case, Nietzsche contends, that "the falsest judgments (to which the synthetic judgments *a priori* belong) are for us the most indispensable ones; that without an acceptance of logical fictions, without an evaluation of reality in terms of the purely invented world of the unconditioned, the immutable, without a constant falsification of the world through numbers, man could not live,—that the renunciation of false judgments would be a renunciation of life, a negation of life" (XII:9).


## V

But if all our "categories of cognition" are merely means by which we interpretatively create "our" world; if they are merely "conventional fictions" (XII:30); and if "in 'Being-in-itself' there exist no 'causal connections,' no 'necessity,' no 'psychological determination' "; if, on the contrary, "it is *we* who alone have invented cause, sequence, reciprocity, relativity, constraint, number, law, freedom, ground, purpose"; if it is *we* who "take this world of signs as being 'in itself' and read and mix it into things"; then we act "as we have always acted—*mythologically*" (XII:30-31); and our "truth" is the truth of myths.

But if "we fabricate the greater part of our experience and can hardly be made to contemplate any event *except* as its 'inventors' " (XII:113; 114), then a proper understanding of why we act as we do is of crucial importance to our whole philosophy. Hitherto, however, (Nietzsche holds) "psychology has been stopped by moral prejudices and fears: it has not dared to plunge into the depth" (XII:33).

The task is, of course, most difficult; for a psychology which dares to "plunge into the depth" has to combat not only the prejudice of the time but "the unconscious opposition in the heart of the investigator himself" (XII:33). Nevertheless, Nietzsche insists, the plunge must be taken. We must recognize not only a *"reciprocal dependence* of the 'good' and the 'bad' impulses" but, beyond this, "the *derivation* of all good impulses from bad ones" (XII:33). We must recognize, in other words, that "even the emotions of hate, envy, covetousness, and imperiousness" are "life-conditioning emotions"; that they "must be present, fundamentally and essentially, in the over-all economy of life and must therefore be intensified if life is to be enhanced" (XII:33).

This thesis of the "derivation" of good impulses from bad ones is as essential to Nietzsche's whole doctrine as is his conception of the Will to Power. And he finds confirmation of it not only by plunging into the depths of the unconscious, but by studying man's history as well.

As Nietzsche sees it, "man is the cruelest animal" (X5:267), and history—"the oldest and longest history of man"—teaches this fact (XIII:75). "It is difficult to imagine," Nietzsche points out, "to what degree cruelty constitutes the great festal joy of ancient man, or is an ingredient in almost all of his pleasures" (XIII:73). "At tragedies, bull-fights, and crucifixions [man] has so far been happiest on earth" (XI:267). He is cruellest towards himself; but, says Nietzsche, let us not overlook "the voluptuousness in the plaints and accusations of all who call themselves 'sinners' and 'bearers of the cross' and 'penitents' " (XI:267).

In Nietzsche's opinion, history shows also "how naïvely and innocently man's need for cruelty manifests itself, and how ancient man posits in principle a 'disinterested malice' . . . as the *normal* characteristic of man" (XIII:73-74). "The time is not too long past when it was impossible to imagine royal weddings and peoples' festivals on a grand scale without executions, torturings, or perhaps an auto-da-fe; similarly, one could not conceive of an aristocratic household as being without creatures upon whom one could vent, without scruple, one's malice and cruel raillery" (XIII:74).

But the history of punishment, especially, reveals man's cruelty. A debtor, "in order to elicit faith in his promise of repayment" and "in order to impress upon his own conscience that the repayment is a duty, an obligation," might, in a contract, pledge as security whatever he still possessed as his own: "his body or his wife or his freedom or even his life (or, under certain religious presuppositions, his salvation, the welfare of his soul, even his peace in the grave)" (XIII:70-71). "The creditor . . . could inflict upon the body of the debtor all kinds of outrages and tortures, cutting off from it, for example, as much as appeared to be proportionate to the size of the debt" (XIII:71). Yet most revealing of all is "the ancient and universal prevalence of precise schemes of valuation which often go into horrible details and minutiae—*legally sanctioned* valuations on individual limbs and parts of the body" (XIII:71).

The "logic" behind this ancient idea of "equalization" is strange indeed; for the equivalence consists in this: that "instead of an equalization in money, in land, or in property of any kind," "the creditor is granted, by way of repayment and compensation, a certain *feeling of satisfaction*—the feeling of satisfaction, namely, which he derives from being permitted to vent without scruple his power upon one who is powerless, the voluptuousness of 'doing harm for the pleasure of doing it,' the joy in sheer violence" (XIII:71-72). This feeling of satisfaction, Nietzsche argues, will be greater in proportion to the lower social rank of the creditor, for "through the 'punishment' of the debtor, the creditor participates in a *right of the masters:* at last he, too, for once attains the elevating feeling of being able to despise as 'inferior' and to mistreat a creature"—or, "if the actual power of punishment, the administration of punishment, has already been transferred to the 'authorities,' " he has at least the satisfaction "of *seeing* the other despised and mistreated" (XIII:72). "The compensation, therefore, consists in a claim and a right to cruelty" (XIII:72); for suffering can be a compensation for "debts" only "in so far as *inflicting* suffering pleases in the highest degree," in so far, that is, "as the injured party gets in exchange for his loss (including his displeasure at his loss) an extraordinary counter-pleasure: the *inflicting* of suffering—a veritable *feast*" (XIII:73).

It is Nietzsche's contention that "in *this* sphere of the law of contract" there was also "first formed that sinister and now perhaps indissoluble association of the ideas of 'guilt' and 'suffering' " (XIII:73). It is his contention, in other words, that "the world of moral concepts—of 'guilt,' 'conscience,' 'duty,' and 'sacredness of duty'—has [here] its origin" (XIII:72). "Its beginning, like the beginning of everything great on earth, has thoroughly and for a long time been drenched with blood. And may we not add that, basically, this world has never completely lost a certain odor of blood and torture?" (XIII:72).

"To see suffering pleases, to inflict suffering pleases even more —this is a hard maxim but, nonetheless, an old, powerful, human-all-too-human and basic maxim" (XIII:74); and "almost everything which we call 'higher culture' is based upon the sublimation and deepening of *cruelty*—such is [Nietzsche's] thesis" (XII:176-177). "The 'wild beast' has not been slain at all; it lives; it flourishes; it has only been sublimated. That which constitutes the painful delight of tragedy is cruelty; that which affects us agreeably in so-called tragic pity and, basically, in everything which is sublime—even up to the highest and most gentle awe of metaphysics—obtains its sweetness only from the intermixed ingredient of cruelty. What the Roman enjoys in the arena, the Christian in the ecstasies of the cross, the Spaniard at the sight of pyres or bullfights, the Japanese of today who pushes and presses to witness a tragedy, the Parisian suburban worker who has a homesickness for bloody revolutions, the Wagnerienne who, with unhinged will, 'surrenders' to a performance of 'Tristan and Isolde'—what all of these enjoy and strive to absorb with mysterious passion is the spicy drink of the great Circe 'Cruelty.' To understand this one must, of course, discard completely the doltish psychology of the past which, with regard to cruelty, could only teach that it originates at the sight of the suffering of *others:* there is an abundant, a superabundant enjoyment even in one's own suffering, in causing oneself to suffer— and wherever man allows himself to be persuaded to self-denial in the religious sense, or to self-mutilation, as among the Phoenicians and ascetics, or to any form of desensualization, decarnalization, and self-crushing, to Puritanical cramps of repentance, to a vivisection of conscience and the Pascalian *sacrifizio dell' intellecto,* he is secretly attracted and impelled forward by his own cruelty, by that dangerous thrill of cruelty *towards himself"* (XII:177-178).

Whether or not what Nietzsche here says about cruelty is true to the facts of human experience is a question which need not concern us at present. What is important, however, is that, for Nietzsche, cruelty is an essential ingredient in human nature; that, as a matter of fact, he regards it as indispensable to man's happiness; and that he sees in the achievement of a "higher culture" but a sublimation and deepening of cruelty.

We shall return to this point later.

## VI

Reference to the essential cruelty of man, and to the rôle which it plays in cultural development, furnishes only part—albeit an important part—of Nietzsche's conception of man. Another part involves his idea of the basic "body-soul unity." What is meant here will become clear, I believe, when we consider, first, Nietzsche's "phenomenalistic" thesis as applied to the "self."

It is Nietzsche's contention that there is no "self" behind the manifestations which are usually attributed to a self, to a person. "There is no such substratum," he tells us; "there is no 'being' behind the doing, the acting, the becoming; 'the doer' has merely been added to the doing by our fancy—the doing is all there is" (XIII:46). If it appears to be otherwise, then this is so "only because of the corruption of language (and the basic errors of reason which are petrified therein) which understands and misunderstands all action as conditioned by an acting being, by a 'subject' " (XIII:45). But just as scientists do not improve matters when they let "lightning lighten" or say that "force moves," "force causes"—since all they mean is but the action, the doing itself—so nothing is gained by ascribing human actions to a "subject," a "doer." "The 'subject' is only a fiction" (XIII:294).

If this thesis be granted—or be accepted at least for the purpose of argument—, then certain consequences follow at once. For example, any reference to a "strong" or a "weak" will is now but "a parable which can lead astray"; for "there is no will and, consequently, neither a strong nor a weak will" (XIV:37). "The multiplicity and disconnectedness of the instincts, the want of a system in their interrelations, constitute a 'weak will'; the co-ordination of the instincts under the dominance of a single instinct constitutes a 'strong will.' In the first case [we have] vacillation and the lack of a chief stress; in the latter case [we have] precision and clearness of the direction" (XIV:37-38).

Furthermore,—so Nietzsche argues—if the "subject" is only a fiction, then "the *ego* of which everyone speaks when he finds fault with egoism, does not exist at all" (XIII:294). That is to say, "the 'ego'—which is not one with the centralized governance of our being—is merely a conceptual synthesis"; and if this is so, then "there can be no action out of 'egoism' " (XIII:295).

As far as Nietzsche is concerned, "the belief in the body is much more fundamental than the belief in the soul"; for "the latter arose from the unscientific contemplation of the agonies of the body" (XV:18-19). Consciousness and intellect exist only to the extent to which they are useful for the unfolding of the life of the body.

To be sure, Nietzsche says that "those who are strongest in body *and* soul are the best"; for "from them springs the higher morality—the morality of the creative ones" (XVI:271). But this "basic principle" (which underlies the whole of *Thus Spake Zarathustra*) must not be interpreted as implying a body and soul dualism—a dualism, that is, which Nietzsche regards as "a doctrine for children" (XI:35). On the contrary, "the awak-ened one, the knowing one, says: I am entirely body, and noth-ing more; and soul is but a name for something pertaining to the body" (XI:35).

The body, Nietzsche holds, is "reason on a grand scale" (XI:35). Even "that small reason," which we call "spirit," is "a tool of [the] body" (XI:36); for "the creative body created for itself spirit, as a hand of its will" (XI:37). "You say 'I,' " Nietz-sche continues, "and are proud of the word. But the greater thing—in which you are not willing to believe—is your body and its big reason. This reason does not say 'I,' but makes 'I' "

(XI:36). "There is more reason in your body than in your best wisdom. And who knows for what purpose your body needs . . . your best wisdom?" (XI:36).

But if the "body" is thus the real core of what we call "Self," it is small wonder, Nietzsche argues, that "most of the conscious thinking of a philosopher is secretly guided and forced into certain channels by his instincts"; that "even behind all logic and the seeming autonomy of its movement there are valuations or, speaking more clearly, physiological demands for the preservation of a specific type of life" (XI:8). "Not only our reason, but our conscience as well, submits to our strongest impulse, to the tyrant within us" (XI:98). In fact, "consciousness, 'spirit,' is for [Nietzsche] a symptom of a relative imperfection of the organism, an experiment, a groping, a mistake, an affliction which consumes an unnecessarily large amount of nervous energy." "We deny," Nietzsche adds, "that anything can be done perfectly so long as it is done consciously. 'Pure spirit' is a pure folly; if we subtract the nervous system and the senses, the 'mortal shell,' we *miscalculate*—that is all!" (XVI:141).

However, if the "body" is all-important, then "it is decisive for the fate of a people and of humanity that culture be started at the *right place";* and this "right place," according to Nietzsche, is *"not* the 'soul' (as was the fatal superstition of priests and half-priests)," but "the body: bearing, diet, physiology—the rest follows therefrom" (XVI:107). But if this is so, then "Christianity, which despises the body, has so far been the greatest misfortune of mankind" (XVI:107).

What characterizes the Christian, Nietzsche contends, is "contempt for, and the wilful turning away from, the demands of the body, from the *discovery* of the body." "The presupposition [of the Christian] is that such [disregard of the body] is in keeping with the higher nature of man,—*that it will necessarily contribute to the welfare of the soul"* (XIV:185). Christianity, in other words, is, for Nietzsche, "the reduction in principle of all feelings of the body to moral values." Sickness itself is conceived as conditioned by morality—perhaps as punishment, or as a trial, or even as a condition of salvation through which man becomes more perfect than he could become in a state of health" (XIV:185-186).

Christianity, moreover, (Nietzsche goes on) has developed certain practices to conform to this conception. Thus, "in order to induce feelings of sinfulness and to prepare the way for contrition, it is necessary to bring about a morbid and nervous condition in the body" (XIV:188). The "religious interpretation" of the "chastisement of the flesh" is thus but "a means of making possible that morbid indigestion known as repentance (the *'idée fixe'* of sin)" (XIV:188). "The mishandling of the body creates the soil for the whole range of 'feelings of guilt,' i.e., for a state of general suffering, which *demands explanation*" (XIV:188).

The Christians, Nietzsche holds, not only "despised the body" and "treated it as an enemy," they also made the fatal mistake of believing "that one could carry a 'beautiful soul' in a body which is a cadaverous abortion" (XIV:185). But in order to make this thesis "comprehensible to others," "they had to define the concept 'beautiful soul' in a [particular] way and had to transmute the natural value [designated by this term] until at last a pale, sickly, idiotically sentimental creature was felt to be perfect, 'angelic,' a transfiguration, a higher man" (XIV:185).

Nietzsche's basic objection to Christianity is thus deeply rooted in his interpretation of the "Self" as essentially "body." His conception of the "man of resentment" completes the picture. This conception, however, is closely tied up with the "will to Power."

## VII

In popular interpretations of Nietzsche's philosophy much has been made of the crucial importance of the "Will to Power"; and, indeed, this conception *is* crucial. But the thesis of the "Will to Power" must be correctly understood. It is a metaphysical doctrine; and whatever personal or political implications it has must be seen and evaluated within this broader framework.

It is Nietzsche's belief that everything which is characteristic of *life* can be reduced to one formula: "Will to Power" (XV:108). But, so Nietzsche holds, not only life manifests this "insatiable desire to display power" (XV:110). The whole universe—physical as well as biological and human—manifests it. In fact, the phenomena which the physicist studies—i.e., "all motions, all 'appearances,' all 'laws,' "—are, for Nietzsche, merely *"symptoms* of an *inner* process," "symptoms," that is, of the "Will to Power" (XV:110); and without reference to this "Will," we are told, all terms of physics remain empty and unintelligible (XV:114).

The ultimate question, Nietzsche points out, is whether or not "we believe in the causality of the will"; and to this question he replies that belief in "the causality of the will" is "simply our belief in causality itself"; that "the causality of the will" is "the only causality" there is (XII:52). "All mechanical happenings, in so far as a force is active therein," are but "effects of a will" (XII:52). In fact, the world "viewed from within," the world "defined and designated in its 'intelligible character' "—this is " 'Will to Power,' and nothing else" (XII:52).

As "will" acts upon "will," and strives to "extend its own power" (XV:121), it "delimits," it "differentiates," and, "relative to itself," it evaluates "every other thing which seeks to grow" (XV:124-125; XIII:89). And in this evaluation is rooted the difference between "good" and "evil."

This "Will to Power," Nietzsche maintains, is clearly in evidence in the realm of life; for "life itself," so he argues, "is *essentially* appropriation, injury, conquest of the strange and weaker, suppression, severity, imposition of one's own forms, incorporation, and, at least and most gently, exploitation" (XII:226). Nietzsche admits that much has been made of the "will to exist"; but reference to such a "will," he contends, is meaningless, for "that which is not, cannot will; and that which already exists—how could it still strive for existence!" (XI:137). "Only where there is life, there is also will: not, however, Will to Life, but . . . Will to Power" (XI:137)—to an ever growing, a richer, a more abundant Life. And this "Will to Power,"—this

"Will" to expand, to dominate—according to Nietzsche, is a *"free* Will" (XV:140). It is the very *"instinct of freedom"* (XIII:104).

At the human level, the "Will to Power" is "the primitive form of passion." All other passions are only its more specific manifestations" (XV:161)—even the "Will to Truth" (XI:134; 137); and "what is believed by the people as good or evil" betrays, according to Nietzsche, but "an old Will to Power" (XI:134), for it is the "Will to Power" which evaluates.

This "Will to Power" is all-pervasive. "Even in the will of the servant," Nietzsche says, "I found the will to be master" (XI:136); and the chain of domination and subservience is uninterrupted. "That the weaker shall serve the stronger—to this the weaker is persuaded by its own will, which wants to be master over what is weaker still" (XI:136). "And as the lesser surrenders itself to the greater in order to obtain pleasure and power over the least: just so even the greatest surrenders and, for the sake of power, hazards life itself. It is the surrender of the greatest that it [itself] is a risk and a danger, and a play of dice for death"; for Life is *"that which must surpass itself"* (XI:136).

"Love," Nietzsche holds, "provides the highest feeling of power" (XIV:147); for "we are godly in love, we become 'children of God'" (XIV:147). And: "He who seeks to create beyond himself has," as far as Nietzsche is concerned, "the purest will" (XI:147). Where, for example, is beauty? "Where I *must will* with all my will; where I want to love and succumb in order that an image may not remain merely an image" (XI:147). There is something of Plato in this Nietzschean conception of the creative Will; for it was Plato who first spoke of "the love of generation and of birth in beauty." [3]

But Will—this "emancipator and bringer of joy"—is also a "prisoner"; for it cannot "will backwards." "It cannot break the time and the desire of the time" (XI:168). " 'That which was'— this is the name of the stone which [the Will] cannot roll" (XI:169). It is the great obstacle—"a fragment, a riddle, a

---

[3] Plato, "Symposium," *Plato Selections,* R. Demos, editor, New York 1927, 262.

horrible incident"—until the creative will transmutes it and says concerning it: "But thus I have willed it!" and "thus I will it! Thus I shall will it!" (XI:170). "Out of itself" Will must thus "ever surpass itself anew" (XI:137), recognizing the past as its own achievement, and reaching out beyond it to ever new horizons. In surpassing itself, however, this Will to Power must of necessity subordinate and exploit whatever it encounters, and must destroy whatever tends to confine it; for such, Nietzsche holds, is "the *nature* of all living things," and such is "the *radical fact* of all history" (XII:227).

This "Will to Power" must not be confused with a desire for happiness or, "with some hypocrisy," with a desire for the happiness of the greatest number (XIV:20). "It is not true," Nietzsche maintains, "that the *unconscious aim* in the development of every conscious being (animal, man, mankind, etc.) is its 'greatest happiness'"; for "a specific and uncomparable happiness" can be attained at each level of development—a happiness which is "intrinsic" to that level (IX:105). Moreover, Nietzsche holds, "it is *not* the satisfaction of the will which is the cause of *pleasure.* . . , but the fact that the will strives forwards and, again and again, becomes master over that which stands in its way. The feeling of pleasure lies precisely in the discontent of the will" (XV:167)—i.e., in "the normal *discontent* of our instincts" which, "instead of making us sick of life," is "the great *stimulus* of life" (XV:168).

But if life is only a "manifestation of the forms of growth of power" (XV:175), then "hedonism, pessimism, utilitarianism, and eudaemonism"—all those doctrines, in brief, which "measure the value of things according to *pleasure* and *pain,* i.e., according to accompanying circumstances and non-essentials"— are "superficial modes of thinking and naïvetés which everyone conscious of *creative* powers and of an artist's conscience will look upon, not without scorn but also not without pity" (XII:-170). It is the "noble feeling," according to Nietzsche, which "*forbids* that we merely *enjoy* life," which "revolts against hedonism." "We want to *accomplish* something!" (XVI:263). We want to *create!* We want to enrich and enhance life! And "man, having become master over the forces of nature, master over his own savagery and licentiousness . . .—this man, compared with his semi-human ancestors, represents an enormous quantum of *power*—not a plus of 'happiness'! How, then, can one assert that he has *striven* after happiness?" (XV:174). From the perspective of this self-disciplined, this creative man, hedonism in all its forms is but a "guide-post to Nihilism" (XIV:29).

And from this perspective, too, utilitarianism also becomes an untenable doctrine. "The value of an action must be judged by its results—thus say the utilitarians—: to measure it according to its origin implies an impossibility—the impossibility, namely, of *knowing* that origin.—But do we know the results? Five steps ahead, perhaps. Who can tell what an action provokes, stirs up, sets in motion against itself? As a stimulus? As the spark, perhaps, which fires a powder-magazine?—The Utilitarians are naïve. In the last analysis, we would have to *know*, first of all, *what* [really] is useful" (XIV:240). And "the value of a man," in particular, "lies not in his utility." It is inherent, Nietzsche holds (with Kant), in the man himself and "would continue to exist even if there were nobody to whom [the man] might make himself useful" (XV:314). Hence, "to appraise the value of a man in accordance with how *useful* he is to other men, or in accordance with what he *costs* them or how much he *harms* them, means as much or as little as to appraise a work of art according to the *effects* which it produces. In this way the value of a man *compared with other men* has not even been touched upon" (XV:314-315); for *value*, according to Nietzsche, is "but the highest amount of power which a man can assimilate" (XV:181), and *"perfection"* is "the extraordinary expansion of . . . the feeling of power, the abundance, the necessary overflowing of all banks" (XV:244).

Pleasure and pain, Nietzsche holds, are "never 'original facts' "; they are "reactions of the will" to given stimuli (XV:142). In them "there already inhere *judgments:* the stimuli are being differentiated as to whether or not they promote the feeling of power" (XV:143)—the ultimate standard of *all* evaluations being *"the enhancement of life"* (XV:145; 146).

There are, of course, interpretations of the Will which are dia-metrically opposed to Nietzsche's interpretation. Schopenhauer's "depreciation of the value of the will" is perhaps a typical ex-ample (XIV:70). Nietzsche maintains, however, that these other interpretations are "fundamental misunderstandings" and the result of a "great confusion." The "psychologists," he tells us, fail to keep two *kinds* of pleasure strictly apart—the pleasure, namely, of *"falling asleep,"* and the pleasure of *"triumph."* "Ex-hausted people," Nietzsche adds, "want repose, relaxation, peace, quiet—it is the *happiness* of the nihilistic religions and philos-ophies; the richly endowed, the people of great vitality, want triumph, defeated opponents, the engulfing by their feeling of power of wider regions than hitherto. All healthy functions of the organism have this need" (XV:173).

Still, the "ascetic man" exists. His *right* to existence, however, stands and falls with the ascetic ideal (XIII:149). The "ascetic man," therefore, fighting for his ideal, fights for his right to existence. "No wonder," Nietzsche points out, "that here we encounter a terrible opponent" (XIII:149). "The idea over which the battle rages is the appraisal of our life." "This life (together with everything to which it belongs: 'nature,' 'world,' the whole sphere of earthly existence)" the ascetic man holds in contempt. He treats it as "a blind alley in which one must ultimately walk back to the place where it began; or he treats it as an error which one refutes—nay, *ought* to refute—by action" (XIII:149).

It is Nietzsche's contention that "the ascetic ideal springs from the protective and healing instincts of a degenerating life which, with all means at its disposal, seeks to maintain itself and fights for its existence" (XIII:154). The "ascetic ideal" thus indicates an *exhaustion* "against which the deepest and as yet unaffected instincts of life ceaselessly fight"; it is "a dodge for the *preservation* of life" (XIII:154). "That the ascetic ideal could rule and dominate over all men to the extent which history discloses, and especially everywhere where the civilizing and taming of man was achieved,—this [Nietzsche holds] reveals but one fact: the *morbidity* of the type of man which has thus far been achieved" (XIII:154).

Among ascetic men "the ascetic priest is the incarnate wish for a 'being-other,' a 'being-somewhere-else'; he is in fact the highest concentration of this wish, its real ardor and passion" (XIII: 154-155). But through the very power of his wishing he is irrevocably bound to the Here. It is through this power that he must "labor to create more favorable conditions" for the existence of "the whole herd of the misbegotten, the depressed, the poorly endowed, the failures, the sufferers-from-themselves of every kind"; and it is through this power that "instinctively" he takes "the lead as their herdsman" (XIII:155). And it is thus that "the ascetic priest, this apparent enemy of life, this *denier*—that he especially belongs to the really great *preservative* and *affirmatively creative* forces of life" (XIII:155). Only the life which he preserves and which he fosters with all his creative ingenuity is *degenerating* life; and therein lies his great danger.

## VIII

"The ascetic priest," Nietzsche tells us, "belongs to no particular race; he thrives everywhere; he grows out of all classes"; and the regularity and universality with which he "puts in his appearance" bespeak "a necessity of the first order which makes this species—*hostile to life,* though it is—always grow again and always thrive again" (XIII:150). "Life itself," Nietzsche continues, "must have an interest in the continuance of such a type of self-contradiction. For an ascetic life is a self-contradiction: here rules resentment without parallel, the resentment of an insatiate instinct and ambition, that would be master, not over some element in life, but over life itself, over life's deepest, strongest, innermost condition" (XIII:150).

The healthy and strong and creative men who say Yes! to Life—the "well-born" and the "noble," as Nietzsche calls them —do not need to "create their happiness artificially by gloating over their enemies"; they need not "lie themselves into happiness." "Being complete men, exuberant with strength and therefore necessarily active, they know enough not to dissociate happiness from action." They live in "confidence and frankness with themselves" (XIII:36-37), and their morality, which "springs from a triumphant affirmation" of Life (XIII:34), is the morality of "love" and "veneration" (XIV:282).

However, not all men are strong, healthy, and creative. Not all are "well-born" and "noble." On the contrary, there are "the weak, the depressed, and those 'festering ones' who suffer from poisonous and malignant feelings"—the "slaves," as Nietzsche calls them—"among whom happiness appears essentially as a narcotic, a stupefaction, a quietude, a peace, a 'sabbath,' a relaxation of the mind and stretching of limbs." Such men are "neither sincere, nor naïve, nor honest and frank with themselves." Their "souls *squint*" (XIII:36-37). Their morality, "from its very inception," says No! to the triumphant Life; and "this No! is its creative deed" (XIII:34). It is the morality of "resentment," of a "bad conscience," of a "slavish soul." Its dominant feelings are "hate" and "contempt" (XIV:282).

There are, thus, two attitudes towards Life—two value scales. But each attitude, in its own way, is a manifestation of Life itself—a manifestation of the same basic impulse, the same "Will to Power." In the one case, however, the "Will" which manifests itself is the "Will to Power" of the "healthy," whereas in the other case it is the "Will to Power" of the "sick," the "botched," and the "broken." (XIII:157). The enmity between these two manifestations of the "Will to Power" is one of the principal themes of all of Nietzsche's thinking; and "preventing the sick ones from making the healthy ones sick, too—this [he says] ought to be our highest aim in the world" (XIII:160). It is the culmination of all his teaching.

But who are the "sick," the "botched," the "enfeebled"? And what has their "weakness" done to them and to others? They are the masses of the "misbegotten" in body and soul who, because of a physiological weakness or a deficiency of spirit, lack the strength or the courage to say Yes! to the triumphant Life— to the Life of an overflowing richness and creativity—and to accept that Life with its inherent dangers. They are the *Herden-*

*menschen* who, afraid to live their own lives as free individuals, band together and seek the security of the "herd." They are the "men of the herd." They are, in Aristotle's sense, born "slaves." The "ascetic priest" is their "herdsman," their "champion," their "savior" (XIII:162).

Since the "ascetic priest" can fulfill his "awful historic mission" only because he himself is "sick"—because he is "kith and kin to the sick" (XIII:162)—the effect which the "sick" and the "botched" have upon the course of history will become clearer, I believe, as we observe their "herdsman" in action. We must remember, however, that the "ascetic priest" "must also be strong, must be master of himself even more than master of others, and must be impregnable in his will to power"; for otherwise he cannot "acquire the trust and the awe of the weak." He must be strong enough or cunning enough to "protect his herd" (XIII:162).

"Protecting the herd," Nietzsche holds, involves two aspects: protecting the herd "against the healthy" (XIII:162) and protecting the members of the herd "against themselves" (XIII:163). The "ascetic priest" accomplishes both in one act. As Nietzsche puts it: "He fights with cunning, hardness, and stealth against anarchy and the ever threatening disintegration of the herd, where *resentment,* that most dangerous explosive, ever accumulates and accumulates. To discharge this explosive in such a way that it blows up neither the herd nor the herdsman—this is his real feat, his highest utility. If one were to express in the shortest formula the value of the priestly existence, one would have to say frankly that the priest is the *deflector of the direction of resentment*" (XIII:163). Instead of allowing the resentment to come to an explosion within the "herd," the "ascetic priest" directs it against the "healthy," the "strong"—against those individuals, in other words, who are not members of the "herd"—, making them the scapegoat, the "villain," the "outlaw," the "incarnation of all that is wicked and evil."

In his efforts thus to deflect the accumulating resentment, the "ascetic priest" can count on a psychological predisposition characteristic of the "sick" and the "weak"; for all sufferers display "a horrible willingness and ingenuity in inventing excuses for painful emotions" (XIII:165). In their "instinctive search" for a "cause of their suffering" they "wallow in torturing suspicion and become intoxicated with the venom of their own malice; they tear open the oldest wounds . . . and make evil-doers out of friend, wife, child, and everything which is nearest to them" (XIII:165). " 'I suffer: it must be somebody's fault' "—so argue all the "sick," the "botched," and the "misbegotten." The "ascetic priest," however, tells them: "It is all your own fault." This preachment, Nietzsche points out, is "bold enough, false enough; but one thing at least is thus attained: the direction of the resentment has been *changed*" (XIII:165). And it is clear, furthermore, "what the remedial instinct of Life has at least *tried* to achieve through the ascetic priest, and for what purpose it has employed a temporary tyranny of such paradoxical and paralogistic concepts as 'guilt,' 'sin,' 'sinfulness,' 'corruption,' 'damnation'—the purpose, namely, of making the sick to a certain degree *harmless,* of inducing the incurable to destroy themselves, and of turning the less sick strictly upon themselves . . . thus utilizing the bad instincts of all sufferers for the purpose of self-discipline, self-surveillance, and self-mastery" (XIII:165-166).

However, it is Nietzsche's contention that the experiment has miscarried; that the "ascetic priest" has attempted to deal only with "symptoms," not with the real cause of the suffering or with the "actual state of the sickness" (XIII:168); and that, through "the exploitation of the feeling of 'guilt' " (XIII:182), he has actually created that horrible monstrosity: the man of "bad conscience." Under the influence of the "ascetic priest," "inveighing against the instincts of life came to be regarded as holy and estimable." The ideal was: "absolute chastity, absolute obedience, absolute poverty," "self-sacrifice, renunciation of the beautiful, of reason, and of sensuality, and a dark frown for all the strong qualities which existed" (XV:233). All instincts, however, (so Nietzsche holds) "which are not discharged outward, *turn inwards*" (XIII:100). And so, under the influence of the ascetic ideal, "all the instincts of wild, free, roaming man [were] turned . . . *against man himself"*; and "this man, who, lacking external enemies and obstacles and being imprisoned in the oppressive narrowness of custom, impatiently lacerated, persecuted, gnawed, frightened, and maltreated himself." Suffering privation and being "consumed by a homesickness for the desert," he was "compelled to create, out of his own self, an adventure, a torture-chamber, an insecure and bad wilderness." This "homesick and desperate prisoner" of the "ascetic ideal" "became the inventor of the 'bad conscience' "; and "with him was introduced [into the world] the worst and most sinister sickness from which, to this day, mankind has not recovered: the suffering of man from a disease called *man*,"—the suffering of man, that is, *from man himself* (XIII:101).

Underlying this thesis of the origin of the "bad conscience" are two basic assumptions. The first is that "the change in question is not a gradual or a voluntary one; that it did not manifest itself as an organic growing into new conditions but as a break, a jump, a compulsion, an inevitable fate against which there was no defense and not even resentment" (XIII:102). The second assumption is that "the pressing into rigid form of a hitherto unrestricted and amorphous population, having had its beginning in an act of violence, could be completed only through acts of violence—that, accordingly, the oldest 'state' [4] came into existence as a frightful tyranny . . . and that it continued to work as such until the raw material consisting of a semi-animal populace was ultimately not only thoroughly kneaded and pliant but was moulded as well" (XIII:102-103).

The men who "organize" the state—the "masters by nature," the "born organizers," who, in "the frightful egoism of the artist," know themselves to be "justified *in advance* in all eternity" (XIII:103-104)—these men do not have a "bad conscience"; the "bad conscience," however, "would not have grown without

---

[4] Nietzsche here means by 'state' "any pack of blonde beasts of prey, a race of conquerers and masters which, organized through war and with the power to organize, puts its terrible paws without hesitation upon a population which, though perhaps vastly superior in numbers, is as yet formless, is as yet roaming about. It is thus that the 'state' begins on earth. And [Nietzsche adds] I believe that we are done with that sentimentality which makes it begin with a 'contract' " (XIII:103).

them" (XIII:104). It would not have developed "had not a tremendous quantity of freedom been destroyed under the pressure of the hammer-blows, the artist violence, of [the born organizers], or had it not at least disappeared from view and become *latent*" (XIII:104). As Nietzsche sees it, "this *instinct for freedom*, made latent by force, . . . this instinct for freedom—repressed, retreating, imprisoned within the self and ultimately discharging itself and finding relief only within itself—this alone is the *bad conscience* in its beginning" (XIII:104).

And at first it is not all bad; for "at bottom" the "bad conscience" is "the same active force which is more magnificently at work" in the great "organizers." It is the same "instinct for freedom," the same "Will to Power" (XIII:104). "Only the material upon which this force vents its form-giving and tyrannous nature is here man himself, his whole old animal self—not . . . other men" (XIII:104-105). And because it is a manifestation of the all-comprehensive "creative Will," "this secret self-tyranny, this artist cruelty, this delight in giving form to oneself as to a difficult, refractory, and suffering material, in burning into it a will, a critique, a contradiction, a contempt, a No!—this sinister and horrible-delightful labor of a soul torn and willingly set against itself, which makes itself suffer from a delight in inflicting suffering; this whole *active* 'bad conscience' . . . , as a real womb of ideal and imaginative events, has also brought forth an abundance of novel and strange beauty and affirmation, and perhaps even *beauty* as such" (XIII:105). The "bad conscience" is thus a "sickness," yes; but it is "a sickness as pregnancy is a sickness" (XIII:106).

However, when we examine "the conditions under which this sickness reached its most terrible and most sublime climax" (XIII:106), we discover "what it really was that, through it, came into the world" (XIII:106).

In order to understand fully the drift of Nietzsche's argument at this point, let us briefly recall what Nietzsche said about the development of justice. In particular, let us recall Nietzsche's interpretation of the relationship of the individual to his community as that of a debtor to his creditor. "Within the original tribal organization," Nietzsche says with explicit reference to "primitive times," "each living generation acknowledges a legal obligation towards the earlier generation, and especially towards the earliest, tribe-founding generation. . . . The conviction prevails [in these early communities] that the tribe *exists* only because of the sacrifices and services of the ancestors—and that one must *repay* them through sacrifices and services" (XIII: 106). "One thus acknowledges a *debt,* which constantly grows because the ancestors, in their continuing existence as mighty spirits and by virtue of their power, never cease to grant the tribe new advantages and advances" (XIII:106-107). "The *fear* of the Ancestor and his power, the consciousness of being indebted to him, necessarily increases, according to this kind of logic, in exactly the same proportion in which the power of the tribe itself increases, in which the tribe itself is ever more victorious, more independent, more honored, more feared" (XIII: 107). Conversely, "each step towards the decline of the tribe, all misfortunes, all symptoms of decay, of approaching disintegration, always *diminish* also the fear of the founder's spirit and detract from the idea of his sagacity, providence, and powerful presence" (XIII:107). "If we conceive this crude kind of logic carried to its conclusion, it becomes evident that, through an imagination inspired by growing fear, the ancestors of the *most powerful* tribes must themselves have grown ultimately into monstrous dimensions and must have been pushed back into the obscurity of a divine mystery and inconceivability;—the Ancestor is at last necessarily transfigured into a *god*" (XIII: 107-108).

"For several thousand years," Nietzsche continues, "the feeling of being in debt to the deity has not ceased to grow but has grown always in the same proportion in which the idea of god and the feeling for god have grown on earth" (XIII:109). "The appearance of the Christian god, as the maximal god so far achieved, has for this very reason brought also the maximal feeling of guilt into the world" (XIII:109).

Nietzsche contends, furthermore, not only that the ideas of "debt" (cf. to owe, owed = ought) and "duty" are interrelated with religious conceptions but that the "moralization" of these ideas leads to "the interweaving of the *bad* conscience with the idea of god" (XIII:110), and that, as the ideas of "debt" (= ought) and "duty" are "pushed back into the bad conscience," the whole course of moral development is changed. As Nietzsche puts it, "now the very hope of an ultimate repayment [of the debt] *shall* imprison itself once and for all in pessimism; now the eye *shall* recoil in despair and rebound from an adamantine impossibility; now the ideas 'debt' and 'duty' *shall* turn backwards—but against *whom?* There can be no doubt about it: [they shall turn] first of all against 'him who owes,' in whom the bad conscience now establishes itself so firmly, drives roots, spreads, and grows polyp-like and with such virulence in every direction and depth that at last, together with the impossibility of repaying what is owed, there is conceived also the impossibility of paying the penalty, [and thus] the idea of inexpiability (of *'eternal* punishment')" (XIII:110-111). Finally, however, this development "turns even against the 'creditor,' whether he be identified as the *causa prima* of man, the origin of the human race, the Ancestor, who is henceforth burdened with a curse ('Adam,' 'original sin,' 'determination of the will'); or as Nature from whose womb man springs and to which, henceforth, the evil principle is ascribed ('diabolization of Nature'); or as existence itself which becomes the ultimate residue of *disvalue as such* (nihilistic flight from existence, yearning for Nothingness or for the 'opposite' of existence, for 'being other,' Buddhism and related views)—until, suddenly, we stand before that paradoxical and horrible expedient through which a tortured humanity has found temporary relief, that stroke of genius of *Christianity:* God sacrificing himself for the debt of man, God himself repaying himself, God as the only one who can relieve man of that which has become unrelievable for man himself—the creditor sacrificing himself for his debtor, from *love* (would you believe it?), from love for his debtor!" (XIII:111).

Here, then, is the crux of the whole matter as Nietzsche sees it: "the man of bad conscience has taken possession of the religious presupposition in order to drive his self-tormentings on to their ghastliest cruelty and intensity. Owing *God* a debt: this thought becomes for him an instrument of torture. He apprehends in 'God' the ultimate antithesis which he can find to his own proper and ineradicable animal instincts; he reinterprets these animal instincts themselves as a debt which he owes God (as enmity, rebellion, revolt against the 'Lord,' the 'Father,' the Original Ancestor, the Beginning of the World); he puts himself at the center of the conflict between 'God' and 'Devil.' Every negation of himself, of the nature, the naturalness and factuality of his own being, he casts out of himself and projects as a Yes!, as existing, living, real, as God, as the holiness of God, the judicial power of God, the hangman's power of God, as the Beyond, as Eternity, as torment without end, as hell, as the infinity of punishment and of guilt. This is a kind of madness of the will in the realm of mental cruelty which is absolutely without parallel: man's *will* to find himself guilty and reprehensible to the point of inexpiability; his *will* to think of himself as punished, although the punishment can never adequately balance the debt; his *will* to infect and to poison the deepest ground of all things with the problem of punishment and guilt in order to cut off once and for all every escape from this labyrinth of 'fixed ideas'; his *will* to set up an ideal—that of the 'holy God'—in order to obtain, through contrast with it, tangible proof of his own absolute unworthiness. Woe! over this mad and wretched beast man! What fancies afflict it, what perversities, what paroxysms of nonsense, what *bestiality of ideas* breaks forth immediately upon the slightest check of its being a *beast of action!*" (XIII:112-113). "Here is disease," Nietzsche continues, "the most frightful disease which has as yet raged within man; and he who is still able to hear (but today one no longer has an ear for this!) how in this night of torment and perversity there has rung out the cry of *love,* the cry of the most yearning ecstasy, of redemption through *love,* he turns away gripped by an invincible horror. There is so much in man that is ghastly! For too long already the world has been a madhouse!" (XIII: 113). "For too long a time man has looked upon his natural inclinations with an 'evil eye,' so that in the end they have become intimately interrelated with the 'bad conscience' " (XIII:116).

## IX

The "bad conscience," Nietzsche contends, took its final form in the hands of that "real artist in the feeling of guilt," the "ascetic priest"; and the "priestly version" of the "inverted cruelty" (which is the "bad conscience") is *"sin"* (XIII:182-183). The idea of "sin," Nietzsche holds, is "the most dangerous and most fateful masterpiece of religious interpretation" (XIII:183). "Man, suffering from himself in one way or another . . . , being unclear as to the why, the wherefore, desiring [to know] the reasons (for reasons bring relief), and desiring also remedies and narcotics—[this man] finally consults one who knows even the hidden; and, lo and behold! . . . from this wizard, the ascetic priest, he gets the first hint concerning the 'cause' of his suffer-ing: he is to search for it *in himself,* in his *guilt,* in a part of his past; he is to understand his very suffering as a *state of punishment.* He has heard, he has understood—has this un-fortunate one, . . . and the sick man has been turned into 'the sinner.' For a few thousand years we can't get away from the sight of this new invalid, this 'sinner'—shall we ever get away from it?" (XIII:183).

The result of this transformation of the sick one into the "sin-ner" was that everywhere in the world we now encounter "the evil conscience"—"a rumination over the past, a distorted view of action," "the *wilful* misunderstanding of suffering [and the] transvaluation [of suffering] into feelings of guilt, of fear, of retribution"; everywhere we find "the sinner breaking himself on the ghastly wheel of a restless and morbidly greedy con-science," "the mute pain, the extreme fear, the agony of a tortured heart, the spasms of an unknown happiness, the cry for 'redemption' " (XIII:183-184). At the same time, however, this transformation of the sick one into the "sinner" has elimi-nated "the old depression, the dullness and fatigue"; life has become *very* interesting again: awake, eternally awake, sleepless, glowing, burnt out, exhausted and yet not tired—thus appears man the 'sinner' who has been initiated into these mysteries." "The grand old wizard, the ascetic priest, has clearly triumphed in the struggle with ennui." "Every emotional excess which hurt; everything which broke, overthrew, crushed, transported, ravished; the mystery of torture-chambers, the ingenuity of hell itself—all this has now been discovered, divined, exploited; all this has been at the service of the wizard; all this has served to promote the triumph of his ideal, the ascetic ideal" (XIII:184).

Under the influence of the ascetic ideal, Nietzsche contends, the sick have become even more sick (XIII:185), the "corrupted health of the soul" has contaminated the whole of European culture (XIII:187), and the most destructive tendencies are masquerading "under the holiest names" (XIV:46). The institutionalized embodiment of this "inversion" of all values Nietzsche sees in the Christian Church.

However, in order to understand clearly Nietzsche's attitude towards Christianity, we must keep in mind that, for him, being "anti-Christian" is by no means the same as being "anti-religious" (XII:72). In fact, Nietzsche points out that " 'Christianity' has become something fundamentally different from what its founder did and wanted" (XIV:159). "Christianity as a *historical reality* should [therefore] not be confused with that one root which its name recalls; the *other* roots from which it has grown have been more powerful by far. It is an unparalleled abuse [of names]," Nietzsche continues, "when such manifestations of decay and such abortions as the 'Christian Church,' 'Christian faith,' and 'Christian life' are adorned by that holy name. What did Christ *deny?*—Everything which today is called Christian" (XIV: 132).

Nietzsche specifically distinguished between the life and teachings of Jesus and the "Christian Church" as founded by St. Paul. Of Jesus he says: "This 'messenger of Glad Tidings' died as he lived, as he *taught—not* in order 'to save mankind,' but in order to show how one ought to live. It was a mode of life which he bequeathed to mankind: his behavior before his judges, his

attitude towards his captors, his accusers, and all kinds of cal-
umny and scorn—his demeanor on the *cross*. He does not resist;
he does not defend his rights; he takes no step to ward off the
most extreme consequence—even more: *he provokes it*. And
he prays, he suffers, he loves *with* those, *in* those, who treat
him ill. *Not* to defend one's self, *not* to be angry, *not* to hold
anyone responsible. But also, not to resist the evil doer—to *love*
him" (XVI:174). That is to say, *"the life which must serve as
an example* consists in love and humility; in the abundance of
heartfelt emotion which does not exclude even the lowliest; in
the formal renunciation of all desire of making its rights felt,
of all defense; of conquest in the sense of personal triumph; in
the belief in salvation in this world, despite all sorrow, opposition, and death; in forgiveness and the absence of anger and
contempt; in the absence of a desire to be rewarded; in the
refusal to be bound to anybody: abandonment to all that is
most spiritual and intellectual;—in fact, [it is] a very proud life
controlled by the will of a servile and poor life" (XIV:138-139).
And Nietzsche adds: "If I understand anything at all about this
great symbolist [Jesus], it is this, that he regarded only *inner*
facts as facts, as 'truth'—that he understood the rest, everything
natural, temporal, spatial, historical, merely as a sign, as an opportunity for parables" (XVI:172); and that "the 'Kingdom of
Heaven' is a state of the heart—not something which [exists]
'beyond this earth' or comes 'after death' " (XVI:173).

Moreover, Nietzsche points out, "the whole psychology of the
'Gospels' lacks the concepts 'guilt' and 'punishment,' and also
the concept 'reward.' " "Sin," "any form of separation between
God and man, has been done away with,—*precisely this constitutes the 'Glad Tidings.'* Eternal bliss is not promised; it is not
made conditional; it is the *only* reality—all the rest is but signs
with which to speak about it" (XVI:171). It is thus "not a 'belief' which distinguishes the Christian: the Christian acts; he
distinguishes himself by means of an action which is *different*.
He does not resist his enemy either by words or in his heart. He
draws no distinction between foreigners and natives, between Jews
and Gentiles. . . . He is angry with no one; he despises no one. . . .

The life of the Savior was nothing else than *this* practice; nor was his death anything else" (XVI:171). "The profound instinct of how one must *live* in order to feel 'in heaven,' in order to feel 'eternal' (while in consequence of every other mode of conduct one does *not* feel 'in heaven' at all): this alone is the psychological reality of 'Salvation.'—A new life, *not* a new belief" (XVI: 172).

But if such is the meaning of the *life* of Jesus, then (Nietzsche holds) "Jesus could not have desired anything else by his death than to furnish publicly the most severe test, the *proof* of his doctrine" (XVI:181), and "one now understands *what* it was that came to an end with the death on the cross, [namely,] a new, a thoroughly original start towards a Buddhistic movement of peace, towards an actual, *not* a merely promised, *happiness on earth*" (XVI:183-184). Jesus's disciples, however, (so Nietzsche's argument continues) "were far from *forgiving* his death— although to forgive it would have been evangelical in the highest sense; nor were they ready, with a gentle and sweet calmness of heart, to *offer themselves* for the same death. Precisely the most unevangelical feeling, *revenge*, once again rose to the top. It was impossible [for the disciples] to let the matter end with this death; 'retaliation,' 'judgment' were needed (—and yet, what could be more unevangelical than 'retaliation,' 'punishment,' 'sitting in judgment'!). Once more the popular expectation of a Messiah came into prominence; attention was fixed upon a historical moment: the 'Kingdom of God' comes to sit in judgment over its enemies. But with this [conception] everything is misunderstood: the 'Kingdom of God' is regarded as the concluding act, as a promise to be fulfilled. But the Gospel had been precisely the existence, the fulfillment, the *reality* of this 'Kingdom.' It was precisely such a *death* [as Christ's] which *was* this 'Kingdom of God' " (XVI:181-182).

And so, according to Nietzsche, it is "the most egregious example of *world-historic irony*" that "mankind is on its knees before the opposite of that which was the origin, the meaning, the *right* of the Gospel; that, in the idea 'Church,' it has pronounced holy precisely that which the 'Messenger of Glad

Tidings' felt as *beneath* him, as *behind* him" (XVI:175); for "Jesus had done away even with the concept 'guilt'; he denied any gulf between God and man; he *lived* this unity of God and man as *his* 'Glad Tidings.' And *not* as a privilege!" (XVI:183).

"The 'Glad Tidings' [of Jesus] were followed very closely by the *worst possible* tidings: those of ["that pernicious blockhead" (XIV:138)] Paul. In Paul," Nietzsche maintains, "is incarnate the type opposite to the 'Messenger of Glad Tidings,' [i.e.] the genius in hate, in the vision of hate, in the relentless logic of hate. What all did not this dysevangelist sacrifice to his hatred! Above all, the Savior himself: he nailed him to *his* cross. The life, the example, the teaching, the death, the meaning and the right of the whole Gospel—nothing of all this was left once this 'counterfeiter out of hatred' had understood what alone he could use" (XVI:184); "nothing remained untouched, nothing remained which even remotely resembled [historical] reality. Paul simply shifted the full weight of [Jesus's] existence *beyond* that existence—into the *lie* of the 'resurrected' Jesus. At bottom, he had no possible use for the life of the Savior—he needed the death on the cross *and* something more"; for "what *he* wanted was *power*" (XVI:184-185). "With Paul," Nietzsche contends, "the priest again aspired to power. He could use only concepts, doctrines, symbols with which masses may be tyrannized and herds be formed" (XVI:185).

As Nietzsche sees it, Christianity, *in its Pauline "distortions,"* "has sided with everything that is weak, low, and botched; it has made an ideal out of the *antagonism* towards the preservative instincts of a strong life; it has corrupted the reason even of the intellectually strongest individuals by teaching [them] to see the highest values of intellectuality as sinful, as misleading, as *temptations*. The most lamentable example," Nietzsche adds, "is the corruption of Pascal, who believed in the perversion of his reason through original sin, whereas it had only been perverted by his Christianity" (XVI:130).

To be sure, "Christianity is called the religion of *compassion*" (XVI:131); but "compassion," as Nietzsche understands the term, is a "suffering with" and is "opposed to the tonic passions

which enhance the energy of the feeling of life" (XVI:131).[5]
Through compassion "suffering becomes contagious" and "the
drain on strength which suffering has already introduced into
the world is multiplied a thousandfold." "In certain circumstances a total loss of life and vital energy may be achieved
through it" (XVI:131). Moreover, "compassion, on the whole,
thwarts the law of development which is the *law of selection*.
It preserves that which is ripe for death; it fights in favor of
life's disinherited and condemned; and because of the multitude
of the botched of all kinds which it enables to cling to life,
it lends life itself a sombre and questionable aspect" (XVI:132).

In this Pauline version of Christianity, "neither morality nor
religion comes in touch with reality"; for here we find "nothing
but imaginary *causes* ('God,' 'soul,' 'self,' 'spirit,' 'free will'—
or even 'non free will'); nothing but imaginary *effects* ('sin,'
'salvation,' 'grace,' 'punishment,' 'forgiveness of sin'). Imaginary

---

5 In order to understand Nietzsche correctly, we must keep in mind that the
German noun *Mitleid* or *Mitleiden* (which I have translated by "compassion")
is derived from the verb *mitleiden*, meaning "to suffer with." That Nietzsche uses
the word *Mitleid* or *Mitleiden* in the sense of "to suffer with" is evident from
the context in which it appears; and it is evident also from certain explicit statements in Nietzsche's works. Thus, Nietzsche says: "Compassion, *in so far as it
actually creates suffering*—and let this be here our sole point of view—is a weakness, as is every indulgence in an injurious emotion. It *increases* suffering in the
world" (IX:144). Again we read: "To look upon our own experiences as we
are accustomed to look upon the experiences of others is very quieting and is an
advisable medicine. But to look upon and adopt the experiences of others *as if
they were our own*—which is demanded of us by a philosophy of compassion—
would ruin us in a very short time; let us simply make the experiment and in-
dulge no longer in fancies" (IX:147; 145). For, "compassion, as principle of
action which demands: 'suffer the misfortune of another as much as he himself
does,' brings it about that the point of view of the self, with all its exaggeration
and excess, must also become the point of view of the other, of the co-sufferer:
so that we should have to suffer at the same time from our own self and from
the self of the other, thus burdening ourselves voluntarily with a double unreason instead of making the burden of our own unreason as light as possible" (IX:
147-148).

However, as Nietzsche sees it, there is another aspect to compassion. Misfortune has befallen "the neighbor." At once "the 'compassionate ones' come and
depict his misfortune for him. At last they go away, satisfied and elevated: they
have feasted upon the terror of the unfortunate one as well as upon their own
terror, and have created for themselves a happy afternoon" (IX:232).

*beings* ('God,' 'spirits,' 'souls') communicate with one another. [Here we find] an imaginary *natural science* ([which is] anthropocentric, lacking completely the concept 'natural causes'); and imaginary *psychology* (nothing but misunderstandings of the self, interpretations of pleasant or unpleasant general feelings, . . . 'remorse,' 'pangs of conscience,' 'temptation of the devil,' 'presence of God'); and imaginary *theology* ('Kingdom of God,' 'Last Judgment,' 'Life Everlasting')" (XVI:141-142). And this "world of pure fiction" "falsifies, devalues, and negates" reality. Having its roots in "the *hatred* of all that is natural," it is an attempt to escape from reality via a *lie* (XVI:142).

There is no need to present here in greater detail Nietzsche's lengthy and, at times, abusive characterizations of Pauline Christianity; the quotations just given are indicative of the rest. Let us recall, however, that, according to Nietzsche, in and through Pauline Christianity the "ascetic priest" strives for power—power over the masses; and that his "perverted Will to Power" has become institutionalized in the Church—"the Church, this deadly hostility to all honesty, to all loftiness of the soul, to all discipline of the mind, to all frank and kindly humanity" (XVI: 176). Against *this* Church and *this* "Christianity" Nietzsche wages a relentless war; and the "morality" of *this* Church and *this* "Christianity" he abhors, repudiates, and seeks to replace because "it aims at destroying the strong, at breaking their spirit, at exploiting their moments of weariness and debility, at converting their proud assurance into anxiety and a troubled conscience"; because "it poisons the noblest instincts and infects them with disease" (XIV:209).

The time for the great "transvaluation of all values" is now at hand, Nietzsche believes, because we have come to know that real Christianity is not a "belief" in something but a "mode of existence," "a life such as he led who died on the Cross" (XVI: 178). We have come to know that "all concepts of the Church" are "the most malicious frauds on earth, calculated to *devalue* nature and all natural values" (XVI:177); that "there is no longer any 'God,' [6] any 'sinner,' or any 'Savior'"; and that " 'free will' and 'a moral order of the universe' are *lies*" (XVI: 176-177). We have come to realize that "a theologian, a priest, or a pope not only errs but actually *lies*" (XVI:177)—and that he lies in order to assure his own dominance over the "herd," to satisfy his own "Will to Power." And with this knowledge, Nietzsche believes, we have liberated ourselves from the shackles of the past. We are now ready for a new point of view, a new morality—the morality of the future.

History, however, reveals only too clearly that "everyone who has overthrown an established law of custom" has been regarded as "wicked" (IX:28), as a "law-breaker." Nietzsche, on the other hand, regards the "law-breaker" in this sense as the real "creator." "Destroyers will they be called [these creators], and despisers of good and evil," Nietzsche tells us; "but they are the reapers and rejoicers" (XI:20). They are the strong, the healthy, the "free men," the men of the future. They are the innovators, the seers of a new future, the creators of new values. But the members of the "herd" will call them "immoral" and will condemn them as "immoralists" (XI:260).

Nietzsche gladly accepts—and revels in—the title "immoralist"; for his aim is "to translate man back again into nature; to master the many vain and visionary interpretations" and "to bring it about that man shall henceforth stand before man as he now, hardened by the discipline of science, stands before other forms of nature . . . deaf to the enticements of the old metaphysical bird-catchers" (XII:181). The realization of Nietzsche's aim necessitates, of course, the annihilation of the "old morality"—of a morality, that is, which "depreciates the joy of living and the gratitude felt towards Life," which "checks the tendency to beautify and to enoble Life," and which "checks the unfolding of Life itself" (XIV:219-220).

---

[6] Cf. "God is dead" (XI:6; 320). And: "God is a conjecture; but I want that your conjecture reach no further than your creating will. Could you *create* a God?—Then, I pray you, be silent about all gods!" (XI:99). "God is a conjecture; but I want that your conjecture be restricted to the conceivable. Could you *conceive* a God? But let this mean for you Will to Truth, that everything be transformed into the humanly conceivable, the humanly visible, the humanly sensible. Your own senses you shall follow to their last ramifications" (XI:99).

Let us now see how Nietzsche hopes to accomplish his task.

## X

"No one yet knows," Zarathustra-Nietzsche says, "what is good or bad;—unless it be he who creates!—It is he, however, who creates man's goal and gives to the earth its meaning and its future" (XI:239-240). And to this "new nobility" of "procreators, cultivators, and sowers of the future" Zarathustra "consecrates" his followers—"not to a nobility which, like traders, [they] can purchase with traders-gold," but to a "nobility" whose "sole honor" is to be creative and to look to the future (XI:247-248; 261).

However, Nietzsche holds that "all who create are hard" (XI:105), and that "entirely hard is only the noblest" (XI:262). In fact, according to Nietzsche, "all great love is above compassion," for "it seeks to create that which is loved" even at personal sacrifice. " 'Myself I offer unto my love, *and my neighbor as myself'*—such [Nietzsche tells us] is the language of all who create" (XII:105).

To be sure, Nietzsche also approves of compassion; but the compassion he approves of is distinctive, for it arises only because of "a wasting of precious capabilities." It arises, in other words, when, "because of the effect of the imbecility of circumstances, someone remains far below the level of development which he might have attained," when we realize "what 'man' might have become, if—!" (XIV:293-294). This "compassion" Nietzsche regards as "higher" and "more farsighted" than that of Pauline Christianity. "We [he says] see how man dwarfs himself, how *you* [i.e. the Pauline Christians] dwarf him! and there are moments when we view *your* compassion with an indescribable anguish, when we defend ourselves against your compassion. . . . You want, if possible—and there is not a more nonsensical 'if possible'—*to do away with suffering;* and we?— it really seems that *we* would rather have suffering intensified and made worse than it ever was! Well-being, as you understand it—that is not a goal, that seems to us to be an *end!* a condition which soon makes man ludicrous and contemptible—and makes his destruction desirable! The discipline of suffering, of *great* suffering—do you not know that *this* discipline has hitherto created all elevations of man?" (XII:170-171). We must not forget, Nietzsche tells us, that "in man *creature* and *creator* are unified. In man there is matter, fragment, excess, clay, filth, folly, chaos; but in man there is also the creator, the sculptor, the hardness of a hammer, the divinity of a spectator, and the seventh day—do you understand this contrast? And (do you understand) that *your* compassion is concerned with the 'creature in man,' with what must be formed, broken, hammered, torn, burned, annealed, purified—with what must necessarily *suffer* and *ought* to suffer? And *our* compassion—do you not comprehend with whom our *reversed* compassion is concerned, when it defends itself against your compassion as the worst of all pampering and enervation?—Compassion thus stands *against* compassion!—But, let it be said again, there are problems higher than all the problems of pleasure and suffering and compassion; and every philosophy which culminates only in these is a naïveté" (XII:171).

Man, as he actually exists—"how poor indeed is he! [so Zarathustra-Nietzsche exclaims] . . . how ugly, how wheezy, how full of hidden shame!" (XV:326). Compared with the rest of nature, he is "the most botched and diseased animal" in existence (XVI:140; 176). This "man of today," therefore, is something to be "surpassed" rather than to be "preserved" (XI:351; XV:326). "He is a transition and a decline" (XI:352), and "even the greatest man" is "all too small," "all too human" (XI:268). "Today," Nietzsche adds, "we see nothing that wants to be greater." "In losing the fear of man, we have also lost the love of man, the respect for man, the hope in man, yes, even the will to be man." "We are tired of *man*" (XIII:44).

If there is to be any change to the better, then it is imperative (Nietzsche holds) that mankind "set its goal above itself—not in a false world, however, but in mankind's own continuation" (XVI:269). *"We must create beyond ourselves!* That is the instinct of procreation, that is the instinct of the deed and the work.—And just as all willing presupposes a goal, *so does man presuppose a creature* which [as ideal] does not exist but which provides the purpose of his existence. Such is the freedom of all volition! Love, veneration, the conceiving of perfection, yearn-ing—they all inhere in a *purpose*" (XVI:269). "We must have a *goal* for the sake of which we all love one another! *All* other goals are only worth annihilation" (XVI:271).

What Nietzsche demands here is that mankind bring forth creatures which stand sublimely above the whole species "man," and that for the sake of this goal we sacrifice "ourselves and 'the neighbor.'" This demand, however, implies at once also a demand for a "new morality," for "all morality which has existed hitherto has had its limits within the species—i.e., it has been useful in providing . . . an unconditional stability for the species." But now that this stability has been achieved, "the goal can be placed higher" (XVI:269); now the time has come to envisage a new ideal—the ideal of *"Superman."*

In order to understand what Nietzsche means by this new ideal, we must first contrast the idea of "Superman" with Nietz-sche's conceptions of the "last man" and the "higher man," and must then view it also as opposed to the idea of (Darwinian) evolution.

The "last man," according to Nietzsche, is in every respect "the opposite of the Superman" (XVI:270). He is the *"multi-farious* man," "the most interesting chaos which has ever existed —*not,* however, the chaos *preceding* the creation of a world, but that following it" (XV:318). He is the sceptic, the dis-illusioned, the uncreative man—"the most contemptible thing" on earth (XI:12). He is the man who "no longer can give birth to a star," who "no longer can despise himself" (XI:12). " 'What is love? What is creating? What is yearning? What is a star?'— so asks the last man, and blinks. The earth has become small, and on it there hops the last man who makes everything small" (XI:12). " 'We have discovered happiness'—say the last men, and blink"; and "they have their little pleasures for the day, and their little pleasures for the night" (XI:12-13). But they are botched and exhausted and no longer capable of a truly creative effort, of pursuing an ideal above and beyond themselves. They are no longer capable of giving birth to a "dancing star" (XI:12).

These "last men" exist "side by side" with "Superman"; but,

Nietzsche adds, "it is by no means the goal to regard the latter as the lords and masters of the former." On the contrary, the "two species" are "as widely separated as possible; the one, like the Epicurean gods, not concerning itself in the least with the other" (XVI:270).

The "higher" men are "higher than kings," for "the highest man [Nietzsche says] shall also be the highest lord on earth" (XI:299). And when these "highest men" are the "last men, and more beast than man, then the rabble rises and rises in value, and at last even the rabble-virtue says: 'Lo, I alone am virtue!'" (XI:299). These "higher men," these "lords on earth," Nietzsche repudiates. They are "not high and strong enough" (XI:345); they are "not sufficiently beautiful and well-born." There is "hidden rabble" even in them; and much in them is "crooked and misshapen" (XI:346). It is "the fate of the higher men" to be *condemned to die out*" (XVI:277). At the very best they are "only bridges," "steps" to the future (XI:346). "Superman" is of different stature. He is the ideal of the future.

The realization of the future, however, is not simply a matter of evolution; for "the process of evolution is by no means of necessity an elevation, an enhancement, or a strengthening" (XVI:129). It would be a complete misunderstanding of Nietzsche were we to regard his doctrine as merely an extension or specific application of the idea of evolution. In fact, Nietzsche clearly and emphatically repudiates "Darwinism." The "struggle for existence," he holds, is "more asserted than proved" (XVI: 71); for "the over-all condition of life is not one of want or famine, but one of abundance, of exuberance, even of absurd squandering,—where there is a struggle, there is a struggle for power" (XVI:71). If a struggle for existence does occur, "its results are unfortunately the reverse of that which the Darwinian school desires"; for that struggle does not lead to "perfection": "The weak always prevail over the strong because they are the great mass, and because they are also more *crafty*" (XVI:71; XV:155). And the idea of "adaptation" "misses the real essence of life." "It overlooks the fundamental pre-eminence of the spontaneous, aggressive, encroaching, re-interpreting, re-directing, and creative forces whose effectiveness alone entails 'adaptation' " (XIII:92; XV:153-154).

Surveying "the great destinies of Man," Nietzsche finds that the reverse of "what Darwin and his school see or *want* to see" is actually the case: instead of a "selection in favor of the better-endowed," there occurs an elimination of the "uncommon," of the "lucky exceptions"; instead of "progress of the species," there takes place "the inescapable advancement to dominance of the mediocre and even of the *lower-than-mediocre types*" (XV:158-159). "Man as a species is *not* progressing" (XV:157). Also, Nietzsche finds, "humanity as such is not a whole: it is an indissoluble multiplicity of ascending-descending processes of life. It does not have a period of youth followed by one of *maturity* and, finally, by one of old age. On the contrary, its strata are confused and do overlap" (XIV:271). "Decadence belongs to all epochs of human history" (XIV:272); but at all times, too, and "in the most varied places on earth and out of the most varied cultures," there arise individuals (the "lucky exceptions" or "lucky strokes," as Nietzsche calls them) who stand far above "mankind in general" and who exemplify what might be, if—. They are "a sort of supermen" (XVI:129) but by no means the full realization of the ideal; for "Superman" *is* an ideal. Man, on the other hand, is "something that is to be surpassed" (XI:6; 53; 64; 241; 243).

In order that human existence have purpose and meaning, Nietzsche argues, man must create something beyond himself; and now that *"God is dead"* (XI:6), he continues, let "Superman" be "the meaning of the earth" (XI:7), the meaning and purpose of human existence (XI:16; 91). As Zarathustra puts it: "In the distant past people said God, when they gazed upon far-flung oceans; but now I have taught you to say: Superman.— God is a conjecture; but I demand that your conjecturing do not reach further than your creative will. Could you *create* a God?—Then be silent about all gods! But you could well create the Superman. Not perhaps you yourselves, my brothers! But you transform yourselves into fathers and forefathers of the Superman; and let *this* be your best creating!" (XI:98-99).

Since "Superman" is an ideal, no "Superman" has as yet existed. "The greatest man and the smallest man [Zarathustra-Nietzsche tells us]—both of them I have seen naked: They are still all too similar to each other. Verily, even the greatest I found—all-too-human" (XI:108). Nietzsche would have loathed and despised Hitler and all he stood for, for even Napoleon was for him but a "synthesis of *Monster* and *Superman*" —an exemplification of "the incarnate *problem* of the noble idea," not of the ideal itself (XIII:56). That ideal, as Nietzsche sees it, is a "Roman Caesar with the soul of Christ" (XV:380).

Nietzsche admits that all who, in the sense of traditional morality, are "the good and the just" will find this ideal—will find "Superman"—*"frightful* in his goodness" (XI:174). We must therefore examine this ideal further and see what it implies.

## XI

"The beginnings of justice, like those of prudence, temperance, and courage," Nietzsche finds, "are of *animal origin*" (IX:33). "Even that interest in truth, which is at bottom an interest in security, man shares with the animals: One does not wish to be deceived, one does not wish to be led astray by one's own nature, one listens distrustfully to the promptings of one's own passions, one controls oneself and lies in wait for oneself; but all this the animal understands as well as does man: in its case, too, self-control grows out of the interest in reality [i.e., out of prudence]" (IX:33). But in the development of man, a *sublimation* of an originally brutish nature occurs; for "all institutions which concede to a passion the *belief in its duration* and the responsibility of this duration" have given that passion "a new rank" (IX:34). "Consider, for example, [Nietzsche suggests] institutions and customs which have created eternal fidelity out of the fiery devotion of a moment, eternal vengeance out of the desires of anger, eternal mourning out of despair, eternal obligation out of a sudden and singular promise. Each time, and as the result of such a transformation, much hypocrisy and false-hood have come into the world; but each time, too, and at that price, a new *superhuman* conception—a conception which elevates man—[has been introduced]" (IX:34).

Our passions, Nietzsche concedes, are rooted in our animal nature; but this is no reason why we should "enfeeble" or "annihilate" them. On the contrary, we must *"enlist them in our service."* "To this end it may be necessary to tyrannize them for a long time (and not only as individuals, but as community, race, etc.); but in the end we should, trustingly, restore their freedom: then, like good servants, they love us and willingly go wherever that which is best in us wants to go" (XIV:307). We may then "love our senses; for we have spiritualized them in every way and have made them artistic" (XIV, 95).

This sublimation of the passions, however, is not a painless or an easy matter. "The worst enemy you can meet [Nietzsche points out] will always be yourself." "You waylay yourself in caverns and forests," and when you are on the "way to yourself," you will always encounter your "seven devils." "To yourself you will be a heretic and a witch and a sooth-sayer and a fool and a doubter and an unholy one and a villain. You must be ready to burn yourself in your own flame; for how could you become new if you had not first become ashes!" (XI:73). Ever anew you must ask yourself: "Are you the victorious one, the self-conqueror, the master of the passions, the lord of your virtues? . . . Or does the animal speak in your wish—your great need, your loneliness, the discord within you?" (XI:79).

"Creating," Nietzsche exclaims, "—that is the great salvation from suffering, and the alleviation of life. But in order that there be one who creates, suffering is needed and much transformation"; for "if he who creates is also to be the child that is to be born, he must . . . [accept] the pain of the child-bearer" (XI: 100). And the greatest creation of man *is man himself*. It is in this sense (but with a change in the metaphor) that Zarathustra says: "My fervent creative will impels me ever anew towards man; thus the hammer is driven to the stone. . . . An image slumbers within the stone—the image of my images [i.e., the ideal]. Alas! that it should slumber in the hardest, the ugliest stone!" (XI:101).

This transformation and sublimation of the passions is also a transformation and a creation of values. One such new value is "the sublimation of sensuality" into *love*—into the "love of the remote" (which, Nietzsche holds, is "a great triumph over Christianity"); another is "the sublimation of *enmity*"—which "consists in this, that one realizes profoundly the value of having enemies" (XVI:28). Just as "almost every [political] party sees its self-preservative interest in preventing the opposition from losing all strength," so "do we behave towards the 'inner enemy': here, too, we have sublimated enmity; here, too, we have understood its *value*. A man is *productive* only at the cost of being rich in contrasts; he remains *young* only under the condition that his soul does not—yearn for peace" (XVI:28-29), for he who renounces "war"—the "war" within him, that is—"has renounced the *great* life" (XVI:29). To be sure, Nietzsche admits that "peace of the soul" need not always be a sign of "age" and of "weariness"; at times it may be "the expression of maturity and mastery in the midst of action, of creative work, of production, of striving—the calm breathing (as it were), the *attained* 'freedom of the will' " (XVI:29). But Nietzsche's main thesis is and remains that "one must still have chaos within one, if one is to give birth to a dancing star" (XI:12); that in the consuming flames of this chaos the passions are sublimated, new values are crystallized, and the ideal—the ideal which gives meaning and purpose to human living—is purified.

And what are the "virtues" embodied in this ideal? There are persons, Nietzsche says, "to whom virtue means writhing under the lash." "There are others who call the slothfulness of their vices a virtue." "There are [still] others who are drawn downwards: their devils draw them"; and what they are not,—"that, that they call God and virtue" (XI:110). "Others are proud of their modicum of righteousness, and for the sake of it do violence to all things: so that the world and its injustice are drowned" (XI:111). "And again there are those who regard it as virtue to say: 'Virtue is necessary'; but fundamentally they believe only that the police is necessary" (XI:111). "And many who cannot see man's loftiness, call it virtue that they can see his baseness all too well. And some want to be edified and raised up, and call it virtue; and others want to be cast down—and call it also virtue.—And thus almost all believe that they participate in virtue; and, at the very least, everyone claims to be an authority on 'good' and 'evil' " (XI:111-112). Against all these conceptions and misconceptions of virtue Nietzsche proclaims: "That *your self* be in your action, as the mother is in the child: let that be *your* formula for virtue!" (XI:112). Virtue, in other words, is the authentic manifestation of the self.

In this ideal, Nietzsche holds, there is "voluptuousness"—a voluptuousness which is "innocent and free to the free hearts, the garden-happiness of the earth, all the future's superabundance of thanks to the present"; a voluptuousness which is "the great happiness symbolic of a higher happiness and of highest hope" (XI:230). And a "passion for power" is there—"this earthquake which breaks and breaks open all that is rotten and hollow; the rolling, roaring, punishing demolisher of whitewashed sepulchres; the flashing question mark beside premature answers." But the term "passion for power" is not adequate to describe what Nietzsche has in mind; for the "drive" is hardly a *passion*. It is a "yearning" instead—a "yearning" *to give* and *to bestow* out of the richness and superabundance of life. " 'Bestowing virtue'—thus Zarathustra once called this unnamable virtue" (XI:231), and he added that "a bestowing virtue is the highest virtue" (XI:86).

But "selfishness" is also included in Nietzsche's ideal—"the wholesome, healthy selfishness which springs from a powerful soul:—from the powerful soul which belongs to the . . . triumphant . . . body, and around which everything becomes a mirror" (XI:232); the "blessed selfishness," which calls *bad* "everything that is broken and niggardly—servile—unfree blinking-eyes, depressed hearts, and that false submissive kind which kisses with broad, cowardly lips" (XI:233). This "healthy and holy selfishness," as Nietzsche calls it, is closely related to the "bestowing virtue"; for it is a "thirst to become a sacrifice and a gift" (XI:86). It is a "selfishness" which enriches itself only in order to bestow the more abundantly—as from a deep fountain. It is a "selfishness" whose core is a "love which bestows" (XI:86). And it is this love—this "bestowing love"—which, according to Nietzsche, is to "give to the earth its meaning, a human meaning" (XI:88). "Let your love to life be love to your highest hope; and let your highest hope be the loftiest thought of life" (XI:53).

Such an ideal includes "greatness"—a "greatness" which is: "to be capable of being just as multifarious as complete, just as wide as full" (XII:155); a "greatness," in other words, which is the superabundant life, perfection in multiplicity of value responses, depths and richness of life, and "the creative abundance of power" (XII:154). In such "greatness," Nietzsche holds, there is *freedom:* "the will to be responsible for oneself; [the will] to preserve the distance which separates us [from the rabble]; [the will] to become more indifferent toward hardships, severity, privation, and even life itself; to sacrifice men, oneself included, for one's cause" (XVI:94-95). "The highest type of free men," Nietzsche adds, "would have to be sought where the highest resistance is constantly being overcome: five paces away from tyranny, on the very threshold of the danger of thraldom. This is psychologically true [Nietzsche points out], if by 'tyrants' one means inexorable and terrible instincts which challenge the maximum of authority and discipline to oppose them . . . ; but it is also politically true; just examine the course of history. The people which were or *became* worth something, never attained that condition under (or because of) liberal constitutions: the *great danger* [what Toynbee has called the "Challenge"] made something out of them which deserved veneration" (XVI:95). "One must *need* to be strong; in no other way does one become strong" (XVI:96).

This ideal of the superabundant and creative life Nietzsche opposes to the conception of "neighbor-love" or "love of the nearest." "Your neighbor-love," he says, "is your bad love of yourself" (XI:68). Instead of "neighbor-*love,*" Nietzsche preaches "neighbor-*flight*" and "the love of the most remote," the love of the future; for "higher than love of the nearest," he says, "is love of the farthest and of what is to come in the future" (XI:69). And for the sake of the future, so Nietzsche continues, we ought to be hard with the present. "Let the future and the most remote [i.e., the ideal] be the motive of your today" (XI:70). Let the love of what is to come prevail over every concern for the present, and "maintain holy your highest hope" (XI:49).

In Nietzsche's opinion, the poet-statesman Goethe—that "most beautiful manifestation" of an "integrated man" (XV:318)—comes closest to a realization of the ideal here envisaged. Goethe —"no mere German, but a European event: a magnificent attempt to overcome the eighteenth century by means of a return to nature, by means of an ascent to the naturalness of the Renaissance"—"bore within him the strongest instincts of his century: its sentimentality, its idolatry of nature, its anti-historic, idealistic, unrealistic, and revolutionary spirit. . . . He enlisted history, natural science, antiquity, as well as Spinoza, and above all practical activity, in his service; . . . he did not withdraw from life, he plunged into it; he was not discouraged but took as much as he could upon his own shoulders and into his own heart. That to which he aspired was *totality;* he fought against the sundering of reason, sensuality, emotion, and will . . . ; he disciplined himself into a harmonious whole; he *created* himself. In the midst of an age of unrealistic trends, he was a convinced realist: he said Yes to everything which in this respect was akin to himself. . . . Goethe [Nietzsche continues] envisaged a strong and highly cultured man; a man skillful in all bodily accomplishments, capable of self-discipline, having respect for himself; a man who can permit himself the enjoyment of the whole fullness and richness of naturalness, who is strong enough for this freedom; a man of tolerance, not out of weakness but out of strength, because he knows how to use to his advantage even that which would destroy mediocre individuals; a man for whom nothing is any longer forbidden, unless it be weakness. . . . Such a spirit [Nietzsche concludes]—such a spirit, *become free,* stands in the midst of the whole universe with a feeling of joyous and confident fatalism, believing that only individual things are bad [but] that, taken as part of the whole, everything redeems and affirms itself; [such a spirit] *no longer denies;* [and the faith manifested in such a spirit] is the highest of all possible faiths" (XVI:109-110). In pursuit of this faith "we must overcome the past in ourselves";

we must "conquer" our instincts and must "consecrate" them anew (XVI:261). Only thus can we realize the highest ideal.

## XII

From the perspective of the ideal just described, Nietzsche attempts the *"revaluation of all values."*

Throughout the longest, the "pre-moral," period of human history, Nietzsche maintains, "the value or disvalue of an action was inferred from its consequences; the action itself was considered as little as was its origin" (XII:46). In the last ten thousand years, however—during the *"moral"* period of history —a gradual change has taken place in this respect. Now the origin of an action—more specifically, the intention behind the action—rather than the consequences, is regarded as determining the value of the action. This "inversion of perspective," Nietzsche holds, has given rise to "a fateful new superstition, to a peculiar narrowness of interpretation," but, nevertheless, taken as a whole, it has been "a great achievement, an important refinement of vision and of standard" (XIII:46). Today, however, because of "a new self-knowledge and an increased profundity of man," Nietzsche holds, we are again "confronted with the necessity of making up our minds" about a "fundamental displacement" or "transvaluation" of values; we are "standing on the threshold of a period" which, negatively, may be described as *"nonmoral."* We have begun to suspect, as Nietzsche puts it, that "the decisive value of an action lies precisely in that which is not intentional," that "all its intentionality, all of it which can be seen, known, or become 'conscious,' still belongs to its surface only" (XII:47). The "intention" is but "a sign and symptom which requires interpretation"; and to the extent to which this is the case, the "morality of intentions" is but "a prejudice, a rashness, perhaps something preliminary . . . something which must be surmounted" (XII:47).

It is the task of the "new philosophers" to initiate the transvaluation of values which is now required (XII:129-130). This task, however, is not an easy one. It inevitably brings the philosopher into conflict with all existing morality.

In order to understand how Nietzsche sees this conflict, let us consider briefly his answer to the question: "Under what conditions did man invent for himself these value judgments, good and evil?" More specifically, *what value do [these conditions] themselves possess?* Have they hitherto hindered or furthered human welfare? Are they a sign of distress, of impoverishment, of degeneration of life? Or, conversely, do they disclose the superabundance, the strength, the will of life, its courage, its self-reliance, its future?" (XIII:4-5).

It is Nietzsche's contention—and this is crucial to his whole position—that "the conceptions of good and evil have a twofold history, namely, *once* in the soul of the ruling tribes and castes," and "again in the soul of the oppressed, the powerless" (VI: 64-65), and that, depending upon this difference in origin, the moral conceptions themselves differ radically. Thus, in the first case, the conceptual opposition is that of good and *bad,* whereas in the second case it is that of good and *evil;* and the very idea of *good* is different in the two cases.[7] In the one case, it is the morality of the noble, the "masters"; in the other case, it is that of the lowly, the "slaves." Within the framework of the "morality of the masters," Nietzsche argues, the term *good* means " 'high-mindedness,' 'noble,' 'exalted-minded,' 'privileged in mind' "; and *bad* means " 'vulgar,' 'plebeian,' 'low' " (XIII:23).[8]

---

[7] In this connection Nietzsche wrote: "I have once called attention to the embarrassment of Hesiod when he conceived the sequence of cultural periods and endeavored to express them in gold, silver, and bronze. He could not dispose of the contradiction with which the magnificent but at the same time terrifying and violent world of Homer confronted him, except by making two ages out of one, which he then placed one behind the other—first, the Age of the Heroes and Demigods of Troy and Thebes, as this world has remained in the memory of the aristocratic families who found therein their own ancestors; next, the Bronze Age, as that same world appeared to the descendants of the oppressed, the despoiled, the ill-treated, the abducted, the enslaved: as an Age of Bronze . . . , hard, cold, cruel, without feelings and without conscience, crushing everything, and spattering it with blood" (XIII:41-42).

[8] The "most eloquent example," Nietzsche points out, is found in the German language; for the word *"schlecht"* is "identical with *'schlict'* (compare *'schlechtweg,' 'schlechterdings'*)." The word *"schlecht,"* in other words, originally and without suspicion-arousing overtones simply denoted the plain, common man in contrast to the man of superior rank. Approximately at the time of the Thirty Years' War, and thus rather late, this meaning changes to the one now customary" (XIII:23).

"The knightly-aristocratic value judgments"—i.e., the value judgments of the "masters," as expressed in the opposition of *good* and *bad*—"have as their presupposition a strong body, robust, rich, and even effervescing health, together with everything which serves their preservation: war, adventure, the chase, the dance, tournaments—everything, in fact, which is included in strong, free, joyous action" (XIII:29). But when "the revolt of the slaves in the realm of morals" begins, all of this is changed. Now "resentment becomes creative and gives birth to values—the resentment experienced by those creatures who are deprived of their proper reaction [which would be that of the deed], and who find compensation only in an imaginary revenge. Whereas all aristocratic morality springs from a triumphant saying Yes! to itself, slave morality, from its beginning, says No! to a 'beyond,' to an 'other,' to a 'nonself'; and this No! is its creative deed" (XIII:34). The revolt of the "slaves" is thus an "inversion of the value-bestowing perspective."

"The 'well-born',," Nietzsche maintains, "simply *felt* themselves as the 'happy ones'; they did not have to construct their happiness artificially . . . or to talk or *lie* themselves into happiness [as is the custom with all men of resentment]; and, as *complete* men, as *necessarily* active men, they knew that action cannot be separated from happiness. . . . All of which is very much in contrast to 'happiness' at the level of the weak, the depressed, and of those afflicted with poisoned and malignant feelings as with festering sores, among whom 'happiness' is essentially a narcotic, a deadening, a rest, a peace, a 'Sabbath,' an enervation of the mind and relaxation of the limbs—in brief, where it is purely *passive*. Whereas the noble man lives with himself in confidence and candor . . . , the man of resentment is neither candid, nor naïve, nor honest and straightforward with himself. His soul squints" (XIII:37). And this "man of resentment" has "conceived 'the evil enemy,' the *'evil one,'* as the root-concept," and, proceeding from this concept, "he now evolves as secondary and contrasting figure a 'good one'—himself!" (XIII:38). This procedure, Nietzsche finds, is "precisely the reverse of the pro-

cedure of the noble man who conceives first of all and spontaneously—namely, out of himself—the basic concept 'good,'
and who, from there, creates for himself an idea of 'bad' "
(XIII:38-39). "This 'bad' of noble origin," Nietzsche continues,
"and that 'evil' out of the cauldron of unsatiated hatred—the
former a secondary creation, an incidental matter, a complementary color; the latter, on the other hand, the original, the
beginning, the real *deed* in the conception of a slave morality—
[this] 'bad' and [that] 'evil,' how different these two words are
despite the fact that both appear to be placed in opposition to
the same concept 'good'!" (XIII:39). Nietzsche is quick, however, to point out that "it is *not* the same concept 'good'." To
realize this, "one need only ask, *Who* really is 'evil' according
to the meaning of the morality of resentment? The answer, in
all strictness, is: *precisely* the 'good one' of the other morality,
i.e., the noble one, the powerful one, the prevailing one—only
re-dyed, re-interpreted, seen differently through the venomous
eye of resentment" (XIII:39).

The "aristocratic men" who, from the perspective of the "man
of resentment," are the "evil ones" but who, *inter pares,* are
"kept rigorously in bounds through convention, respect, custom,
and gratitude, though much more through mutual vigilance and
jealousy"; who, "in their relations with one another find many
new ways of manifesting consideration, self-control, delicacy,
loyalty, pride, and friendship";—these same "aristocratic men"
are in reference to what is outside their circle "not much better
than beasts of prey which have been let loose" (XIII, 39). In
contact with the "outsider," with what is "foreign"—"in the
wilderness," as Nietzsche calls it, where they can "give vent with
impunity to that tension which is produced by enclosure and
imprisonment in the peace of society"—"they *revert* to the
innocence of the beast-of-prey conscience, like jubilant monsters
who, after a ghastly sequence of murder, arson, rape, and torture,
perhaps move on with bravado and a moral equanimity as if
merely a student's prank had been played, convinced that, for a
long time, the poets have again something to sing about and to

praise" (XIII:40). The study of history shows, Nietzsche holds, that it would be a mistake "not to recognize the beast of prey—the magnificent *blonde beast,* avidly rampant for spoils and victory—at the bottom of all aristocratic races" (XIII:40). At all times, the "aristocratic races" have been the "barbarians"; and even man's highest cultures still reflect "a consciousness of, and a pride in," this "barbarism." Pericles's "famous funeral oration," Nietzsche finds, is but one example of this (XIII:40). On the basis of historical fact, therefore, "one may be perfectly justified in remaining afraid of the blonde beast at the core of all aristocratic races, and in remaining on guard; but [Nietzsche adds] who would not a hundred times rather be afraid when he may at the same time admire, than be not afraid but be unable any longer to get rid of the loathsome sight of the failures, the dwarfed, the stunted, the envenomed? And is not this *our* fate?" (XIII:42). *"Not* fear; rather that we have nothing more to fear in man; that the vermin 'man' is in the foreground and pullulates; that the 'tame man,' the incurably mediocre and disagreeable creature, has already learned to regard himself as goal and pinnacle, as the purpose of history, as 'higher man'" (XIII:43) —this, Nietzsche holds, is the curse of our age.

"When the oppressed, the down-trodden, the overpowered say to themselves with the vindictive guile of weakness: 'Let us be otherwise than the evil ones, namely, good! and good is every one who does not oppress, who hurts no one, who does not attack, who does not strike back, who hands over revenge to God, who holds himself, as we do, in hiding; who goes out of the way of all evil, and who, like us—the patient, the meek, the just—, demands but little from life;—[when the weak say this, then all of what they say], considered coldly and without prejudice, means nothing more than: 'We weak ones are indeed weak; it is good not to do anything *for which we are not strong enough';* but this dismal state of affairs, this prudence of the lowest order, which even insects possess . . . has, thanks to the counterfeiting and self-deception of weakness, dressed itself up in the pomp of an ascetic, quiet, patiently waiting virtue, just as though the very weakness of the weak . . . were a voluntary achievement, something intended, chosen, a *deed,* a *meritorious act"* (XIII:46-47). A radical *falsification* has here taken place: weakness has been falsified into merit, "the impotence which does not requite into 'goodness,' timid baseness into 'meekness,' submission to those whom one hates into 'obedience.' . . . The inoffensiveness of the weak, cowardice itself . . . here gain a good name: 'patience,' and are perhaps even called *the* virtue; the inability to revenge oneself is called not-intending-to-avenge-one-self, perhaps even 'forgiveness' " (XIII:48). "They are miserable, there is no doubt about it, all these whisperers and counterfeiters in the corners," Nietzsche concedes; but, he at once adds, "they tell me that their misery is a favor and distinction given to them by God . . . ; that perhaps this misery is also a preparation, a probation, a training; that perhaps it is even more—something which some day will be compensated and will be paid back with tremendous interest in gold, nay in happiness. This they call 'Blessedness' " (XIII:48-49). But "this workshop *where ideals are manufactured,"* Nietzsche finds, "stinks because of all the lies" (XIII:49). Here revenge is falsified into "the triumph of righteousness," and the "phantasmagoria" of "the last judgment," of "the advent of the 'kingdom of God,' " serves as "a solace against all the troubles of life" (XIII:50). Here, "eternal life is necessary to make up for ever for that earthly life 'in faith, in love, in hope' " (XIII:51), which is the life of the botched and misbegotten, of the "men of resentment."

In conformity with these two points of view—the point of view of the "aristocratic man" and the point of view of the "man of resentment"—men (so Nietzsche holds) have given themselves all their values (XI:67). And let there be no mistake about it— "It was man who assigned values to things in order to preserve himself; it was he who created the meaning of things—a human meaning!" And "through valuation only is there value" (XI:67). But "valuing is creating" (XI:67); and it does make a basic difference whether the creator of values is an "aristocratic man" or a "man of resentment." In Nietzsche's words, "values and their modifications are related to the *growth of power of him who posits values"* (XIV:16). Exhaustion, for example, "alters the appearance of things, the value of things." "In contrast to him who involuntarily *gives* to the things of the fullness which he himself represents and feels, and who sees the things fuller, more powerful, richer of promise—who at all events *can* bestow—, the exhausted one belittles and disfigures everything he sees; he impoverishes value; he is pernicious" (XIV:40). The facts, Nietzsche believes, are clear; but history shows that "the exhausted ones have always been confused with the most vigorous, and the most vigorous with the most pernicious" (XIV:40).

"I found," Nietzsche writes, "that all supreme value judgments, all who have attained full sway over mankind, or at least over its tamer portion, can be traced back to the judgments of exhausted people" (XIV:46). "I unearthed," he continues, "the destructive tendencies hidden under the holiest names. All that which weakens, teaches weakness, infects with weakness, people have called God; I found that the 'good man' is a form of self-affirmation on the part of decadence" (XIV:46). By contrast, Nietzsche wants to "teach the negation of all that which makes weak, which exhausts." He wants to "teach the affirmation of all that which strengthens, which accumulates strength, which justifies the feeling of strength." And he adds, "up to now neither the one nor the other has been taught; [up to now] virtue, disavowal of self, pity, even negation of life have been taught. All these are values of exhausted people" (XIV:46).

Throughout history, however, the valuations of the "aristocratic man" and those of the "man of resentment" have been intermixed. "Every kind of decay and disease has constantly shared in the work of formulating the collective value judgments," and "in the value judgments which have become dominant, decadence has even attained preponderance" (XIV:32). The result is that "we not only have to fight against conditions consequent to all present misery of degeneration, but that *all previously developed* decadence has remained with us, has remained *active*" (XIV:32). As a result, the struggle for a new orientation is all the more difficult; but, Nietzsche contends, without a radical transvaluation of all the values which are now commonly accepted there is no hope for the future.

We have seen in what sense Nietzsche speaks of a "morality of masters" and a "morality of slaves." "In all higher and mixed cultures," Nietzsche finds, "attempts are made at the reconciliation of these two moralities, still oftener there is an intermixture of the two, and a mutual misunderstanding, at times even a solidified coexistence—even within the same man, within one soul" (XII:227); and this is the very situation which bodes ill for the future.

In so far as the "masters" determine the meaning of "good," "the elevated and proud states of the soul" are felt as providing the value accent, the determination of the order of rank. "The noble man separates from himself all beings who are the expression of the opposite of such elevated and proud states: he despises them." "Good" and "bad" simply mean "noble" and "despicable," respectively. "The opposition 'good' and 'evil' is of a different origin." "Despised is the coward, he who is afraid, who is paltry and mean, who thinks only in terms of a narrow utility; and despised is also the distrustful one with his unfree glances, he who debases himself, who accepts mistreatment like a dog, the begging flatterer, and, above all, the liar" (XII:228). By contrast, the noble man feels himself as determining values, as creating values. "What is harmful to me is in itself harmful." "In the foreground is the feeling of fullness, of power, which wants to overflow, the happiness of high tension, the consciousness of a wealth which desires to give and to share:—the noble man also helps him who is in need, but not (or almost never) out of compassion, [he does it] out of a drive created by the surplus of power. The noble man honors in himself the man of power, even him who has power over himself, who knows when to speak and when to be silent, who, with pleasure, practices strictness and hardness against himself and shows reverence for all that is strict and hard" (XII:228). "The noble and courageous ones who think thus are farthest removed from that morality which sees precisely in pity, or in action for others, or in disinterestedness the mark of distinction of the moral; faith in oneself, pride in oneself, a radical enmity and irony toward "selflessness"—these belong just as definitely to aristocratic morality as do an easy disregard of, and a caution with respect to, feelings of sympathy and the 'warm heart' " (XII:229).

It is otherwise with "slave-morality." The "common element" in the morality of "the abused, the oppressed, the suffering, the unfree, of those who are uncertain of themselves, and of the weary" is "a pessimistic mistrust of the entire situation of man" and "a condemnation of man together with his situation" (XII: 230). "The eye of the slave is envious of the virtues of the powerful; he has a scepticism and distrust, a *refinement* of distrust of everything 'good' which is there honored;—he would fain persuade himself that happiness itself is there not genuine. Conversely, those attributes are brought into prominence and flooded with light which serve to alleviate the existence of sufferers; it is here that pity, the kind helping hand, the warm heart, patience, diligence, humility, friendliness attain honor, for they are here the most useful qualities and almost the only means of withstanding the pressure of existence. Slave-morality is [thus] essentially a morality of utility. Here is the seat of the origin of that famous antithesis 'good' and *'evil'* " (XII:230-231). It is Nietzsche's doctrine that "the herd seeks to preserve a type [of man], and that it defends itself on both sides: as much against those who are degenerates of the type (criminals, etc.) as against those who tower above it. The tendency of the herd is directed toward stagnation and preservation; in it there is nothing which is creative" (XIV:236). And Nietzsche wants that "the sense of the herd shall rule within the herd—but shall not reach beyond it" (XIV:237). He "aims at an *order of rank, not* an individualistic morality" (XIV:237). The morality of the herd, however, is directed against all "order of rank" (XIV:236).

But behind this herd-drive for equality Nietzsche discerns "the tyrant-madness of impotence"—"secret tyrant-longings" which "disguise themselves in virtue-words" (XI:117). And when the "preachers of equality" "become subtle and cold, it is not the spirit, but envy, which makes them subtle and cold" (XI:117). With these "preachers of equality" Nietzsche does not want to be confused; for "thus speaks justice . . . : 'men are not equal.' And neither shall they become so!" (XI:118-119). "Good and evil, and rich and poor, and high and low, and all the names of values: weapons they shall be and sounding signs of the fact that life must again and again surpass itself!" (XI:119). But the distinctions of "rich" and "poor," of "high" and "low" are not a matter of wealth. "Rabble above, rabble below! What are 'poor' and 'rich' nowadays!" Nietzsche is filled with "disgust at our richest—at the culprits of wealth who, with cold eyes and lascivious thoughts, pick up their profit out of all kinds of rubbish —at this rabble which stinks to heaven—at this guilded, falsified rabble" (XI:330).

Surveying his own Age, Nietzsche finds much decadence; but, he argues, "decadence belongs to all epochs of mankind; everywhere there is refuse and decaying matter, [for] the elimination of all decaying and waste materials is itself a process of life" (XIV:272). "Indeed all abundant growth involves also a terrible *crumbling away* and *decay:* suffering and the symptoms of decline *belong* to the ages of enormous progress; every fruitful and powerful movement of mankind has always *created also* a nihilistic movement. Under certain circumstances, the birth of the *most extreme* form of pessimism, of *Nihilism* proper, might be the sign of an incisive and most essential growth, of the transition into new conditions of existence" (XIV:92). Nietzsche therefore warns us "not to confuse the instincts of decadence with those of *humanity;* not to confuse the *dissolving means* of civilization *which necessarily drive us into decadence* with *culture;* not to confuse *debauchery,* the principle of *'laisser aller,'* with the *Will to Power* (—the latter is the *counter*-principle of the former)" (XIV:100).

Decadence itself, therefore, is *not* "something to be fought"; "it is absolutely necessary and is proper to every age and every people. But what must be combatted with all power at our disposal [Nietzsche maintains], is the spreading of the contagion among the healthy parts of the organism" (XIV:33-34).

What Nietzsche meant by decadence may be gathered from some of the Notes which constitute the bulk of *The Will to*

*Power.* "Scepticism," Nietzsche writes, "is a result of decadence, as is debauchery of the spirit. The corruption of morals is a result of decadence (weakness of will, need for strong stimulants)" (XIV:34-35). "Nihilism is not a cause of decadence, but only its logic. . . . The *social problem* is a result of decadence. Illness, in particular the illness of the nervous system and the mind, are signs that the *defensive* strength of a strong constitution is lacking" (XIV:35). "There is decadence in everything which characterizes modern man. But close to the sickness there are signs of a still untried strength and powerfulness of the soul. *The same causes which bring about the diminution of man, force the stronger and rarer individuals upwards to greatness*" (XIV:91).

Decadence, for Nietzsche, is not simply a symptom of radical cultural changes; it is found in individuals as well as in cultures. "Not to be able to have done with an experience is already a sign of decadence. This tearing-open again of old wounds, this wallowing in self-contempt and contrition, is an additional sickness from which no 'salvation of the soul' but only a new form of its sickness can ever result"(XIV:190).

Reference has been made to Nihilism. But "what does Nihilism mean"? For Nietzsche it means *"that the highest values lose their value";* that "there is no goal"; that "there is no answer to the question: 'to what purpose?'" (XIV:8). *"Radical Nihilism* is [thus] the conviction that existence, as far as the highest values are concerned which one has acknowledged, is absolutely unjustifiable; this, together with the *insight* that we do not have the smallest right to assume a Beyond or an In-itselfness of things which might be 'divine' or be morality incarnate" (XIV:8).

The dilemma which here confronts us, Nietzsche holds, has arisen because of the very *truthfulness* which is a consequence of our faith in morality; for, "in the end, this truthfulness turns against morality itself, discovers the *teleology* of the latter, and its *biased* point of view" (XIV:9). The conflict is now real—the conflict, namely, "of *not* valuing what we know, and of no longer being *allowed* to value that with which we would like to deceive ourselves" (XIV:9-10). "This antagonism results in a process of dissolution" (XIV:10). "The highest values in the service of which man was to live, especially when they disposed of him in a very severe and costly manner—these *social values* (for the purpose of *strengthening their power*) were built up above man as if they were God's commands, as 'Reality,' as 'true' world, as hope and as world *to come*. Now, when the lowly origin of these values becomes known, the whole universe seems to have lost its value, to have become 'meaningless' " (XIV:10). "We realize that we cannot reach the spheres in which we have placed our values—but, with this insight, that other sphere in which we live has *by no means* gained in value; on the contrary, we are *tired,* because we have lost the main incentive" (XIV:11).

"As a *psychological state,* Nihilism is [thus] bound to appear, *first,* when we have sought in everything which happens a 'meaning' which is not there; so that the seeker ultimately loses courage. Nilhism is in this case our becoming conscious of the prolonged *waste* of strength; it is the torture of the 'In vain,' the insecurity, the lack of an opportunity to recuperate in some way or to set one's mind at rest about something—the shame before oneself, as if one had *cheated* oneself too long" (XIV:12). "As a psychological state, Nihilism appears, in the *second* place, when one has assumed a *totality,* a *systematization,* or even an *organization* in and behind everything which happens, so that the soul, thirsting to admire and revere, revels in the idea of a higher form of sovereignty and of stewardship" (XIV:13).

But "Nihilism, as a psychological state, has yet a *third* and *final* form. Given the two *insights:* that Becoming aims at nothing, and that within all Becoming there prevails no great unity in which the individual might immerse himself as in an element of the highest value—there still remains the *subterfuge* of condemning this whole world of Becoming as an illusion, and of inventing a world, as the *true* world, which lies beyond it. But as soon as man realizes that this world has been fashioned only out of psychological needs and that he has no right whatsoever to do this, there comes into being the final form of Nihilism, which comprises the *disbelief in a metaphysical world* and forbids itself belief in a *true* world" (XIV:13-14).

What has happened in all these cases of Nihilism? "The feeling of *valuelessness* was achieved when it was understood that the total character of existence may not be interpreted by means of the concept 'Purpose,' or by means of the concept 'Unity,' or by means of the concept 'Truth' " (XIV:14). And Nietzsche draws the conclusion that *"belief in the categories of reason is the cause of Nihilism*—[that] we have measured the value of the world by means of categories *which pertain only to a purely fictitious world"* (XIV:15). More specifically, "All values by means of which we have hitherto tried to make the world valuable to us and, once the values proved inapplicable, have thereby *deprived it of value,*—all these values are, psychologically considered, results of certain perspectives of utility for the preservation and enhancement of human forms of dominance, and are only falsely *projected* into the nature of things. It still is the *hyperbolic* naïveté of man to posit himself as the meaning and value standard of all things" (XIV:15). "The most extreme form of Nihilism would [therefore] be the insight that *all* belief . . . is necessarily false because a *real* world does not exist at all: only a *perspective illusion,* whose origin lies within us" (XIV:16).

In Nietzsche's view it is "the most general sign of modern times" that, "in his own eyes, man has lost unbelievably much in *dignity.* For a long time he was the center and the tragic hero of existence in general; then he endeavored at least to demonstrate his kinship with the decisive and in itself valuable part of existence—as all metaphysicians do, who wish to retain the *dignity of man,* in their belief that the moral values are cardinal virtues. He who has let God go, clings all the more strongly to the belief in morality" (XIV:19). Modern man—this is Nietzsche's argument—"believes that he can get along with a moral doctrine which has no religious background; but with this belief the road to Nihilism has become inevitable" (XIV:19).

Nihilism, however, is itself ambiguous, Nietzsche finds it necessary to distinguish between "Nihilism as a sign of *enhanced power of the spirit: active* Nihilism"; and "Nihilism as *decline* and *retrogression of the power of the spirit: passive Nihilism"* (XIV:21). Nietzsche himself accepts *"active* Nihilism" as the deliberate procedure requisite to the transvaluation of values he hopes to achieve.

## XIII

One last idea which is central to Nietzsche's doctrine must be considered. It is the idea of *"eternal recurrence."* "Not only man [Nietzsche says] but Superman will recur eternally!" (XVI:279).

Nietzsche confesses that this is "the most *oppressive* thought," and that the only means of enduring it at all is "the transvaluation of all values" (XV:424). He maintains, however, that in this idea "the two extremes of thought—the materialistic and the Platonic—are reconciled" (XV:425), and that, for this reason, it marks "The turning point of history" (XVI:267). It is "the highest formula of saying Yes! to life which can ever be attained" (XVII:96).

The moment of conception of this idea (in August 1881) was for Nietzsche himself a tremendous emotional experience. It was conceived, he tells us, "six thousand feet beyond man and time" (XVII:96); and the moment of its conception is "immortal." "For the sake of that moment alone [Nietzsche adds] I will endure recurrence" (XVI:274).

In Nietzsche's mind several lines of reasoning converge and crystallize in the idea of "eternal recurrence." There is, first, the argument based on general considerations of the nature of the universe. "If the universe had a goal," Nietzsche maintains, "that goal would have been reached by now. If any sort of unforeseen final state existed, that state also would have been reached" (XV:425). Nietzsche, therefore, denies a "final purpose" of the world (XIV:49). At any given moment, "the absolute conditions of a new distribution of all forces are present," and change and time are of the "essence" of the world (XV:427-428).

The principle of the conservation of energy, Nietzsche holds, "inevitably involves eternal recurrence" (XV:427); for if that principle is true, then the universe is "nothing which grows into existence and which passes out of existence" (XV:428). It simply "exists." And "we need not concern ourselves for one instant with the hypothesis of a *created* world" (XV:428). But "if the universe can be conceived as a definite quantity of energy, as a definite number of centers of energy—and every other concept remains indefinite and therefore useless—it follows that the universe must go through a calculable number of combinations in the great game of chance which constitutes its existence. In infinity, at some moment or other, every possible combination must have once been realized; not only this, but it must have been realized an infinite number of times. And inasmuch as between every one of these combinations and its next recurrence every other possible combination would necessarily have been undergone, and since every one of these combinations would determine the whole series in the same order, a circular movement of absolutely identical series is thus demonstrated: the universe is thus shown to be a circular movement which has already repeated itself an infinite number of times, and which plays its game for all eternity" (XV:430; XVI:237-243).

However, this universe with its eternal recurrence of events is not merely matter in motion. On the contrary, it is "a sea of forces storming and raging in itself, for ever changing, for ever rolling back over incalculable ages to recurrence, with an ebb and flow of its forms . . . ; producing the most ardent, most savage, and most contradictory things out of the quietest, most rigid, and most frozen material, and then returning from multifariousness to uniformity, from the play of contradictions back into the delight of consonance, saying Yes! unto itself, even in this homogeneity of its courses and ages; for ever blessing itself as something which recurs for all eternity—a becoming which knows no satiety, or disgust, or weariness:—this, my Dionysian world of eternal self-creation, of eternal self-destruction, this mysterious world of twofold voluptuousness; this, my 'Beyond Good and Evil,' without aim, unless there is an aim in the bliss of the circle, without will, unless a ring must by nature keep good will to itself . . . *this world is the Will to Power—and nothing else!*" (XV:431-432).

As Nietzsche sees it, his doctrine of "eternal recurrence" is the only alternative to "theism," to faith in an "arbitrary God"

(XVI:244). But we must not ascribe any "aspiration" or "goal" to this "circular process" which, being "beyond rationality" (XVI:247), is "simply an irrational necessity, absolutely free from any formal ethical or aesthetic significance" (XVI:248). The universe does not aim at "becoming more beautiful, more perfect, more complicated." Such ideas merely betray the "anthropomorphism" of human interpretations (XVI:248). And yet, for Nietzsche, the idea of "eternal recurrence" has profound moral significance, because from it he derives his basic imperative: "Live so that you may desire to live again!" (XVI:251). Let us always act remembering that "eternity is at stake" (XVI:251). "Let us stamp the impress of eternity upon our lives! This thought," Nietzsche adds, "contains more than all the religions which have taught us to condemn this life as something ephemeral, which have admonished us to squint upwards to another and indefinite existence" (XVI:254). "We must live so that we would fain live again and live for ever so, to all eternity!" (XVI:254). And if we accept this imperative, then, Nietzsche holds, "our duty is present with us every instant" (XVI:254).

This doctrine of the "eternal recurrence," Nietzsche maintains, imposes upon man the "heaviest burden." As he puts it: "What if a demon crept after you into your loneliest loneliness some day or night, and said to you: 'This life, as you live it at present, and have lived it, you must live it once more, and also innumerable times; and there will be nothing new in it, but every pain and every joy and every thought and every sigh, and all the unspeakably small and great in your life must come to you again and all in the same series and sequence—and similarly this spider and this moonlight among the trees, and similarly this moment, and I myself. The eternal sandglass of existence will ever be turned once more, and you with it, you speck of dust!'— Would you not throw yourself down and gnash your teeth, and curse the demon that so speaks? Or have you once experienced a tremendous moment in which you would answer him: 'You are a God, and never did I hear anything so divine!' If that thought acquired power over you as you are, it would transform you, and perhaps crush you; the question with regard to all and everything: 'Do you want this once more, and also for innumerable times?' would lie as the heaviest burden upon your activity! Or, how would you have to become favorably inclined to yourself and to life, so as *to long for nothing more ardently* than for this last eternal sanctioning and sealing?" (X:270-271). The idea of "eternal recurrence" is thus, for Nietzsche, "the ideal of the most world-approving, exuberant and vivacious man"—of the man, that is, "who has not only learned to compromise and arrange with that which was and is, but wishes to love it again *as it was and is,* for all eternity, insatiably calling out, *da capo,* not only to himself, but to the whole piece and play; and not only to the play, but actually to him who requires the play—and makes it necessary; because he always requires himself anew—and makes himself necessary" (XII:74).

In its "worst form" this idea of "eternal recurrence" means: "existence, as it is, without either a purpose or a goal, but inevitably recurring, without an end in nonentity"; and this, Nietzsche holds, is "the extremest form of Nihilism: nothing (purposelessness) eternal!" (XIV:48). "Everything goes, everything returns; eternally rolls the wheel of existence. Everything dies, everything blossoms forth again; eternally runs on the year of existence. Everything breaks, everything is integrated anew; eternally builds itself the same house of existence. All things separate, all things again greet one another; eternally true to itself remains the ring of existence. Every moment begins existence, around every 'Here' rolls the ball 'There.' The middle is everywhere. Crooked is the path of eternity" (XI:266). "All things eternally return, and ourselves with them. . . . We have already existed times without number, and all things with us. . . . Souls are as mortal as bodies. But the complexus of causes in which I am intertwined returns—it will again create me! I myself pertain to the causes of eternal return. I come again with this sun, with this earth, with this eagle, with this serpent—*not* to a new life, or a better life, or a similar life:—I come eternally to this identical and selfsame life, in its greatest and smallest" (XI:269-270). And in this thought of "eternal recurrence" Nietzsche rejoices: *"I love you, O Eternity!"* (XI:283); and he finds in it the greatest affirmation of Life. "Joy does not want heirs, it does not want children—joy wants itself, it wants eternity, it wants recurrence, it wants everything eternally-like-itself" (XI:395-396). "All joy wants the eternity of all things. . . . It wants love, it wants hate, it is over-rich, it bestows, it throws away. . . . So rich is joy that it thirsts for woe, for hell, for hate, for shame, for the lame, for the *world*—for this world. . . . Joys want the eternity of *all* things; they want *deep, profound eternity!*" (XI:396-397). And on this note Nietzsche ends his doctrine:

"Sing now yourselves the song, the name of which is 'Once more,' the significance of which is 'Unto all eternity!'—sing, you higher men, Zarathustra's roundelay!

O man! Take heed!
What says deep midnight's voice indeed?
I sleep my sleep—
From deepest dream I've woke, and plead:—
The world is deep,
And deeper than the day could read.
Deep is its woe—
Joy—deeper still than grief can be:
Woe says: Hence! Go!
But joys all want eternity—
Want deep, profound eternity!" (XI:397-398; 279).

## XIV

I have devoted so much space to an exposition of Nietzsche's philosophy that the question may well be raised, Was all this necessary? My justification is, not that Nietzsche's philosophy is in itself unchallengeable or, at least, right in all essentials. I quite agree that, at times, the strident tones and gross exaggerations of Nietzsche's "arguments" (if that is what one wishes to call his aphorismic assertions) are offensive rather than convincing. Nor do I mean to minimize the contradictions and distortions which any tyro in philosophy can readily find in Nietzsche's writings. And yet, it remains true that Nietzsche's philosophical intent has hitherto been largely misunderstood; that his conception of "Superman," in particular, has been falsified;

and that his whole approach to values and matters of morality has been placed into perspectives which, like distorting mirrors, have warped even his noblest ideas. Few philosophers in the past have suffered as much as has Nietzsche from his would-be followers who made a travesty of his doctrine and lacked the sensitivity and perceptiveness requisite to seeing his genuine contributions to the problem of morals. If, in a measure, I have succeeded in setting the record straight, the lengthy exposition is already justified.

However, there is more to be said.

Nietzsche, properly understood, is still the radical challenge to any complacency in moral matters. His extreme views require an answer—and now, in our times of positivism, emotivism, and persuasive definitions, more than ever; for how would the emotivists and the hedonists answer Nietzsche? To set dogma against dogma is hardly sufficient. And Nietzsche has already branded them "nihilists" and has pointed up the necessity of a positive reconstruction of morals.

Moreover, in the philosophies of Max Scheler and Nicolai Hartmann (which we shall discuss in the next chapter) some of Nietzsche's positive contributions to ethics have brought forth admirable fruit. When Sartre speaks of "authentic existence" and of the fact that existentialism dares to draw the conclusion from two premises: (a) there is no God, and (b) there is no determinate human nature, he but echoes in his own way the two premises basic to Nietzsche's philosophy. And are not the characters in Sartre's play, No Exit, but living in their own morbid ways Nietzsche's "eternal recurrence"—without the joy and exultation, however, that comes from creative living?

That much of our modern understanding of man's unconscious motivations owes its inception to Nietzsche's psychological insights need be mentioned only in passing.

When we put all of these facts together, we discover that Nietzsche marks a turning-point in moral philosophy—a turning-point and a challenge which we neglect only to our own disadvantage. Sooner or later, in one way or another, we must come to terms with, and must surpass, Nietzsche. This is the ultimate justification of the detailed exposition which I have given here. Let us not again see Nietzsche's ideal of "Superman" —this ideal which towers high above even the "highest men" as man himself towers above the primates, this ideal of a radically new being in the sense of S. S. Alexander's "deity"—let us not again see this ideal through the "squint-eyes" of the champions of some "swastika," and let us not again misunderstand so grossly Nietzsche's intention.

Yet, Nietzsche's raptures at his conception of the "eternal recurrence," his *amor fati* strike us as perversions rather than exultations of human existence. To say "Yea" to everything, as Nietzsche bids us to do, implies that we say Yea to murder and rape and the distortions of human sensibilities. It means that the slave wants his master, the sick his illness, the dying man his own death. And this in itself is a perversion of the value scale, and a contradiction of the very urge to an abundant life which culminates in a new species of being—the creative, responsible, self-forming and self-determining being which, at his ideal best, is Superman: a new creature, far beyond present man; a "mutant," but a gigantic step forward to a new mode of existence and of moral and intellectual responsibility. This is the transvaluation of values which Nietzsche so ardently desired.

## REFERENCES

1. Bertram, E., *Nietzsche: Versuch einer Mythologie,* Berlin, 1918.
2. Ewald, O., *Nietzsches Lehre in ihren Grundbegriffen: Die ewige Wiederkunft des Gleichen und der Sinn des Uebermenschen,* Berlin, 1903.
3. Förster-Nietzsche, Elisabeth, *Das Leben Friedrich Nietzsches:*
     I. *Der junge Nietzsche,* Leipzig, 1912.
     II. *Der einsame Nietzsche,* Leipzig, 1914.
4. Hildebrandt, K., *Gesundheit und Krankheit in Nietzsches Leben und Werk,* Berlin, 1926.
5. Jaspers, K., *Nietzsche: Einführung in das Verständnis seines Philosophierens,* Berlin, 1936.
6. Kaufmann, W., *Nietzsche: Philosopher, Psychologist, Antichrist,* Princeton, 1950.
7. Klages, L., *Die psychologischen Errungenschaften Nietzsches,* Leipzig, 1926.
8. Simmel, G., *Schopenhauer und Nietzsche,* Leipzig, 1907.
9. Vaihinger, H., *Nietzsche als Philosoph,* Berlin, 1902.

# Moore, Scheler, Hartmann and
# the Conception of the Good

The three thinkers here brought together represent a school of
thought which holds that, in its crucial meaning, "good," or
"value," is indefinable; that, nevertheless, the word denotes something accessible to intuitive inspection; and that the *ought* is essentially entailed by the good. No matter how much Moore, Scheler
and Hartmann may differ in other respects, all three adhere to this
basic creed. The fact that, in the end, Moore's views terminate in
"language analysis" whereas Hartmann's culminate in a Platonic
realism of value essences does not eliminate the common elements in their (and Max Scheler's) respective positions; it merely
underscores the need for further study and a more detailed comparison of their theories.

I

We begin our study with the views of G. E. Moore.

Professor Frankena expressed but a generally held opinion
when, in 1942, he wrote: "The impact of Moore's thought on
twentieth-century moral philosophy has been a powerful one. . . .
Possibly no other living moralist has had so great an influence"

(8:110). And W. David Ross stated, in 1930, that Moore's theory is "the culmination of all the attempts to base rightness on productivity of some sort of result."[1] In Johnson's opinion, Moore's position is the strongest statement of an "*ideal* ultilitarianism"; and it is against this position that "much of the deontologists' critique of axiological ethics is directed."[2] Let it be understood, however, from the very beginning that Moore "did not follow the lines marked out by modern idealism" (29:387); that, in fact, he dismisses idealism rather summarily (18:110-140); and that he has no love for metaphysics.

To the question, What is Ethics?, Moore replies that it is "the whole truth" about that which is at the same time common and peculiar to all judgments involving such terms as "virtue," "vice," "duty," "right," "ought," "good," and "bad" (18:1). Of these "common" and "peculiar" terms, he selects "good" for further analysis, taking it, in a sense, as representative of all others.

But now the question is, What is good? And this question may have at least three different meanings. It may mean, first, What particular things are good? It may mean, secondly, What sort of things are good? And it may mean, lastly, How is "good" to be defined?

The first of these meanings is not a question of ethics; for "it is not the business of the ethical philosopher to give personal advice or exhortation" (18:3). The second meaning is of the type, Is pleasure good? Are books good? And here Moore agrees with philosophical tradition in holding that answers to such questions "do indeed belong to Ethics" (18:3-4; 27; 77; 118). Indeed, in *Principia Ethica* he discusses and evaluates a number of the traditional answers. His own interest, however, centers in the third meaning of the question—in the question, that is, How is "good" to be defined?; for this is "the most fundamental question in all Ethics" (18:5; 223; 19:8; 10).

Moore is explicit in stating, however, that his "business" is not with the proper use of the word "good," "as established by custom"; it is "solely with that object or idea, which I hold,

---

[1] Ross, W. D., *The Right and the Good,* Oxford, 1930, 16.
[2] Johnson, Oliver A., *Rightness and Goodness,* The Hague, 1959, 2.

rightly or wrongly, that the word is generally used to stand for" (*18*:6). "The direct object of Ethics is knowledge and not practice" (*18*:20; 63); but knowledge includes not only a direct apprehension, it also includes "valid reasons" (*18*:20).

Although "good" is the key term for Moore, the meaning of this term is ambiguous (*19*:69-75; 161; 250). Even in *Principia Ethica* Moore distinguished between "good in itself" or the "intrinsically good," and "good as a means" (*18*:171), and he distinguished both from "my own good" or "good for me" (*18*: 97-98; *20a*:611). However, in 1903 Moore did not yet distinguish between "intrinsic good" and "ultimate good." In 1912, on the other hand, he specifically refused to "take '*ultimately* good' or 'good *for its own sake*' to be synonyms for 'intrinsically good' " (*19*:74). What the "ultimately good" and the "intrinsically good" have in common is that "both of them will apply to things whose existence *would* be good, even if they existed quite alone" (*19*:75). What distinguishes them is the fact that "a whole which is 'intrinsically good' may contain parts which are *not* intrinsically good . . . ; anything which is 'ultimately good' or 'good for its own sake' can contain no such parts" (*19*:75).

The most important distinction for Moore's views is that between "good in itself" and "good as a means" (*18*:23-24). "The arguments brought forward in ethical discussion," he points out, "have always been of both classes": those that would prove a specific conduct to be "good in itself," and those that would prove it to be "good as a means" (*18*:24). In the case of actions which are "good as means" only the "balance of good" in the world must be "greater than if any other possible action had been performed" (*18*:22-23). But in the case of the "intrinsically good," the action must be good in itself and without reference to effects. It is the "intrinsically good" which has always been of concern to Moore (*20a*:554; *19*:69-73), his central thesis being that the "intrinsically good" cannot be defined.

Reacting to Stevenson's analysis of some of his arguments (*26*), Moore is "inclined" to accept the "emotive" interpretation and he is "inclined" not to accept it (*20a*:554). In the end, however, he does not accept it (*20a*:554). In fact, the "attitude" theories seem to have confirmed Moore in his conviction that "good" is indefinable (*19*:90ff). To be sure, Moore admits that, "whenever any man judges an action to be right [or good], he always . . . *has* a certain feeling towards it, and even that he makes the judgment only *because* he has that feeling." But this "only proves" that *"what* he is judging is not merely *that* he has the feeling" (*19*:103). The "good" transcends the "attitude" (*19*:90-125; *20a*:535-554).

However, even though it is indefinable (*18*:17), the term "good" denotes *something*. It is cognitive in significance. And what it refers to is "a simple, indefinable, unanalyzable object of thought" (*18*:21). The nature of this "object" can be apprehended only by inspection of our own experience. We must "attentively consider what is actually before [our] mind"; and if we try this "experiment" "with each suggested definition," we may become "expert enough" to recognize that in every case we have before our mind "a unique object" (*18*:16). Moore thus stands committed to a form of intuitionism which is also characteristic of the views of Scheler and Hartmann.

But let us examine Moore's position in greater detail.

To begin with, Moore holds that a definition "states what are the parts which invariably compose a certain whole" (*18*:9); and if this is what is meant by a definition, then "good" cannot be defined "because it is simple and has no parts" (*18*:9). If now the attempt is made to define "good" in terms of an identity with some other notion, then the result is what Moore calls the "naturalistic fallacy." The fallacy lies in *the identification of any two notions which are distinct* (*18*:10; 38; 61; 173). The name, "naturalistic fallacy," is therefore somewhat misleading; for the fallacy is committed even if "good" is identified with some other non-natural notion (*18*:39; 114). There is, however, a narrower sense in which the fallacy means the confusion of "good," "which is not . . . a natural object," "with any natural object whatever" (*18*:13); and in this sense it may well mean a confusion of an "ought" with an "is" (*18*:14).

All intuitionists would heartily agree with Moore on these points; for all of them hold that we just *see* that ethical propositions cannot be identified with propositions concerning "natural properties," whether simple or complex. But as to the distinction between "natural" and "non-natural" properties Moore is, unfortunately, rather vague (*18*:40-41). We are told that each natural property of a natural object could exist by itself in time, whereas non-natural properties cannot so exist. But if we accept this statement at face value, then we can hardly regard "yellow" or "square" as "natural" properties, for, surely, neither "yellow" nor "square" exists by itself in time. Indeed, in the sense of "natural" and "non-natural" here suggested, *no* properties at all can possibly be regarded as "natural" (*3*:59). Moore's distinction between "natural" and "non-natural" is, therefore, meaningless.

But let us return to Moore's thesis. He specifically tells us that "whether good is defined as yellow or green or blue, as loud or soft, as round or square, as sweet or bitter, as productive of life or productive of pleasure, as willed or desired or felt, whichever of these or of any other object in the world, good may be held to *mean,* the theory, which holds it to *mean* them, will be a naturalistic theory" (*18*:40). Every naturalistic theory, however, necessarily rests upon or involves the "naturalistic fallacy" (*18*:47-49; 59-61; 73) and must, therefore, be repudiated (*18*:chpt. III). At best they provide different *criteria* for calling certain things good. "Good" as such, however, is intuited, not defined.

"If I am asked," Moore states, " 'What is good?' my answer is that good is good, and that is the end of the matter. Or if I am asked 'How is good to be defined?' my answer is that it cannot be defined and that is all I have to say about it" (*18*: 6; 9). And he adds: "My point is that 'good' is a simple notion, just as 'yellow' is a simple notion; that, just as you cannot, by any manner of means, explain to any one who does not already know it, what yellow is, so you cannot explain what good is (*18*:7; 21; 41; 110-111; *20*:chpts. VIII; X).

Even though Moore is thus explicit and emphatic in maintaining that "good" is indefinable, he is equally explicit in asserting that it is quite possible to give an account of the "good."

In fact, a major part of his work in Ethics is devoted to giving us such an account. His starting-point is our self-revelatory experience of "good" as such. As he puts it: We must "become aware" of the "good," and must become aware also of the fact "that it is different from other notions" (*18*:17; 173-174). In this "inspective procedure" he is in full agreement with Scheler and Hartmann, although he never developed the detailed analyses which characterize the work of the two German philosophers.

Again, however, it is important to keep in mind the distinction between "good as means" and "good in itself" (*18*:21-23; 74; 90), and that it is only the latter, or the "intrinsic good," which involves us into difficulties and which now concerns us (*18*:xi; 2-3; 21; *20*:257).

Moore holds that when something is "intrinsically good" its goodness is completely independent of all relations to surrounding circumstances (*18*:187). The assertion, "X is good in itself or is intrinsically good," "cannot be reduced to any assertion about reality, and therefore must remain unaffected by any conclusion we may reach about the nature of reality" (*18*:114); it is synthetic, intuitive, incapable of proof or disproof and logically independent of all judgments of existence (*18*:viii-x; 7; 74-75; 118; 143-144; *19*:223-224; *20*:chpt. X). It is, in Scheler's and Hartmann's terminology, *a priori*.

However, in 1942, Moore conceded that to say "X is an intrinsically good world" is logically equivalent to saying that "it would be better that the world in question should exist than that there should be no world at all" (*20a*:555-557). But even in 1903 Moore admitted that "very many different things are good and evil in themselves" (*18*:ix-x; chpt. VI; *19*: chpt. VII), although the question, What kinds of things are intrinsically good?, has to be answered "intuitively," there being no way of proving "ultimate" answers (*18*:65; 74; 77; 143; 148).

Among the "immense variety" of things which are intrinsically good, Moore mentions "the pleasures of human intercourse and the enjoyment of beautiful objects," "courage," "compassion," and "appreciation of tragedy" (*18*:*passim*; *19*:237; 247-

250). Any questioning of, or objection to, such a list must, on Moore's theory, inevitably culminate in an appeal to "intuition." "Anything which is good as an end must be admitted to be good without proof" (*18*:65). There is and can be no proof of ultimates.

But what sense can the term "ultimately good" have that is irreducible and undefinable? If the term is meant to denote a simple quality which all the "intrinsically good" things have in common, then that quality must be of a kind which neither an inspection of sense objects nor an introspection of personal experience reveals. A thing "could be completely described without its goodness being mentioned" (*3*:60). It is at this point, as we shall see later, that Nicolai Hartmann takes refuge in a Platonic realm of value essences. Moore, however, does not take this step. But neither does he take that other step which would lead to an interpretation of "good" as an evaluative rather than a descriptive term, and thus to a theory which sharply distinguishes between description and evaluation, interpreting the latter as a specifically definable act.

As far as Moore is concerned, "good" is just "good"—and "that's the end of it"; no further account of it can be given. But precisely this claim—the claim, namely, that no further account of "good" can be given—is open to challenge. Moore himself gives us no reason why certain things are "good in themselves" and others are not, and there is nothing in his whole doctrine to indicate how we could possibly come to know "things in themselves," be they "good" or "bad." We—the subjects of our experience—are always already present whenever there is knowledge of the world and of things; and since this is the case, just what does it mean to say that something is "good" or "beautiful" *in itself?* "Good" and "beautiful," let us remember, are, according to Moore, not descriptive properties. Hartmann's Platonism, hypostatizing as it does a self-existent "realm of values," shows a way out of the difficulty; but Moore is not ready to take so drastic a step. Neither, however, is Moore willing to accept a more empirical approach and to regard "good" and "beautiful" as terms of evaluation.

To be sure, in his contribution to the symposium, "Is Goodness a Quality?," [3] Moore equates the expression "intrinsically good" with "worth having for its own sake" (*ibid.* 122-125), implying that only something experienced in a certain manner can be "intrinsically good." But this interpretation, since it introduces a basic complexity into the meaning of "good," contradicts his earlier contention that "good" denotes something simple and unanalyzable, and Moore repudiates the idea. His whole argumentation shows, however, that Moore was and remained troubled by the meaning of the term "good."

Moreover, he specifically distinguished between "good" (which is indefinable) and "good things" (*18*:viii; ix), regarding the latter as definable. But what Moore here means by "definition" is obviously an enumeration of instances (*13*:430), not a conceptualist definition; and the meaning of "good" is and remains an abstraction from those instances. Thus, aesthetic enjoyment is "good," personal affection is "good," pleasant feelings are "good"; but "good" is "good." And what might that mean separated from, and independent of, awareness? We have no access to a "good in itself," isolated from experience, only to ends and goals which we value because of their relation to us or to some other experiencing subject.

One problem remains: the problem, namely, of moral obligation. We get a glimpse of Moore's solution of this problem in his assertions (a) that "every judgment in practical Ethics may be reduced to the form: This is a cause of that good thing" (*18*:146); (b) that the "business" of Ethics is finished "when it has completed the list of things which ought to exist, whether they do exist or not" (*18*:119); and (c) that our "duty" is "that action which will cause more good to exist in the Universe than any possible alternative" (*18*:148). It is clear, therefore, that, in Moore's theory, "good" is the primary concept, the "basic category." "Duty" or the "ought" is derivative only. In this fact may be seen Moore's "ideal Utilitarianism."

However, a fuller discussion of Moore's position must take

---

[3] *Aristotelian Society, Supplementary Volume* 11 (1932), 116-31.

cognizance of the fact that, for Moore, "right," "duty," "ought," and "virtue" are closely interrelated; that they are essentially connected with "good as means" (*18*:180); and that "all moral laws . . . are merely statements that certain kinds of actions will have good effects" (*18*:146; 172; *19*:250-252). The "best ideal" which we can construct is "that state of things which contains the greatest number of things having positive value, and which contains nothing evil or indifferent" (*18*:185). But, our world being what it is, this "ideal" state is ideal indeed, and not actual. Still, through our actions we can, and ought to, contribute to the total "good" of our world. In fact, so Moore holds, we are "morally bound" to perform that action which will "produce the greatest possible amount of good in the Universe" (*18*:147; 23-27; *19*:chpts. I; II). "Our 'duty' is merely that which will be a means to the best possible" (*18*:167); and, in this sense, "duty" and the "expedient" are one and the same (*18*:167), and both are identical with the "useful" (*18*:147; 167). We cannot distinguish "duty" and the "expedient" by saying that "the former is something which we ought to do, whereas of the latter we cannot say we 'ought'" (*18*:167). "Whatever is expedient is always *also* a duty, and whatever is a duty is always *also* expedient" (*19*:172). "The only fundamental distinction is between what is good in itself, and what is good as a means" (*18*:168). The question, What ought we to do?, being concerned with means only, must therefore be carefully distinguished from the question, What kinds of things are intrinsically good? (*18*:24-6), although it is the answer to the latter question which inevitably determines what our "duty" is or what we "ought to do." The "intrinsically good," therefore, since it is the end for the sake of which means are employed, is the ultimate norm of all our actions.

Let us note, finally, that "virtues," according to Moore, are "habitual dispositions to perform actions which are duties, or which would be duties if a volition were sufficient on the part of most men to ensure their performance" (*18*:172). "In order to decide whether any particular disposition or action is a virtue or a duty . . . we must be able to prove that the disposition or action in question is generally better as a means than any alternatives possible or likely to occur" (*18*:172-173). Again the reference to the "intrinsically good" as ultimate norm is clear. But now certain difficulties arise. There is, first, the peculiar relationship of "duty" and "expediency." To be sure, Moore maintains that he does not mean to *identify* "duty" and "expediency," holding, rather, that the two *"coincide"* (*19*:172). But even such "coincidence"—that an action which is "expedient" is also our duty—rests either upon a purely verbal stipulation and is of no significance for Ethics; or it entails a conception of "duty" which lacks all the moral fiber usually associated with it. Here, I believe, Kant and the deontologists, making a sharp distinction between "duty" and the merely "expedient," have been more faithful to the facts of moral experience than was Moore. After all, "duty" and the "expedient" may at times be in radical conflict; and when this is the case, doing what is "expedient" entails the violation of a "duty" and, far from being "good," is morally reprehensible.

A second consideration, however, is more crucial for an ultimate evaluation of Moore's position, for it concerns his conception of the basic norm. It is evident from Moore's arguments that he regards the "intrinsically good" as something which *ought to exist*. In fact, he specifically equates the meaning of "intrinsically good" with "ought to exist" (*18*:17). However, as Paton has pointed out (*22*:115), such an identification is unwarranted within the framework of Moore's philosophy because, for Moore, "good" is simple, whereas "ought to exist" is clearly a complex notion. Moreover, as Frankena has shown (*8*:99), "intrinsic goodness can have a normative character . . . only if it essentially or analytically involves a reference to an agent on whom something is actually or hypothetically enjoined" (*8*:99). But, again, if "good" is simple, it cannot have this relation to an agent, for the relation is obviously complex. It would seem, then, that Moore's conception of the "good" as simple, unanalyzable, and undefinable is irreconcilable with his ideas of "good" as normative, no matter how understood.

In the third place, Moore specifically tells us that "duty"

"can only be defined as that action, which will cause more good to exist in the Universe than any possible alternative" (*18*:148). "Dutiful" actions are, thus, "good-producing" actions, and the statements "This action is my duty" and "This action, when done by me, is good-producing" are asserting the same thing. But if this were true, the question "Why is this my duty?" could never be answered by "Because it is good-producing," for, strictly speaking, such an answer would be equivalent to "Because it is my duty" and, thus, to an empty tautology. Now, either we accept this tautology—in which case our theory is completely sterile; or we define "duty" in some other way and regard "good-producing" as reason or ground for assuming or acknowledging a duty—in which case we have repudiated Moore's theory. But it is this latter alternative which alone holds promise for the future.

In 1942, Moore himself accepted the view "that the fact that an action, which I could do, would produce *some* intrinsically good thing is always some reason (though far from a conclusive one) in favor of the hypothesis that I ought to do that action" (*20a*:565). But if "the fact that a state of affairs would be intrinsically good is 'always and necessarily' *some* reason [although 'only a very weak reason indeed'] in favor of the hypothesis that an action which would produce that state of affairs ought to be done" (*20a*:565), then the "ought" finds no decisive support in the conception of the "intrinsically good" and must therefore be justified on other grounds. Moore does not provide such justification. Nicolai Hartmann attempts one in metaphysical terms; but, in a sense, the bridge between Moore and Hartmann is the "material value ethics" of Scheler, and to this we turn next.

## II

"In England, Moore has presented an interpretation of the problem of value which in many respects is similar" to my own (*25*: 13). In these words Max Scheler himself points up the similarity of his views and those of G. E. Moore. It is, therefore, not amiss to discuss Scheler's "material value ethics" along with Moore's conception of "good" as an irreducible quality. But we shall discover almost at once an immensely more varied and a more detailed interpretation of our value experience than Moore ever attempted.

Two aspects characterize Scheler's work: (a) Scheler was the first to apply Husserl's phenomenological method to the sphere of values, and (b) he stressed the interrelations of values and the *ought,* founding the *ought* upon values. Our discussion will stress both aspects. This means, however, that, prior to a discussion of the relation of the *ought* to its "founding" values, we must consider not only the role which "value-feelings" play in Scheler's philosophy, but also the "essence" and the "order of rank" of values. Only after we are clear on these points can we fully understand how the *ought* can have its "ground" in values.

We turn, first, to the problem of "value-feelings."

It is Scheler's contention that values are "ideal objects"—like color and tone qualities—and that they belong to an absolute and invariable "value realm." They are "given to us in feeling" (*25*:57). We must be sure, however, that we do not misunderstand the term "feeling." Scheler himself is meticulous in distinguishing between *"Gefühl"* and *"Fühlen."* The former pertains to an essentially physiological state of affairs; the latter, however, has "intentional" or cognitive significance. It is a form of knowing distinct from, and supplementary to, sensation and reason. Instead of being a "felt state" (such as being tired, being nauseated, being elated), the "value feeling" is a specific kind of act in and through which values are "given." It is an "emotional act," to use Scheler's terminology, which is independent and nonderivative in character (*25*:267-269). That "value feeling" is not the same as a "feeling state" is especially clear whenever a "feeling state" itself is "felt" as a value or as a disvalue. "Value feeling," in other words, is always directional, intentional, cognitive, and is concerned with, or directed towards, something objective—values (*25*:271).

However, Scheler rejects the thesis that values exist only *as felt,* and he repudiates the idea that their content or quality as values consists in their being related to "feeling" (25:257; 259). It is his contention that values are as independent of feeling as colors are of seeing.[1] They, and their order of rank, are simply disclosed in "value feeling" as the colors of the rainbow are disclosed in sight, or the tonal sequences of a symphony are disclosed in hearing.

The comparison with colors of the rainbow and the tonal sequence of a symphony already suggests that in "value feeling" there is given not only each value as a simple quality but also an "order of rank" of "higher" and "lower" values. This "order of rank" which is immediately apprehended in the "act of preferring" is foundational and, therefore, essential to the "feeling of values" as such (25:109); for "preferring" is not a striving or willing; it is simply the act in which the "being higher" of a value is directly disclosed (25:108). But "value feeling" and "preferring" are, in the last analysis, a form of "loving"; and it is this "loving" as a cognitive act which is the ground of every value apriori (25:108). It is this "loving" which, roughly, corresponds to Pascal's *raison du coeur*.

Moreover, as here understood, love is the discoverer of values. "It does not follow our value feeling and preferring but moves ahead of them as their guide" (25:275). Love is "creative"— not of the value realm as such, however, but of what values an individual may "feel" and "prefer" (25:275). And we must take note of the fact that for every person the "orientation of loving or hating," of value preferences, is different; and it is different for the same person at different times. Each and every one of us has his own "attitudinal predisposition" *(Grundgesinnung)* which determines what we are capable of knowing and doing and which, therefore, determines also in a large measure "our" world, the world in which we "live," in which we "love" and "hate."

Values are "primary phenomena" *(Urphänomene)* which are "given" in our "value-feeling"; they are not susceptible to further explanation (25:267). They are "irreducible basic phenomena of an emotive intuition" (25:278) and cannot be further ana-

---

[1] This is Scheler's own example and is obviously valid only at the level of naïve realism.

lyzed. Scheler, therefore, repudiates all efforts to resolve values into relations—be it the relations of objects to objects, of objects to subjects, or of subjects to subjects (25:256). Only when we "bracket" every reality—in the fashion of Husserl's phenomenology—can the manifoldness, the full richness, of value qualities in the universe be adequately apprehended. As long as our orientation is restricted to the sphere of those values which are related to our desires or to real things, neither the mass nor the content of the absolute value sphere can be discerned. After all, values are "ideal objects" which constitute a self-existent, absolute, and invariable "value sphere"—or at least so Scheler maintains.

To be sure, things and situations have characteristics or "dispositions to values" which, in fact, make them suitable to be or to become "bearers of values." But this fact must not be confused with the erroneous assertion that the value of anything is itself nothing but a certain disposition or capacity (25:39-40). Moreover, the relation "to me" also is not a proper foundation of value; for only something which is a good "in itself" can also become a good "for me." But in so far as the relation to me of a thing which is good "in itself" is also "good," the goodness of the relation is in addition to the value of the thing itself. Lastly, to maintain that values have their "ground and being" in God as the highest person makes values relative to a supreme being and, therefore, distracts from the absoluteness of the values themselves. Scheler thus repudiates the view that "values do not have 'being' but are merely 'valid' " (25:202). Values, according to his theory, are ultimate and nonderivative "givens" of a certain kind.

However, values as such or by themselves cannot become "real" or "actual" in the world of things. The interrelations which connect them with things Scheler develops in his doctrine of "goods" (25:42-45). A good, he tells us, is "a 'thinglike' unity of value qualities" and "is related to value quality as the thing is related to those qualities which are its attributes" (25:43). As Scheler puts it, "thingness" is present in a good, but not the "thing." That is to say, in order that something be a good, it need not first be a thing. Being a good is itself a primary value fact. Indeed, in a good there is given such intimate relation to value that we can speak of a "value-thing" *(Wertding),* the unity of which is constituted by the value, and the essence of which is "saturated," as it were, with value.

In contrast to such "value-things" there exist also "thing-values" *(Dingwerte),* values, that is, which make a thing valuable but do not constitute it a good. In the case of "thing-values" the thing itself exists independently of any relation to value, and the value is only externally attached to the thing; it does not "found" its unity. "In their givenness," however, goods and things are "of equal ultimacy" (25:44). It is impossible to reduce the one to the other.

That Scheler's whole distinction makes sense only on the basis of his stipulation of an absolute and independently existing value realm need be noted only in passing; for it is obvious that without such prior stipulation the whole idea of a "value-thing" reduces to the idea of "valuable things" and is, therefore, amenable to an interpretation in terms of "things" and "ascribable values." But about this more will be said in another context.

Still, values as qualities require some subsisting mode of being —a "value-bearer" *(Wertträger)*—for their actualization; and in the relationship of value to "value-bearer" the interrelation of "value" and "being" becomes clear. Thus, by their very essence, and of necessity, ethical values have persons as their "bearers," and only derivatively also acts of will and actions. On the other hand, aesthetic values are values of objects; but they are values of only those objects whose reality is "suspended" and whose mode of being is that of "appearances." They are values, moreover, which belong to the objects only because the objects are "intuitive picturizations" (as distinguished from objects which are merely thought) (25:106). By virtue of their essence, the values of life *(Vitalwerte)* have only "living beings" as "bearers"; and, similarly, the sensuous values are essentially values of things and events.

Of special significance to us is, of course, the relation of "moral values" to their "bearers." Scheler maintains—and this must be especially noted—that "the value 'good' appears when we realize the higher positive value (which [in any concrete situation] is given in the experience of preference). It appears as attached to our act of will. For this very reason, however, this value can never itself be the content of our act of will. The value 'good' appears, as it were, 'upon the back' of the act and does so necessarily *(wesensnotwending)*. It can therefore never be intended in the act itself" (25:49). That is to say, we can never directly aim at the (morally) "good." But as we realize in any given situation the highest value possible in that situation our act is *good*. It is "bad" to the degree to which we fall short of the realization of the highest possible value.

Despite all relations to "value-bearers," however, the values themselves, according to Scheler, have a being all their own and are independent of their "bearers" (25:40). Scheler stipulates, in other words, that there exists an independent realm of values. But a difficulty arises, because such a realm can be known only from the perspective of a subject; and the human subject experiences values in varying perspectives and at different levels. It is significant, therefore, that even according to Scheler the value modalities of the "agreeable" and the "vital" depend, not upon pure intentional value-feeling, but upon organs of the body at the subpsychic level (25:117). Thus, Scheler explicitly makes the value modalities of the "agreeable" and the "vital" dependent upon and, therefore, relative to actual factors in experience. In the case of the modalities "agreeable-disagreeable," "the whole value sequence is 'relative' to the essence of a sensuous nature as such" (25:125). But a similar relativism with respect to bodily feelings pervades the "vital" values of "ascending" or "descending" vitality (25:127). As a consequence, the absoluteness of these two value modalities has in principle been abandoned, and it is only a matter of degree to make the value modalities in question relative to the bodily conditions of any given subject which experiences the values. This fact, however, affects Scheler's whole value theory; for either values are taken to be ideal objects—in which case it must be possible to apprehend all values in their absolute transcendence and regardless of their "modality" through a phenomenologico-intuitive act of "value-feeling"; or values must be interpreted as real qualities, as constituents of actual things—in which case their being is relative to real things and apprehensible only to subjects bodily experiencing those things. Scheler cannot have it both ways at the same time.

At least as far as the value modalities of the "agreeable" and the "vital" are concerned, Scheler himself has brought the values back into the sphere of bodily experience. Drives and interests, therefore, must be reconsidered in their relations to values and, thus, once more the door has been opened to naturalistic and relativistic theories of value—the very thing which Scheler hoped to make impossible. The absoluteness of values can be maintained only under two closely interrelated conditions: First, values must be "given" in experience in a manner which removes them from the flux of experience and its relativity (i.e., only a strictly phenomenological method might accomplish the goal); and, secondly, values must be apprehensible in an immediate and direct way. Scheler does not consistently observe the first of these conditions. His realistic faithfulness to the fact of experience surpasses his phenomenological intention, and his theory suffers from this inconsistency.

For the time being, however, let us brush aside further criticism and let us consider another aspect of Scheler's value theory which is essential to his ethics: the order of rank of values.

As independent phenomena values "are 'material' *(materiale)* qualities which have a certain order of 'high' and 'low' with respect to one another, and which have this order irrespective of their form or mode of being *(Seinsweise)* which they assume" (*25*:40). A theory of value, therefore, must investigate this "order of rank" and must provide criteria which enable us to place any given value in its appropriate position within that order. Scheler, unfortunately, gives us only a schematic outline of the order as he saw it. We must wait for Nicolai Hartmann (next section) to provide the details. Still, even in Scheler's theory certain features stand out clearly.

Actually Scheler recognizes two great scales of order: One

pertains to the height of values as determined by the nature of the "value-bearers"; the other is an order of pure value modalities, i.e., of the content of the values themselves (25:120).

As far as the order of values with respect to their "bearers" is concerned (25:120-125), Scheler holds that the highest level is that of the "values of the person." Included here are the values of the person as person, and the values of virtues. Below this level is that of the "values of things"; and here we find, in descending order, "spiritual values," the "biologically valuable," and "material goods."

In different perspective we find in this same realm "intrinsic values" *(Eigenwerte)* and "extrinsic values" *(Fremdwerte)*. But these two groups contain values of essentially "equal height." That is to say, we find intrinsic and extrinsic values at each of the previously mentioned levels.

The complexities of the value realm become still more apparent when Scheler finds it necessary to distinguish also, in decending order, between values of acts, values of functions, and values of reactions—all of which are below the values of the person proper.

Still another sequence is that of values of attitudes, values of actions, and values of success. Of these three groupings the first two belong to the sphere of moral values. Still other value distinctions which Scheler makes need not concern us here.

However, crucial to Scheler's whole position is the order of rank of value modalities (25:125-130). As he puts it: "The most important and most basic of all apriori relations exist . . . in the sense of an order of rank among the complexes of qualities of the 'material' *(materiale)* values, which we shall designate value modalities. They constitute the real 'material' *(materiale)* apriori of our insight into values and value preferences" (25:125).

Basic to this order of rank, according to Scheler, is an "intuitive value preference." But this immediately "given" foundation of a value scale is augmented by four derivative criteria: (a) Duration (the value which endures is higher than is a value which is transient) (25:110-113). (b) Extensionality and divisibility (the value which can be shared by many without being "fragmented" is higher than is a value which cannot be so shared) (25:113-114). (c) A value which is foundational to another value is lower than is the value for which it is the foundation (25:114-116). (d) The depth of the satisfaction achieved in the value experience (a value which gives but superficial satisfaction is lower than is one which profoundly satisfies us, (25:116-117). When these criteria are applied, so Scheler maintains, then an ascending scale of values of four distinct levels emerges.

1. There is the lowest level, constituted by the values of the senses. This is the level of the "agreeable" and the "disagreeable," and of their respective degrees and modifications. The entire series of these values is "relative" to the "sensuous nature in general" (25:125).

2. Next higher is the level of the values of vitality or life: The level of the "noble" and the "ignoble" or ordinary, including the feeling of an "ascending" or "descending" life, the feeling of "well-being" or of "sickness," of "being strong" or "being feeble," etc. (25:127).

3. The third level comprises the spiritual values, including the "beautiful" and the "ugly," and their modifications; but also the "right" and the "wrong" as basis of an objective order of law. And it includes the values of cognition and "truth" which underly all sciences and philosophy. It includes the cultural values: the values of "approval" and "disapproval," of "respect" and "contempt," and so on (25:128).

4. Lastly there is the level of the values of the holy: "Bliss" and "despair" (which are completely independent of happiness and unhappiness), "reverence," "worship," etc.—values, that is, which are apprehended only in love (25:129). However, the ultimate justification of the value of the "holy" Scheler finds in grounding the entire value realm in "an infinite personal spirit" (25:116), i.e., in God. And at this point his phenomenology turns into a metaphysic—a fact which we shall merely register at this time.

In analogy to the levels of value modalities Scheler recognizes a series of "value-persons" (Wertpersonen). He specifically mentions, in ascending order, the "artist of sensuality," the "leading spirit," the "hero," the "genius," and the "holy one" (25:129). These "universally valid pure types of value-persons" result from "a combination of the idea of the value-person as the highest value" (in contrast to the values of things and conditions), "with the order of rank of the modalities of values" (25:585-586). That is to say, the values characteristic of each level indicated above become the primary basis of the person and, thus, become constitutive of the unity of each separate type of person. But again the "realism" of Scheler asserts itself, and he maintains that, although the pure forms are discernible, in actual existence only mixtures of varying degrees of purity of the types occur. "St. Augustine is, thus, a mixture of holiness and heroness" (25:587, n. 1).

Still, the various types of value-defined persons play an important part in Scheler's ethics; for the highest moral sense of the world is "the possible existence of persons of the highest and most positive values" (25:573). Moreover, in view of his own ideal self-image, a person experiences an *ought*—"not merely as 'I am obliged to follow,' but as 'it obliges me to follow'" (25:579). Such followership under the pressure of an *ought* "is neither imitation nor obedience but, stemming from an attitude of devotion to the ideal, is a 'growing into' the person and into the disposition and the character of the ideal. . . . We become *as* the ideal is as a person, not *what* it is" (25:581).

One critical remark seems in order before we turn to a more detailed discussion of the problem of the *ought;* it is this: Love and hate, as the highest forms of man's "intentional-emotional life" *(unseres intentionalen emotionalen Lebens)* (25:274), are not directly concerned with an absolute ideal value realm but with actual goods and persons. That is to say, they are concerned with "givens" in the realm of actualities. Hence, what Scheler originally repudiated—our concern with goods as the starting-point of a value theory—becomes, in the end, his own approach to values; for love and hate concern themselves directly with specific value realizations, not with values in the abstract. But to the extent to which this is true, values are bound up with given cultural situations and it is impossible to apprehend value essences immediately and in their absoluteness. Values thus become dependent upon our apprehension and comprehension of *being;* and in the background lurk always man's drives and specific interests. Scheler is right, of course, in holding—against Kant—that man's drives are not simply chaotic (*25*:163; 87; 93); that they cannot be reduced to a single drive—such as the drive for self-preservation (*25*:177; 293-296); and that egoism is not a "primary tendency of life" (*25*:292). Man's drives and interests themselves are factually structuralized and are indicative of that "value cosmos" which is the *"valu milieu"* of any given individual no less than of the human species—a cosmos whose constituent, value-accented things affect man's drives in manifold and specific ways. This is true of all "spiritual acts" no less than of biologically conditioned acts. And Scheler admits as much (*25*:176-178). Scheler's absolute and independent value realm is, thus, a mere hypostatization. His genuine insights must be salvaged by placing them into a radically different framework. But there is no time to develop that framework here; I shall deal with it in another book.

We now return to the problem of the *ought* as Scheler sees it and as he attempts to solve it. It should be clear, however, that, for Scheler, his value theory is the basis for his interpretation of moral obligation, although he does not work out the problem with as much care and in as much detail as one might wish. Scheler himself regards his discussion as "preliminary" only. The really constructive effort along the lines indicated by Scheler was made by Nicolai Hartmann; and so we shall return to the problem in the next section. It is important, nevertheless, to get Scheler's own views clearly before us.

The "emotional apriori"—feeling, preferring, loving, hating, willing—has a "primary" value content which it derives neither from thought nor from sensation; but it is precisely this content which is foundational to the moral *ought* (*25*:83-86). The *logique du coeur* (*25*:269; 286-287) which Scheler here introduces rests upon the following specifically formulated axioms:

Ia. "The existence of a positive value is itself a positive value."
  b. "The nonexistence of a positive value is itself a negative value."
  c. "The existence of a negative value is itself a negative value."
  d. "The nonexistence of a negative value is itself a positive value" (25:48).
IIa. "In the sphere of volition, good is that value which adheres to the realization of a positive value."
  b. "In the sphere of volition, evil is that value which adheres to the realization of a negative value."
  c. "In the sphere of volition, good is the value which adheres to the realization of a higher (the highest) value."
  d. "In the sphere of volition, evil is that value which adheres to the realization of a lower (the lowest) value" (25:49).
III. "The criterion for 'good' (and for 'evil') consists in the agreement (in the conflict) of the value intended in the realization with the value to be preferred, or, respectively, in the conflict (the agreement) with the value not to be preferred" (25:49).

It is evident that these axioms are themselves of a purely formal nature and are "independent of all types of values and all value qualities (as well as of the idea of the 'value-bearer'), and are grounded in the nature of values *as values*" (25:102). Moreover, "good" and "evil" are clearly not primary values but "adhere" only to the realization or nonrealization, respectively, of values which *ought* or *ought not* to be realized. The value "content" to be realized is supplied by the facts of concrete situations and is specific to those situations. The axioms, however, provide Scheler with criteria for his interpretation of the *ought*—the *ought* pertaining to the "realization" of values in conformity with the axioms. "Whenever we say that something ought to be done or ought to be, we grasp a relation between a positive value and a possible bearer of this value: a thing, an event, etc." (25:200).

The objection that the *ought* cannot encompass contents which do not yet exist and which, for this reason, have as yet no value, Scheler brushes aside. It is his thesis that values are independent of empirically concrete "bearers" and that, therefore, we can "ascribe an actual value to a nonactual content"— as when, in anticipation, we ascribe a value to a fruit that has not yet ripened. Actually, "the *ought* is always founded," Scheler tells us, "upon a value which is being viewed as to its possible real existence" (25:200). But the *ought* here involved is only the "ideal *ought*." Opposed to it is that other *ought* "which, in addition, is viewed also in connection with a possible volition that will realize its content" (25:200). It is this latter *ought* which is "the *ought* of duty" and, therefore, the crux of moral obligation.

Let us consider, first, the "ideal *ought*" and its relation to values (25:218-225), for it will turn out that, according to Scheler, the *"ought* of duty" is dependent upon the "ideal *ought*" in so far as "every duty is always also an ideal *ought-to-be* of an act of volition" (25:218). That is to say, "wherever a concrete content of an ideal *ought* is given and is related to a striving, there a demand emanates from it"—a demand which, "through an inner knowing that one is 'obliged' or through an external act, such as a 'command,' . . . is somehow *made emphatic*" (25:218). However, the relation of this "ideal *ought*" to values is determined by two axioms: "Everything that is positively valuable ought to be; and everything that is negatively valuable ought not to be" (25:221). The relation of the *ought* to values is thus clearly marked as one-directional: "Every *ought* is founded upon values—whereas values are by no means founded upon an ideal *ought* (25:221). If this fact is combined with the axioms previously given as Ia, b, c, d; IIa, b, c, d; and III, and with the additional fact (as Scheler sees it) that, in principle, values are indifferent with respect to existence and nonexistence, then only in volition can values be effectively related to existence and nonexistence. It is the *ought* which takes the values out of their indifference to existence; and, in this sense, every *ought* is the *ought-to-be* (or *ought-not-to-be*) of something (25:221). This means, however, that wherever we say of something that it *ought* to be, the something, whatever it may be, is understood to be nonexistent (25:221).

But opposed to every *ought-to-be* is always an *ought-not-to-be* (25:223). The *ought-to-be* pertains to positive values, whereas the *ought-not-to-be* pertains to negative values. But the connection between the *ought-to-be* and the *ought-not-to-be* is such that the very meaning of every positive *ought* (such as: there ought to be justice in the world) necessarily entails a reference to a disvalue: the reference, namely, to the nonbeing of the positive value in question (25:223). Still, the relationship is such that, by itself, the *ought* can *never* disclose what the positive values are. The most it can accomplish is to imply that the positive value is the opposite of a certain negative value which *ought not to be.* "Every *ought,* therefore, (not only the *ought-not-to-be*) aims at the exclusion of certain disvalues; but it does not itself posit positive values" (25:223). There is no positive *ought* which is in itself necessary and inescapable; there is only a necessary *ought-not-to-be* of the opposites of positive values (25:224). Nevertheless, basic to every *ought* there is a positive value. But this value is not given in the *ought* itself; it is in each case disclosed in the "value feeling" (25:224). Only because we start with the idea of a *value* which is indifferent with respect to the sphere of existing things as well as with respect to the sphere of volition but which is the basis of every *ought,* can we overcome the destructive negativism which besets Kantian ethics (25:225).

What Scheler here intends is laudable. However, his suggested relationship of values and the "ideal *ought*" is at best but a step toward the solution of the prudential *ought.* It does not concern the essentially moral *ought,* the "*ought* of duty," at all. The question is, does Scheler's interpretation of the "normative *ought*" help us to a solution of the moral problem?

Scheler accepts Herbart's questionable contention that "*every* idea of duty can be traced back to an obligation established through a command" (25:225). What this means will become clear when we consider Scheler's further thesis that "every kind of imperative" presupposes "the positing of a value to which our striving is not related in primary intention" (25:226), and to which it must therefore be directed by a command—even if this command is only negative. As Scheler puts it, "basic to every imperative is an (ideal) *ought-not-to-be* of some striving" (25:226). Historically, therefore, "commandments" are, first of all, negative rather than positive. And if our ethics takes as its starting-point the idea of obligation, it must remain essentially negative and repressive (25:226). That Scheler is wrong here can readily be seen when we take as the basis for moral obligation commitments made on the basis of value considerations. Thus, when I have promised to meet you tomorrow, I am under the positive obligation to carry out my promise—even though I am at the same time under the obligation to negate desires on my part which, when permitted their course, would interfere with my keeping the promise.

As Scheler sees it, *all* imperatives (including the categorical imperative) are themselves justified only when, in the last analysis, they rest upon an "ideal *ought*" and, therefore, indirectly upon some value (25:227). The imperatives themselves must find justification (25:228). This implies, however, that, despite their acknowledgment of *the same value,* all imperatives may vary in the course of history or from culture to culture, for man's value comprehensions may vary (25:229). In extreme cases diametrically opposed imperatives may be grounded in the same value. Thus, if we accept the premise that, at a given level, "intrinsic value equals extrinsic value"—a premise which Scheler accepts—we may find, based upon this value premise, the imperative, "Love thy neighbor more than thyself," but also the quite different imperative, "Make something of yourself so that you can give to others out of the richness of your being" (25:229). Historically developed imperatives are therefore never a dependable clue to the real *ought* (25:230-231).

The situation, then, is this: all cases of an imperatival *ought*— that is, all cases of an *"ought* of duty"—presuppose on the part of the subject a striving to which is directed a command which finds its justification in an "ideal *ought*" (25:232). Every duty is, thus, immediately an obligation to do something—and to do something with respect to a certain person (25:232)—but it finds its ultimate justification in value considerations.

That Scheler has seen the complex interrelations of values and duties is evident from what has been said; that he has seen them clearly and correctly, however, may well be doubted. One of the difficulties inherent in his thesis is Scheler's commitment to

Herbart's erroneous thesis; for if obligations are established only "through a command," then (a) it is difficult to understand self-imposed duties, and (b) why is not the command itself sufficient to establish the duty? Perhaps the emotivists would assert that it is. However, moral obligation or the *"ought of duty"* is justifiable only in terms of value-determined personal commitments. Value considerations justify the commitment; but the *ought* is entailed by the commitment, not by the value considerations. We must see clearer here than did Scheler.[1]

## III

The ethics of Nicolai Hartmann is closely related to that of Max Scheler. In some respects it is but an extension, a systematization and a modification of Scheler's views. Still, there are new insights and new perspectives in Hartmann's theory, and these warrant special consideration.

Like Scheler, Hartmann insists that "there is a pure value a priori which, directly, intuitively, emotionally permeates our practical consciousness, our whole conception of life, and which lends to everything that falls within the range of our vision the mark either of value or of disvalue" (*10*:177).[2] There is, in other words, an *ordre du coeur,* a *logique du coeur,* "a cognition *sui generis*" (*10*:104), which is a cognitive "value-feeling that rejects and accepts, condemns and justifies" (*10*:100), and is "a genuine cognition of Being" (*10*:219). "Wherever anyone has a real value consciousness, this is an immediate testimonial in him of the value itself" (*10*:102), "the annunciation of the being of values in the subject in their peculiar idea-like mode of being" (*10*:185). This value-feeling in its general sense is "embodied in acts of preference, of approval, and of conviction" (*10*:185). More specifically, however, "the phenomenon of conscience is

---

[1] Werkmeister, W. H., Value Theory and the Problem of Moral Obligation, *Proceedings of the Inter-American Congress of Philosophy,* Buenos Aires, 1958.

[2] Although, for the convenience of the English speaking reader, I have keyed all references to the readily available translation of Hartmann's *Ethik* by Stanton Coit, all quotations are my own translations from the German of the 1926 edition of Hartmann's work.

clear proof of the actuality of values" (10:236); for it is "the revelation of moral [as distinguished from all other] values in actual consciousness" (10:202). But, in any case, the value consciousness is, in Scheler's sense, "a consciousness of 'material' and objective content" (10:179). "Value consciousness, then, —whatever else it may be—is in the first place a value-feeling, a primal, immediate capacity for being in touch with the valuable" (10:86).

If we accept this thesis of the basic value intuition, then there appears to be no criterion of dependability, no means of checking on whether or not our value-feeling actually discloses a value or goes astray. The value-feeling itself is its own ultimate justification and vindication. Only blind trust seems required. But can such trust become a dependable basis for a moral *ought?* It may well be doubted.

Moreover, according to Hartmann, "not everyone possesses a consciousness attuned to every moral value" (10:102). "The process of ethical evolution [in particular] is a genuine process of discovery, a genuine unveiling and disclosing of values. On the other hand, however, it is, at the same time, always a loss of values, a forgetting of values, a vanishing of values" (10:89). According to Hartmann, this very fact of a shifting value consciousness bespeaks, not a relativity of values, but "a kind of 'narrowness' of the value consciousness" (10:89), "a restriction of the value view" (11:66). But this "narrowness" or "restriction" of our value consciousness raises anew the question concerning the validity and dependability of the primal value-feeling. At the very least it makes all known values, *as known,* dependent upon the nature of the value consciousness in which they are given; and there is no faculty of man which can probe beyond this "given."

Hartmann himself holds that "the sole responsibility for the legitimacy and objectivity of the standard of values falls upon the aprioristic value intuition proper, i.e., in the last analysis it falls upon value-feeling" (10:192). "In the realm of values nothing can be anticipated, deduced, or proved universally; one can only follow step by step the phenomena of value consciousness" (*11*:69). Whatever our value-feeling discloses is as objective as "mathematical insight" (*10*:227); for value-feeling does not allow itself to be transformed, without resistance, by something that is a pure fabrication. It is in itself something unaccommodating, something incapable of being disconcerted, "a unique being, a law unto itself, a distinctive value orientation" (*10*:86).

It is hardly possible to emphasize more strongly the basic significance of the value-feeling. And yet, a lingering doubt remains; for, surely, we cannot deny the fact of error even in basic value judgments. Hartmann himself holds that "where there are delusion and error, these consist of a non-agreement with the fact. The fact as . . . something independent of truth and error in cognition . . . , as something existing in itself, is precisely the presupposition of delusion. . . . But in this case the 'fact' is the value itself" (*10*:227).

Forceful as this argument may appear to be at first glance, it is considerably weakened when we remember that in the natural sciences as well as in ordinary, every-day experience—and even in mathematics—there are various ways of checking up on a presumed "fact." An object seen may be tested within the context of causal relations. But when it comes to values, Hartmann maintains that "the criterion of the genuine and the spurious is nothing other than the primal value consciousness itself" (*10*:103). This criterion would still be acceptable if Hartmann did not maintain at the same time that what is disclosed in value-feeling is a self-existent realm of values in themselves, not simply a felt quale of the experience in question. No matter how sympathetic we may be towards the idea of a primal value-feeling, the further contention that the values disclosed in that feeling are self-existent essences can find support only in blind trust. There is nothing in Hartmann's theory—as there is nothing in Scheler's—that would change this fact.

However, let us accept, for the sake of argument, Hartmann's dependence upon a primal value-feeling. There is still another aspect of value cognition which must be clearly understood. Hartmann himself regards the primal value consciousness as not in itself capable of discerning fully the interrelations of values and, therefore, the structure of the value realm. Value-feeling must here be supplemented by reflection and philosophical analysis.

The values disclosed in value feeling are, of course, the starting-point for all reflection and analysis (*10*:63-64). In a sense, reflection and analysis are but means of bringing into fuller view or into clearer consciousness the facts disclosed in value-feeling. "Analysis leads only to the other, the deeper phenomenon, which is in itself independent and is independently discerned, namely, the phenomenon of value proper which is no longer a phenomenon of something else . . . [but] can only be comprehended purely for itself and purely as an ideal phenomenon" (*10*:104). The roundabout way through reflection and analysis means only "a leading or guiding of one's own perception of value towards that which would not otherwise fall within the range of one's vision" (*10*:104). Reflection and analysis may thus broaden one's experience of values. One may even say that "philosophical ethics discovers values." "But rarely is this a really original discovery." Generally it is "a secondary discovery" (*10*:87). That is to say, reflection and analysis, as secondary value cognitions, disclose more clearly what is only dimly given in the primal value-feeling. They bring into the clear light of consciousness in particular the interrelations of values. As Hartmann puts it, they "can do nothing except draw forth from the total emotional phenomenon [which is our value experience] the aprioristic content already contained therein" (*10*:178). Hence, in value cognition, "the consciousness of law is precisely what is secondary" (*10*: 179). But this "secondary cognition" is important just the same.

According to Hartmann, then, value experience involves two aspects: a primal value-feeling which directly apprehends and "discovers" values, and a secondary but rational comprehension and clarifying discernment of what is "given" in the value-feeling. One might argue that the "secondary" approach to values could provide a much-needed corrective to value-feeling; but Hartmann does not take this position. He stands committed to the dependability, the intrinsic reliability of the primal value-feeling as such. Only the structure of the value realm is fully disclosed in analysis.

The primal value-feeling occurs, of course, always within the context of our actual experience of the world around us. "Here as everywhere else, that which is actually experienced is the 'springboard' to an intuition of ideas" (*11*:367). In this relatedness of our value-feeling to the facts of experience lies the a posteriori element of our value experience (*10*:chpt. VII). The cognition of values as such, however, is always a priori (*10*: chpt. XIIId). But this combination of a posteriori and a priori elements in value experience creates certain difficulties. On the one hand, empiricists may well argue that only "after the fact" do we know what in our experience is (or was) valuable. On the other hand, however, every apriorism is under suspicion of being subjective and arbitrary, for, in some specific sense, even prejudices, imaginative constructions, and errors are a priori. Hartmann hopes to escape from both horns of the dilemma by maintaining that we must carefully distinguish between the experiencing of a value "content" (which, depending upon actions, situations, and factual conditions, is always a posteriori) and the "content" itself (which is a priori and which, relative to the experiencing subject, is "as independent as are spatial relations in geometric cognition and things in the cognition of things") (*10*:219). As Hartmann puts it: "One can experience as valuable only that which in itself is valuable" (*10*:227).

At once, however, we are taken a step beyond the actualities of experience; for "something is valuable only through its relation to a value itself. The value must already be fixed. It is the condition of the possibility of there being anything of value" (*10*:89). It is "the 'condition of the possibility' of conscience" (*10*:202; 93). But a still further step must be taken, for the mode of being of the value proper has as yet not been defined. Ethics, however, is concerned not only with the cognition of values but also—and most importantly so, according to Hartmann—with the values themselves (*10*:219). How, then, are the values in themselves to be understood?

"In their mode of Being," Hartmann tells us, "values are

Platonic ideas" (*10*:184). They are "essences" (*10*:185), which one can spiritually intuit but which one cannot see or grasp (*10*:185; 183-205). They do have an "ideal self-existence" (*10*:217-231). Indeed, "there is a realm of values which subsists in itself, a genuine κόσμος νοητός which exists as much beyond reality as beyond consciousness—an ethical ideal realm, which is not constructed, not invented or dreamed up, but is actually existing and capable of being apprehended in the phenomenon of value-feeling" (*10*:226).

As essences subsisting in their own value realm values are derived neither from things or actual conditions, nor from the subject and its mode of being; they are not purely "formal" and empty constructions, but concrete "material" contents and structures which can be actualized in things, conditions, or persons (and which in that case constitute a specific quale of the latter) but which never become part and parcel of the world of things and of persons (*10*:chpt. XVI). Values, therefore, are always absolute, never relative (*10*:206-216). To be sure, "the substance of the value already includes a relation to the person" (*10*:214); but "the values themselves are not affected by this relation; they are absolute. The relational structure is nothing but a presupposition of their manifestation; it is a categorial (not an axiological) pre-condition" (*10*:216).

There is in all of Hartmann's arguments a kernel of truth which, freed from his misinterpretations, ought to be preserved. There is, for example, the fact that, although a person may in a large measure create the content of experience, he cannot change the fact that this content is either valuable or not. The "being valuable" remains, in principle, distinct from the experiential content. Thus, the value of justice is not itself justice. We observe "just conduct," and we know that "being just" is a value. We are clearly moving on two planes of cognition. Moreover, Hartmann is right when he holds that an "ideal object" offers resistance to any attempt to change it arbitrarily. The meaning of "square root of minus two" cannot be changed at will if the rest of the mathematical system is retained. Similarly, if, in a given situation, mutual trust is a value, then it does not become a disvalue simply by our thinking it to be such. And, finally, if we experience one thing as useful and another as agreeable, a knowledge of the values "useful" and "agreeable," and their respective differences, is already presupposed; and so with all other values.

But from these facts of experience Hartmann draws unwarranted conclusions. Let me illustrate his logic in one specific instance. The moral value of justice Hartmann transforms into a moral value called justice and then he speaks of "justice" as an ideal object, a value essence, which differs characteristically from other value essences and, with them, constitutes the Platonic realm of values. The argument is essentially the same in the case of all the values which Hartmann discusses. But when we examine carefully the steps involved in this argumentation, we observe that, by a sequence of unwarranted transformations of meanings, Hartmann moves from undeniable facts of experience to be hypostatization of an ideal in-it-self-ness. The steps in the arguments have no logical justification; and the facts of experience with which he is concerned can be accounted for in terms of empirically oriented value theories. Hartmann's recourse to a Platonic realm of "essences" is both unwarranted and unnecessary.

There are, however, still other considerations which make Hartmann's position untenable. One of these pertains to man's creative endeavors, especially to his artistic creations. According to Hartmann, the artist apprehends a pre-existing value which he then actualizes in the work of art. The really constitutive and "creative" prius are thus the values. One might argue, however—and with good reason, I believe—that no values but persons are creative, and that through the creative acts of persons values come into being which did not exist previously. To be sure, Hartmann might reply that through the creative acts of persons previously unrealized value essences become embodied in the factualities of our human world, and that this fact in no way disproves his contention that all values already subsist as essences in a Platonic value realm.

However, the situation is not as simple as this, and the argument previously raised cannot be brushed aside so easily. After all, the uniqueness of a work of art is inseparable from its value matter. The Venus de Milo, for example, is *this particular* crystallization of Greek art. Its sole value lies in the unique combination of all that makes it the Venus de Milo and not something else. But if this is so, then we face a significant dilemma: We must hold either that the unique combination of value elements which makes the Venus de Milo the valuable object it is did exist in the Platonic value realm prior to its embodiment in the actual statue, or that the creative genius of the artist who carved the Venus de Milo brought forth a combination of values which, as such, is itself a value and is the result of that artist's creative action. If we accept the first of these alternatives, the hypostatized Platonic realm of values becomes crowded with all the prototypes of the created and the as yet uncreated works of art; and this is certainly not what Hartmann wanted. But if we accept the second alternative, then man can create values which previously did not exist in the value realm; and if he can do it as far as some values are concerned, there is no reason for believing that he cannot do it as far as all values are involved. Hartmann's thesis has been impaired in any case.

What has just been shown to be the case with respect to aesthetic values can equally well be demonstrated with respect to moral values; for every act of generosity, of neighborly love, of love of the remote, every manifestation of justice, of trust, or of courage is unique because the person involved and the factual situation are unique. Courage as such is but an abstraction. What is real is the courageous act here and now, under these unique circumstances. And courage under these particular conditions differs from courage under other conditions. The abstract idea of courage lacks all the gradations and shades of meaning which distinguish one act of courage from another. And one wonders, indeed, if courage as a value, separated from all content of actual situations, can even be apprehended in its in-itself-ness. The point is, Does a reference to a self-existent realm of values—to a realm of values detached from, and independent of, the actualities of human existence—add anything to our understanding of values and value interrelations? Hartmann, of course, believes that it does. An empirically oriented value theory, however, may be able to deal directly with the facts of man's value experience, and may do so most effectively.

But now Hartmann will point out that, if we stipulate the existence of a Platonic realm of values, the intricate interrelations of values can be clarified and understood most readily; and much of his work—the entire second volume of the *Ethics,* in fact—is devoted to a clarification of the value relations and the entailed problem of a value scale.

The first relation of far-reaching importance is that in which the lower value is the "foundation" of the higher *(Fundierungsverhältnis).*[3] This relation holds "between the values of a wider sphere and those of a narrower sphere." "It is a univocal and irreversible relation which makes the higher value dependent upon the lower" (*11*:25). The dependence, however, is purely "material," not axiological. That is to say, the lower value becomes "matter" for an axiological higher value, being only the *condicio sine qua non* of the latter. "In every other sense the higher value is independent of it" (*11*:25). The value of goods is thus foundational to moral values. "Where moral values and disvalues appear in real persons, there a world of actual goods is already at hand—a world of value-objects to which the acts of the person pertain" (*11*:25). But the relationship cannot be reversed. The existence of a world of goods does not in itself entail the emergence of moral values or disvalues.

Moreover, the relation of foundational dependence cannot be universalized for the value realm as a whole. The structuralization of that realm, according to Hartmann, is much more complicated. In fact the dependence of moral values upon goods has no bearing upon the order of rank of the moral values proper. However, it is Hartmann's basic conviction that "every morally selective consciousness of value is necessarily a consciousness

---

[3] Hartmann here reverses the order of dependence inherent in Scheler's theory.

of the order of rank of values" (*11*:47), and that reflective analysis can discern this order in detail.

It is Hartmann's further contention that "behind every moral conflict, as the situations of life bring it about in manifold forms, there can always be found, in one form or another, the opposition of value against value, not the opposition of value against disvalue" (*11*:47). "No one does evil for evil's sake; it is always something good (something valuable) that entices him" (*11*:46) and that leads him into a value conflict. This conflict must be resolved and must be resolved in favor of the higher value. The order of rank of values thus takes on crucial significance for all morality.

The order of rank of values, however, is not a simple, one-dimensional scale (*11*:50). One basic diversity lies in the difference between the "strength" and the "height" of values (*11*:51-52). On the whole, the higher value is "weaker," the lower is "stronger" (*11*:52). The higher is also the more complex, the lower the more elementary value; and "to sin against the lower value is, in general, more grievous than to sin against a higher. The fulfillment of a higher value, however, is morally more valuable than is that of a lower" (*11*:52).

Since Hartmann finds that Scheler's five criteria of an order of rank of values are inadequate (*11*:54-57), and since "it is impossible to discern one single supreme value, as to content" (*11*:68), the question is, Just how does Hartmann interpret the "value structure" dimly "given" in our primal value-feeling?

He recognizes, first of all, a group of "foundational values" which, through their content or "matter," condition all higher values. Here he enumerates and discusses "life," "consciousness," "activity," "suffering," "strength," "freedom of the will," "foresight," and "purposive efficacy" (*11*:131-154). All of these values are somehow "attached" to the subject; but they are not moral values proper. In fact, one might argue, against Hartmann, that they are not values at all but are facts of human existence which *are being valued* by human beings. No recourse to a Platonic realm of values is necessary to account for the *value of* life, consciousness, activity, suffering, and so on.

Hartmann's next group consists of the values of "goods": the value of "existence," of a "situation," of "power," and of "happiness" (*11*:155-164). But these values, too, important as they are in human affairs, are not moral values. They enter into the discussion only because human volition, human intention, is largely concerned with them. But, again, it is a fact that existence, power, and happiness, etc. *are valued*. They are not themselves values, but value is attributed to them. And once more recourse to a Platonic realm of values is unnecessary to account for man's valuations.

The moral values proper Hartmann divides into four groups. There are, first of all, the "foundational moral values"; "the good," "the noble," "richness of experience," and "purity" (*11*: 171-222). There are, secondly, the ancient virtues: "justice," "wisdom," "courage," and "self-control" (*11*:228-252). But there are also in a separate group the predominantly "Christian" virtues of "brotherly love," of "truthfulness and uprightness," of "trust and faith," of "modesty, humility, aloofness," and "values of social intercourse" (*11*:267-308). And there are lastly the more "philosophical" virtues of "love of the remote," "radiant virtue," "personality," and "personal love" (*11*:311-381).

It must be pointed out, however, that the four "strata" of moral values are inhomogeneous in one important respect. The "foundational moral values" (the "good," the "noble," "richness of experience," and "purity") are essentially attributes of acts and/or intentions, whereas all other moral values, being "virtues," are the "content" of those acts and/or intentions. More specifically, if I intend to be "just" or "modest" or to "love the remote," my intention is "good." If I pursue my intention against great obstacles and with a certain magnanimity, my intention may be "noble." But neither the "good" nor the "noble" is a content of my intention; "justice," "modesty," and the "love of the remote" are. In this difference we discern a certain heterogeneity even within Hartmann's realm of moral values.

This heterogeneity is increased by the fact that neither "richness of experience" (being a responsiveness to many values) nor "purity" (being the nonviolation of any value) can strictly be classified with the "good" and the "noble." In fact, one may wonder if "richness of experience" and "purity" (in Hartmann's sense) are moral values at all.

Hartmann is at his best when he discusses the remaining three strata of "moral values." But it is impossible to present here his analyses and reflections in all their richness of detail. Suffice it to say that there is little in his whole discussion, however, to which the hypostatization of a Platonic value realm is an indispensable presupposition. Even if our approach to the whole question of values is empirical, we can learn much from the detailed and illuminating discussion of virtues here presented.

Our immediate problem, however, may be put in the form of a question: What principles of order determine the structure of the realm of values which, according to Hartmann, has been discerned in the detailed discussion of the four groups of moral values?

The first thing that strikes us as we read Hartmann's analyses is the fact that the "unitary meaning of the morally good has been dissolved into a whole firmament of values" (*11*:385). There is not even a completed system of values. The most we can hope for is "a kind of schematic arrangement of the values," and even then much will remain arbitrary and accidental. Still, the situation is not entirely hopeless, for certain "regularities" stand out even in our incomplete "table of values"; and these regularities are the "structural laws" of the table and, thus, of the value realm (*11*:389). Specifically, Hartmann recognizes six types of such laws, which he arranges in three groups (*11*: 389):

1. Laws of Stratification ⎫ First Group
2. Laws of Foundation ⎭
3. Laws of Opposition ⎫ Second Group
4. Laws of Complementation ⎭
5. Laws of Value Height ⎫ Third Group
6. Laws of Value Strength ⎭

Of special interest for our purposes are the laws of the first and the third group, respectively. "Opposition" and "complementation" are essentially concerned with a dialectic which is inherent in the whole value realm and which, on the one hand, points up value conflicts but which, on the other hand, demands a synthesis of the conflicting values (*11*:420). "Justice" and "brotherly love," according to Hartmann, are thus in conflict; but morality demands a synthesis of the two. And "brotherly love" *(Nächstenliebe)* and "love of the remote" *(Fernstenliebe)* are also in conflict; and Hartmann does not see that a synthesis of both is given in "love of humanity."

But let us consider the "laws of stratification." Hartmann distinguishes three.

a. In the stratification of values, the lower value recurs as an element in the higher value. It is contained in the higher value in modified form but cannot be removed from its substance (*11*:400).

b. In the stratification of values, the realization of the higher value necessarily entails the realization of the constituent lower values. But if the lower value is only a foundation of the higher, the realization of the value for which it is the foundation does not necessarily entail the realization of the lower value (*11*:400-401). Thus, the value of a moral attitude is dependent upon the value of some object or situation intended; but the realization of the moral value in the person does not depend upon the achievement of the intended goal; it depends only upon the intention itself.

c. In the stratification of values, not only is the "matter" of the higher value determined, at least in part, by the "matter" of the lower value, but the height of the higher value is also conditioned by the height of the lower value (*11*:401). This relationship, however, does not hold when the lower value is only the "foundation" of the higher, for the "intended value" and the "value of the intention" stand in no discernible order of rank to each other (*11*:402).

There are two laws governing the interrelations of "value height" and "value strength." They are:

a. The higher value is always the more conditioned, the more dependent and, in this sense, the "weaker." Its fulfillment is significant only in so far as it rises above the fulfillment of the lower value. The "stronger" value is always the lower; it is the axiological foundation of the moral life, not its fulfillment (*11*:451-452). "Justice" is, thus, the lower, "radiant virtue" distinctly the higher value.

b. The second law is the equivalent of the first but casts additional light upon the relationship here involved. The law states: The most grievous transgressions are violations of the lowest values, whereas highest merit attaches to the fulfillment of the highest values (*11*:452).

The interrelations of "value strength" and "value height," however, reveal a double aspect of the order of rank of values: "Throughout the value realm two equally important orders of rank hold sway, and to these two orders two opposed laws of preference correspond" (*11*:457). According to the one law, the higher value ought to be realized. According to the other law, the lower value ought to be preserved. The solution of the problem lies, of course, in a new synthesis, in a twofold moral demand, "not to violate the lower values and yet, at the same time, to realize the higher" (*11*:258). Even so, however, the opposed laws reveal a basic antinomy within the value realm itself—an antinomy which is rooted in the very essence of the good and which encompasses all moral values (*11*:460). It is part of the tragedy of human existence that in our actual existence value antinomies cannot always be resolved. Thus, problems pertaining to the value realm still remain—and they remain despite Hartmann's Herculean efforts to solve them.

We have repeatedly deplored Hartmann's hypostatization of an ideal and self-existent value realm for the structuralization of which the "laws" which we have just considered are, presumably, constitutive. In his actual analyses, however, Hartmann deals primarily with actualities of human experience. There is a strong empirical flavor to his method. For example, when Hartmann discusses the relationship of complementation (*11*:433-443), it seems evident that the relationship in question—"wherever value A appears, there value B ought also to appear" (*11*:435)—the relationship, that is, between "trust" and "trustworthiness," between "faith" and "fidelity," between "worthiness" and "esteem," etc.—consists not so much in the interrelations of the "matter" of the values in question as in the attitude of one person toward

another. The relationship, in other words, is not one of entailment but derives from the idea of a morally responsive person.
Hartmann himself actually speaks of "an organic interpenetration
of the heterogeneous conduct on the part of different persons"
(*11*:441). Again and again he thus returns to the actualities of
human existence, and without this contact even he is unable to
discern the "essences" of the various values and their interrelations.

One problem we have not yet touched upon—the problem,
namely, of the moral *ought*. To be sure, Max Scheler's interpretation of the *ought* is basic to Hartmann's theory; but there
are in Hartmann certain modifications of the theme, and these
are important.

According to Hartmann, "the ideal ethical world is not only
that of the moral subject and his acts; it is also that of the
subject's living creations and his self-propagating and self-
perpetuating works" (*10*:240). It is a world in which values
are being realized and in which unresolvable conflicts may make
such realization impossible. And in this complex and ever-chang-
ing world the moral *ought* occurs. It occurs because the relations
between values and the actualities of man's existence constitute
a tension between two heterogeneous kinds of principles. In
metaphysical language, the *ought* arises from "the coexistence
of ontological and axiological determination in one world" (*10*:
239). It is as if the value realm were imbued with the tendency
to transform the ideal into the real. Or, as Hartmann puts it:
"The *ought-to-be* is in its nature an *ought-to-be-real*" (*10*:304).
The *ought,* according to this interpretation, "belongs to the
essence of a value and must already be contained in its ideal
mode of existence" (*10*:247).

But the *ought* in this sense is not an *ought-to-do;* "it is only
an ideal and pure *ought-to-be*" (*10*:247). The fact that something is in itself valuable does not yet entail that someone ought
to do it; it does mean, however, that whatever is valuable ought
to be. The *ought-to-do* is always determined by an *ought-to-be;*
but this relation cannot be reversed. Nor does every *ought-to-be*
entail an *ought-to-do;* for what ought to be may already be

realized or prevailing conditions may prevent me from realizing it (*10*:248). The *ought-to-do*, therefore, is narrower in scope than is the *ought-to-be*. Moreover, as actual, the *ought—any ought*—depends upon Being. More specifically, the actual *ought-to-be* presupposes the non-being of that which, in a given situation, ought to be; it can therefore occur only in a real, self-existent world (*10*:250).

However, as far as Hartmann is concerned, actuality is the highest mode of Being. "It is the synthesis of possibility and necessity , . . . their blending in one and the same existent" (*10*:307). This means that "necessity . . . belongs to the essence of actuality" (*10*:307). But in the *ought-to-be* something is intended which lies beyond actuality and, therefore, is unreal. Its mode of Being is not a blending of possibility and necessity; it is, rather, a necessity which extends beyond possibility and, therefore, beyond the actual. In Hartmann's words: "In the modality of the actual *ought-to-be* two basic factors are clearly discernible: a deficiency of possibility and an excess of necessity. The former is seen in the unreality of the content, in the fact that 'it cannot yet be'; the latter is the no less existing categorical demand for the content, the *ought-to-be* proper of that which is not and is ontologically not yet possible" (*10*:308). The mode of Being of the *ought,* therefore, is "below" reality. It is that which a given reality does not satisfy, that which "makes a demand for the realization of its content and, in doing so, elicits in the subject sensitive to this demand a tendency towards its realization" (*10*:308).

"Modally speaking," Hartmann asserts, "the ideal *ought-to-be* is a necessity which exists for itself, and exists this side of possibility and impossibility" (*10*:309). However, "value is inseparably connected with the ideal *ought-to-be,*" the modality of the *ought-to-be* being "contained in the value essence" (*10*: 309; 304). And, thus, "from the pure essence of value proceeds the *ought-to-be*" (*10*:314).

But, again, alternative interpretations of the *ought* are possible. An empirical approach, for example—deriving the *ought* of moral obligation from man's basic commitments to values—

could avoid entirely the metaphysical entanglements which beset Hartmann's theory. But, having hypostatized values into self-existent ideal entities, Hartmann is caught in the consequences of that initial step—a step which could easily have been avoided.

In addition, however, Hartmann's proposed solution of the problem of the *ought* in terms of modalities of Being prevents him from seeing that there are not only an *ought-to-be* and an *ought-to-do,* but that the *ought-to-do* is itself twofold, embracing the prudential and the moral *ought;* that the prudential *ought* is essentially an *ought* of means, whereas the moral *ought* takes on the form of specific imperatives which, having nothing to do with means, may well be called categorical, and which are entailed by our commitments rather than by the values which induce us to make the commitments. In other words, not only is Hartmann's theory overburdened with unnecessary metaphysical baggage, it fails in crucial respects to account for the facts of moral experience.

## REFERENCES

1. Altmann, Alexander, *Die Grundlagen der Wertethik,* Berlin, 1931.
2. Bosanquet, B., Review of G.E. Moore's *Principia Ethica, Mind,* XIII (1904), pp. 254-261.
3. Broad, C. D., "Certain Features in Moore's Ethical Doctrines," *The Philosophy of G. E. Moore,* Paul Arthur Schilpp, editor, Evanston, 1942.
4. Edel, Abraham, "The Logical Structure of G. E. Moore's Ethical Theory," *The Philosophy of G. E. Moore,* Paul Arthur Schilpp, editor, Evanston, 1942.
5. Edwards, Paul, *The Logic of Moral Discourse,* Glencoe, 1955.
6. Ewing, A. C., *Second Thoughts in Moral Philosophy,* New York, 1959.
7. Frankena, William K., "The Naturalistic Fallacy," *Mind,* XLVIII (1939), pp. 464-477.
8. Frankena, William K., "Obligation and Value in the Ethics of G. E. Moore," *The Philosophy of G. E. Moore,* Paul Arthur Schilpp, editor, Evanston, 1942.
9. Greiner, Joseph Gottfried, *Formale Gesetzes-Ethik und materiale Wert-Ethik,* Heidelberg, 1932.
10. Hartmann, Nicolai, *Ethics,* translation by Stanton Coit, London, 1932, I.
11. Hartmann, Nicolai, *op. cit.,* II.

12. Hartmann, Wilfried, *Die Philosophie Max Schelers in ihren Beziehungen zu Eduard von Hartmann*, Düsseldorf, 1956.
13. Jones, E. E. C. "Mr. Moore on Hedonism," *International Journal of Ethics*, XVI (1905-06), pp. 429-464.
14. Koehle, Eckard J., *Personality: A Study According to the Philosophies of Value and Spirit of Max Scheler and Nicolai Hartmann*, Newton, 1941.
15. Mackenzie, J. S., Review of G. E. Moore's *Principia Ethica*, *International Journal of Ethics*, XIV (1903-04), pp. 377-382.
16. Mayer, P. Emmanuel, *Die Objektivität der Werterkenntnis bei Nicolai Hartmann*, Meisenheim, 1952.
17. Mettrick, Edward F., "G. E. Moore and Intrinsic Goodness," *International Journal of Ethics*, XXXVIII (1927-38), pp. 389-400.
18. Moore, George Edward, *Principia Ethica*, Cambridge, 1903.
19. Moore, George Edward, *Ethics*, London, 1912.
20. Moore, George Edward, *Philosophical Studies*, London, 1922.
20a. Moore, George Edward, "A Reply to My Critics," *The Philosophy of G. E. Moore*, Paul Arthur Schilpp, editor, Evanston, 1942.
21. Nowell-Smith, P. H., *Ethics*, New York, 1957.
22. Paton, H. J., "The Alleged Independence of Goodness," *The Philosophy of G. E. Moore*, Paul Arthur Schilpp, editor, Evanston, 1942.
23. Riddell, J. G., "The New Intuitionism of Dr. Rashdall and Dr. Moore," *Philosophical Review*, XXX (1921), pp. 545-565.
24. Ross, W. David, *The Right and the Good*, Oxford, 1930.
25. Scheler, Max, *Der Formalismus in der Ethik und die materiale Wertethik*, 4th edition, Bern, 1954.
26. Stevenson, Charles L., "Moore's Arguments Against Certain Forms of Empirical Naturalism," *The Philosophy of G. E. Moore*, Paul Schilpp, editor, Evanston, 1942.
27. White, Alan R., *G. E. Moore; A Critical Exposition*, Oxford, 1958.
28. Wittmann, Michael, *Max Scheler als Ethiker*, Düsseldorf, 1923.
29. Wright, H. W., "The Objectivity of Moral Values," *Philosophical Review*, XXXII (1923), pp. 385-400.
30. Hancock, Roger, "The Refutation of Naturalism in Moore and Hare," *Journal of Philosophy*, LVII (1960), pp. 326-334.

# CHAPTER VIII

# The Morality of Freedom and
# Human Dignity

If, through a dishonest act, a man has amassed a fortune and now, as the result of a searching self-analysis, has "to say to himself, 'I am a worthless man, though I've filled my purse,' he must have a different criterion of judgment than if he approves of himself and says, 'I am a prudent man, for I've enriched my treasure'" (B, C:149).[1] In this simple manner did Kant hint at the radical difference between a morality of human dignity and a morality of empirical ends. His whole theory of ethics is in fact but an explication of this difference—a staunch defense of the former and a disproof and repudiation of the latter.

However, Kant's ethics must be viewed within the framework

---

[1] The interpretation of Kant's moral doctrines here attempted is based essentially upon his *Critique of Practical Reason* and his *Foundations of the Metaphysics of Morals*. The translations by Abbot (*1*) and Paton (*17*) have been consulted; but all references are given to the excellent and readily available translation by Beck (*3*). Since references to Beck's translation may be either to the *Foundations of the Metaphysics of Morals* or to the *Critique of Practical Reason,* identification by letters has been deemed necessary. Thus, B, F: (followed by the page number) refers to Beck's translation of the *Foundations,* whereas B, C: (followed by the page number) refers to his translation of the *Critique.* All references, however, are to the same book (*3*). All crucial passages have been checked against Otto (*9*) or Vorlander (*8*) and, occasionally, have been re-translated.

of his philosophy as a whole (B, C:211); and when it is so viewed, there emerges behind all references to freedom and human dignity the crucial problem of ethics itself—the problem, that is, of the nature and meaning of *the moral.* This crucial problem (and its manifold ramifications) will be the topic of the discussions which follow.

## I

The essential unity of the Kantian system involves two inter-related aspects. On the one hand, the theoretical and the practical employments of reason, to use Kant's own terminology, must culminate in the unity of a single principle; for reason, whatever its employment, is one and the same and differs only in its applications (B, C:54). On the other hand, Kant's "critical" point of view necessitates one and the same logical approach in every field of inquiry. Of these two aspects, the unity of principle will become evident as we consider in detail Kant's theory of ethics; the unity of the methodological approach, however, must be kept in mind from the very beginning of our discussions, for otherwise we cannot understand or evaluate correctly Kant's moral philosophy as a whole.

In the field of cognition, Kant assumes as "given" our ordinary human experience and the knowledge, embodied in the sciences, which is concerned with this experience. He then asks: What is the nature of human experience, and how is such experience possible? His epistemology, as presented in the *Critique of Pure Reason* and the *Prolegomena to any Future Metaphysics,* is but an attempt to answer these questions.

In the field of action, Kant similarly assumes as "given" the fact of our moral evaluations, and he asks: What is the nature of moral phenomena, and how is morality itself possible? In his attempt to answer these questions, he introduces into the field of ethics the same radically critical considerations which mark the great turning point in his epistemology. Where other philosophers are satisfied with the elaboration of moral codes or with the construction of a "calculus of pleasures," Kant demands that we investigate the nature of morality as such, and that we inquire into the presuppositions upon which alone it depends.

The investigation which Kant here demands is epistemic rather than psychological or anthropological. This does not mean that Kant is opposed to psycho-anthropological research in the field of morals. On the contrary, he explicitly states that "natural and moral philosophy can each have its empirical part" (B, F:50). As events in our personal existence, moral decisions and evaluations, like all other mental events, are the legitimate object of psychological studies; whereas moral codes and maxims of actions, as historically evolved parts, may be studied by historians, anthropologists, and sociologists alike. Kant's critical ethics is not in conflict with any of these investigations; for Kant is concerned not with the *content* of the moral laws or maxims which guide our actions, but with the concept of law itself, or with the meaning of *the moral*. He is concerned, that is, with the question, In what sense and under what conditions can our decisions and actions be called *moral?* And to this question neither psychology nor anthropology nor any of the other social sciences can give an answer, for, implicitly or explicitly, all of them presuppose and therefore assume that answer. They are concerned with the origin and development of moral codes, with the factors of training, of contacts, and the cultural interrelations of moral maxims and codes with all other factors in a given culture pattern. But in all of these investigations they assume that we know what is meant by *the moral,* that we know what constitutes the concept or law of morality as such. Kant's critical ethics, on the other hand, is devoted to a clarification of this presupposition of all the sciences which deal with moral matters.

Kant finds the uniquely characteristic nature of *the moral* in man's experience of an *ought*. That this experience is real cannot be doubted; that it is general is attested to by thinkers of all ages and all countries. For Kant, however, it is "an identical and therefore a self-evident proposition" (B, C:139) that the moral law implied in an *ought* is a universal law (B, F:71; B, C:148); for, according to Kant, "the consciousness of this principle," i.e., the consciousness of the moral law, is "a fact of reason" (B, C:142). It is "the sole fact of pure reason, which by it proclaims itself as originally legislative" (B, C:143). The basic question of critical ethics is, therefore, not whether or not an *ought* is ever experienced, but how such experience is possible and how and in what sense it can be valid for all men.

Kant is well aware of the fact that universality of assent does not prove the objective validity of a judgment; that, even if sometimes that which is universally assented to is also correct, this is no proof of the necessity of such agreement. He knows that, on the contrary, "only objective validity affords the ground of a necessary universal agreement" (B, C:127), and, knowing this, he sets out to uncover the grounds of the objective validity and meaning of the *ought*. His system of ethics, as a clarification of *the moral*, is therefore essentially an analysis of the *ought*— of its validity, its presuppositions, and its ultimate ramifications; and this analysis is epistemic. That, as a mental event, the experience of an *ought* can also be studied psychologically is from Kant's point of view completely irrelevant.

## II

If the ought and the experienced objective necessitation which it implies are of the essence of *the moral*, then our first question may well be, To what extent have older theories of ethics done justice to this fact? More specifically, have the theories which attempt to ground moral maxims in some object or objects of desire successfully accounted for the meaning and the necessitation of the *ought*? But, here again, we must carefully distinguish the psychological problem from the epistemic. "Why something pleases or displeases, how the pleasure of mere feeling differs from taste, and whether this is distinct from a general satisfaction of reason . . . ; how desires and inclinations arise, and how, finally, maxims arise from desires and inclination under the co-operation of reason"—"all these matters belong to an empirical psychology" (B, F:85) and do not concern us here. What must be investigated, however, is the hedonistic thesis that pleasure (or satisfaction) and displeasure (or dissatisfaction) are the determining ground of man's moral conduct, that they are the basis of the *ought*.

It is Kant's contention that a principle of conduct which is "based only on the subjective susceptibility to a pleasure or displeasure" may be counted among the subjective maxims of a person thus susceptible, but it cannot function as a moral law even to that person (to say nothing about its being a law "for rational beings"); for such a principle "lacks objective necessity" (B, C:132-133). It does not establish an *ought*.

The reasons for this insufficiency of the hedonistic principle are obvious. (i) The pleasure expected or actually enjoyed by a person always depends upon "the presence of an object" (B, C:133), and whether or not a particular object gives pleasure or displeasure depends upon the "susceptibility" of the experiencing subject. It follows, therefore, that, as a guide for action, the hedonistic principle depends on whether or not "the faculty of desire is determined by the sensation of agreeableness which the subject expects from the actual existence of the object" in question (B, C:133); and this relation of dependence implies the subjectivity of the principle as a guide for life. Not all persons derive pleasure from the same object (B, C:139), nor does the same person at different times derive pleasure from the same object. Each judgment concerning the pleasure derivable from an object "rests on mere data of experience" and therefore depends "on the very changeable opinion of each person" (B, C:147), and therefore cannot establish the objective necessitation of an *ought*.

(ii) The hedonistic principle may, of course, be interpreted as the principle of self-love—as the principle, that is, of one's own happiness (B, C:133). But even this interpretation, although it seems to free us from a dependence upon ephemeral pleasures, does not avoid the basic difficulties; for the concept 'happiness' is "merely the general name for subjective grounds of determination" and "determines nothing specific concerning what is to be done" in any given situation (B, C:135). It "contains no other determinants for the will than those which belong to the lower faculty of desire" (B, C:135-136). Although to be happy may be the desire of every rational but finite being, "where one places his happiness is a question of the particular feeling of pleasure or displeasure in each man, and even of the differences in needs occasioned by changes of feeling in one and the same man" (B, C:136-137). The principle, therefore, remains objectively contingent (B, C:137) and "does not prescribe the same practical rules to all rational beings, even though all the rules go under the same name—that of happiness" (B, C:148).

Given the enormous variety of interests and feelings of all men, it is only natural that some desires for happiness are in irreconcilable conflict.[2] Although there may be agreement and harmony in somes cases, this fact is purely accidental and by no means the general rule (B, C:139); and from such an accidental harmony no universal law of conduct, no objectively valid *ought,* can be derived. Too many exceptions would have to be granted.

(iii) But even if we were to suppose that all "finite rational beings were unanimous in the kind of objects their feelings of pleasure and pain had, and even in the means of obtaining the former and preventing the latter," "the unanimity itself would be merely contingent" (B, C:137), for it would be based upon their sensuous nature and its responsiveness to objects (which is accidental) and not upon their rational nature (which, in Kant's opinion, is essential). The determining ground for action would therefore still be "only subjectively valid and empirical" (B, C:137), and moral rules justified on such grounds, although on the average more often right than not, "will not be rules which must hold always and necessarily" (B, C:147). Only "universal rules of skill," i.e., universal rules determining the selection of means for the realization of a stipulated end, are implied by the principle of self-love (B, C:137).

(iv) There is one and only one condition under which the principle of self-love yields a universal moral law or an *ought* and that is, to include in the very conception of one's own happiness the happiness of every other rational being (B, C:

---

[2] *Cf.* "The pledge which is said to have been given by Francis I to the Emperor Charles V, 'What my brother wants (Milan), that I want too' " (B, C:139).

146). Such an extension of the principle of self-love, however, cannot be justified on empirical grounds. "Not only would one have to presuppose that we find in the welfare of others a natural satisfaction but also one would have to find a want such as that which is occasioned in some men by a sympathetic disposition" (B, C:145-146). Such a "want," however, "we cannot presuppose in every rational being" (B, C:146). Hence, if the extension of the principle of self-love can be justified at all, it can be justified only on grounds of reason. But if reason warrants the extension, then "the form of universality" rather than some additional content of self-love is the determining ground of the will. Through the "form of universality" I restrict my maxim to do as I please, which is "founded on inclination," and make it conformable to a universal law; and from this limitation to make my actions conform to a universal law, and not from the addition of any external incentive, "obligation arises to extend the maxim of self-love also to the happiness of others" (B, C:146).

(v) If it now be argued that the hedonistic principle can be saved by distinguishing between lower and higher pleasures, Kant repudiates all such contentions. "It is astonishing," he says, "how otherwise acute men believe they can find a difference between the lower and the higher faculty of desire by noting whether the conceptions which are associated with pleasure have their origin in the senses or in the understanding" (B, C:133). "It is not a question of where the conception of this enjoyable object comes from, but merely of how much it depends on whether the latter can be agreeably affected. . . . However dissimilar the conceptions of the objects . . . the feeling of pleasure, by virtue of which they constitute a determining ground of the will . . . is always the same" (B, C:134).

To be sure, "a man can find satisfaction in the mere exercise of power, in the consciousness of his spiritual strength in overcoming obstacles in the way of his designs, and in the cultivation of his intellectual talents. We correctly call these the more refined joys and delights, because they are more in our power than others and do not wear out, but, rather, increase our capacity for even more of this kind of enjoyment; they delight and at the same time cultivate. But [Kant goes on] this is no reason to pass off such pleasures as a mode of determining the will different from that of the senses. For the possibility of these pleasures, too, presupposes, as the first condition of our delight, the existence in us of a corresponding feeling" (B, C:135). And "if the determination of the will rests on the feelings of agreeableness or disagreeableness" which a man expects, then "it is all the same to him through what kind of notion he is affected." "The only thing he considers in making a choice is how great, how long lasting, how easily obtained, and how often repeated this agreeableness is" (B, C:134). From such a "calculus of pleasures" no objectively necessitating *ought* can be derived.

(vi) But the principle of self-love encounters other difficulties; for "what is to bring true lasting advantage to our whole existence is veiled in impenetrable obscurity" (B, C:148). Not only is the concept of happiness an indefinite concept—since all the elements which enter into its meaning must be taken from experience whereas the whole designated by the term, the happiness of a life-time, comprises future as well as present well-being (B, F:77)—but even the elements are not constant. What gave us pleasure yesterday and today may not do so tomorrow or the next day. We can never be sure of the as yet unrealized satisfactions of a life-time, for our pleasures depend not only on the objects which we desire but also on our capacity and physical ability to realize and enjoy them (B, C:148); and over these matters we have little control. The principle of self-love, therefore, is at best only a maxim of prudence, not a moral command, not an *ought* (B, C:148), and, in Kant's opinion, "it would be better to maintain that there are no practical laws but merely counsels for the service of our desires than to elevate merely subjective principles to the rank of practical laws" (B, C:137).

If nature had really intended man for happiness, so Kant concludes, she "would have taken over not only the choice of ends but also that of the means and with wise foresight would have intrusted both to instinct alone"; for all the actions man now has to perform guided only by reason, "and the entire rule of conduct," "would be dictated much more exactly by instinct," and the end—one's own happiness or that of every human being —"would be far more certainly attained by instinct than it ever could be by reason." In fact, "the more a cultivated reason deliberately devotes itself to the enjoyment of life and happiness, the more the man falls short of true contentment" (B, F:57).

(vii) If it be maintained that the desire to avoid pain and to obtain pleasure is man's true basis for the moral law, Kant argues against this idea also. In order to imagine, he points out, that a person is "tormented with mortification by the consciousness of his transgressions" or that he is "delighted by the consciousness of doing dutiful [i.e. moral] acts," we must presuppose that this man is "at least to a certain degree morally good." That is to say, "the concept of morality and duty [i.e., the concept of the *ought*] must precede all reference to this satisfaction and cannot be derived from it." "One must already value the importance of what we call duty, the respect for the moral law, and the immediate worth which a person obtains in his own eyes through obedience to it, in order to feel satisfaction in the consciousness of his conformity to law or bitter remorse which accompanies his awareness that he transgressed it. Therefore, this satisfaction or spiritual unrest cannot be felt prior to the knowledge of obligation, nor can it be made the basis of the latter" (B, C:150). Kant is willing to grant that frequent practice in doing one's duty, i.e., in following the *ought,* can "finally cause a subjective feeling of satisfaction," but he denies that the concept of duty, the *ought,* can be derived from it (B, C:150).

(viii) Equally untenable, according to Kant, is the position of those philosophers "who assume a certain particular moral sense which, instead of reason, determines the moral law, and in accordance with which the consciousness of virtue is directly associated with satisfaction and enjoyment, whereas consciousness of vice is associated with mental restlessness and pain" (B, C:150). In the end, this so-called moral sense reduces to nothing but man's desire for his own happiness. The moral sense doctrine thus turns out to be but a more refined form of hedonism and is therefore subject to the criticisms already advanced against all hedonism.

(ix) Still other considerations come before us when the idea of perfection is made the supreme principle of morality (B, C: 151). According to Kant, "the concept of perfection in its practical meaning" signifies "the fitness or sufficiency of a thing to any kind of ends"; and "only if ends are already given can the concept of perfection in relation to them . . . be the determining ground of the will" (B, C:151). The ends themselves, however, are not determined by the idea of perfection and must be chosen on some other grounds. As applied to the problem of conduct, perfection can pertain only to "talent" or to the "skill which strengthens or completes talent" (B, C:151). That is to say, the idea of perfection presupposes something in the character of man which can be perfected. But if talents are to be perfected, then the reason for this is that their cultivation will either contribute to the advantages of life or bring our own will into closer agreement with the will of God. Whichever is the case, the motive and determining ground for our actions is the happiness expected from them (B, C:152). And, thus, even the principle of perfection is but a veiled form of the principle of self-love.

(x) One final point of criticism of the views under consideration is in order. Kant maintains that morality presupposes freedom, for without the assumption of freedom there is no meaning to the *ought*. However, all empirical grounds of determination, if they really determine our actions, completely eliminate freedom of choice. Moreover, "to look upon all punishment and reward as machinery in the hand of a higher power, which by this means sets rational beings in action toward their final purpose (happiness), so obviously reduces the will to a mechanism destructive of freedom that it need not detain us" (B, C:150).

Kant thus finds that, as determining grounds of the will, "all material principles" are "wholly unfit to be the supreme moral law" (B, C:150), and that the ground of moral obligation "must not be sought in the [empirical] nature of man or in the circumstances in which he is placed" in this world (B, F:52). The "practical necessity" of acting according to a moral law, i.e., the experiencing of an *ought,* cannot possibly rest on feelings, and inclinations (B, F:92), for all such empirical grounds for action do not justify the necessity and universality of the *ought,* —a necessity and universality without which morality itself is meaningless (B, C:139).

What, then, is left as determining ground of a moral will? What is the objective basis of the *ought?* Kant maintains that there is left a basic "concept of pure reason" (B, C:155)—a concept of the lawfulness of reason as such. The material content of our subjective maxims may remain, but it does not remain as the determining ground of the *ought* or of moral conduct (B, C:146). This ground, according to Kant, is "the mere form of universal legislation" (B, C:138)—a formal law, that is, which is imposed by pure reason alone.

## III

It is Kant's contention that where there is no freedom there can be no morality, no conduct determined by a moral law, no choice based on an *ought.* "The question of freedom [therefore] lies at the foundation of all moral laws and [our] accountability to them" (B, C:202). "These laws are possible only in relation to the freedom of the will; but, if the will is presupposed as free, then they are necessary" (B, C:156), for, "freedom and unconditional law reciprocally imply each other" (B, C:140), and "the moral law expresses nothing else than the autonomy of the pure practical reason, i.e., freedom" (B, C:144).

That such freedom exists, Kant believes, is evident from the facts of moral experience itself. The first of these facts is man's responsiveness to the moral law; his feeling of an *ought.* Because a man knows that he *ought* to do something, Kant argues, he realizes that he *can* do it; that "he is free" (B, C:142-143; *12*:145; 157). The experience of an *ought* would be meaningless without the presupposition of man's freedom.

The second revelatory experience, according to Kant, is man's bad conscience when he has violated the moral law. "The advocate who speaks in his [the guilty man's] behalf cannot silence the accuser in him when he is conscious that at the time when he committed the wrong he was in his senses, i.e., he was in possession of his freedom" (B, C:204).

But if freedom is crucial to the problem of morality and if its reality is revealed by the facts of moral experience, then the question arises, How is this freedom to be conceived? This question is pressing because every event in nature is determined by antecedent causes, and in the whole of nature there is no break in the immutable chain of cause and effect relations. Yet in this world of a thorough-going causal determination man lives: and in this world he must preserve his moral freedom. How is this possible?

One might, of course, call the actions of a man *free* because they are caused not by external conditions as constraints but by internal factors only—by ideas, let us say, "whereby desires are evoked;" because they are actions, in other words, "brought about at our own pleasure" (B, C:202). It is a fact, too, that many persons are satisfied with this spurious argument. They "allow themselves to be put off and believe that with a little quibbling they have found the solution of the difficult problem" (B, C:202). We must be candid, however, and must admit that if the ideas which determine a man's actions "have the ground of their existence" in antecedent states (even though all of these states are without exception internal and have a psychological rather than a mechanical causality), they are nonetheless "determining grounds of past time" which are no longer in a man's power when he acts (B, C:202), and they preclude all psychological freedom. That is to say, if the freedom of our will were nothing but our being determined by purely internal factors, "it would in essence be no better than the freedom of a turnspit, which when once wound up also carries out its motions of itself" (B, C:203). We would be "marionettes" or "automatons," "fabricated and wound up by the Supreme Artist," and the consciousness of our freedom "would be a mere illusion" (B, C:206). Morality could not be justified on such a basis, for the *ought* would be meaningless.

The freedom demanded by moral considerations cannot be a freedom which breaks through or suspends the causal chain of events, either internal or external; it must be something quite different. As Kant puts it: "If it were possible for us to have so deep an insight into a man's character as shown both in inner and outer actions, that every, even the least, incentive to these actions and all external occasions which affect them were so known to us that his future conduct could be predicted with as great a certainty as the occurrence of a solar or lunar eclipse, we [must] nevertheless still assert that the man is free" (B, C:204).

That the conception of freedom here indicated is difficult to conceive, Kant readily admits. He is convinced, however, that the arguments of the *Critique of Pure Reason,* although they have not established the *reality* of freedom, have at least demonstrated that, as a transcendental idea, freedom is *"not inconsistent with nature"* (8:479).

It cannot be our purpose to review here the whole argument of the *Critique of Pure Reason.* It may be well, however, to remind ourselves of a few crucial points.

Kant distinguishes between two kinds of causality: "Causality is either according to *nature* or [it] arises from freedom" (8: 464). By the first type of causality Kant means "the connection in the sensible world of one state with a preceding state on which it follows according to a rule." By the second type he means "the power of beginning a state *spontaneously"* (8:464). But this power of spontaneous origination of an act "is a pure transcendental idea." It "contains nothing borrowed from experience," and it "refers to an object that cannot be determined or given in any experience" (8:464). "The practical concept of freedom" which is needed in ethics "is based on this transcendental idea" (8:465). The denial of transcendental freedom must, therefore, involve "the elimination of all practical freedom" (8:465). But if transcendental freedom is conceivable, then practical freedom is at least possible. In the *Critique of Pure Reason* Kant tried to show that transcendental freedom and nature "can exist together, without any conflict, in the same actions, according as the actions are referred to their intelligible or to their sensible cause" (8:469). That is to say, if reason, "as a purely intelligible faculty" which is not subject to the "conditions of succession in time," can "have causality in respect of appearances"(8:475), then man, as noumenon, may be regarded as free from the empirical determinations of sensible nature and thus as capable of starting spontaneously a new sequence of events. Kant, of course, holds that our reason *has* causality in this sense, or that "we at least represent it to ourselves as having [this] causality" (8:472). The evidence in support of his view Kant finds in the fact that in all matters of conduct we impose imperatives as rules upon our active powers (8:472), and that we thus acknowledge an *ought*. The *ought*, Kant points out, "expresses a kind of necessity and of connection with grounds which is found nowhere else in the whole of nature" (8:472-473); for "when we have the course of nature alone in view, *'ought'* has no meaning whatsoever. It is just as absurd to ask what ought to happen in the natural world as to ask what properties a circle ought to have" (8:473). Thus, as Kant sees it, throughout the whole of nature strict causal determination prevails: the *ought,* however, "expresses a possible action the ground of which cannot be anything but a mere concept" (8:473). In other words, it is Kant's view that reason does not follow "the order of things as they present themselves in appearance, but frames to itself with perfect spontaneity an order of its own according to ideas, to which it adapts the empirical conditions, and according to which it declares actions to be necessary, even although they have never taken place, and perhaps never will take place. And at the same time reason also presupposes that it can have causality in regard to all these actions, since otherwise no empirical effects could be expected from its ideas" (8:473).

## IV

At this point it will be helpful to re-orientate ourselves with respect to the arguments covered and with respect to the discussions yet to come, for Kant's system as a whole is not easily understood. Its ramifications are far-flung and complex, and the arguments which support it are involved.

Kant holds that "nature, in the widest sense of the word, is the existence of things under law" (B, C:153). Things, however, have their noumenal as well as their phenomenal aspects, and this distinction of aspects carries over into the meaning of nature as here defined. The phenomenal aspect of rational beings, for example, is their "existence under empirically conditioned laws," whereas their noumenal aspect is their "existence according to laws which are independent of all empirical conditions and which therefore belong to the autonomy of pure reason" (B, C:153). In other words, as phenomena all rational beings are subject to the law of strict causal determination, but as noumena they are under the law of "pure practical reason," i.e., under "the moral law" (B, C:153).

The moral law, as here understood, is thus "the idea of a supersensuous nature, a nature not empirically given yet possible through freedom" (B, C:154). It "ideally transfers us into a nature in which reason would bring forth the highest good were it accompanied by sufficient physical capacities; and it determines our will to impart to the sensuous world the form of a system of rational beings" (B, C:154). "The difference, therefore, between the laws of a system of nature to which the will is subject and a system of nature which is subject to a will . . . rests on this: in the former, the objects must be the causes of the conceptions which determine the will, and in the latter the will is the cause of the objects. Consequently, in the latter the causality of the objects has its determining ground solely in the pure faculty of reason" (B, C:154-155). These ideas, however, are anticipations of conclusions yet to be derived within the framework of the Kantian system. We must first consider the arguments which support them, and thus we come back to the problem of freedom.

There can be but little doubt, I am sure, that freedom in some sense is essential to morality. The question is, In *what* sense is it to be understood? For Kant, so we have seen, freedom does not mean an interruption or suspension of the causal chain of natural events; it means autonomy or the power of rational self-determination. "The will," he says, "is a faculty of determining itself to action *in accordance with the conception of certain laws.* Such a faculty can be found only in rational beings" (B, F:85). And if that which serves the will as the objective ground of its self-determination is given by reason alone, it must hold alike for all rational beings (B, F:85). As we have seen, it was the task of the *Critique of Pure Reason* to show that freedom in this sense, though "problematic" and "the stumbling block of all empiricists" (B, C:122), is "not impossible" (B, C:118). Morality, however, demands a firmer basis; and the question is, Can we transcend the problematic concept of freedom and demonstrate its *reality?*

Before this question can be answered, we must distinguish between two points of view from which the interrelation of freedom and the moral law may be interpreted. In Kantian terminology, "freedom is certainly the *ratio essendi* [i.e., the very basis] of the moral law," but the moral law as such is "the *ratio cognoscendi* [i.e., the source of our knowledge] of freedom" (B, C:119n; B, F:104). It follows at once that two lines of approach to the problems of morality are open to us: Either we start with the moral law as given, as a "conditioned" of experience—in which case the reality of freedom, as the indispensable condition of the moral law, is revealed in and through the givenness of that law (B, C:119); or we assume the reality of freedom and attempt to "find the law which alone is competent to determine it necessarily" (B, C:140)—in which case "morality together with its principle follows from it by mere analysis" (B, F:102). Both approaches, however, come ultimately to the same thing, namely, the complete elucidation of the morality of human freedom. For methodological reasons we shall here consider first the moral law as the *ratio cognoscendi* of freedom, and shall thereafter analyze freedom as the *ratio essendi* of morality.

## V

As Kant sees it, moral experience is a state of consciousness in which a man submits himself and his actions to that peculiar kind of evaluation in which he asks, not whether or not his inclinations, needs, or moods demand or oppose contemplated actions, but whether or not the intended actions are necessary or are objectively justified. It must be noted, however, that in the case of actions which are necessary merely for the attainment of an end which seems desirable to us, we have the unmistakable feeling that our actions themselves are contingent; that they depend on the end in question, and that we shall cease to pursue them as soon as we no longer desire this end. But in the case of moral actions—in the case of actions, that is, in which an *ought* determines what we do—the will has "no freedom to choose the opposite" (B, F:79). Here we are under a constraint to follow through irrespective of our desire. "The law of morality commands" (B, C:48).

Furthermore, the experience of an *ought* or constraint or obligation—call it what you will—entails an evaluative attitude towards all inclinations, drives, and desires—be they sensuous or intellectual or anything else—and permits none of them to culminate in action without the explicit sanction of reason. Even an acknowledged duty may require revaluation as our own development or a change in our environment alters the circumstances under which we are living. But the standard of such an evaluation or revaluation—the criterion, that is, by which we determine which actions ought to be done and which ought not to be done—must always remain the same. If it is not universally valid, it does not define *the moral* as such and is, in Kant's sense, no standard at all. Since no empirically grounded standard can possibly be universally valid (see Section II, above), Kant holds that the criterion and basic law of *the moral* must be a law of reason itself; that it must be *"derived from the universal concept of a rational being as such"* (B, F:71). Only such a law can hold true for all rational beings and, being grounded in unchanging reason itself, is subject to no change at all.

As we follow the argument further, it will be helpful to keep in mind certain distinctions and definitions which are basic to Kant's point of view. Kant thus speaks of *practical rules,* meaning specific rules for the guidance of conduct—rules, that is, which prescribe particular actions as means to a desired end; and he speaks of *practical principles,* meaning "propositions which contain a general determination of the will, having under it several practical rules" (B, C:130). If the practical principles are subjective only, i.e., if they are regarded by the subject as valid only for his own will, Kant calls them *maxims;* but if they are objective, i.e., if they are recognized as valid for the will of every rational being, he calls them *practical or moral laws* (B, C:130).

In terms of these distinctions the Kantian problem of ethics is to find a criterion which enables us in all cases to distinguish between mere maxims and moral laws. This problem arises because in the will of a rational being (such as man) which is affected by feeling and sense impressions "there can be a conflict of maxims with the practical laws recognized by this being" (B, C:130). The criterion in question Kant calls the *"principle or law of morality"* (B, C:79). For an understanding of Kant's ethics and a critical evaluation of his position it is of the utmost importance that this *law of morality,* as criterion of *the moral,* be not confused with a *moral law,* which is a principle of action valid for every rational being. The former is indispensable for the definition of the term "moral," whereas the latter is merely a constituent part of an acceptable moral code. Thus, a maxim of action which meets all the requirements imposed upon principles of action by the law of morality is, according to Kant, a moral law and should be accepted as such, but it is not itself a law of morality.

The distinctions are clear. Kant, unfortunately, has not always kept them in mind and, as a result, has contributed much to the confusions which still prevail with respect to his doctrine.[3]

---

[3] The confusion arises, in part, from peculiarities of the German language. The "law of morality" is, of course, *das Gesetz der Sittlichkeit;* and the "moral law" is *das sittliche Gesetz.* But the term *Sittengesetz,* though usually to be translated as "moral law," may in some contexts mean "law of morality." Kant himself is not consistent in its use.

We shall here attempt to adhere strictly to the definitions just given, even though this means an occasional reformulation of Kant's explicit statements—an occasional deviation, that is, from the language of Kant for the sake of his basic intention. Such a procedure will accomplish two things: (i) It will bring into sharp focus the very essence of critical ethics; and (ii) it will enable us to evaluate Kant's whole system of ethics in the light of his own assumptions.

Let us start with the question, What, precisely, is the principle or law of morality?

Kant holds that "everything in nature works according to *law.*" A rational being alone has "the capacity of acting according to the *conception* of laws, i.e., according to principles" (B, F:72). Its will, being nothing but "practical reason," is "a faculty of choosing only that which reason, independently of inclination, recognizes as practically necessary, i.e., as good" (B, F:72). Its freedom, in the *negative sense,* is its capacity to choose a course of action without being determined by sensuous desires; in the *positive sense* it is the capacity of reason to be its own ground of practical determination (*11*:10; 11). And the freedom, both in its positive and negative sense, is possible only as *a determination of the will through the conception or idea of a law.*

Now, "the conception of an objective principle, so far as it constrains a will," Kant calls an *imperative* (B, F:72). All imperatives are experienced as a constraint. They express the idea that it would be good to do or to refrain from doing something, even though our inclinations may determine us otherwise. Not all imperatives, however, express an *ought* in the moral sense; for imperatives as such are merely the form in which reason imposes its practical demands upon the will of an acting subject. A perfectly good will would at all times and necessarily act "in unison with the law," i.e., in unison with the practical demands of reason; and in a case of such a will the *ought* would be out of place. But in the case of human beings, imperatives are "formulas expressing the relation of objective laws of volition in general to the subjective imperfections of the will" (B, F:73).

That is to say, since man's maxims of action are derived from subjective sources and are therefore not of themselves always in harmony with the practical law, imperatives impose that law as a command (*11*:11).

"All imperatives command either hypothetically or categorically. The former present the practical necessity of a possible action as a means to achieving something else which one desires (or which one may possibly desire). The categorical imperative would be one which presented an action as of itself objectively necessary, without regard to any other end" (B, F: 73). "The hypothetical imperative, therefore, says only that the action is good to some purpose, possible or actual." The categorical imperative, on the other hand, "declares the action to be of itself objectively necessary without making any reference to a purpose, i.e., without having any other end" (B, F:74).

The hypothetical imperatives are as numerous as are the ends or purposes to which they refer in concrete situations. All sciences, for example, have "some practical part" which consists of problems pertaining to ends which are possible for us, and of "imperatives" as to how these ends can be reached. However, the concern of such applied sciences—medicine, engineering, agronomy, and the like—is not whether or not the ends in question are themselves reasonable and good but, rather, what must be done to attain them. The imperatives here involved Kant calls *rules of skill* (B, F:75; 76).

According to Kant "there is one end, however, which we may presuppose as actual in all rational beings so far as imperatives apply to them"—one purpose which they not only *can* have but "which we can presuppose that they all *do* have by a necessity of nature"—and that is happiness (B, F:75). The imperatives which refer to the choice of means to one's own happiness, although assertorical (because they are "necessary to a purpose which we can a priori and with assurance assume for everyone"), are still only hypothetical. Kant calls them *counsels of prudence* (B, F:75; 76).

Categorical imperatives do not concern the material or end

of an action but only the form and the principle from which that action results. They tell us, not *what* to do, but *how* to act (*11*:13). For this reason they alone can determine the will prior to, and independently of, every empirical ground of determination. They alone, therefore, imply "the concept of an unconditional and objective and hence universally valid necessity" (B, F:76) and are thus capable of serving as the basic *principle* or *law of morality*, as the law or concept of *the moral* as such.

When we now ask how imperatives of any kind are possible, Kant replies that no difficulties whatsoever are encountered with respect to the rules of skill; for "whoever wills the end, so far as reason has decisive influence on his actions, wills also the indispensably necessary means to it that lie in his power. This proposition, in what concerns the will, is analytical" (B, F:76).

Difficulties arise, however, in connection with the counsels of prudence. If it were possible to give a definite and satisfactory definition of happiness, or if "the means to happiness could be infallibly stated" (B, F:78), "the imperatives of prudence would completely correspond to those of skill and would be likewise analytical. For it could be said in this case as well as in the former that whoever wills the end wills also (necessarily and according to reason) the only means to it which are in his power" (B, F:77). An imperative or counsel of prudence "differs from the imperative [or rule] of skill only in that its end is given, while in the latter case it is merely possible" (B, F:78). Kant finds, however, that the concept of happiness is indefinite. "The reason for this is that all elements which belong to the concept of happiness are empirical, i.e., they must be taken from experience, whereas for the idea of happiness as such an absolute whole or maximum of well-being is needed in my present and in every future condition" (B, F:77). No such whole can be empirically constructed and be objectively valid under all circumstances, for "happiness is an ideal not of reason but of imagination" (B, F:78). If happiness is our goal, only the counsels of prudence—i.e., the counsels of "diet, economy, courtesy, restraint, etc., which are shown by experience best to promote welfare on the average" (B, F:78)—can be given; and these counsels, being empirically grounded, cannot serve as the basic law of morality, as the definition, that is, of *the moral*.

When we come to the categorical imperatives, certain preliminary considerations are in order. As Kant points out, we cannot show by example, or empirically, whether or not there is such an imperative. On the contrary, we may well suspect that "all imperatives which appear to be categorical be yet hypothetical, but in a hidden way" (B, F:78). But if an empirical demonstration is imposible—if, as Kant maintains, "the categorical imperative or law of morality . . . is an a priori synthetical practical proposition"—then we must investigate the possibility of such an imperative in a purely a priori manner (B, F:79).

Pursuing this approach, Kant finds that when we merely think of a hypothetical imperative as such, we do not know what specific prescription it will contain until the conditions are stated under which it is to be an imperative (B, F:80), for only the end desired entails the specification of the means necessary to its realization. But when we think of a categorical imperative, we "know immediately what it contains"; "for since the imperative contains besides the law only the necessity of the maxim of acting in accordance with this law, while the law contains no condition to which it is restricted [such as an end or goal], there is nothing remaining in it except the universality of law as such to which the maxim of the action should conform; and in effect this conformity alone is represented as necessary by the imperative" (B, F:80).

Kant is here saying that the law of morality cannot be a hypothetical imperative, for all such imperatives—be they rules of skill or counsels of prudence—prescribe only such actions as depend, as means to its realization, upon an antecedently chosen end or goal; and although the imperatives themselves are objective principles of action, the ends which they serve are chosen on subjective grounds only and cannot be derived from the imperatives themselves. Hypothetical imperatives thus lack that objectively compelling and universal necessity which is the basic requirement for the law of morality. For this reason they do not and cannot define *the moral.*

But all of this is different in the case of categorical imperatives; for these imperatives, by definition, *command unconditionally,* i.e., they command without any reference to an end or goal. They can do so, however, only by neglecting content altogether and by referring to the mere form of laws, i.e., by referring to the mere form of those practical principles which are valid for the will of every rational being (B, C:130). The categorical imperatives, therefore, contain nothing but a reference to the form of laws *and* the command that any maxim of action which is to become a moral law conform to that form.

But if all categorical imperatives thus reduce to a reference to the mere form of laws and to the command that our practical maxims conform to this form, then there really is only one categorical imperative. In Kant's language it is this: *"Act only according to that maxim by which you can at the same time will that it should become a universal law"* (B, F:80). Or, more briefly: *"Act according to a maxim which is at the same time valid as a universal law"* (*11*:22; 23). And such an imperative is possible because reason, in its practical employment, is independent of all determination through the senses and therefore capable of acting in conformity with its own requirement, which is *universal validity* (*11*:19).

The categorical imperative, as just formulated, Kant accepts as the basic *principle* or *law of morality,* as the criterion of *the moral.* This means that any action the maxim of which fulfills the requirement of universality is sanctioned as a moral law, whereas any action the maxim of which does not fulfill that requirement is disqualified as a law. It is of utmost importance, however, to note again that the categorical imperative itself is the principle or law of morality (B, F:78; 79), and that it is *not* a moral law.

By way of illustrating the function of the categorical imperative as the criterion of *the moral,* Kant points out that "some actions are of such a nature that their maxim cannot even be *thought* as a universal law . . . without contradiction, far from it being possible that one could will that it should be such" (B, F:82). These actions, Kant holds, can never be regarded as moral. In the case of other actions "this internal impossibility is not found, though it is still impossible to *will* that their maxim should be raised to the universality of a law . . . because such a will would contradict itself" (B, F:83), i.e., its different maxims of action would be in irreconcilable conflict and for this reason, when taken together, could never be regarded as universally valid. The will involved in an action according to one maxim would be pitted against itself as it is engaged in actions according to other maxims also. Its maxims, though each is conceivable in itself, can never constitute a coherent system of laws for a unified will.

Certain negative considerations, according to Kant, also disclose the effectiveness of the categorical imperative as a criterion of moral actions. Thus, "when we observe ourselves in any transgression of a duty, we find that we do not actually will that our maxim should become a universal law. . . . We only take the liberty of making an exception to it for ourselves or for the sake of our inclination, and for this one occasion. . . . If we weighed everything from one and the same standpoint, namely, reason, we would come upon a contradiction in our own will, viz., that a certain principle is objectively necessary as a universal law and yet subjectively does not hold universally but rather admits exceptions" (B, F:83). The action would therefore be immoral. We thus find again that universality, i.e., the form of a universally valid law, is the touchstone of the moral value of all maxims of our actions (B, F:82).

### VI

Let us repeat: "What is derived from the particular natural situation of man as such, or from certain feelings as properties, or, even, from a particular tendency of the human reason which might not hold necessarily for the will of every rational being (if such a tendency is possible) can give a maxim valid for us but not a law: that is, it can give a subjective principle by which we might act only if we have the propensity and inclination, but not an objective principle by which we would be directed to act even if all our propensity, inclination, and natural tendency were opposed to it" (B, F:84). Subjective ends, resting on incentives, are grounds for hypothetical imperatives only (B, F: 86); they do not in themselves ground universally valid laws. Such laws are encountered only where the maxims of action conform to the form of a law as demanded by the basic norm of *the moral*, i.e., by the categorical imperative.

In so far as the categorical imperative stresses the *form* of a law rather than its *content,* it may be said to be empty. But in order to understand correctly what is meant here, we must distinguish between content in the sense of "reference to form" or "content of law," and content in the sense of "reference to action" or "material content." When it is said that Kant's ethics is an empty formalism and that it has no moral content, the charge is correct only if by content is meant a material content, a moral maxim or moral code; but, so understood, the charge is no argument against Kant. On the contrary, since no material content can be determined a priori, none can be included in the basic law of morality without impairing the universal validity of that law. Kant is therefore right in excluding all material content from the principle which defines *the moral.* But the true meaning of the categorical imperative pertains to the nature of laws, not to the matter of action; and this content, being but "the mere form of a universal legislation" (B, C:138), defines what is moral and what is not. It would be a misunderstanding of Kant to expect anything else from the categorical imperative.

As Kant sees it, reason alone does not bring forth ends or goals or maxims of action; on the contrary, it presupposes them as something derivable or derived from our needs, desires, and inclinations. But given this material content—and our experience abounds with it—reason, by applying to all maxims of action the formal requirement of universality, stamps some of them as moral and others as not moral. It thus evaluates, approving and rejecting and accepting as *moral laws* only those maxims of action which are universally valid. The categorical imperative itself, as criterion of *the moral,* is thus above all actions and is clearly distinct from all moral laws—the latter being but maxims of action which fulfill the demand of reason for universal validity.

Since the categorical imperative, as the law of morality, is nothing but the principle of morality itself, and since, moreover, it is the principle "by which reason determines the will to action" (B, C:152), we can say that man's consciousness of freedom is inextricably bound up with it and is, in fact, identical with it (B, C:152). The categorical imperative, in other words, is but an expression of the freedom or autonomy of our will. Or, to put it still differently, "the sole principle of morality consists in independence from all material of the law (i.e., a desired object) and in the accompanying determination of choice by the mere universal legislative form which a maxim must be capable of having" (B, C:144). Freedom of autonomy, understood in this sense, is "itself the formal condition of all maxims, under which alone they can all agree with the supreme practical law" (B, C:144-145). Only a will which is thus autonomous, i.e., a will which is determined only by the law of morality itself, is a good will (B, F:62). It is a will which acts exclusively from respect for the law as such.

However, we have here again enunciated conclusions for which the supporting arguments must yet be developed. We return, therefore, to a consideration of the categorical imperative and its most direct implications.

## VII

Kant's interpretation of the law of morality places reason above the affections and makes it the sole judge of all our actions. The morally good, Kant maintains, is that which is done, not from inclination or desire, but for the sake of the law. When a conflict arises between our inclinations and a moral law, the principle of morality demands that we disregard the former and act only in accordance with the law. But since the essence of a law lies in its universality, Kant's position reduces to this, that we ought to act only in conformance with the formal principle of universality.

It is at this point and with specific reference to Kant's emphasis on the formal aspect of moral laws that various critics have accused Kant of adhering to a radical *rigorism* in moral matters—to a rigorism so extreme that it does violence to human nature and to our best and most unselfish acts.

Most critics who raise the charge of rigorism base their arguments upon the contention that Kant's critical ethics *suppresses* all human desires, inclinations, and affections and upholds only those actions as moral which are done from duty alone. The charge, I believe, rests upon a basic confusion; but, unfortunately, Kant has himself given aid and comfort to his critics. Thus he says, for example, that our inclinations are "so lacking in absolute worth that the universal wish of every rational being must be to free himself completely from them" (B, F:86); that the "sublimity and intrinsic worth of the command is better shown in a duty the fewer subjective causes there are for it and the more they are against it" (B, F:84); that a man is to obey the moral law "from duty and not from a spontaneous inclination or from an endeavor unbidden but gladly undertaken" (B, C:191); that the moral law demands obedience "even though the creature does not like it" (B, C:191); that the submission to the law "contains no pleasure but rather displeasure proportionate to the constraint" upon the sensuously affected subject (B, C:188); and that "the majesty of duty has nothing to do with the enjoyment of life" (B, C:195). Kant also says: "It is a very beautiful thing to do good to men because of a love of order. But this is not the genuine moral maxim of our conduct, the maxim which is suitable to our position among rational beings as men. . . . We stand under a discipline of reason, and in all our maxims we must not forget our subjection to it" (B, C:189). And, finally: "The essential point in all determination of the will through the moral law is this: as a free will, and thus not only without co-operating with sensuous impulses but even rejecting all of them and checking all inclinations so far as they could be antagonistic to the law, it is determined merely by the law" (B, C:181).

Close examination of the passages shows, however, that all of them, in so far as they emphasize the form of a law as against the content of a maxim of action, far from entailing a disastrous rigorism, are perfectly reconcilable with the facts of man's moral experience. In the last quotation, for example, the phrase, "so far as they could be antagonistic to the law," is crucial. Properly interpreted the passage as a whole means that, although many of our inclinations must be checked or suppressed completely, those which are in harmony with the formal property of a law, i.e., with the demand for universality, are quite acceptable as grounds for action. All other passages quoted can be similarly reconciled with Kant's basic thesis. After all, the rigorism of which Kant has been accused and which seems to underlie the passages referred to is not analytically implied by his rationalism. It is implied only by the conjunction of two independent premises—the premises, namely, that (i) only actions done exclusively out of respect for, and therefore in harmony with, the law of morality deserve to be called moral, and that (ii) moral laws as such are in irreconcilable conflict with all inclinations and desires. The first of these premises is an essential part of Kant's rationalism and of critical ethics in general; the second, however, is no such ingredient element of the system but is, instead, an intrusion from entirely different sources. We shall consider both premises in the order in which they are given.

(i) It is inconceivable that form and content should ever be in conflict. To speak as if they were is to assume implicitly a particular content where only form was to be assumed. Form by itself, being a logico-epistemic abstraction, is nothing real and, for this reason, has no power to oppose anything. It attains reality only to the extent to which it is the form of something. Hence, just as in the field of theoretical knowledge a universally valid law, without addition of empirical data and their given interrelations, is a mere form of a law and therefore incapable of being constitutive of nature or of determining things and events, so in the field of action the law of morality is but the mere form of a law from which neither our maxims of action nor our moral laws can be derived. Here, too, empirical data are required to make the principle of universality applicable and useful. Far from finding form in conflict with the content of volition, we find thus that in actuality there can be no content without form, as there can be no form without content. Every appeal to the principle of universality, i.e., every appeal to the law of morality, must therefore take into consideration man's sensuous nature as the source of all content of actions. A repudiation of our inclinations and desires would deprive morality of its sole contact with the real; and Kant never intended this.

The crux of the matter is that Kant's separation of form and content is logico-epistemic, not psychologico-real. His distinction, therefore, does not preclude a factual harmony between the law of morality and at least some of our inclinations, moods, and desires. In order to be moral we need not suppress or eradicate all our desires; it is necessary only that we restrict our willingness to follow them indiscriminately or blindly. As Kant puts it: "Pure practical reason merely checks selfishness" and restricts it to agreement with the law of morality (B, C:181); "it limits all inclinations, including esteem, to the condition of obedience to its pure law" (B, C:186). This demand for a *restriction* of inclinations and desires through moral reason is so far removed from the assumption of a radical opposition between all inclinations and the moral law that it actually implies that pure reason, in order to achieve moral ends at all, must presuppose the material content, i.e., the maxims of action, of man's desires and drives. Reason merely approves or disapproves the subjective maxims, using their agreement or disagreement with the principle of universality as sole criterion of their moral worth.

It may happen, of course, that the restrictions thus imposed by reason are in opposition to some, or even most, of our desires; but there must always be at least one inclination or one desire which entices us in the direction sanctioned by the law of morality; otherwise we cannot act at all. The maxim of this inclination or desire fully meets the requirement of universality and is therefore a moral law. This means, however, that if reason has evaluated the alternative courses of action suggested by desires and inclinations and has sanctioned one particular course, then the law of morality does not compel us to refuse the approved desire or inclination any and all influence on our will. If, for example, as Kant himself says, "to be kind where one can is duty" (B, F:59), then one can hardly deny that our impulse or inclination to be kind is itself morally sanctioned and therefore of moral worth—even though its character *as moral* is determined, not by the fact that it is an inclination, but by the fact that its maxim is a universal law. And if a rational self-love, i.e., selfishness restricted by the law of morality to agreement with that law (B, C:181), is also sanctioned, then the desires and inclinations which are the constituent elements of this self-love have themselves moral sanction and may be permitted to affect our will. No moral law restricts or inhibits them.

It is true, of course, that Kant says: "A command that everyone should seek to make himself happy would be foolish, for no one commands another to do what he already invariably wishes to do" (B, C:148); and that therefore the desire for happiness does not ground a moral *ought*. But this argument is beside the point; for it is not the function of reason to discriminate between inclinations and disinclinations but to evaluate *all* inclinations and disinclinations and to approve or disapprove of them in accordance with the requirements of the law of morality. Inclinations and disinclinations to act in certain ways provide the content, the maxim of action, which is subject to an evaluation. If the content or maxim in question is in harmony with the law of morality, it belongs to the moral content sanctioned by the law; and it does so irrespective of our inclination or disinclination toward it.

Kant explicitly states that "pure practical reason does not require that we should renounce the claims of happiness; it requires only that we take no account of them whenever duty is in question" (B, C:199); and that "as far as our nature as sensible beings is concerned, our happiness is the only thing of importance" (B, C:170). After all, "man is a being of needs, so far as he belongs to the world of sense, and to this extent his reason certainly has an inescapable responsibility from the side of his sensuous nature to attend to its interests and to form practical maxims with a view to the happiness of this and, where possible, of a future life" (B, C:170). In fact, happiness, though "not of itself absolutely good in every respect," is at least an indispensable element in the highest good; for "virtue and happiness together constitute the possession of the highest good for a person" (B, C:215). Kant's sole concern is to make clear to his readers that man is "not so completely an animal as to be indifferent to everything which reason says on its own and to use it merely as a tool for satisfying his needs as a sensuous being"; for "that he has reason does not in the least raise him in worth above mere animality if reason only serves the purposes which, among animals, are taken care of by instinct" (B, C:170). What Kant thus insists upon is that, irrespective of whether or not a desire for happiness is involved in an action, the true moral worth of that action stems only from the fact that its maxim is sanctioned by the law of morality as such.

Even Kant's references to a "holy will" do not exclude inclination from the realm of moral perfection. Any maxim of action which has stood the test of expansion into universality and which is therefore a moral law, is part of the volitional content sanctioned by the law of morality. For a perfect being it is "a law of holiness" (B, C:189). That is to say, "in the supremely self-sufficing intelligence choice is . . . incapable of any maxim which could not at the same time be objectively a law, and the concept of holiness, which is applied to it for this reason, elevates it not indeed above all practical laws but above all restrictive practical laws, and thus above obligation and duty" (B, C:144). More pointedly still, Kant states that in the case of the holy will "the volition of itself is necessarily in unison with the law" (B, F:73), and that "the will whose maxims necessarily are in harmony with the laws of autonomy [i.e., with the law of morality] is a holy will" (B, F:96). The phrase, "the will whose maxims are necessarily in harmony with the laws," is a clear reference to the *content* of actions even in the case of the holy will. What Kant is saying is that a "holy being" is one who can act only according to maxims which are moral laws—which means, not that a "holy being" has no inclinations whatever, but that the maxims of his inclinations necessarily have the forms of universality requisite for moral laws.

We thus reach the conclusion that, despite his occasional lapses in linguistic formulations, Kant denies not that moral actions are also actions of our sensuous nature but that their moral worth lies in the material or sensuous motives which tend to induce them. It is Kant's position that, no matter what their inception may be, actions are moral only if their maxims fulfill the requirements given in the categorical imperative which, as the principle of universality, is the law of morality itself; and that fulfillment of these requirements transforms mere subjective maxims of action into objectively valid moral laws. Actions are moral not because they have no content at all but because their maxims fit into a context of laws other than that found in the sensible world. Without content no action is possible or even conceivable; and the law of morality itself, being but the formal demand for universality and having no content or maxim of its own, would be meaningless were it not for the fact that its demand is superimposed upon the material content of desires and inclinations. Thus, far from implying the complete suppression and eradication of all desires and inclinations, Kant's law of morality presupposes them as given and would be a vacuous abstraction without them.

## VIII

We have said earlier that the rigorism of Kant's ethics stems from the conjunction of two independent premises—the premises, namely, that (i) only actions done exclusively out of respect for, and therefore in harmony with, the law of morality deserve to be called moral, and that (ii) moral laws as such are in irreconcilable conflict with inclinations and desires. So far we have discussed only the first of these and have found that it entails no suppression or eradication of inclinations and desires which could be regarded as rigoristic. We shall now examine the second premise given above and shall attempt to clarify its relation to the Kantian system.

(ii) Since Kant's rigorism is not implied by his rationalism, its source must be extraneous to the system. Following this lead, we find that Kant's own conscience has at times supplied content where only questions of form were involved, and that his habits and attitudes—habits and attitudes of a "cool correctness" in conduct which reflect, in a measure, his protestant middle-class Prussian origin—have intruded upon purely theoretical discussions and have more than once colored his views. Kant himself, however, gives us another hint when he says: "In our times, when men hope to have more effect on the mind through yielding, soft-hearted feelings or high-flying puffed-up pretensions, which wither instead of strengthening the heart, than through the dry and earnest idea of duty which is more fitting to human imperfection and progress in goodness, attention to this method is more needed than ever" (B, C:254). Here Kant seems to point out that his rigorism is an implied but deliberate attack upon the sentimentalism of his Age. This interpretation gains support from another passage in the *Critique of Practical Reason*. "Can it be thought," Kant asks, "that there is any reason why we like to degrade [the moral law] to the level of our familiar inclination and why we take so much trouble to make it the chosen precept of our well-understood interest, other than the fact that we want to be free of the awesome respect which so severely shows us our own unworthiness?" (B, C:185). As opposed to this natural tendency to degrade the law Kant wants to uphold the dignity of the law; for he maintains that "if we search carefully, we shall find for all actions which are worthy of recommendation a law of duty which *commands* and does not leave to our pleasure what may be agreeable to our propensity" (B, C: 192).

Whatever the reason—be it unconscious intrusion or deliberate design—moral content creeps into Kant's arguments and illustrations where reference to form alone would be in order; and it is this content, surreptitiously introduced, that entails the rigorism of his ethics.

Kant's deviations from the basic premise of critical ethics are especially marked when, in illustrating the application or function of the law of morality, he confuses that law with the highest moral law. Since the law of morality, i.e., the categorical imperative, is but the demand for universal validity, it can be applied only in the sense of using it as the criterion by means of which we determine which maxim of action is a moral law and which is not. No specific moral law can be derived from it. At times, however—and especially in his *Metaphysics of Morals*—Kant seems to attempt such a derivation, thus confusing the issue.

Since moral laws, as universally valid maxims of action, have specifiable content, they can be derived only from more comprehensive moral laws which also have content; and in this whole chain of derivation even the highest laws from which specific moral laws are derivable must still have content—which is to say that they must be moral laws and not the law of morality. The situation here is analogous to that which we encounter, for example, in classical mechanics, where the principle of causality is not itself a law within the system (of the order, for instance, of Newton's three basic Laws of Motion of their derivatives), but is instead a metalinguistic stipulation specifying what kind of equations are to be admitted as constituent parts of the integrated system. Kant, however, writes at times as if for him the law of morality were the highest moral law; and whenever he deduces practical laws from the law of morality it can be shown that he implicitly assumes some moral law as inherent in his major premise.

The origin of the laws which Kant thus assumes is not and cannot be the categorical imperative; it is, rather, a comprehensive evaluation which has been empirically obtained. It is content pertaining to health, wealth, power, happiness, and other objects of inclination and desire. Take, for example, the case of a man "for whom things are going well" and who resolves to "let each one be as happy as heaven wills, or as he can make himself," but who refuses to contribute to the welfare of others or to come to their assistance in time of need (B, F:82). Kant maintains that if such a way of thinking were a universal law of nature, the human race could exist but it would be "impossible to *will* that such a principle should hold everywhere as a law" because a will acting upon such a maxim would conflict with itself, for "instances can often arise" in which a man acting upon the above maxim would himself "need the love and sympathy of others" but "would have robbed himself . . . of all hope of the aid he desires" (B, F:82) because he refused aid to others. Kant's argument here assumes not only the basic law of morality (which is but the demand for universality in the maxims of action) but also a principle of happiness involving explicit references to love, sympathy, and aid—references, in other words, to content; and the force of Kant's argument stems from these references to content rather than from any application of the principle of universality. The argument, in other words, depends in its essentials upon the assumption of a moral law (the law of happiness and enlightened self-interest) and not upon the law of morality. It thus involves a basic confusion; and only confusions of this type give rise to Kant's rigorism.

## IX

In the preceding section reference has been made—albeit only in passing—to a highest moral law. From the point of view of the systematics of a moral code, the question of whether or not there is an ultimate or highest moral law from which all other moral laws can be derived is, of course, of great importance; but we are here not concerned with this problem. We are at present interested only in clearing up or preventing certain confusions; for even if there is a highest moral law in the sense indicated, it must not be mistaken for the law of morality as such. The former, as the all-comprehensive maxim of action, has specifiable content pertaining to man's desires, inclinations, or needs; the latter, as the criterion of *the moral,* is but the demand for the universal validity of all moral laws, the highest included.

Nevertheless, the idea of a highest moral law contains systematic suggestions which are not without bearing upon the role and function of the law of morality itself. It will be best, however, to approach the problems here involved in an indirect way.

To begin with, Kant's law of morality—since in itself it imposes no moral laws and, as formal criterion of *the moral*, is not restricted to any particular stage in man's cultured advancement—is beyond all changes and transformations of accepted moral codes and is itself unchanging. What is in evolution in our cultural development is the specific moral code accepted at any given time, not the law of morality as such. In fact, it is the latter which defines the framework within which alone any reference to the evolution of morals makes sense; for only when the nature of *the moral* is specifically and definitely defined is it possible to speak intelligibly about the difference in moral codes and the discovery of new moral laws.

It is, of course, true that the desires and inclinations of human beings are many and varied, and that the ends men set themselves are therefore likewise many and varied. And it may well happen that one man regards as desirable what another considers to be most undesirable, and both may be right in their judgments; for both may have different needs and desires and, for this reason, may pursue different ends. Moreover, no two men ever find themselves in absolutely identical situations; for, strictly speaking, each moment of choice or of action is unique as a space-time event. It must be admitted, of course, that normal human beings living in the same cultural environment may find themselves in *similar* situations, facing *comparable* problems; and within the limits of such similarities rules of conduct may be evolved. Such rules, however, are empirical maxims, not moral laws.

Nevertheless, in so far as man's actions—even the most unique of his actions—are moral at all, they must possess or contain that quality which alone makes them moral, i.e., they must fulfill the requirements of the principle or law of morality. Since Kant's categorical imperative is not a generalization of some particular maxim of action but is the demand that the maxim of every action which is to be judged moral must be conceivable as a universal law, even a completely unique action is moral if its maxim fulfills the stated requirement.

Hence, to maintain that Kant's principle of morality is irreconcilable with the facts of cultural evolution, or to accuse Kant of upholding a formalism which leaves no room for the uniqueness of individual human situations is to distort his basic principle—even though Kant has repeatedly done this himself. Precisely because the law of morality is not a generalization of some empirically derived maxim of action, i.e., precisely because that law is but the formal definition of *the moral,* can Kant's critical ethics allow for the uniqueness of actual situations in a manner in which no other ethical doctrine can do so. Because Kant's law of morality is the purely formal demand for universal validity of the maxims of action, it is beyond changes in moral codes and is effective as a criterion of *the moral* with respect to *any* maxim which requires evaluation anywhere, at any time, under any circumstances.

So conceived there is, of course, danger in the purely formal law of morality; for it might be argued that if every action is unique, then the maxim of every action is at once universally valid—valid, that is, for its unique single instance. If this is admitted without qualification, then all actions are moral and Kant's criterion of *the moral,* since it does not differentiate between the immoral and the moral, is no criterion at all. Such a conclusion, if it were sustained by the rest of the Kantian system, would be fatal to that system as a whole. It can be shown, however, that this conclusion is not sustained, for the formal criterion so far considered is specifically qualified in the larger context; and it is in that context that the systemic suggestions referred to above come into their own.

## X

The universality of law, Kant maintains, is the formal condition of nature in the widest possible sense. That is to say, it is the formal condition of a nature which includes noumenal as well as phenomenal objects. It must be noted, however, that in the world of phenomena the laws of nature, as necessary connections of the "manifold of intuition," can be "given a priori in conformity to concepts of the understanding, i.e., as schemata" (B, C:176-177), whereas in the world of noumena, in which alone moral laws are valid, nothing can be found which corresponds to sensuous intuition. Kant, nevertheless, holds that it is possible to think of the laws of morality as constitutive of a realm of "intelligible nature" in much the same way in which the law of causality is constitutive of the realm of "sensible nature." If this be granted, then we can conceive the moral laws, in their universal and formal aspects, after the manner of laws of "sensible nature." The latter, therefore, may be regarded as "the *type* of the moral law" (B, C:177). A moral law, in other words, as a universal and necessary law of "intelligible nature," plays in the noumenal realm the very same role which a law of nature plays in the phenomenal realm; and the law of morality is as constitutive of "intelligible nature" as the law of causality is of "sensible nature."

If the analogy here indicated is accepted, then it is possible to reformulate the categorical imperative and to state it thus: "Act according to maxims which can at the same time have themselves as universal laws of nature as their objects" (B, F:94). However, this new formulation requires clarification and is at best but a transition to Kant's ultimate "third principle." Kant himself has reworded it twice and has made significant additions. Thus he says at one time: "Act as though the maxim of your action were by your own will to become a universal law of nature" (B, F:80). And at another time he says: "Ask yourself whether, if the action which you propose should take place by a law of nature of which you yourself were a part, you could regard it as possible through your will" (B, C:178). In these formulations the implications of such phrases as "by your own will" and "through your will" are particularly significant and require special attention.

According to Kant, every law expresses a necessary relation

between specified terms. It is therefore an analytic truth that all laws are universally valid; for if the statement of a relation between terms admits of exceptions and is thus *not necessary*, it is not a law—although it may be an empirical rule having a determinable probability value. The indispensable formal ground of any law—as of any other propositional statement—is, of course, the basic axiom of intelligibility, i.e., the principle or law of non-contradiction. It is obvious that a contradictory statement cannot be a law. But it is equally obvious that the interrelated axioms of intelligibility—the principle of identity, the principle of non-contradiction, and the principle of the excluded middle—do not by themselves establish the validity of any particular law. Moreover, it is evident that we must distinguish between the objective validity of a law and its applicability to real things or events. It is possible, for example, that a law expresses a relation between terms which have no counterpart in the real world or which are defined for an imaginary world only. In so far as a law actually expresses a necessary relation between the terms in question, it is objectively valid; but in so far as the terms have no counterpart in the real world, the law is not applicable to real things or events. Hence, if the moral laws no less than the laws of nature are to be applicable as well as objectively valid, they must contain at least one reference to empirical facts. In the realm of nature such facts are our sense impressions; in the realm of morals they are our preferences and valuations.

One other aspect of the laws must be noted. In the realm of nature every applicable and valid law is, in principle, a constituent element in a systemic context. The necessity expressed in the law is grounded, not in empirical data or in inductive generalizations from such data, but in a deduction (be it actual or only conceived as possible) of the law itself from some assumption or theory. It is a systemically determined necessity and is therefore one which transcends mere empirical generalization. The applicability of the law, on the other hand, does not depend on systemic context but is assured only by determinable relations of the law itself to the empirical data.

The systemic context of which an individual law is a constituent element contains, as a rule, many laws which vary in scope and which thus form discernible levels of generality. The context of laws, in other words, is a systemic hierarchy within which all laws depend ultimately upon the assumed premises of the system and are derivable from those premises by chains of reasoning of varying length. The premises of the system themselves, however, can be justified only by still broader assumptions which, in turn, require other assumptions for their justification. Whether or not the progression of reason from assumed premises to ever more comprehensive premises finally culminates in some ultimate and all-inclusive premise (as some metaphysicians believe) is a question which need not concern us now. It is sufficient to note that the projection of such a goal is not contradictory but finds support even in the nature of reason itself—in so far at least as reason is comprehension in terms of principles only. Kant acknowledged and used the projection in his doctrine of transcendental ideas.

If laws are not only constituent elements of a system but are also applicable to things, then they are descriptive of the interrelations of these things; and the system of the laws is descriptive of a world. It is in this sense, for example, that the systemically connected laws of physics and chemistry describe a world. Ideally, a unified science, as an all-inclusive system of laws applicable to all data of observation, would describe the whole of "nature." But let us return now to the Kantian analogy between moral laws and the laws of nature, and to Kant's second formulation of the law of morality.

The objective validity of the laws of nature, so we have seen, is grounded in systemic context; and the necessity which these laws express is derived from the premises of the system. In so far, therefore, as the laws of nature, in their formal aspect, are "the *type* of the moral law" (B, C:177), what is true of the former must also be true of the latter. That is to say, the validity of the moral laws, and the necessitation which they express, are likewise grounded in and justified by systemic context. As integral parts of the system, the moral laws no less than the laws of nature have a significance which transcends particularized whims and wishes and is independent of purely subjective desires and feelings. They have the weight and validity of the system as a whole. There is this difference, however: whereas the laws of nature express a univocal and necessary relation between actual things, the moral laws assert that such a relation connects the termini of possible actions. But this difference does not disrupt the analogy to which Kant refers; for that analogy involves only the formal aspects of the two kinds of laws, and from the purely formal point of view, it is irrelevant whether the laws in question pertain to actual or to possible "things." From the purely formal point of view, therefore, an integrated system of moral laws is as descriptive of a world as is the system of the laws of nature. That the world described by the system of moral laws is a possible rather than an actual world is from this point of view of no importance. But since Kant defines nature as the existence of things in so far as that existence is determined by universal laws, it is clear that a system of moral laws, in so far as it determines the existence of things, also determines nature. If we keep this fact in mind, then, I believe, we come to a better understanding of Kant's second formulation of the law of morality: "Act according to maxims which can at the same time have themselves as universal laws of nature as their object" (B, F:94).

What Kant means is that our actions are moral whenever we act as if the maxims of our actions, conceived as integral parts of the systemic context of laws, were themselves the object of the actions involved. Or, rendered more freely, what Kant means is that any actions must be regarded as moral if the maxim on which we proceed can be included as an integral part in that context of laws which determines nature. The term "nature" refers here to a possible rather than to an actual realm—to a possible realm, however, which is in itself perfectly consistent and coherent, and which man, as a free and rational agent, conceives and projects beyond the actual world.

We must note, however, that although the inclusion of the maxims of our actions as laws in a systemic context entails their universal validity within the scope of that context, it does not assure their applicability. It is possible, in other words, to conceive a world which is completely determined by a system of laws but which has no connection whatever with the actualities of human existence. Such a world would be as irrelevant to our actions as our actions would be irrelevant to it. The moral realm, therefore, has real significance only if the maxims which are admitted as laws are expressive of human desires and inclinations and are thus germane to our existence—a conclusion which is well substantiated by our earlier arguments.

## XI

Two other problems can now be clarified. The first involves the relation of a universally valid law to a particular instance or case where that law applies. The second pertains to the relation of particular laws to the systemic context as such. Both problems arise with respect to the laws of nature as well as with respect to moral laws. Kant's analogy between the two kinds of laws is therefore borne out again, and our interpretation of the moral laws can follow once more the pattern set by our understanding of the laws of nature.

As integral parts of a systemic context, all laws of nature and all moral laws are categorical statements asserting necessary relations. The application of these laws, however, depends on specifiable conditions and is therefore essentially hypothetical. The theorems of Euclidean plane geometry, for example, considered as part of the deductive system, are universally valid categorical assertions. Their applicability to the world of things depends, however, on whether or not ideally rigid bodies exist, and is therefore conditional or hypothetical only. Similarly, the generalized gas law, considered merely as a law, is also a universally valid categorical assertion. Its applicability, too, assumes certain conditions as fulfilled in a given case and is thus hypothetical only, for if the gas in question is not an ideal gas, the law may give an approximate description of its behavior but does not apply in all strictness. That the moral laws, too, are applicable only under specifiable conditions pertaining to given situations follows not only from the Kantian analogy but from the nature of these laws themselves. For example, the law, *Contribute to the welfare of others,* can have practical significance only if in a given situation I actually have the means and the power to contribute to their welfare. Although the law itself is unequivocally categorical in its demand, its applicability in a given case is conditional only. To disregard the condition reduces the law itself, as a practical demand, to an absurdity.

We can now understand how it is possible for Kant to maintain that all moral laws are universal in the sense that they hold for all rational beings, and yet to allow for the uniqueness of concrete situations. So far as this problem is concerned, the moral laws are in exactly the same position as are the laws of nature formulated in our sciences. The latter, too, are universal in scope and must be applied to unique situations; and the solution of the problem is the same in both cases.

We must note, however, that the processes and things to which the laws of nature apply are rarely, if ever, completely described by a single law. Each individual law which is applicable in some concrete situation pertains only to an isolated aspect of that situation. Numerous other laws are simultaneously applicable to other aspects of the same situation; and only all laws together describe fully what is the case. For example, the range, R, of a bomb dropped from an airplane in level flight is determined by the law

$$R = v\sqrt{\frac{2h}{g}}$$

where 'v' is the velocity of the plane, 'h' is the height from which the bomb is dropped, and 'g' is the gravitational attraction of the earth. The law states that R is a function of v, h, and g—where v, h, and g are specifiable factors in the concrete situation. It is evident, however, that v, h, and g are not the only factors in a given situation which can and do affect R. The resistance of the air, the direction and force of the wind (if there is any), a premature explosion of the bomb, a collision of the bomb with some other object in mid-air—all of these (and still others) are or may be further factors affecting the range of a particular bomb; and their effects upon R can also be described by laws. Moreover, each of these factors is in turn determined by other factors operating according to still other laws. The actual value of R in a concrete situation is therefore fully described only by the whole complexus of interrelated laws which have a bearing upon any or all of the factors involved in the case. That we usually disregard most of the factors and laws merely means that we are satisfied with an approximation or an abstractive description; it does not prove that only a single law completely determines what is the case. The point is that where moral laws are concerned the situation is analogous.

No moral decision is ever made in a vacuum, and no moral situation is ever simple. A number of issues are simultaneously involved whenever, under given circumstances, we adopt a definite course of action. The action itself, in order to be adequate to the situation, must be the resultant of all the moral laws germane to the issues involved. The question, for example, whether or not in a given situation I should contribute a certain amount of money to the support of a specified charity cannot be answered exclusively on the basis of the law which demands that I contribute to the welfare of others. To act on the basis of this law alone would mean to decide the issue without due regard for all the factors involved in the concrete situation. It might well be the case, for instance, that I need the money for a surgical operation which will save my life; or that I need it to pay for my own education; or that I need it to support my invalid mother. Surely, each one of these alternatives suggests a course of action which would be in harmony with the moral law; and each one, in turn, entails its own complexus of issues and thus involves still other moral laws. Thus, to aid my mother rather than to contribute to the specified charity comes itself under the law which demands that I contribute to the welfare of others; but in my choice between the charity and my mother still other laws are involved—such as, for example, that I ought to contribute to the welfare of the greatest number of people, and that I ought to support first those who are closest to me. It is obvious, therefore, that we cannot make a decision which is adequate to the total moral situation on the basis of one isolated law; and it is my contention that, despite his own aberrations in this respect, Kant fundamentally did not think that we could. Not only is the interpretation here given in perfect harmony with Kant's explicit statement that the categorical imperative is "the only condition under which a will never comes into conflict with itself" (B, F:94), but is entailed by the Kantian analogy between moral laws and the law of nature. Just as in the realm of nature an individual event in all its concreteness is determined only by a complexus of harmoniously interrelated laws, so in the realm of morals an individual action is morally justified in its full concreteness only when it is determined by the harmoniously integrated complexus of all those moral laws which are germane to the given situation. This means, in principle, that an action in all its situational concreteness is fully justified only if it conforms to all relevant moral laws which, as part of a systemic context, must themselves be consistent with that context as a whole.

We are here brought back to the second problem mentioned at the beginning of this section—the problem, namely, of the relation of particular laws to the systemic context.

The necessity expressed in a moral law, like the necessity expressed in a law of nature, is grounded in the systemic context of which the law itself is an integral part. That is to say, it is grounded in the fact that the law is deducible from the assumptions or postulates which define and, in this sense, determine the systemic context. All moral laws taken together in their systemic unity describe a world—albeit a conceivable or possible rather than an actual world. The analogy between moral laws and the laws of nature is in all formal respects beyond question.

However, in the case of the laws of nature the deduction of a validly applicable system is assured because the laws in question derive concrete meaning and content from their relation to the manifold sense data which are the given of our experience. In the case of the moral laws, however, sense content is irrelevant; for moral laws are not directly or essentially concerned with what *is*. Their concrete meaning is not derivable from the world of things and sense impressions; it is, however, intimately bound up with human volitions, with desires and inclinations. The system of moral laws is, in fact, the projection of a trans-cendental realm of volitions which, in its integrated unity, is but the expression of a self-consistent will—the individual volitions being the particularized manifestations of that will. Hence, when we evaluate the maxim of a contemplated or proposed action in the light of Kant's law of morality, we actually evaluate it in terms of the total system of moral laws or—what amounts to the same thing—in terms of a self-consistent will through the exercise of which a conceivable world is to be actualized. That in the over-all situation the conceivable world which we attempt to actualize is, in a sense, but a continuation in projection of the world we live in is obvious. Were it otherwise, our actions would lose that touch with reality which makes them effective in the world of things, and we ourselves would be lost in Utopian dreams or, in the extreme, in schizophrenic disintegration. The fact that we are rational beings living in an actual world thus delimits our projections of a moral realm; it restricts the freedom we might otherwise have in selecting the highest moral law from which all other laws must be deducible.

Of course, the restriction here referred to leaves still room for choice in the construction of our system; for the same or nearly the same laws can be deduced from different premises; and valid laws may be derived from false as well as from true assumptions. However, since the particular moral laws, in order to be relevant to our actions, must have definable content, the highest moral law, as the major premise of the system, must likewise have content. If this condition is not fulfilled, the re-quired deduction is not possible. Since the categorical imperative, as the law of morality, i.e., as the criterion of *the moral,* is (i) a meta-systemic stipulation and therefore not an integral part of the system, and (ii) a stipulation concerning the purely formal requirements of a law, it is not itself the highest moral law and is not the premise from which the particular laws or the context of these laws can be derived. We still face the question: Is there a highest moral law as demanded by the conception of a system; and if so, what is it?

## XII

The question which we have just raised cannot be answered at once or by a simple Yes or No. It admits, however, of an indirect approach which may yield a satisfactory conclusion.

Moral laws, as Kant understands them, are maxims of action which fulfill the formal requirement of universal validity. Man's actions, however, are inseparably related to ends—i.e., to objects or states of affairs—which men desire or wish for. Since there are countless ends which men may or actually do desire, there are countless maxims of action; but only some of these qualify as moral laws. As we now know, the maxims which do qualify as moral laws constitute a context; and this context, in order to preserve the universal validity of all laws which are included in it, must be self-consistent and, therefore, essentially systemic. Since the Kantian thesis is, not that no law can pertain to an end, but only that universality rather than the end involved is the criterion of a law, it follows that the systemic context of laws actually defines or determines a self-consistent realm of ends. And since the ends which men seek are conceived and understood in terms of value, the realm of ends is really a self-consistent realm of values. Hence, if there were "something the existence of which in itself had an absolute worth," then this something, "as an end in itself," "could be a ground of definite laws." "In it and only in it could lie the ground of . . . a practical law" (B, F:86). Is there such a highest value, such an end in itself?

Let us assume for a moment that such a "something" actually exists. Then, "if there is to be a supreme practical principle . . . , it must be one that forms an objective principle of the will from the conception of that which is necessarily an end for everyone because it is an end in itself" (B, F:87). If this is admitted, then we can formulate an implicit premise of Kant's system thus: Act so that you treat anything the existence of which is itself an absolute worth always as an end and never as a means only. And if we now hold, with Kant, that *"rational nature exists as an end in itself"* (B, F:87), that therefore man and every rational being is "an end in himself and not merely a means to be arbitrarily used by this or that will," and that, as a consequence, "in all his actions, whether they are directed to himself or to other rational beings, [man] must always be regarded at the same time as an end" (B, F:86), then we can reformulate the law of morality in this way: *"Act so that you treat humanity, whether in your own person or in that of another, always as an end and never as a means only"* (B, F:87). "This principle of humanity and of every rational creature as an end in itself is the supreme limiting condition of freedom of the actions of each man" (B, F:88-89). It means, however, that "the ends of any person . . . must as far as possible also be my end"; for only thus does the "conception of an end in itself . . . have its full effect on me" (B, F:88).

Kant's conception of a "realm of ends" and his thesis that rational beings as such are "ends in themselves" entails significant consequences.

Let us note first, however, that, for Kant, "rational beings" are "persons"; that "their nature indicates that they are ends in themselves, i.e., things which may not be used merely as means" (B, F:86-87); that "without them nothing of absolute worth could be found" (B, F:87); and that, therefore, a person is an object of respect which restricts or sets limits to arbitrary choice. Persons, in other words, "are not merely subjective ends whose existence as a result of our action has a worth for us but are objective ends, i.e., beings whose existence in itself is an end" and "for which no other end can be substituted" (B, F:87).

If persons are ends in themselves, i.e., if they are ends the very existence of which is as such of absolute worth, then, surely, they must be distinguished from all other ends, i.e., they must be distinguished from ends the existence of which is of value only to us. We must distinguish, in other words, between *persons* which, as existing beings, must be respected as having absolute worth, and *ends* which, conceived as values, are to be realized through our own actions. The former are objects (or "ends") of respect; the latter are objects (or "ends") of action. But *as ends* they are all included in the "realm of ends"; for "if we abstract from the personal difference of rational beings and thus from all content of their private ends, we can think of a whole of all ends in systemic connection, a whole of rational beings as ends in themselves as well as of the particular ends which each may set for himself" (B, F:91).

So understood, the realm of ends takes on new significance. As a realm it is "a whole of all ends in systemic connection." The connections which constitute this whole are common laws (B, F:91), i.e., they are the maxims of action which have qualified as particular laws. The idea of a realm of ends is thus further proof that Kant thought of moral laws not as isolated maxims but as integral parts of a system of laws; and the inclusion of persons as ends of respect in the realm of ends enabled him to maintain that the law demanding this respect might well serve as the basis for the entire system of laws which is constitutive of the realm of ends, i.e., that this law, in effect, is the highest moral law.

The realm of ends which centers around the absolute worth of a person is, for Kant, not only a systemic context of moral laws but also the basis of moral society; and it is this in a two-fold sense. (i) The law which demands respect for a person as absolute worth—be it one's own person or somebody else—imposes upon everyone the duty to rise above the level of "animality" to that of "humanity" and thus to become worthy of the "humanity" which dwells within him (*11*:190). In the state of nature, i.e., prior to the establishment of a moral society, the individual is motivated by envy, by a desire for power, by an urge to possess, and by all the related inclinations which are antagonistic to harmonious interrelations. The mere presence of other human beings brings the anti-social traits into prominence (*12*:190). The "dominance of the good principle," in so far as men can contribute to its realization, can therefore be assured only through the establishment of a society which is grounded in moral laws. To establish such a society is the rational task and, therefore, the duty of all mankind (*12*:190). It is a duty, that is, which "the human race has to itself," not one which one person has to another (*12*:195).

(ii) Moral society, even though it is only partly realized, is "a connection of men under moral laws" (*12*:190). And since the highest moral law demands respect for the "humanity" within each person as an end having absolute worth, it also prescribes— at least in a broad way—the conduct of individuals as members of a society. In so far as the highest moral law finds expression in legislative acts and thus becomes part of the positive law of a given society, it is essentially proscriptive and determines what is legal and what is not. An action is *legal,* according to Kant (*11*:27), if, in conformity with a general law, the maxim of that action allows the freedom of choice of each person to exist together with the same freedom of all; and positive law is from this point of view but the totality of those conditions under which co-existence in freedom is possible (*11*:27). Hence, if my action is such that, in conformity with the general law, it is reconcilable with the freedom of all persons, then "anyone does me an injustice who prevents my action" (*11*:28), for his interference cannot be reconciled with the idea of freedom. It must be clearly understood, however, that in legal actions only external conformity to the law is required; for "anyone can be free although his freedom is a matter of indifference to me—nay, even if I desire with all my heart to destroy it—if only I refrain from external actions which interfere with it" (*11*:28). Morality, however, demands more than legality—more, that is, than the merely external conformity of actions with the general law of freedom; and it does so along two distinct lines.

In so far as I act from respect for the humanity within me, my own perfection is an "end which is at the same time a duty" (*11*:195); for "combined with the humanity as an end within our own person there is the rational will and, therefore, the duty" to cultivate all capacities which are necessary for the furtherance of those ends which reason prescribes as pertaining to man (*11*: 195). It is thus a man's "duty to supply the defects of his knowledge by instruction and to correct his errors . . . in order for him to be worthy of the humanity that resides in him" (3:356). But the duty here involved is only general, and the maxim of action should be: "Cultivate your faculties of mind and body so as to be effective for all ends which you may encounter, uncertain as to which of them might some day become your own" (11:196). Beyond this, however, it is a man's "duty to cultivate his will to the purest disposition of virtue, to raise it to the point where the law becomes the incentive to his actions which accord with duty, and to obey the law from duty—this being inner morally practical perfection"—a perfection which makes "each practical end, which is also a duty, our object" (11:190-191).

In so far as the happiness of others is "an end which is also a duty" (11:197), it is necessary to distinguish between benevolent wishes and benevolent actions. The former, since they do not imply the doing of anything, may be unlimited. The latter, since they may entail personal sacrifices, do involve limits; "for the maxim that one should sacrifice one's own happiness (one's own true wants) in order to promote that of others, if made a universal law, would be self-contradictory" (11:197). The limits, however, must remain indeterminate. "Much depends on what would be the true want of each according to his own feelings, and it must be left to each to determine this for himself" (11:197). The law, therefore, "holds for the maxims only, not for particular actions" (11:197).

Included in the happiness of others, which it is my duty to promote, is their moral well-being. However, our duty here is purely negative. "The pain which man feels from remorse, although moral in origin, is yet physical in its effect—like grief, fear, and every other diseased condition. To see to it that he is not deservedly smitten by this inner reproach is not *my* duty but *his* concern. Nevertheless, it is my duty to do nothing which, because of the nature of the man, might induce him to do that for which his conscience may afterwards torment him; that is, it is my duty not to give him occasion for stumbling" (11:197-198).

There emerges thus, from Kant's point of view, a general pattern of moral society based upon the principle of respect for the humanity within us as an end in itself. The laws governing such a society, as distinguished from the laws of nature, are moral laws which, in so far as they regulate external actions only, define what is legal, but which, in so far as they themselves become the ground of determination of our actions, are moral laws proper (*11*:11) and define virtues (*11*:183; 186). Through the realization of moral society man rises from the level of animality to that of humanity (*11*:190), for the realization of moral society is the perfecting of man as a rational and free individual (*11*:195) and thus as a person.

To be sure, Kant admits that the realm of ends, this "systemic union of rational beings through common objective laws"—this moral society—is "only an ideal" (B, F:91); but "a rational being belongs to the realm of ends as a member when he gives universal laws in it while also himself subject to these laws. He belongs to it as a sovereign when he, as legislating, is subject to the will of no other" (B, F:91). When this idea is followed through, a still different formulation of the categorical imperative becomes possible.

## XIII

In the original formulation of the categorical imperative Kant emphasized "universal validity for every rational being" as the sole characteristic of the moral law. In this formulation he provided us with the criterion which alone separates the moral law from mere subjective maxims. In the second formulation of the law of morality Kant gave us "the supreme limiting condition of freedom" by stipulating that "the subject of ends, i.e., the rational being itself, be made the basis of all maxims of actions and [that it] thus be treated never as a mere means but as . . . an end" (B, F:95). This second principle is, of course, universal —because it applies to all rational beings; and it does not commit us to relative ends—because "humanity" is here not thought of as an object which we ourselves, subjectively, make our end, but as "the objective end which should constitute the supreme limiting condition of all subjective ends" (B, F:89).

However, being only the supreme limiting condition of freedom—a condition, that is, which prevents freedom from becoming arbitrary and lawless—even the second formulation of the categorical imperative is not final. It does not clarify the *basis* of the moral law itself.

Kant's position, briefly stated, is this: The two basic ideas—that of universality and that of an end in itself—can be brought together in a "third practical principle of the will" which is "the supreme condition of [the will's] harmony with universal practical reason" (B, F:89). Only this new formulation will disclose the ultimate basis of the moral law.

The "third practical principle" can be obtained, Kant believes, when the will of every rational being is taken as *"making* universal law" (B, F:89); i.e., it can be obtained when each individual person takes his own maxims of action "from the point of view which regards himself, and hence also every other rational being, as legislative" (B, F:95)—"as giving universal law through all the maxims of [his] will" (B, F:91). The will of a rational being is in that case not only subject to laws but is "self-legislative" and therefore subject to those laws only "of which it can regard itself as the author" (B, F:89). The freedom of the moral will is thus preserved; for "there is no contradiction in positing for one's self an end which is also a duty since in doing so I constrain myself, and this [self-constraint] is quite consistent with freedom" (*11*:185). The duty (and therefore the moral law) is self-imposed.

If Kant's argument is accepted, then morality "consists in the relation of every action to that legislation through which alone a realm of ends is possible" (B, F:91), and the moral imperative demands that every person, as self-legislative rational being, "act as if he, by his maxims, were at all times a legislative member in the universal realm of ends" (B, F:95); or, in Kant's final formulation: *"So act that the maxim of your will could always hold at the same time as the principle of universal legislation"* (B, C:142).

The interrelation of the basis *(ratio essendi)* and the criterion *(ratio cognoscendi)* of the moral laws—to which attention was called earlier—is now clear. The former is the self-legislative will of a rational being; the latter is the principle of universality. When the former is given, the latter follows from it analytically (B, F:102); but when the latter is given, the former is its only possible "unconditioned ground" (B, F:101-115). That is to say, the autonomous or self-legislative will of a rational being is in itself the basis or source of all moral laws, whereas the principle of universality is the criterion of moral laws as distinguished from mere maxims (*11*:23). If the will, as lawgiver, is conceived only as "will in general, which might also be the will of others," it is the basis of morality proper (*11*:192). Universality, however, is in any case the criterion of laws as such.

## XIV

Before we continue with the main argument, we must consider briefly one additional aspect of the realm of ends.

It is Kant's contention that in the realm of ends "everything has either a *price* or a *dignity*" (B, F:92). "Whatever has a price can be replaced by something else as its equivalent; on the other hand, whatever is above all price, and therefore admits of no equivalent, has a dignity" (B, F:92). It is Kant's contention, furthermore, that everything related to "general human inclinations and needs" has a "market price," but that "that which constitutes the condition under which alone something can be an end in itself" has an "inherent worth" or dignity (B, F:92). Since "morality is the condition under which alone a rational being can be an end in itself, because only through it is it possible to be a legislative member in the realm of ends," it follows that "morality and humanity"—the latter in so far as it is capable of morality—"alone have dignity" (B, F:92). The idea of man as autonomous legislator in the intelligible world thus "places before our eyes the sublimity of our own nature" (B, C:194).

"Skill and diligence in work have a market value; wit, lively imagination, and humor have an affective price; but fidelity in promises and benevolence on principle (not from instinct) have intrinsic worth. Nature and likewise art contain nothing which could replace their lack, for their worth consists not in effects which flow from them, nor in advantage and utility which they produce; it consists only in intentions, i.e., in maxims of the will, which are ready to reveal themselves in this manner through actions even though success does not favor them" (B, F:92).

There emerges, thus, at the end of the present argument an idea with which Kant opened the First Section of his *Foundations of the Metaphysics of Morals*—the idea, namely, of an unconditioned good will. As Kant puts it: "Intelligence, wit, judgment, and the other talents of mind . . . or courage, resoluteness, and perseverance as qualities of temperament are doubtless in many respects good and desirable. But they can become extremely bad and harmful if the will, which is to make use of these gifts of nature . . . , is not good. It is the same with the gifts of fortune. Power, riches, honor, even health, general wellbeing, and the contentment with one's condition which is called happiness make for pride and even arrogance if there is not a good will to correct their influence on the mind and its principles of action, so as to make them conformable to a universal end." "The good will seems to constitute the indispensable condition even of worthiness to be happy" (B, F:55). And so Kant can say that *"nothing in the world—indeed nothing even beyond the world—can possibly be conceived which could be called good without qualification except a good will"* (B, F:55).

But we know now that that will alone is unconditionally good "whose maxims, when made a universal law, can never conflict with itself" (B, F:94), whose freedom is restricted by respect for the humanity within us as an end in itself, and whose very essence is self-legislative autonomy in the realm of ends. So at least Kant views the situation.

## XV

Let us now remind ourselves of the fact that, beginning with Section XII, our whole argument rests upon an assumption—upon the assumption, namely, that there is "something" which, as an end in itself, can be "a ground of definite laws." This "something" turned out to be the self-legislative will of a rational being. A will, however, cannot give laws to itself unless it is autonomous or free (B, F:103). Freedom of the will is therefore the only condition under which alone moral laws are possible (B, F:115). The question now is, Do we, as individual persons, have such freedom; and if we do, how do we know that we have it?

We have seen in Section III that Kant's arguments in the *Critique of Pure Reason* lead to the conclusion that freedom in the sense required is at least thinkable without contradiction, and that, as transcendental idea, it is reconcilable with the idea of a thorough-going causal determination in the realm of phenomena (B, C:153). But this conclusion alone is insufficient for morality because it does not in itself entail the reality of such freedom. The world of phenomena, conceived as a system of nature in the narrow sense, is confirmed by experience; it is the realm of "the objects of the senses interconnected by universal laws" which "reveals its reality by examples of experience" (B, F:110). But no corresponding confirmatory evidence of freedom can be found in the world of phenomena since, as a purely intelligible world, the world of noumena lies beyond experience. Does this mean that we have no evidence at all which has any bearing on the question of freedom, and that therefore freedom itself must always remain a transcendental idea?

It is Kant's contention that "it is as impossible for the subtlest philosophy as for the commonest reasoning to argue freedom away" (B, F:110). This is so because the pure practical or moral laws "are possible only in relation to the freedom of the will; but, if the will is presupposed as free, then they are necessary. Conversely, freedom is necessary because those laws are necessary" (B, C:156).

Kant's argument here hinges on the distinction between the

*conditioned* (which is the given) and the *unconditioned condition* (which alone makes the given possible). That is to say, if moral laws are the conditioned given, then, if it can be shown that freedom of the will is the only unconditioned condition which makes them possible, the experiential givenness of those laws entails as the indispensable condition of their possibility the givenness of a free will. Actually, according to Kant, the condition (which is the *ratio cognoscendi*) and the unconditioned condition (which is the *ratio essendi*) are one and the same reality *taken in different respects.* "A free will and a will under moral laws are identical" (B, F:102).

However, as far as *knowledge* is concerned, we "cannot start from freedom, for this we can neither know immediately . . . , nor infer from experience, since experience reveals to us only . . . the mechanics of nature, [which is] the direct opposite of freedom. It is therefore the moral law, of which we become immediately conscious as soon as we construct maxims for the will, which first presents itself to us; and . . . it is the moral law which leads directly to the concept of freedom" (B, C:140-141).

We come to know the moral law "in the same way we know pure theoretical principles, by attending to the necessity with which reason prescribes them to us and to the elimination from them of all empirical conditions, which reason directs" (B, C: 141). There are situations, Kant points out, in which our actions are clearly determined by objects of desire or by inhibitory stimuli (B, C:141). In these situations we act under compulsion and know that we are not free. But there are other situations in which we experience an *ought,* an obligation to do or not to do a certain act; and, irrespective of our acceptance or rejection of this obligation, through our experiencing an *ought* at all we recognize our freedom (B, C:141-142); for freedom is the only unconditioned ground which makes the experience of an *ought* possible (B, C:210). The moral law, therefore, "expresses nothing else than the autonomy of the pure practical reason, i.e., freedom" (B, C:144). That is to say, we know that freedom is real because it is "the necessary presupposition of reason" in a being whose actions are known to be determined, not by objects of desire, but by "laws of reason independently of natural instinct" (B, F:113).

As far as Kant is concerned, man, being both sensuous and rational, lives in two worlds. As phenomenon, i.e., as an object of sense experience, he belongs to the "sensible world"; but as a noumenon, i.e., as an object of reason alone, he is a member of the "intelligible world." However, so long as we had no definite conception of morality and freedom, we could not even make conjectures concerning the essential nature of a noumenon, which is "posited as the ground of the alleged appearance" (B, C:121). This situation has now changed; for if there is any force to the preceding arguments, then "the law of pure will, which is free" (B, C:145), implies that "as a rational being and thus as belonging to the intelligible world" (B, F:107), i.e., as a noumenon, man is a self-legislative will in the realm of ends.

But if this is so, then it is really our membership in two worlds, the "sensible" and the "intelligible," which explains morality. When we think of ourselves as free, "we transport ourselves into the intelligible world" (B, F:107), which is under universal laws of reason. But if we were members of the intelligible world only, then our actions "would completely accord with the principle of the autonomy of the pure will" (B, F:108), and our will would be absolutely good and, thus, holy. Such, however, is not the full story of our existence; for when we intuit ourselves as beings of flesh and blood, we belong to the world of phenomena, which is under the universal law of causal determination. And if we were a member of this world only, then our actions would have to "conform only to the natural law of desires and inclinations" (B, F:108). Neither our membership in the intelligible world nor our membership in the sensible world, each taken by itself, can therefore account for the experience of an *ought*. But given our membership in both worlds, then, whenever we, as actual human beings, think of ourselves as obligated, we recognize that our actions *ought* to conform to the laws to the intelligible world, whereas inclination and desires hold us in the world of sense. Only because we live in both worlds do we experience the laws of the intelligible world as imperatives, and the "actions in accord with these principles as duties" (B, F:108; 104).

## XVI

The question now arises why I, a creature of "sensible nature" as well as a rational being, should accept and obey the moral law (which is a law of reason only) whenever this law is opposed to my inclinations and desires. As Kant puts it: "In order to will that which reason alone prescribes to the sensuously affected rational being as that which he ought to will, certainly there is required a power of reason to instill a feeling of pleasure or satisfaction in the fulfillment of duty, and hence there must be a causality of reason to determine the sensibility in accordance with its own principles" (B, F:114). This "causality of reason" must be a power of reason itself, for otherwise something extraneous to the moral law would determine our will and, as a consequence, we would not be free. In other words, "the objective determining ground [which is the moral law] must at the same time be the exclusive and subjectively determining ground of action if the latter is to fulfill not merely the letter of the law but also its spirit" (B, C:180). Our task, therefore, is, first, to make clear "in what way the moral law becomes an incentive," and, then, "since the moral law is such an incentive, to see what happens to the human faculty of desire as a consequence of this determining ground" (B, C:180).

A self-legislative or free will can be determined only by laws which are self-imposed in conformity with the principle of universality. Such laws, however, by determining our will and thus "thwarting all our inclinations," produce in us, as sensuous beings, "a feeling which can be called pain" (B, C:181). The reason for this is obvious. Since our inclinations, when taken together as a system of desires the satisfactions of which are personal happiness, constitute our "selfishness," i.e., our "self-love" and our "self-conceit," pure practical reason checks our selfishness. By bringing our self-love into harmony with the moral law, it reduces our selfishness to a *rational* self-love and completely destroys our self-conceit (B, C:181; 182). But, "if anything checks our self-conceit in our own judgment, it humiliates. Therefore, the moral law inevitably humbles every man when he compares the sensuous propensity of his nature with the law" (B, C:182); and this humiliation is painful.

But if the moral law humiliates me, why should I accept it at all as binding for me? To this question Kant replies that when the idea of something as the determining ground of our will humiliates us in our self-esteem, then this something, "in so far as it is positive and the ground of determination," awakens *respect* for itself. "Respect for the moral law is therefore the sole and undoubted moral incentive" (B, C:186); in fact, "it is morality itself, regarded as an incentive" (B, C:183). More specifically, the moral law is *objectively* "a formal determining ground of action through practical pure reason" (B, C:183); and it is *subjectively* "a cause of respect" (B, C:182) and therefore "also a subjective ground of determination" (B, C:183; 186).

As Kant sees it, "the moral law determines the will directly and objectively in the judgment of reason" (B, C:186). Its effect on my feelings is humiliation. "This humiliation occurs proportionately to the purity of the law." But "the lowering of the pretensions of moral self-esteem (humiliation) on the sensuous side is an elevation of the moral, i.e., practical, esteem for the law on the intellectual side" (B, C:186). Taken by itself, the moral law fails to express its effect in action because subjective causes, i.e., desires and inclinations, hinder it; but respect for the moral law, being an indirect effect of the law on feeling, "weakens the hindering influence of the inclinations through humiliating self-conceit" (B, C:186). Respect for the moral law is therefore "an incentive for obedience to the law" and is "the ground of maxims of a course of life conformable to it" (B, C: 186).

To charge Kant at this point with bad psychology is no refutation of his argument; for if the humiliation of which Kant speaks is actually felt, it is necessarily the negative aspect of a feeling of respect. Only because we respect something do we feel humiliated when we fall short of its norm. Kant, therefore, is unquestionably right in maintaining the inseparable connection between respect and humiliation. Nor can we escape his conclusion by trying to avoid altogether the experience here in question. Such an attempt would require that we abandon Kant's basic belief that man, in his very essence, is a rational being; for the humiliation which we experience is, according to Kant, the humiliation of our "sensuous nature," whereas the respect which is the cause of this humiliation is respect for the law of reason itself and thus for the very ground of our existence as rational beings. That is to say, a moral law, as a law of reason, expresses our very nature as rational and self-legislative beings— of beings, that is, who, in order to be true to themselves, must adjust their empirical practical acts to the laws of their essential nature.

If man were merely a sensuous creature, he would be incapable of respect for a particular law of reason and would follow at all times his desires and inclinations. If he were holy, he would, as a matter of course, act always in accordance with the moral law and would therefore have no occasion to experience the humiliation of his sensuous nature. But man is neither a mere sensuous creature nor a completely rational or holy being. He is "certainly unholy" (B, C:193). His inclinations and desires often oppose actions sanctioned by the moral law, i.e., by reason. If, nevertheless, man freely submits to the law and, through his own will, imposes a constraint on all inclinations, then he acts from respect for the law (B, C:187). He acts as a rational being which, though inextricably tied to a sensuous nature, yet treats "humanity," in his own person at least, as an end in itself and as "holy to him" (B, C:193). In doing this, he reaches the highest attainment of moral man and "places before our eyes the sublimity of our own nature" (B, C:194).

If it is now argued that motives other than respect for the law determine the will in moral actions, Kant points out that all such arguments, if they do not miss the point entirely, confirm rather than disprove his doctrine and rest upon it.

One might argue, for example (as did Epicurus), that the real motive for doing morally right acts is the enjoyment or pleasure —"the most intimate joy" (B, C:219)—expected as a result of these acts, and that therefore "the virtuous disposition" is already in the persons to whom incentives to virtue are to be given (B, C:220)—to wit: their desire to obtain pleasure and to avoid pain. Or one might argue (as did Hutcheson) that man is endowed with a special sense or "moral feeling." Confronted with these arguments, Kant admits that "the upright man cannot be happy" unless he is "conscious of his righteousness"; for "with such a character the moral self-condemnation to which his own way of thinking would force him in case of any transgression would rob him of all enjoyment of the pleasantness which his condition might otherwise entail" (B, C:220). That is to say, "a man, if he is virtuous, will certainly not enjoy life without being conscious of his righteousness in each action, however favorable fortune may be to him in the physical circumstances of life" (B, C:220). But Kant argues rightly that we must not confuse "the moral ground of determination" with the pleasures and joys—"the ever joyous heart"—which are "only its consequences" (B, C:221). "It is a very different thing to make a man happy from making him good, and to make him prudent and farsighted for his own advantage is far from making him virtuous" (B, F:98-99). Moreover, "in order to imagine the vicious person as tormented with mortification by the consciousness of his transgressions," one must "presuppose that he is, in the core of his character, at least to a certain degree morally good," just as one has to "think of the person who is delighted by the consciousness of doing dutiful acts as already virtuous." A man must already value respect for the moral law "in order to feel satisfaction in the consciousness of his conformity to law or the bitter remorse which accompanies his awareness that he has transgressed it" (B, C:150).

The appeal to a special moral sense or feeling, lastly, is, in Kant's opinion, "superficial"; for "feelings naturally differ so infinitely in degree that they are incapable of furnishing a uniform standard of the good and the bad," and, also, "one cannot validly judge for others by means of his own feelings" (B, F:99).

There is, thus, nothing left as subjectively determining ground for moral actions except respect for the law.

In order to distinguish the gratifications of desire and inclination from the satisfactions derived from actions done from respect for the moral law, Kant calls the former, when taken together, man's "happiness," and he calls the latter "self-contentment" (B, C:221). He explains and justifies the distinction thus: Pure practical reason, by imposing the moral law, "can produce a consciousness of mastery over inclinations and thus of independence from them and from the discontentment which always accompanies them, bringing forth a negative satisfaction with one's condition, i.e., contentment, whose source is contentment with one's own person. Freedom itself thus becomes in this indirect way capable of an enjoyment. This cannot be called happiness, since it does not depend upon a positive participation of feeling; nor can it be called bliss, because it does not include complete independence from inclinations and desires. It does nevertheless resemble the latter so far at least as the determination of the will which it involves can be held to be free from their influence, and thus, at least in its origin, it is analogous to the self-sufficiency which can be ascribed only to the Supreme Being" (B, C:222-223).

Kant is willing to admit that "a natural and necessary connection between the consciousness of morality and the expectation of proportionate happiness as its consequence may be thought at least possible," but he is adamant in maintaining that morality is basic and that happiness can constitute an element of the supreme good only as "the morally conditioned but necessary consequence" of morality as such (B, C:223). He argues, in other words, that only the moral, i.e., the virtuous, person is "worthy of happiness" (B, C:232).

## XVII

We have just spoken of the highest, the "supreme" good without, however, making clear what was meant. Since Kant uses the term with a special meaning and assigns to it an important part in his system, we must now consider it further.

To begin with, certain basic distinctions must be noted. The Latin expressions *boni* and *mali,* Kant finds, "contain an ambiguity due to the poverty of the language" (B, C:168). German and English, however, have words which enable us to make the required distinctions. Thus, for *bonum,* the German language has *das Gute* and *das Wohl,* and, correspondingly, the English language has *the good* and *the well-being.* For *malum,* German has *das Böse* and *das Übel* or *Weh,* and English has, respectively, *the evil* or *wicked* and *the bad* or *woe.* There are, therefore, "two very different judgments if in an action we have regard to its goodness or wickedness or to our weal or woe" (B, C:168). "Well-being or woe indicates only a relation to our condition of pleasantness or unpleasantness, or enjoyment or pain. . . . But the *good* or *evil* always indicates a relation to the will so far as it is determined by the law of reason" (B, C:169). Good and evil are therefore "properly referred to actions and not to the sensory state of a person." Hence, "if something is to be, or is held to be, absolutely good or evil in all respects and without qualification, it cannot be a thing but only the manner of acting, i.e., it can be only the maxim of the will, and consequently the acting person himself as a good or evil man" (B, C:169).

To be sure, our weal and woe are very important in the evaluation of our practical reason; "and, as far as our nature as sensible beings is concerned, our happiness is the only thing of importance" (B, C:170). But Kant, the rationalist, finds that man "has reason for yet higher purpose, namely, to consider also what is in itself good or evil, which pure and sensuously disinterested reason alone can judge" (B, C:170).

Now, "*either* a principle of reason is thought of as already the determining ground of the will without reference to possible objects of the faculty of desire"—in which case action in accordance with the principle is in itself good, and "a will whose maxims always accord with this law is absolutely and in every respect good and the supreme condition of all good"; "*or* a determining ground of the faculty of desire precedes the maxim of the will, and this determining ground presupposes an object of pleasure or displeasure"—in which case the maxim of reason "determines actions which are good only with reference to our inclination," the object of our inclination being itself "not a good but only well-being" (B, C:171). The idea of an absolute good is thus derivable only from the first alternative. This means, however, that "the concept of the good and evil is not defined prior to the moral law" but "must be defined after and by means of the law" (B, C:171). What this implies will become clear in a moment.

We have seen that moral laws are "the sole determining ground of the pure will," that these laws constitute a systemic context which is meta-systematically determined by the principle of universality, and we know that this meta-systemic principle is merely formal. But we have also seen that reason always seeks "the unconditioned" for the conditioned (B, C:212). This unconditioned, Kant now points out, "is not only sought as the determining ground of the will but, even when this is given (in the moral law), is also sought as the unconditioned totality of the *object* of the pure practical reason, under the name of the *highest good*" (B, C:113).

The term "highest," however, may mean either the "supreme" or the "perfect" (B, C:214). Understood in the sense of "supreme," it designates "the unconditional condition, i.e., the condition which is subordinate to no other" (B, C:214). Understood in the sense of "perfect," it refers, in the language of Kant, to "that whole which is no part of a yet larger whole of the same kind" (B, C:215).

It is Kant's contention that "virtue (as the worthiness to be happy) is the supreme condition of whatever appears to us to be desirable and thus of all our pursuit of happiness" (B, C:215); and in this sense it is the supreme good (B, C:215). But this fact does "not imply that [virtue] is the entire and perfect good as the object of the faculty of desire of rational finite beings" (B, C:215). In fact, only "virtue and happiness *together* constitute the possession of the highest good for a person, and happiness in exact proportion to morality (as the worth of a person and his worthiness to be happy) constitute [the highest good] of a possible world"—the term "highest good" being taken to mean "the perfect good, wherein virtue is always the supreme good" (B, C:215). Happiness, therefore, "though something always pleasant to him who possesses it, is not of itself absolutely good in every respect but always presupposes conduct in accordance with the moral law as its condition" (B, C:215). Happiness and morality, in other words, are "two specifically different elements of the highest good" (B, C:217).

However, the idea of the highest good, as a *"synthesis* of concepts," being neither derivable from experience nor deducible analytically and yet being necessary for the ultimate interpretation of morality, is, in Kant's sense, a transcendental idea—i.e., it is thinkable but not experienceable for a finite being (B, C: 217-218); and as transcendental idea it is "the necessary highest end of a morally determined will and a true object thereof" (B, C:219). The maxims of the will, "which refer to it by their material, have objective reality" (B, C:219).

As Kant sees it, "the complete fitness of intention to the moral law is the supreme condition of the highest good" (B, C:225). Such complete fitness, however, is holiness—"a perfection of which no rational being in the world of sense is at any time capable" (B, C:225). This perfection "can be found only in an endless progress toward the complete fitness of intention to the moral law (B, C:225; 226)—a progress, which, "on principles of pure practical reason," must be assumed to be "the real object of our will" (B, C:225).

In this way, i.e., via the idea of an "endless process from lower to higher stages of moral perfection" (B, C:226), the highest good becomes indirectly an object of the will. However, the highest good is not conceivable or possible as an object "unless three theoretical concepts are presupposed," namely, freedom, immortality, and God (B, C:236). All three are "pure concepts of reason," for "no corresponding intuition can be given and consequently no objective reality for them can be found *in a theoretical way"* (B, C:236). But since "practical reason inexorably requires the existence of these objects for the possibility of its practically and absolutely necessary object, the highest good," Kant holds that "theoretical reason is justified in assuming them" (B, C:237).

To be sure, no "positive use" can be made of these three objects (freedom, immortality, and God) "for theoretical purposes" (B, C:237). In particular, "no synthetic proposition is made possible by conceding their reality"; for "Nothing more has here been accomplished by practical reason than to show that those concepts are . . . transcendent thoughts in which there is nothing impossible" (B, C:237). Because they are "necessary conditions of the possibility of that which [an apodictic practical] law requires to be made an object," i.e., because they are practical postulates of morality, these ideas "acquire objective reality" in the sense that "they have objects"—although we cannot even indicate *how* their concepts can refer to objects (B, C:237).

As practical postulates the ideas of freedom, God, and immortality are "immanent and constitutive," being "the grounds of the possibility of realizing the necessary object of pure practical reason (the highest good)" (B, C:238). Considered in any other way they are "transcendent and mere regulative principles of speculative reason" (B, C:238).

Kant is fully aware of the fact that in his philosophy of morals he has "*widened* our knowledge beyond the limits of the world of sense" (B, C:160) and has entered the field of metaphysics. He finds, however, that once a self-legislative autonomous will is admitted (as in his opinion it must be) as the indispensable and objectively real basis for the moral law, then the objective reality of this will—as *causa noumenon* (B, C:165)—"gives objective reality to all other categories" in so far as they "stand in a necessary connection with the determining ground of the pure will (moral law)" (B, C:166) and that, therefore, without metaphysics there can be no moral philosophy (B, F:52).

Since we are here interested in ethics rather than in metaphysics, we shall not pursue Kant's arguments further but shall conclude our expository presentation with a brief reference to certain key ideas which place those arguments in proper perspective.

"Two things," says Kant, "fill the mind with ever new and increasing admiration and awe, the oftener and more steadily they are reflected on; the starry heaven above me and the moral law within me. . . . I see them before me, and I associate them directly with the consciousness of my own existence. The former begins from the place I occupy in the external world of sense, and it broadens the connection in which I stand into an unbounded magnitude of worlds beyond worlds and systems of systems and into the limitless times of their periodic motion, their beginning and continuance. The latter begins from my invisible self, my personality, and exhibits me in a world which has true infinity but which is comprehensible only to the understanding. . . . The former view of a countless multitude of worlds annihilates, as it were, my importance as an animal creature, which must give back to the planet (a mere speck in the universe) the matter from which it came, the matter which is for a little time provided with vital force, we know not how. The latter, on the contrary, infinitely raises my worth as that of an intelligence by my personality, in which the moral law reveals life independent of all animality and even of the whole world of sense" (B, C:258-259). And as a person, as a rational being under the moral law, my destination "reaches into the infinite" (B, C:259).

## XVIII

We have completed our exposition and interpretation of Kant's ethics. Although we have omitted many details, we have considered at least the essential ideas which provide the basis for his system. In the course of our discussions we have distinguished implicitly between Kant's idea of critical ethics as such and the concrete content of his specific moral code; and, interpreting the former as seemed most consistent with Kant's theoretical intentions, we have met and repudiated some of the commonest criticisms of the Kantian position. We shall now attempt an evaluation of Kant's doctrine which, it is hoped, will reveal crucial inadequacies of critical ethics itself and will prepare the ground for a more adequate conception of ethics.

It has often been pointed out that in the history of ethics two schools of thought stand in radical opposition to each other. There are the thinkers (and their names carry us back to Greek classicism) who, emphasizing the significance of the *good,* make the *ought* derivative: Everything *good* is *what ought to be,* and it ought to be *because* it is good. But there are also the thinkers (and the Mosaic Commandments reflect their spirit) who, emphasizing the significance of the *ought,* make the *good* derivative: Everything which *ought* to be is *good,* and its *goodness* stems from the *ought.* There can be no doubt as to where Kant stands in this controversy. For him, the *ought* is the very core of morality. In fact, no other thinker before Kant has made quite as much of the *ought* as did he, or has stressed *duty* to the same extent. In a special sense, therefore, Kant typifies one of the extremes in ethics. He disregards the significance for ethics of values and their manifold interrelations, and seems entirely unaware of the whole content of value theory. When he repudiates all attempts to derive moral laws from a consideration of *goods* or *ends,* he fails to notice that things are goods only because of the values ascribed to them, and that ends are worth pursuing only because of the values they embody. Hence, when Kant repudiates—rightly—an ethics of goods and ends, he believes to have accomplished much more than he actually has. The whole range of values and its significance for ethics has not even been considered by Kant.

Because of this neglect of values, Kant's ethics is formalistic in a sense much more profound than that usually implied in the charge of formalism. The usual charge is that Kant's categorical imperative, demanding that we act always in conformance with the requirements of universality, provides itself no moral code to guide us. We have seen, however (Section VI), that this charge misses the point as far as Kant's theory is concerned. We are now saying that, in neglecting the role which values play in human affairs and in stressing the mere universality of the moral law, Kant has given us an incomplete definition of *the moral.* He has failed to augment his formalism with a concrete value-content which, *together with the ought,* provides the only adequate conception of *the moral.*

In opposing Kant on this crucial issue of the definition of *the moral,* I hold no brief for thinkers who would derive the *ought* from the *good,* or who, like Scheler and Hartmann, assume an independent realm of values. Their view, it seems to me, goes to the other extreme. It is my contention—and I have argued the point elsewhere (*23*:119-123; *24*:499-500)—that only within the range of man's value experience and valuations has an *ought* moral relevance, and that only because of the *ought* do our valuations attain moral significance. That is to say, value experience and valuations *together with* the *ought* establish the sphere of *the moral.* Interpretations in terms of values alone or in terms of the *ought* alone distort the facts in the case. The former lead to aesthetic analogies and approbations only; the latter deprive the *ought* of all morally relevant content and reduce it to an empty form. Neither view is adequate to man's moral experience.

But let us consider Kant's position from still a different angle. All "lawgiving" in the moral sense, Kant tells us, involves "two parts: first, a law which represents the act to be done as objectively necessary, i.e., which makes that act a duty; secondly, a motivation which subjectively connects the ground of deter- mination of the will to do this act with the conception of the law" (*11*:15); and, Kant adds, only that act is moral in which the idea of duty itself is the motivation (*11*:16). In other words, according to Kant, "it is not sufficient to do that which should be morally good that it *conform* to the law; it must be done *for the sake of* the law. Otherwise the conformity is merely con- tingent and spurious" (B, F:52; italics added). "Though it might happen that the action occurs as the law prescribes, and thus in accord with duty but not from duty, the intention to do the action would not be moral, and it is the intention which is precisely in question" in moral matters (B, C:189).

Against this position it has been argued that "Kant's fallacy lies in thinking that just the bare knowledge that an action is of a certain kind [e.g., that it conforms to the idea of duty] is sufficient to move us to do that action" (7:488). Such knowledge, so the objection goes on, "has no influence on us unless we have an interest in . . . that kind of action, unless, that is, we have some feeling towards it" (7:488). But this argument hardly does justice to Kant's position; for Kant himself clearly recognized that the moral law, although it is *objectively* "a formal determining ground of action," is *subjectively* a "cause of respect"; and that only because it is a "cause of respect" it is "also a subjective ground of determination" (B, C:183; 186). Kant does not maintain that "the bare knowledge that an action is of a certain kind" will in itself induce us to carry out that action. He holds, rather, that *respect*—as distinguished from bare knowledge—is "an incentive for obedience to the law" (B, C:186); that, in fact, "respect for the moral law is . . . the sole and undoubted moral incentive" (B, C:183).

Kant's error—if such we want to call it—is of a different kind and is much more fundamental than is the "fallacy" with which Field charges him. It is rooted in his conception of a *person;* and it is crucial for his whole position because only a person, being alone capable of autonomous determination through law, is the subject of the moral law (B, C:193).

To be sure, Kant's conception of a person, despite its importance for his system, is not fully developed and must largely be inferred from scattered references to it. Three statements, however, come close to being explicit definitions. Thus, Kant says, "Rational beings are designated 'persons,' because their nature indicates that they are ends in themselves" (B, F:86-87). Again, "The moral personality is nothing other than the freedom of a rational being under moral laws" (*11*:26). And again, the only origin "worthy" of duty is "nothing else than personality, i.e., the freedom and independence from the mechanism of nature regarded as a capacity of a being which is subject to . . . pure practical laws given by its own reason" (B, C:193). In all three of these statements two references stand out. One is to freedom, the other to reason; and with respect to both freedom and reason man "belongs to the intelligible world" (B, C:193);

i.e., he is *homo noumenon* (*11*:291). Only as *homo noumenon,* therefore, is he a person. As a creature of nature, however, man is for Kant what he was for Hobbes—a merely sensuous being, a hedonist and absolute egoist, who can be elevated to the level of morality only through the stern law of practical reason.

It may be granted that reason and freedom are essential to being a person. Kant's interpretation, however, implies that a person is *nothing but* autonomous rational will; and this conception leads to two grave difficulties. (i) If to be a person means nothing more than to be the point of origin of an autonomous rational will, then all persons are essentially alike; and this is obviously what Kant meant to emphasize, for each person can then act for all rational beings, and the maxim of his action is a law universal. But with such an interpretation, the unique character and concrete richness of the individual person, as we encounter him in actual life and as he manifests himself in every decision and free act, has, in principle, been denied or has been ascribed to something which, in Kant's view, is not essential to being a person, i.e., to man's "sensuous nature." In either case, I believe, the facts of experience have been distorted. Kant escapes these consequences only because he does not carry through rigorously his rationalistic interpretation.

(ii) If a person is *nothing but* autonomous rational will, then all feelings and affections, all emotions and passions—except the "feeling of respect for the law"—are irrelevant to the nature of a person and therefore to the whole range of morality. Love and hate, sympathy and cold aloofness, reverential awe and sneering disdain are, on this view, as devoid of any essential connection with the nature of a person as they are of moral significance. They are manifestations of man's "animality" only, and what moral value they have is derived from their conformance or non-conformance to the moral law imposed by "practical reason." Such an interpretation, it seems to me, deprives our affections of a moral significance which rightfully belongs to them by virtue of their relation to man's value experience and valuations. To say, for example, that an act of love is morally good only because its *maxim* conforms to the requirement of universality deprives that act of any moral significance which belongs to it, I am sure, by virtue of the fact that it is an act of *love,* and is to this extent a distortion of our moral experience.

Moreover, as Scheler has pointed out (*19*:247), in ascribing all feelings and affections to man's sensuous nature, Kant obliterated all distinctions of quality and depth between sensuous pleasure, joy, and happiness so that, for him, Aristotle's eudae-monism and Aristippus's radical hedonism were essentially equivalent and equally false. Here again, I believe, the facts of value experience and of our valuations contradict Kant's theory. His rationalism, I fear, has prevented him from understanding the role which values play in the realm of *the moral.*

It is Kant's thesis, as we have seen, that "nothing in the world —indeed nothing even beyond the world—can possibly be conceived which could be called good without qualification except a good will" (B, F:55). But the crucial point is that "the good will is not good because of what it effects or accomplishes or because of its adequacy to achieve some proposed end; it is good only because of its willing, i.e., it is good of itself" (B, F:56). C. D. Broad has pointed out—and I think rightly—that the facts upon which Kant bases his arguments justifying the conception of the intrinsic goodness of a good will merely prove that "a good will is a *necessary constituent* of any whole which is intrinsically good"; they do not prove "that a good will has itself any intrinsic value" (*4*:117). Broad's criticism, however, does not go far enough. It must be augmented in at least two respects. (i) Inherent in Kant's conception is the idea that a good will is but will acting in accordance with, and for the sake of, the law. This means that any value consideration is irrelevant to the definition of a good will, and the "good" here is but the equivalent of "for the sake of the law." I find it difficult to accept this equivalence as providing the crucial element in the definition of a good will. Here again it is Kant's disregard for values and value interrelations which troubles me. If we interpret Kant strictly, then, so long as I act "for the sake of the law," it is immaterial to the idea of a good will whether I intend something noble or something base, whether I tend to realize values or disvalues; and this seems to me to be a perversion of our value experience in so far as that experience is relevant to morality. I can see nothing so sacred in the idea of law *per se* that for its sake all other values should be regarded as irrelevant to a good will. On the contrary, I find it much more plausible to define the good will in terms of an intended realization of values (*24*:499). That is to say, I find it much more plausible to regard a will as good when that will tends to realize the highest possible value inherent in a given situation, and to regard it as evil when it tends in the opposite directions.[4]

(ii) The second respect in which Broad's argument must be augmented pertains to his agreement with Kant that "the rightness or wrongness of a volition depends wholly on the nature of its motive. It does not depend on its actual consequences. And it does not depend on its intended consequences except in so far as the expectation of these forms part of the motive" (*4*:117). When we interpret Kant strictly—as I believe we must—even "intended consequences" can have no bearing upon the rightness or wrongness of an act, for, as material content, they can be no part of the "ground of determination" of a thoroughly good will, i.e., of a will which acts "for the sake of the law" only. But even if we admit values and value considerations (and this includes the value aspects of "intended consequences") to be part or all of the motive of an action, it does not follow that the action is right (or that it is wrong, as the case may be). The motive alone is not sufficient. Even with the best of intentions we can do the wrong thing simply because we do not sufficiently take into consideration the objective facts in a given situation. Good intentions, therefore, are only one of the requirements of right action. They are a necessary but not a sufficient condition. At least one other requirement is the understanding of and insight into the factors and conditions which objectively delimit the concrete situation within which we must act. That is to say, a right action is an action which, inspired by an enlightened good will *and* carried through with due consideration of all the factual

---

[4] On this point at least I am in essential agreement with Scheler and Hartmann.

conditions involved in a given situation, does lead (unless frustrated by extra-situational forces) to the realization of the highest values possible under the given conditions. By contrast, a wrong action is one which does not lead to the realization of the highest values possible because it was either not inspired by an enlightened good will or it was carried through without due consideration for the factual conditions; it is the action of an unenlightened or of an evil will (24:499-500).

I find myself in agreement with Kant in holding that good and evil, being characteristic qualities of the will, are not value content (like all other values) towards which the will is directed; but I disagree with Kant in holding that will is not intrinsically good (or evil) but is so only because of its direction towards values. If I am right in my position, then the value-intention of the person determines the quality of the will, and an individual act is morally significant only as the expressed will of a person of such and such value-orientation. The individual person in his concreteness and richness of value commitments—not some abstract "rational being"—thus becomes the existential focus of morality, both as the subject and the object of moral actions. Such an interpretation, I believe, is more adequate to the facts of moral experience than is Kant's rationalistic formalism with its emphasis upon "rational beings." It does do full justice to the actualities of moral decisions and to the character of moral acts in and through which the person as a whole finds expression and concrete realization. Compared with it, Kant's reference to "rational beings" remains an empty abstraction.

To be sure, Kant refers to the "humanity" within us and within every other person, and bids us to respect it as "an end in itself" (B, F:87); but nowhere does he give us a clear definition of what he meant by "humanity." We shall not go too far astray, however, if we assume that for Kant the term designates at least a rational being capable of spontaneous action. But beyond this Kant seems to have had in mind also the "idea of humanity" which was the ideal of the Enlightenment. Because of this ideal Kant held that it is our "duty to supply the defects of [our] knowledge by instruction and to correct [our] errors"; that it is our duty, in other words, "to be worthy of the humanity that resides within [us]" (*3*:356; B, F:88). Although Kant specifically opposed the ideal of humanity to the "crudity" of our nature and to the "animality" of our being (*3*:356), he at no time said anything more positive about it than that it is "that by which alone" we are "capable of setting ends" for ourselves (*3*:356); i.e., that it is rational free will. And this, it seems to me, is a startlingly empty conception of the "humanity" within us. There is here no reference to compassion, to love, to friendship, to loyalty, to trustworthiness—to any of the emotions, sentiments, and affections which somehow are at the human core of all of us; and this is a grave omission. Granted that reason and an autonomous will are indispensable to our being human. It seems to be true, nevertheless, that our humanity lies even more in our enobled passions, in the value responses which engage our whole being—including the utilitarian and aesthetic as well as the moral values (*25*:306-307). Moreover, Kant's conception of humanity gives us at best only a generalized ideal, whereas the fact of the matter is that each and every one of us must represent or realize humanity in his own specific way, as this particular person here and now, and in the concrete richness of individual existence. Whatever is essential to our humanity must therefore be capable of great variability without self-abandonment; and reason alone is not so variable. Finally, the humanity within us is an evolving ideal (*cf.* the emergence of the Greek and the Christian conceptions of man) to whose slow development centuries of cultural effort and striving have contributed content and meaning. Such facts, it seems to me, bespeak clearly the necessity of defining humanity in terms of our value commitments rather than, as with Kant, in terms of reason alone. One last point may require consideration. Kant clearly saw and emphasized the independence of the moral sphere. For him, morality is dependent neither upon metaphysics nor upon religion. "By virtue of pure practical reason" morality is "self-sufficient." It "does not need religion at all" (*12*:3). In fact, "pure *moral* legislation" is what "really constitutes true religion" (*12*:95). Nevertheless, metaphysical elements appear in Kant's arguments and, in the postulates of practical reason, his whole doctrine culminates in metaphysical stipulations.

The metaphysical elements which appear in Kant's arguments are primarily of a teleological nature. Thus, Kant writes: "As nature has elsewhere distributed capacities suitable to the functions they are to perform, reason's proper function must be to produce a will good in itself" (B, F:58). And, more importantly: "Complete fitness of the will to the moral law is holiness, which is a perfection of which no rational being in the world of sense is at any time capable. But since it is required as practically necessary, it can be found only in an endless progress to that complete fitness; on principles of pure practical reason, it is necessary to assume such a practical progress as the real object of our will" (B, C:225). Kant's reference to "reason's proper function" and "the real object of our will," i.e., to the "endless progress" toward "complete fitness of the will to the moral law," are essentially teleological—and they are teleological, not in the acceptable sense of heuristic principles in science, but in a speculative metaphysical sense which clearly places them beyond all possibility of verification.

However, let us look at the metaphysics of Kant's doctrine from another angle. Kant speaks of postulates of pure practical reason and means by them theoretical propositions which, though not demonstrable, are "an inseparable corollary of an a priori unconditionally valid practical law" (B, C:226). Thus, the postulate of immortality "derives from the practically necessary condition of a duration adequate to the perfect fulfillment of the moral law" (B, C:235). That is to say, it derives, according to Kant, from the fact that "the infinite progress" toward "complete fitness of the will to the moral law" is "possible only under the presupposition of an infinitely enduring existence and personality of the same rational being"; i.e., it is possible only under the presupposition of the "immortality of the soul" (B, C:226). The soul, therefore, is immortal.

What makes Kant's argument plausible at all is his initial assumption of a cosmic teleology—his assumption, in other words, that the ultimate goal of the universe is "the complete

fitness of the will to the moral law" and thus the achievement
of perfection or holiness on the part of every rational being.
However, once we repudiate this metaphysical assumption and
take the position that, although the moral law challenges us to
bring our will into complete harmony with it, this challenge
is itself a moral *ought* rather than an inevitable cosmic *must,*
then Kant's argument for personal immortality collapses. Actually, of course, Kant's reference to an "infinite progress" is an
admission on his part that "complete fitness of the will to the
moral law," i.e., moral perfection or holiness, can never be
attained by human beings. The startling thing is, however, that
Kant's argument implies a morally perverse conclusion; for if
a person should ever become morally perfect, his "infinite progress" would obviously come to an end. There would then be
no longer any ground for his immortality, and he should cease
to be immortal. I have called this a morally perverse conclusion
because the person achieving moral perfection would have no
longer any ground for existence at the very moment when he has
become worthy of eternal bliss. I am sure that this is not what
Kant intended; but his justification of immortality entails this
perverse conclusion.

Let us consider next Kant's postulate of the existence of God,
for this postulate "gives significance to what speculative reason
could indeed think but had to leave indeterminate as a mere
transcendental ideal" (B, C:235).

"If we inquire into God's final end in creating the world,"
Kant tells us, "we must name not the happiness of rational beings
in the world but the highest good, which adds a further condition to the wish of rational beings to be happy, viz., the condition
of being worthy of happiness" (B, C:233); and we are worthy
of happiness only as our will is fitted to the moral law. Again
Kant's teleological way of thinking is in evidence, for he is
saying that the realization of the highest good is the very goal for
which the world was created. But we shall not press this thesis
of speculative metaphysics at present, for Kant also states (a)
that all men desire to be happy, (b) that morality demands that
we be worthy of happiness, (c) that being worthy of happiness

and being happy is to have attained the highest good, and (d) that "the prospect of the highest good" leads to the postulate of the existence of God (B, C:235). Upon closer inspection we find that (d) resolves itself into the following argument: "In the mere course of nature happiness exactly proportionate to moral worth is not to be expected and is indeed impossible and that therefore the possibility of the highest good from this side cannot be granted except under the presupposition of a moral Author of the world" (B, C:246); and "since the promotion of the highest good and thus the presupposition of its possibility are objectively necessary" (B, C:247), the "moral Author of the world" exists. To put it more briefly, I have "a duty [based on an apodictic law] to make . . . the highest good the object of my will so as to promote it with all my strength. In doing so, I must presuppose its possibility and also its conditions, which are God, freedom, and immortality" (B, C:244). Kant is arguing, in other words, that what ought to be must be realizable; since the highest good ought to be, and since God is indispensable to its realization, God exists.

In evaluating this argument we must keep in mind that the highest good consists of two components, namely, conformity to the moral law (which makes us worthy of happiness), and happiness perfectly proportionate to that worthiness (B, C:246). Of these two components only the first is within our own power; the second is "impossible" in the "mere course of nature" and requires for its realization "a moral Author of the world" (B, C:246). Now the moral *ought,* as defined in the categorical imperative, is concerned only with the first component. I *ought* to make my actions conform to the moral law. But this *moral ought* to which I am unconditionally subject does not imply that the highest good *ought to exist* or that it ought to be possible for me to realize the highest good; only Kant's thesis—no matter how cautiously advanced—that God's final end in creating the world is the realization of the highest good, implies it. Hence, if the highest good is not realizable because the "mere course of nature" prevents us from attaining a happiness commensurate to our worthiness, the *moral ought* remains unaffected by this fact. This means, however, that not the demands of morality but Kant's metaphysical assumption of a just world order implies the existence of a "moral Author of the world." His argument thus proceeds on a purely speculative hidden premise and is therefore unacceptable. If the premise is explicitly assumed, the argument is a *petitio*.

# REFERENCES

1. Abbott, T. K. *Kant's Critique of Practical Reason and other Works on the Theory of Ethics,* 4th edition, London, 1889.
2. Bache, K., "Kants Prinzip der Autonomie im Verhältnis zur Idee des Reiches der Zwecke," *Kant-Studien,* Ergänzungshefte No. 12, 1909.
3. Beck, L. W., *Critique of Practical Reason and other Writings in Moral Philosophy,* Chicago, 1949.
4. Broad, C. D., *Five Types of Ethical Theory,* London, 1934.
5. Cohen, H., *Kants Begründung der Ethik,* Berlin, 1877.
6. Eklund, H., "Die Würde der Menschkeit," *Uppsala Universitets Årsskrift,* 1947:8.
7. Field, G. C., "A Criticism of Kant," *Readings in Ethical Theory,* W. Sellars and J. Hospers, editors, New York, 1952.
8. Kant, I., *Critique of Pure Reason,* Norman Kemp Smith translation, reprint edition, New York, 1950.
9. Kant, I., *Kritik der praktischen Vernunft,* Karl Vorländer edition, Leipzig, 1944.
10. Kant, I. *Grundlegung zur Metaphysik der Sitten,* Rudolf Otto editor, Gotha, 1930.
11. Kant, I., *Metaphysik der Sitten,* Voländer edition, Leipzig, 1945.
12. Kant, I., *Religion innerhalb der Grenzen der blossen Vernunft,* Hartenstein edition, vol. 6, 1868.
13. Kant, I., *Religion Within the Limits of Reason Alone,* T. M. Greene and H. H. Hudson, translators, Chicago, 1934.
14. Koppelmann, W., *Die Ethik Kants,* Berlin, 1907.
15. Messer, A., *Kants Ethik,* Leipzig, 1904.
16. Müller, C., "Die Methode einer reinen Ethik," *Kant-Studien,* Ergänzungshefte No. 11, 1908.
17. Paton, H. J., *The Categorical Imperative; A Study in Kants Moral Philosophy,* Chicago, 1948.
18. Paton, H. J., *The Moral Law, or Kant's Groundwork of the Metaphysics of Morals,* New York, 1950.
19. Scheler, M., *Der Formalismus in der Ethik und die materiale Wertethik,* 2nd edition, Halle, 1921.
20. Schwarz, H., "Der Rationalismus und der Rigorismus in Kants Ethik," *Kant-Studien, II,* (1898).

21. Simmel, G., *Kant,* Leipzig, 1904.
22. Sternberg, K., "Beiträge zur Interpretation der kritischen Ethik," *Kant-Studien,* Ergänzungshefte No. 25, 1912.
23. Werkmeister, W. H., "Ethics and Value Theory," *Proceedings of the XIth International Congress of Philosophy,* Brussells, 1953, X.
24. Werkmeister, W. H., "Problems of Value Theory," *Philosophy and Phenomenological Research,* XII (1952).
25. Werkmeister, W. H., "Prolegomena to Value Theory," *Philosophy and Phenomenological Research,* XIV (1954).
26. Werkmeister, W. H., *Outlines of a Value Theory,* Istanbul, 1959.
27. Singer, Marcus G., "The Categorical Imperative," *Philosophical Review,* LXIII (1954).

# CHAPTER IX

# The Deontologists

Our criticism of Kant's ethics centered around three main points: (i) Kant's neglect of values and their interrelations; (ii) Kant's conception of the nature of a person; and (iii) Kant's metaphysical assumptions. There remain, however, significant insights into the nature of morality not found outside the Kantian framework, and it is not astonishing that in recent years various attempts have been made to revise the Kantian position in such a way as to preserve these insights. The most notable of these attempts is associated with the names of Price (*1*), Prichard (*2*), and Ross (*3*). I shall here try to present and evaluate the revised Kantianism of these three men, keeping in mind their basic agreements as well as their individual differences.

The problem which all three thinkers face, and which they share with Kant and other ethicists, was well stated by Price: "Some actions we all feel ourselves irresistibly determined to approve, and others to disapprove. Some actions we cannot but think right, and others wrong, and of all actions we are led to form some opinion, as either fit to be performed or unfit; or neither fit nor unfit to be performed; that is, indifferent. What the power within us is, which thus determines, is the question to be considered" (A:13). Although the idea of the "fitness" or "unfitness" of an action is itself as yet undefined and, therefore,

366

ambiguous, all three thinkers agree at least in holding that our "perceptions of moral right and wrong" must denote either some discernible character of the actions in question or only our feelings concerning those actions (A:16); and that, if the latter is the case, ethics loses all significance. That is to say, these men agree with Kant, as against Hume and Stevenson, that morality is a matter, not of emotive approbation or disapprobation, but of insight and knowledge, of genuine cognition. "As to the schemes which found morality on self-love, on positive laws and compacts, or the Divine Will"—we are told—they either mean that "moral good and evil are only other words for advantageous and disadvantageous, willed and forbidden"; or they relate not to the question of "what is the nature and true account of virtue" but to the entirely different question of "what is the subject matter of it" (A:16).

## I

To the question, "What is the power within us that perceives the distinctions of right and wrong?," Price replies: "The *understanding*" (A:17). It is necessary, however, to view this brief reply in its proper perspective. When we do so, we find that Price distinguishes sharply between "sensation" and the "understanding." By "sensation" he means "the effects arising from the impressions made on our minds by external objects" (A:17). Sensation is, thus, concerned exclusively with particulars and "cannot rise to any *general* ideas"; "it lies prostrate under its object" (A:19). The intellect, on the other hand, "examines and compares the presented forms," "rises above individuals to universal and abstract ideas" and, taking in at one view an infinity of particulars, is "capable of discovering general truths" (A:19-20). Sense and understanding are, thus, totally different: the one involving only particulars, the other dealing with universals; one being not discerning but suffering, the other not suffering but discerning—"surveying and examining all things, in order to judge them" (A:21). Since "imagination," like sense, can give us particulars only, the understanding alone is capable of transcending particulars and of giving us universals and, thus, is itself a "source of new ideas"—*the most important source of our ideas*" (A:18; 36. Italics added). But the understanding is not "the power of reasoning" (A:40). It is, rather, a faculty of "intellectual discernment" (A:23) through which we obtain such ideas as "proportion" (with respect to quantities), "identity and diversity, existence, connexion, cause and effect, power, possibility and impossibility" (with respect to all things) (A: 36-37). And it is this faculty of "intellectual discernment" which, according to Price, gives us also our ideas of moral right and wrong (A:37).

"Our ideas of *right* and *wrong*," Price maintains, "are simple ideas," for "there are, undoubtedly, some actions that are *ultimately* approved, and for justifying which no reason can be assigned" (A:41). Were it not so, Price goes on, "there would be an infinite progression of reasons and ends, and therefore nothing could be at all approved or desired" (A:41). But if right and wrong are "simple ideas," then they "must be ascribed to some power of *immediate* perception"; and this "power," Price contends (against Hutcheson, Hume, and Locke) (A:41-43), can only be "the Understanding" (A:41).

By way of positive justification of his thesis Price refers, first, to "common sense" (A:43-46) and points out, secondly, that, whereas all sensations are but "feelings of a sentient being, which must be of a nature totally different from the particular causes which produce them" (A:46), right and wrong are asserted of actions as such and are "absolutely unintelligible, and void of sense and meaning, when supposed to signify nothing true of actions, no essential, inherent difference between them" (A:47). What Price thus points out most emphatically is the fact that judgments of moral rightness and moral wrongness have an objective validity which they never could have if they did not affirm some essential characteristics of the very actions themselves which are being judged. "The more we enquire, the more indisputable . . . it will appear to us," Price continues, "that we express necessary truths, when we say of some actions, they are right; and of others, they are wrong" (A:47). If this were not so—that is, if, in themselves, no actions are either right or wrong—then, in themselves, all actions are morally indifferent; and this conclusion, Price holds, is "contrary" to our own "discernment" (A:48). As he sees it, a rational agent who is "incapable of perceiving a difference, in respect to fitness and unfitness to be performed, between actions, and acting from blind propensions without any sentiments concerning what he does, is not possible to be imagined" (A:48-49). Rationality and discernment of the fitness or unfitness of actions are inseparable. "Do what we will, we shall find it out of our power, in earnest to persuade ourselves, that reason can have no concern in judging of and directing our conduct; or to exclude from our minds all notions of right and wrong actions" (A:49).

But if right and wrong "express *real characters* of actions" —namely, their fitness or unfitness, respectively—then no one can call an action right which is not so objectively or in itself— provided we mean by "action," "not the bare external effect produced, but the ultimate principle of conduct" (A:50-51)— i.e., the intent. An action is right, in other words, when it is done from an insight into its fitness in the given situation, Price holds. Morality is "fixed on an immovable basis." It is "equally everlasting and necessary with all truth and reason," and is not "the arbitrary production of any power human or divine" (A:52).

To be sure, "approbation and disapprobation of ourselves and others, as our own actions and dispositions, or those of others, are observed to be right or wrong, are unavoidable" (A:72-73). Let it be noted, however, that the rightness or wrongness of the actions and dispositions is the basis of the approbation or disapprobation, respectively; and that approbation and disapprobation are not the basis for calling an action or disposition right or wrong (A:59; 104-105). Moreover, "obligation to action, and rightness of action, are plainly coincidental and identical" (A:105). In fact, "right, fit, ought, should, duty, obligation, convey . . . ideas necessarily including one another" (A:105). Hence, when we discern the fitness of action, we at once know also what we ought to do.

Price admits that there are difficulties in determining what is right or wrong in concrete situations. It is his contention, however, that, "in many particular cases," the difficulties arise because of an "interference" or conflict of "the different general principles of virtue" (A:166-167). That is to say, although each principle by itself is self-evident (A:168) and its truth is as "irresistible" as is the truth of the axioms of geometry (A:169), "so variously may different obligations combine with or oppose each other in particular cases, and so imperfectly are our discerning faculties, that it cannot but happen, that we should be frequently in the dark, and that different persons should judge differently, according to the different views they have of the several moral principles" (A:167-168).

In order to understand fully Price's position on this point, let us note briefly that among the "axioms" of morality which he regards as self-evidently true are the following: "Gratitude is due to benefactors; reverence is due to our Creator; it is right to study our own happiness; an innocent being ought not to be absolutely miserable; it is wrong to take from another the fruit of his labor" (A:169). "It cannot be shown," Price adds, "that there have ever been any human beings who have had no ideas of property, gratitude, benevolence, prudence, and religious worship. All the difference has been about particular usages and practices" (A:170). "The most depraved never sink so low, as to lose all moral discernment, all ideas of right and wrong, justice and injustice, honour and dishonour" (A:173). But if this is so, then why have men erred so often and so much in their interpretation of what is right in a given situation? "The *practical* errors of men," Price holds, "have arisen plainly from their *speculative* errors; from their mistaking facts, or not seeing the whole of the case" (A:171). To put it in another way, "the rules of judging are universally the same. Those who approve, and those who disapprove, go upon the *same principles*" (A:175. Italics added). In different ages and circumstances, however, the same practices have often not the same effects. "The state of human affairs is perpetually changing, and, in the same period of time, it is very different in different nations. Amidst this variety, it is impossible that the *subject-matter* of virtue should continue precisely the same. . . . Many practices, very warranted and proper under one form of government, or in the first establishment of a community, and where particular regulations and opinions prevail, may be quite wrong in another state of things, or amongst people of other characters and customs" (A:179). The general principle of morality, however, remains unaltered and unalterable.

But now a further problem arises as far as Price is concerned. It centers around the distinction between "objective rectitude" and our "consciousness of rectitude." As Price himself puts it: "From knowing the nature and capacities of a being, his relations, connexions, and dependencies, and the consequences of his actions, the whole of what he ought to do [in the sense of "objective rectitude"] may be determined, without once attending to his private judgment" (A:179). But the individual himself who acts in a given situation must depend entirely on his own "private judgment concerning what is right." He cannot escape the limitations of his judgment and, because of these limitations, his action may fall far short of what is demanded by "objective rectitude." The difficulty which Price thus encounters is obvious. The solution which he suggests is "to follow our consciences steadily and faithfully, after we have taken care to inform them in the best manner we can; and, where we doubt, to take the *safest* side, and not to venture to *do* any thing concerning which we have doubts, when we know there can be nothing amiss in *omitting* it" (A:184).

But it also follows from the distinction between "objective rectitude" and "consciousness of rectitude" that "what is *objectively right* may be done from any motive good or bad; and, therefore, from hence alone, no merit is communicated to the agent; nay, it is consistent with his greatest guilt" (A:184). What Price here recognizes is the fact that, because of limitations of insight, what is "objectively right" may by sheer accident be done with evil intent. Thus, it turns out that what is "most essential" for the moral evaluation of the "agent" (as distinguished from the act) is his intention. When this intention is good, Price holds, "there is so far virtue, whatever is true of the *matter* of the action: for an agent, who does what is *objectively wrong,* may often be entitled to commendation" (A:184).

With this paradoxical conclusion we have reached the end of Price's argument. In evaluating his position we must keep in mind that, against all irrationalists and hedonists, he holds that "the ultimate spring of virtuous practice in reasonable beings, is the reasonable faculty itself, the consideration of duty, or the perception of right" (A:199). So far so good. Difficulties arise, however, when "duty" and "right" are defined in terms of fitness; for not all actions whose "fitness" at a given occasion is beyond dispute can be regarded as morally relevant. "Fitness," in other words, may define purely expeditious or prudential as well as moral acts. *Moral* acts and *moral* fitness require further specification. The question now is, How do other deontologists deal with this crucial problem?

## II

We turn first to an examination of the position defined and defended by H. A. Prichard, restricting our discussion to his "essays and lectures" which, although covering the period from 1912 to 1947, were posthumously published in 1949 under the apt title, *Moral Obligation.*

In the past, Prichard tells us, the "moral question" has been answered in two distinct ways: some philosophers have argued that "we ought to do so and so, because, as we see when we fully apprehend the facts, doing so will be . . . for our advantage or . . . happiness"; others have maintained that "we ought to do so and so, because something realized either in or by the action is good" (B:2). Both lines of reasoning "break down," Prichard holds; although they do so for different reasons (B:4).

The first type of answer, which Prichard calls "Utilitarianism in the generic sense," amounts to the assertion that "if something which is not an action is good, then we *ought* to undertake the action which will, directly or indirectly, originate it" (B:4). But, as Prichard is quick to point out, this argument assumes an "intermediate link"—the premise, namely, that "what is good ought to be"; and it assumes, in addition, that our apprehension of *this* ought culminates in a "feeling of imperativeness or obligation" (B:4). Both of these assumptions—typically made, for example, by Nicolai Hartmann—Prichard regards as false. They do not correspond to "our actual moral convictions." For instance, we ought to be just in deciding between two parties; but "the balance of resulting good may be, and often is, not on the side of justice" (B:4). We are, thus, driven to the view "that the act is good in itself and that its intrinsic goodness is the reason why it ought to be done" (B:5). But this view, too, is untenable, for "it leads to precisely the dilemma which faces everyone who tries to solve the problem raised by Kant's theory of the good will" (B:5). The dilemma is this: If the reason why we call an act *good* is our sense of obligation, then, instead of our sense that we ought to do this act being derived from its goodness, our apprehension of its goodness presupposes our sense of obligation; but if the reason why we call the act *good* is some "intrinsically good desire," then the ground has been cut from under the meaning of moral obligation, "for we cannot feel that we ought to do that the doing of which is *ex hypothesi* prompted solely by the desire to do it" (B:6). The crucial point as far as both horns of the dilemma are concerned is that in either case the rightness of an act is made to depend upon a motive; and it is Prichard's contention that "in reality the rightness or wrongness of an act has nothing to do with any question of motive at all" (B:7); that, in fact, the rightness or wrongness of an act is "absolutely underivative or immediate." It neither requires, nor is it capable of, supporting reason.

The rightness of action [Prichard holds] consists in its being the origination of something of a certain kind A in a situation of a certain kind, a situation consisting in a certain relation B of the agent to others or to his own nature. To appreciate its rightness two preliminaries may be necessary. We may have to follow out the consequences of the proposed action more fully than we have hitherto done, in order to realize that in the action we should originate A. Thus we may not appreciate the wrongness of telling a certain story until we realize that we should thereby be hurting the feelings of one of our audience. Again, we may have to take into account the relation B involved in the situation, which we had hitherto failed to notice. For instance, we may not appreciate the obligation to give X a present, until we remember that he has done us an act of kindness. But given that by a process . . . of *general and not of moral* thinking we come to recognise that the proposed act is one by which we shall originate A in a relation B, then we appreciate the obligation immediately or directly, the appreciation being an activity of *moral* thinking" (B: 7-8. First Italics added).

This lengthy quotation, I believe, sums up concisely Prichard's position and reveals at the same time the utter inadequacy of his analysis of the moral situation. But about this more will be said later; let us first consider a few supplementary observations which clarify Prichard's thesis.

"The rightness of a right action," Prichard says, "lies solely in the origination in which the act consists, whereas the intrinsic goodness of an action lies solely in its motive; and this implies that a morally good action is morally good not simply because it is a right action but it is a right action done because it is right, i.e., from a sense of obligation" (B:10). To put it differently: "When, or rather so far as, we act from a sense of obligation, we have no purpose or end"—if by "purpose" or "end" we mean "something the existence of which we desire, and the desire of the existence of which leads us to act" (B:10); it does not mean, however, that in so far as we act from a sense of obligation we have no *motive*. The sense of obligation may itself be our motive; for, as far as Prichard is concerned, "desire and the sense of obligation are co-ordinate forms . . . of motive" (B:11).

There remains, however, a crucial difficulty; for the "rightness of an action" is, and must be, a characteristic of the action itself, whereas the "sense of obligation" is, and can be, only a subjective experience. As experienced, the *sense* of obligation is immediate and underivative; the obligation itself, however—that is, the rightness of an action in its objective significance—is not necessarily underived or known immediately. Unless the distinction here indicated is made, no one can have an obligation which he does not also feel, and there would then be no way of deciding on objective grounds—that is, in terms of rightness—between felt but conflicting obligations or between felt and actual obligations. It is imperative that in our interpretation of obligation we do not confuse the objective ground with the subjective feeling of obligation. There are passages in Prichard's writings which indicate that he was aware of the importance of this distinction; but there are other passages in which his position is not so clear.

In dealing with Prichard, it is necessary also to distinguish between "morality" and "virtue" as two "independent, though related, species of goodness" (B:11); for an act may be "virtuous"—here Prichard agrees with Aristotle—in the sense that it is "done willingly or with pleasure," and it is then done not from a sense of obligation alone. This implies, however, that obligation can no more be derived from virtue than virtue can be derived from obligation (B:12). After all, "we can only feel an obligation to *act;* we cannot feel an obligation to *act from a certain desire"* (B:13). To have overlooked this fact is one of the crucial errors of Aristotle.

But now a basic question arises: "If a man has an obligation, i.e., a duty, to do some action, does the obligation depend on certain characteristics of the situation in which he is, or on certain characteristics of his thought about the situation?" (B:18). It may be remembered that Price faced essentially the same question when he distinguished between "objective rectitude" and our "consciousness of rectitude," and that, as a way out of the difficulty, he suggested, rather weakly, that we "follow our consciences steadily and faithfully" and, when in doubt, refrain from action. Prichard, on the other hand, considers the question to be of special importance and devotes an entire essay to it. His arguments depend on his conception of *action* as "originating, causing, or bringing about the existence of something, viz. some new state of an existing thing or substance, or, more shortly, causing a change of state of some existing thing" (B:19). It is not essential to an action that we originate something *"knowing* that we are doing so" (B:19): but it is important, that some things we bring about "directly," whereas other things we bring about "indirectly." If this is kept in mind, then, Prichard maintains, "the meaning of a moral rule has the form: 'A man ought, or ought not, to bring about a thing of a certain kind indirectly'" (B:20).

It must be noted, however, that, when we bring about something indirectly, "the result is not wholly due to us" (B:20), for other causes may intervene. Also, in stating a moral rule, we are "in two respects speaking elliptically" (B:20); for (i) "we never think that an action can be a man's duty unless he is able to do it,"—as Kant put it: 'I *ought*' presupposes 'I can'; and (ii) we assume that the situation to which the moral rule is applied is such that a thing, or a group of things, which the man can bring about directly, will, when produced, bring about a stipulated other thing indirectly. A moral rule, therefore, when fully stated, will be of the following form: "When a situation in which a man is contains a thing of the kind A capable of having a state of the kind X effected in it, and when also it is such that some state or combination of states Y which the man can bring about directly would, if brought about, cause a state of the kind X in A, the man ought to bring about that state or combination of states" (B:21).

Analysis of this formulation of a moral rule shows that, according to Prichard, the obligation referred to depends solely on certain characteristics of the situation and is thus "wholly independent of our knowledge and thought about the situation" (B:22). Although this idea—implying, as it does, an objective ground of moral obligation—has its attraction, it leads to "very awkward consequences." The most awkward of these emerges as soon as we ask: "How am I to *know* that some moral rule is applicable to me here and now?" That is, "How am I to *know* that the situation satisfies the two conditions necessary for the application of the rule?" (B:22) It is obviously possible that, in terms of the objective situation, I have a duty to perform a certain act "without knowing, or even being able to discover, that I have" this duty (B:23). We are, thus, forced back to the extreme conclusion that "we cannot know but can only believe that we have" a duty—a conclusion which renders uncertain the whole conception of duty (B:24).

But to the thesis that duty or obligation "depends on certain facts of the situation" the only alternative is that "obligation depends on our being in a certain attitude of mind towards the situation"; that "the ground of an obligation lies in some state of [our] own mind" (B:25). If we accept this view of the "subjective ground of duty," it is at least "possible to *discover* our duties." But a complete disregard of the facts in a given situation destroys the very meaning of duty by making it dependent on our changing attitudes (B:26). This difficulty, however, can be overcome, Prichard believes, by modifying the thesis slightly: We ought to act only "*after* having considered the circumstances fully" and having obtained "the best opinion" we can about them (B:27). But this admonition is itself "not free from difficulty"; for "our having a duty to consider the circumstances cannot be based on the possibility of our having a future duty of another kind if we were to consider them." Prichard's solution is that, in order to "vindicate" the duty to consider circumstances, "we must represent the two so-called duties as respectively an element and a possible element in a *single* duty, viz. to consider the circumstances, and then *if,* but only if, as a result, we reach a certain opinion, to do a certain future action" (B:27). In other words, according to Prichard, our's is "a single duty," but it is one the full nature of which is not known to us so long as we are ignorant of the facts (B:28). It cannot be said, however, that this thesis eliminates all difficulties inherent in Prichard's position; for it is obviously not true that all "facts" in a given situation are equally relevant to our moral obligation in that situation; and, moreover, mere facts are not in themselves a sufficient ground for a moral *ought*. Only facts of a certain kind can provide such ground.

So far Prichard has assumed that an obligation is simply an "obligation to do something." Upon analysis he finds, however, that this assumption must be modified. To be sure, "an obligation must be an obligation to perform some *activity*"; but it is an obligation to perform that "special kind of *mental* activity for which the proper phrase is 'bringing about something' " (B:31-32); and this activity, according to Prichard, is "that of *setting* or *exerting ourselves* to do something" (B:35. Italics added). An obligation is, thus, an obligation "not to bring about something directly but to set ourselves to do so" (B:35). Not the act itself but our intention is crucial. It follows at once that "the obligation cannot itself be a property which the action [as such] would have, if it were done" (B:37). What does exist, so Prichard maintains, is "the fact that you, or that I, ought, or ought not, . . . to set ourselves to do a certain action" (B:37). The "ought" and the "ought not" here clearly refer not to a "certain action" but to "a certain man." But if this is the case, then the obligation we are under depends "not on the nature of the situation but on that of our thought about it," and the subjective view of the ground of obligation is true (B:38).

This conclusion, however, falsifies our moral experience; for the crux of that experience is the objective significance of the *ought*. Prichard himself was dissatisfied with the conclusion he had reached and, in later essays, augmented in several respects his position and the arguments which support it (B:87-163).

His starting point now is a re-appraisal of Kant's distinction between hypothetical and categorical imperatives. The distinction, Prichard finds, is not, as Kant thought, "one between two statements concerning the word 'ought' made on different grounds, but one between two statements in which 'ought' has a completely different meaning" (B:91). The *moral* ought, i.e., the ought which Kant tried to express in the form of categorical imperatives, is, according to Prichard, "simply the equivalent of 'duty' or 'morally bound' " (B:91). "X ought to do so and so" then means "X is under moral obligation to do so and so." And "being under a moral obligation," Prichard holds, is an attribute *sui generis* of the person involved and is therefore "incapable of having its nature expressed in terms of the nature of anything else" (B:94). However, to regard "being under an obligation" as an attribute *sui generis* and, therefore, as beyond analysis does not advance our understanding of the nature of that obligation or of its ground. Moreover, to regard being under a moral obligation as an attribute of the person involved, although perfectly legitimate under certain conditions, obfuscates the crucial distinction between the nature of an obligation as such and the psychological fact of accepting an obligation. It is true, nevertheless, that, objectively considered, a person can be under a moral obligation to perform a certain act when, psychologically, he fails (or refuses) to accept his obligation. Although the moral obligation is that of a person, *as obligation* it arises in a given situation and is not simply an attribute of the person. Prichard has failed to interpret and justify obligation in this objective sense.

The question, Why should a man accept a moral obligation to do so and so?, has been answered in the past by an assurance that doing his duty contributes to his own happiness, either indirectly through the results of his actions (Butler), or directly insofar as, by its very nature, doing one's duty "carries happiness with it" (Plato and Aristotle). In the former case, however, it can be readily shown that considerations of "conduciveness to our advantage" are "irrelevant to the question whether it is a duty to do some action" (B:97), for we may be duty bound to do something even if doing it is not conducive to our advantage. And if this is so, then the disadvantages and personal frustrations which may result from doing one's duty may continue to pile up until they outweigh the satisfaction or the good which a man derives from knowing that he is doing his duty. Thus, the second form of the argument—the argument, namely, that doing one's duty is its own sufficient reward—also breaks down. To the question, therefore, " 'Will doing our duty be for our happiness?' the only possible answer must be: 'It all depends; in some instances it may be and in others it may not' " (B:108). And on such shaky ground the idea of moral obligation cannot rest.

Neither does a teleological theory of duty solve our problem. No matter what form it takes, such a theory is "open to a fatal objection of principle"—the objection, namely, that "it resolves the moral 'ought' into the non-moral 'ought,' representing our being morally bound to do some action as if it were the same thing as the action's being one which we must do if our purpose is to become realized" (B:117; 119). Prudential considerations are not a sufficient basis for the obligatoriness of the moral ought. And there is the further difficulty that teleological theories assume that "in all deliberate action we have a single final aim or purpose" (B:128)—be this aim happiness (Bentham), enjoyment (Mill), satisfaction (Green), or whatever—whereas no such assumption accords with the facts of human experience.

The situation is not changed for the better by the quasi-teleological thesis that we *ought* to aim at a single something, be it our own happiness or the general happiness, be it our own perfection or that of human beings generally (B:129), for "to aim at something is to have the desire of it as our motive and there cannot be an obligation to have a certain motive" (B:135).

If it be maintained that "no act can be a duty unless there is something good connected with the action"—be it that the action *causes* something good, or that it itself *is* good (B:142) —then again obligation has been resolved into something which is not an obligation. More specifically, the obligation to *do* something has been resolved into an "ought-to-existence" (B: 158; 160)—a thesis which is central to the Ethics of Nicolai Hartmann. Prichard insists, however—and I think rightly—that "the 'ought' of obligation is not that of 'ought-to-exist'" (B: 163). Resolving the former into the latter falsifies the whole meaning of the moral ought. Prichard, therefore, comes back to the conclusion, previously reached, that moral obligation is an attribute *sui generis* of a person; that it cannot be further analyzed; and that it itself is an impelling motive. But this conclusion we cannot accept for reasons already indicated and for reasons yet to be given.

### III

Many of the ideas advanced by Price and Prichard have been augmented and developed more fully by Sir W. David Ross. In fact, the position of the deontologists has in many respects found its most adequate formulation in Ross's two books, *The Right and the Good* (1930), and *Foundations of Ethics* (1939).

It is only natural, therefore, that we shall center our final evaluation of this revised form of Kantianism on the work of Ross, selecting for analysis especially the definitive statement of his views as given in the *Foundations*.

Ross's starting-point is "moral consciousness," i.e., "the existence of a large body of beliefs and convictions to the effect that there are certain kinds of acts that ought to be done and certain kinds of things that ought to be brought into existence, so far as we *can* bring them into existence" (D:1). We must not assume, however, "that all of these convictions are true," or "that they are all consistent," or even "that they are all clear" (D:1). By and large, however, two "main strands" are discernible in the complex fabric of common opinion about moral questions: There is (i) the idea of human life envisaged as obedience to laws; and there is (ii) this same ideal envisaged as the progressive satisfaction of desires and the attainment of ends. In the former case the idea of *right* is basic; in the latter case the idea of *good* is basic (D:5; 10-11). Ross holds, however, that anyone who tries to work with one of these ideas only "will sooner or later find himself forced to introduce the other," for it may be the case that neither "right" or "good" "can be elucidated without remainder in terms other than itself" (D:5). Nevertheless, Ross holds, right is more basic than is good. The question of what is right, therefore, receives his main attention. And for his answer Ross claims universal validity.

He acknowledges, of course, the facts revealed by anthropologists and comparative sociologists that there exists a great variety of views with respect to moral matters in different societies and even within the same society. According to Ross, however, this diversity of opinion on moral questions rests ultimately "not on a disagreement about fundamental principles, but partly on differences in the circumstances of different societies, and partly on different views which people hold, not on moral questions but on questions of fact" (D:18; 19). For Ross, therefore, as for Kant, the ultimate principles of morality are universal in scope.

Moreover, according to Ross, in spite of the great differences of opinion in moral matters which prevail at any given time, "we need not doubt that man progresses fairly steadily towards moral truth as he does towards scientific" (D:20)—although evolutionary theories as such do not offer us "anything that can be accepted as a definition of 'right' or 'obligation'" (D:21). Nor can we expect any help from the approval theories, either private or public; for if moral approval presupposes the conviction that the action is right, then we cannot mean by calling an action right that it awakens in us the emotion of approval (D:23); and the thesis that an action is right *because* we approve, is too preposterous to deserve serious consideration (*cf.* Chapters I and II).

When the positivists now contend that ethical terms are purely emotive words, and that ethical judgments assert nothing but are "mere expressions of a state of mind in which we are liking certain kinds of conduct and wishing others to behave accordingly" (D:34), then, so Ross points out, this theory "simply falls into a confusion." The theory starts with the fact, long known to moral philosophers, that moral judgments cannot be verified by an appeal to sense experience; it combines with this fact the view of the positivists that synthetic judgments have meaning only when they *are* so verified (D:37). This theory itself, however, is unverifiable by sensory experience and is therefore meaningless—as measured by its own criterion (D:38). We may agree with Ayer (so Ross holds) that, when two persons differ on a question of right or wrong, it is by considerations of fact that they try to remove the difference of opinion on the moral question. But it remains true, nevertheless, that the point of any attempt at persuasion of this kind is to convince the other person that the liking, or the disliking, of a certain act is justified, i.e., that "the act has a character which *deserves* to be liked or disliked, is good or is bad" (D:41). And so Ross comes back to the question, What constitutes a right act?

After evaluating G. E. Moore's theory as set forth in *Principia Ethica,* Ross concludes that "the more we think of the term 'right,' the more convinced we are likely to be that it is an indefinable term, and that when one attempts to define it one will either name something plainly different from it, or use a term which is a mere synonym of it" (D:43).

Moral rightness, as Ross views it, includes, of course, the "generic quality of suitability," but it includes also "the differentia which distinguishes it from every form of rightness but itself" (D:54). This distinguishing mark lies, in part at least, in the nature of the ought which is implied in "moral rightness"; and this ought, this obligatoriness, according to Ross, pertains to persons rather than acts, for, strictly speaking, we cannot say that "such and such an act is obligatory." After all, the act is not yet there to be either obligatory or anything else. Nor, so Ross, concludes, "can we say 'such and such an act would be obligatory if it were done'; for, clearly, its obligatoriness, if it has any, does not depend on its being done" (D:56).

It is Ross's contention that, when we say that such and such an act is our duty, "we are already satisfied of the rightness of the act by a consideration of its nature apart from its motive" (D:131). The motive, to be sure, also is relevant, for it determines the "moral goodness" of the act (D:139). But right now we are interested in the "rightness" rather than the "goodness" of an act—even if, in the end, we cannot escape the problem of goodness altogether. Our specific question is, What constitutes the rightness of a right act?

To begin with, let us say (with Ross) that "right" means "suitable"—in the "unique and indefinable" sense of "morally suitable"—to "the situation in which an agent finds himself." This statement, of course, does not mean very much. It is clear, however, that any situation in which an agent finds himself contains two aspects: It contains an *objective* aspect, which consists of "the facts about the various persons and things involved in the situation"—facts, in virtue of which a certain act would be "the best possible fulfillment of the various *prima facie* obligations resting on the agent"; and it contains a *subjective* aspect, "which consists of the agent's thoughts about the situation" (D:146). From this distinction of aspects it follows that "an act which the agent, in view of his opinion about the situation, thinks will be the maximum fulfillment of obligation, will be in that respect right; while in order to be *completely* right an act will have to be suitable both to the objective and to the subjective element, which it can be only if the agent's opinions correspond to the realities of the situation" (D:146). It also follows from this distinction that "when people express different opinions about the rightness or wrongness of an act, the difference is often due to the fact that one of them is thinking of objective and the other of subjective rightness" (D:147). The distinction thus makes possible a reconciliation of apparently contradictory views.

However, the real question is, "Which of the characteristics —objective or subjective rightness—is ethically the most important, which of the two acts is that which we ought to do?" (D:147) Ross finds that there are various considerations which seem to require that we regard *objective* rightness as decisive. In difficult moral situations, for example, "we *want* to know not what act we think likely to produce certain results, but what act *will* produce certain results. And we are often driven to admit that we do not know what we ought to do" (D:147)— i.e., what is required by the objective aspects of the situation. Also, moral laws—such as, Keep your promises, and, Do that which will produce most good—are often expressed in a form which implies an objective standard. Ross, nevertheless, holds that *"it is the subjectively right act that is obligatory"* (D:148. Italics added). In this he follows Prichard, pointing out that the objective view—although "not fatal to the possibility of knowing moral rules"—is "fatal to the possibility or recognizing particular duties incumbent on us here and now," for we can never know absolutely that we can produce the intended result. But if it is "my state of knowledge or opinion about the facts of the case" (D:150), then it is at least possible for me to discover my duties; for "we can always or almost always know what it is that we think likely" (D:151).

But Ross also agrees with Prichard in holding that an agent "should set himself to *act*" only when either action is immediately required or when he has reached that point in the analysis of a situation when no further thinking about it "would enable him to judge better of the circumstances and of the probable effects of alternative exertions" (D:157). In the latter case he is as near to the objectively right act as he can reasonably be expected to come.

It is important to note, however, that, for Ross as for Prichard, any reference to "setting oneself to bring about a certain result" is not the same as "desiring to bring about that result"; that is, it is not the same as being activated by a certain motive, for "we may set ourselves to produce the result from any one of a variety of motives." Hence, if the self-exertion as such is our duty, then "it is not the self-exertion from any particular motive that is our duty" (D:158). Nevertheless, "an action done from a certain motive is . . . morally suitable to a situation in a sense in which a mere action, irrespective of its motive, is not" (D: 159). Thus, if, from a sense of duty, we "set ourselves" to produce a maximum of good, our act is "more completely fitting" than it would be if we should "set ourselves" to do an act which produces a maximum of good only accidently, or one which is induced by an unworthy motive. It is Ross's contention, however, that neither the actual result nor the particular motive is decisive. What alone makes an act right or wrong is "the nature of what is intended" in that act; and the only thing which can be "obligatory or disobligatory" is a self-assertion on our part: the "setting ourselves to perform a certain act" (D:160).

But now new difficulties arise. "Suppose that of two men one does that act which he mistakenly believes to be his objective duty, and the other does that which is his objective duty, believing it not to be so." In this case, Ross holds, "we should regard the former as at least less blameworthy than the latter; and in fact we should not regard the former as directly blameable for the act, but only, if at all, for previous acts by which he has blunted his sense of what is objectively right" (D:163-164). But does not such an evaluation of the two men introduce a vicious subjectivity into ethics?

Before we answer this question, we must consider just what is meant by "subjectivity" and in what sense subjectivity is vicious. It is Ross's thesis that the only *vicious* subjectivity lies in the thesis that "acts are made to have some moral characteristic by being thought to have it" (D:164). But this sort of subjectivism is not involved in the situation just described.

As Ross sees it, any given situation involves three possibilities: (i) There is one act in this situation which would be the objectively right act and which a man would recognize as such *if* he had "complete knowledge about the circumstances and a completely correct moral insight." (ii) But if the man is mistaken about the circumstances, there is one act which is right "in the sense of being appropriate to his opinion about the circumstances." This act is not *made* right by being thought so, but it *is* right relative to the supposed situation, just as in the first case the act *is* right relative to the actual situation. "The harmony is not created by being thought to exist, it exists independently of the agent's thought about it" (D:164). (iii) The agent may be mistaken, not about the facts in the case, but in his moral judgment as to what is his duty. Still, so long as this man thinks as he does, the act he performs has "the same sort of harmony with his conviction as an act in which a man acts in a correct conviction has with that conviction"—a harmony which is there "for all to apprehend" (D:164-165). Not one of these three possibilities thus involves a *vicious* subjectivity.

But now the question may be asked, "Can we be said to *know* our duty? And if we can, how do we acquire this knowledge?" (D:168) To begin with, rightness is not an attribute which is directly perceived, as a color or a noise is perceived. It is only because I know or think that a given act has a particular character that I know or think (at a second level of knowing and thinking) that it is right. In view of this fact, "we might feel inclined to say that our perception of particular duties is always an act of inference, in which the major premise is some general moral principle" (D:169). Ross maintains, however, that this interpretation will not do, for man, who "was a practical being before he became a theoretical one," has somehow answered "the question how he ought to behave in particular circumstances before he engaged in general speculation on the principles of duty" (D:169); and, more importantly, reflection upon our own experience shows that "it is not by deduction but by direct insight that I see [particular acts] to be right, or wrong" (D:171). "We can hardly fail to recognize in the best and most enlightened of men an absolutely original and direct insight into moral principles, and in many others the power of seeing for themselves the truth of moral principles when these are pointed out to them" (D:172). The truth of moral principles, in other words, is self-evident.

It is true, of course—so Ross admits—that it is "often justifiable to accept the fact that an act falls under one of the basic principles of morality as sufficient reason for regarding it as right (or wrong) without further consideration," because "mankind has for more generations than we can tell been exploring the consequences of certain types of acts and drawing conclusions accordingly about the rightness or wrongness of types of acts" (D:174). Nevertheless, in any given situation various principles may be involved. In the last resort, therefore, "we must use our own judgment as to what is right and what is wrong" (D:175).

However, in using our own judgment, we must not only anticipate the consequences of alternative actions, we must also "estimate the comparative goodness of these consequences" (D:175); and in both respects we encounter great difficulties in the actual and concrete situations. Thus, forecasting the consequences of alternative actions is made difficult, if not at times impossible, because there are many "agencies, factors and forces and other persons, at work in altering the course of events" (D:178); and "estimating the *goodness* of the results of alternative actions" is made extremely difficult by the fact that an accurate calculus of goods—as an accurate calculus of pleasures —is impossible of achievement (D:179-185). Moreover, there are other duties besides our duty to produce the maximum good —duties such as "fulfilling promises," "making reparation for wrongs we have done," "making a return for good we have received." And "where such a special *prima facie* duty exists, as well as the general *prima facie* duty of producing the maximum good, our final judgment about our duty depends not on a comparison of goods but on a comparison of *prima facie* duties" (D:186). In view of all these facts there is nothing for us to

do but study in detail the situation in which we find ourselves—
and to do so "till the morally significant features of it become
clear to us" (D:186).

Such a study of the situation in which we find ourselves may
be guided (a) by teleological considerations, or (b) by intuition.
It is Ross's contention that a teleological interpretation "over-
simplifies the moral life; that it recognizes only one type of claim,
the claim that we shall act so as to produce most good, while
in fact there are claims arising from other grounds, arising from
what we have already done (e.g., from our having made a
promise, or inflicted an injury) and not merely from the kind of
result our action will have, or may be expected to have" (D:189).
He therefore accepts Intuitionism as the preferable alternative.
His Intuitionism, however, is closely linked up with his conception of the rational nature of man.

As will be remembered, Kant also emphasized man's rational
nature, in fact, Kant went so far as to maintain that an action
done from a sense of duty could not be motivated by desire, for,
in Kant's view, desire belongs to man's sensuous nature. According to Ross, however, "this complete degradation of desire
is not justified"; for, "quite apart from a desire to do our duty,
we have many desires which we could not have if we were not
rational beings" (D:205). There is, for instance, our desire
to understand," which hardly belongs to "the purely animal part
of our nature" but "springs directly from our possession of
reason." And there is the desire "to follow a certain career or
occupy a certain position—which we should never feel unless
reason had been at work, apprehending the nature of human
relationships and the consequent desirability of such a career
or such a position" (D:205). It will not do, therefore, (as did
Kant) simply to oppose man's rational nature (which alone has
moral worth) to his sensuous nature (which does not have such
worth). The truth is, Ross holds, that man's moral life is "a
struggle between a multiplicity of desires having various degrees
of worth" (D:206). And "if it be granted that we have desires
that spring from our possession of reason, it is only natural that
there should arise a desire, itself springing from our rational

apprehension of principles of duty, not to be the slave of lower desires but to regulate our life by these principles" (D:206).

Here we find Ross arriving at a strange conclusion. Starting originally from the Kantian premise of a clear separation of "desires" and "reason," he now conceives man, the moral agent, as simply a creature of desires. To be sure, he distinguishes between a desire which stems from our "rational apprehension of principles," and various "lower desires"; but what Kant had in mind when he spoke of our "respect" for the law is strangely missing or has been distorted, and man's moral life has thereby been falsified. Ross's interpretation, reducing all motivation to some form of desire, leaves little room for man's free and, therefore, moral choice. Moreover, if all our motives stem from desire, is there still any sense left to the notion of duty? It would not seem so.

## IV

In our arguments so far we have completely neglected the problem of goodness and, in particular, the problem of moral goodness which, as we have seen earlier, necessarily augments the problem of rightness. We are now ready to make amends for this neglect.

Ross admits that the only universal precondition of our using the word "good" in connection with an object is "the existence of a favorable attitude in ourselves towards the object." "What we *express* when we call an object good is our attitude towards it" (D:254). However, what we *express* is not what we *mean*. "What we *mean*," Ross holds, "is something about the object itself and not about our attitude towards it," some specific characteristic of the object "which we think it would have whether we were commending it or not" (D:255).

When we now ask what this specific characteristic is by virtue of which we call something *good*, Ross replies that the answer depends on whether "we are speaking of (1) a person or of (2) a thing" (D:255). When we are speaking of a person, then "the root idea expressed by 'good' seems to be that of success or efficiency" (D:256). Thus, we may say of someone who is playing the violin that he is a good violinist—"if we think him comparatively successful in his endeavour." But when we are speaking of a thing, the predominant meaning of "good" is "ministering to some particular human interest." Thus, "a good knife is essentially one that can be successfully used for cutting, a good poem one that arouses aesthetic pleasure in us" (D:256). From the point of view of ethics, however, only those meanings of "good" are important in which we say "such-and-such a man is morally good," or in which we say "(rightly or wrongly) 'virtue is good,' 'knowledge is good,' 'pleasure is good'" (D:256-257). And the question is "whether 'good' in this predicative sense can be defined in a purely naturalistic way, or can be defined at all" (D:257).

In his attempt to answer this question, Ross distinguishes two main types of the predicative applications of "good," namely, (i) "good" in the sense of "useful as a means" to something else, and (ii) "good" in the sense of "good in itself," "intrinsically good," or "good apart from its results." "But what is good *in itself* may be so in either of two senses." If (a) what we call good in itself contains bad or indifferent elements as well as good ones, we may speak of it as "good on the whole"; but if (b) it contains good elements only, we may speak of it as "good through and through." "Only things that are good through and through will be good in the strictest sense of the word" (D:258); and with respect to these things Ross now asks: (i) "What is the nature of that which we are ascribing when we say of something that it is good in this sense?" (ii) "What are the things that *are* good in this sense?" (D:258).

In attempting to answer these questions Ross first repudiates the thesis that "goodness is a relation or a relational property." This thesis, he finds, is most plausibly expressed by saying that "nothing possesses the kind of intrinsic characteristic which we ascribe to things when we call them good; that some things are, however, the actual or possible objects of a favorable emotion, and that on the strength of this we mistakenly ascribe to them goodness in themselves" (D:261). To be sure, no one can *prove* that conscientiousness and benevolence are good in themselves, but, then, neither can we *prove* ultimates in any other field of experience. Some truths must be apprehended without proof; "and we apprehend that conscientiousness or benevolence is good with as complete certainty, directness, and self-evidence as we ever apprehend anything" (D:262).

If it now be objected that not all men acknowledge the same intrinsic goods or place them in the same "order of value," Ross replies that "here, as elsewhere, varieties of opinion are no indication that there is not an objective truth that is there to be apprehended." After all, "different ages and different communities differ in their degree of mental maturity"; and what seems self-evident to one age or one community, need not be so to some other age or community. The history of science itself shows this clearly. And "it cannot really . . . be contended," Ross concludes, "that there is more variation between the opinions of different ages or communities about what things are good, than there is between their opinions about matters of natural science" (D:269).

Now, the only ground, Ross holds, on which a thing is "worthy of being thought to be good," of being admired, is that it actually *is* good; that its goodness is an intrinsic quality of it. It cannot be said, however, that "the only ground on which a thing is worthy of our interest or liking it is that it is good in itself"; and, as a matter of fact, "we often take satisfaction in things that we do not think good, but only pleasant" (D:279). Admiration and satisfaction are therefore entirely different reactions; and satisfaction is not in itself crucial in moral matters. What is crucial are the *"admirable* activities of the human spirit," i.e., "certain moral dispositions and actions, and certain activities of the intellect and of the creative imagination," which "appear to be good in a way which depends entirely on their intrinsic nature" (D:283); and, "by a self-evident necessity," we have a *prima facie* duty to produce the things which are good in this intrinsic sense. This "duty to produce what is intrinsically good always takes precedence over the *prima facie* duty of producing pleasure for others"; and we have no duty at all of producing pleasures for ourselves (D:284).

However, not all goods which are "worthy objects of admiration" are morally good. "Excellent scientific and artistic activity is good but not morally good" (D:290). What, then, is characteristic of the *morally* good? Ross does not follow Kant in identifying the morally good with "goodness of will," for (so he argues) "if we hold that actions are morally good when and because they proceed from certain motives, we can hardly fail to ascribe moral goodness to those same desires when they do not lead to action," and if we include certain desires in our conception of what is morally good, "we cannot refuse to include also certain emotions." Hence, "if desire for another's pleasure is good, so also is satisfaction at his actual pleasure" (D:290-291). But predispositions to act or to react in certain ways—"the relatively permanent modifications of character," as Ross calls them (D:292)—are also morally good. In fact, "a character is a larger and grander bearer of moral goodness than any single manifestation of character—whether it be an action, a desire, or an emotion—can be" (D:293).

Still, it is generally agreed that "action owes its goodness, and the measure of its goodness, to the motive from which it springs" (D:293). The problem of goodness, therefore, resolves itself into a problem of motives. The Hedonist, of course, recognizes only one ultimate motive—pleasure. But although Ross admits the force of the hedonistic arguments at a certain level of analysis, he finds that at least twelve types of motives are readily discernible.

We have, of course, "desires for particular pleasures"; and such desires are "probably the commonest of all." But out of them "there arises in some people, and actuates them in some of their actions, a desire for their own pleasure on the whole." When so actuated, these people may give up some particular pleasure or pleasures which they desire in order to obtain the greatest amount of pleasure "on the whole" (D:296). But—so Ross holds—we also have "desires for some particular good activity, or for the attainment of some particular virtue, or knowledge, or skill" (D:296). Although such desires may be closely related to our desires for particular pleasures, we can distinguish between these two kinds of desires as "two distinct elements in our total mental state, and can say that in some cases the one desire and in others the other predominates" (D:296).

In some people, however, there arises—corresponding to the desire for the greatest amount of pleasure on the whole—"a generalized wish for good activity." "This is the motive which Aristotle describes as dominating the good man, and it is also the motive in what T. H. Green describes as the life of self-realization" (D:296-297). Beyond this, Ross argues, "there are desires that particular people other than oneself should have particular pleasures" (D:297); and in some people we find, in addition to this restricted altruism, "a generalizing altruism in which the pleasure or happiness of all human beings, or even of all sentient beings, becomes an object of desire" (D:298). But there are also "desires for the exercise of good activities by, or the improvement of character or intellect in, some particular person or persons, other than the desirer"; and there is a generalized form of these desires, which is "the desire for the perfection of all human beings" (D:298). We must recognize also as a distinct motive of action "the desire that some one else should suffer," and, possibly, "a generalized desire that every one except oneself should suffer" (D:298). There is, in addition, "the wish to make another person's character worse in some respect"; and a generalized form of this wish is at least conceivable—the wish, namely, that all other men be "as bad as possible" (D:298). But even Ross admits that such a motive would be "the motive not of a man but of a devil" (D:299).

The thesis of these twelve types of motives contradicts, of course, the contention of the hedonists that "only states of activities of the desirer himself can be the object of desire" (D:299); but the hedonists' contention, so Ross points out, rests upon a basic confusion anyway—the confusion, namely, "between the fulfillment of desire and the satisfaction of the desirer." "The fulfillment of desire is simply the coming into existence of that which is desired; the satisfaction is a new mental experience in the mind of the desirer. The latter naturally does not arise unless the desirer knows or thinks he knows that the desire has been fulfilled, whether or not in fact it has been fulfilled" (D:300).

It is Ross's contention that the twelve types of motives mentioned above can be arranged "in order of excellence." If we disregard "the generalized wish to cause moral evil as falling below the level of human nature," then, Ross holds, we must "rank lowest the wish to produce moral evil in some other person," it being an object worthy not only of dissatisfaction but also of condemnation (D:301). The wish to produce pain is next in "the scale of demerit. The pleasures, which follow next as we ascend the scale, Ross groups under three headings: those which are "morally bad"—such as "the pleasure of hurting another"; those which are "morally indifferent"—such as "the sensuous pleasures"; and those which are "morally good"—such as "the pleasure of helping another" (D:302).

The respective desires share the corresponding places in the "order of excellence." Ross continues: "The wish to promote some good activity, or some improvement of character or of intellect, in another, appears to be as certainly better than the wish to produce pleasure for another, as the wish to corrupt a character is worse than the wish to produce pain" (D:302). Ross concludes by arguing that "the desire to do one's duty, both in its particularized and its generalized form," "ranks above all other motives"; for, "in its typical manifestation, the sense of duty is a particularly keen sensitiveness to the rights and interests of other people, coupled with a determination to do what is fair as between them; and it is by no means the case that it tends to be divorced from warm personal feeling; it tends rather to be something superadded to that" (D:303-304).

In a combination of higher and lower motives—which is the usual situation in actual living—Ross, differing from Kant, holds that the action has less moral worth only if the lower motive is in itself positively bad. If the lower motive is itself good, it adds to the goodness of the act (D:305). "Kant's picture of the ideally good man as going through life never animated by natural kindness but only by the sense of duty has always been felt by most readers to be unduly narrow and rigoristic." If we avoid Kant's mistake, "we can think of the ideally good man as having many good motives in addition to the sense of duty, but with a sense of duty strong enough to induce him to do his duty even if the other motives were absent" (D:306).

It has been Ross's thesis so far that the goodness of actions depends on the goodness of *motives*. Ross realizes, however, that to ascribe the goodness of actions *solely* to the goodness of their motives "would be to simplify matters far too much" (D:306-307). After all, an act done from a good motive may be wrong when considered objectively, and, similarly, when the good motive is lacking or a bad motive is present, "an objectively right act may be morally bad, or indifferent" (D:166; 308). But if the motive is morally good, the act itself is "far more likely to conform to objective duty," and thus be right, than is any other act (D:166). Ross concludes therefore: "An action will be completely good only if it manifests the whole range of motivation by which an ideally good man would be affected in the circumstances, a sensitiveness to every result for good or for evil that the act is foreseen as likely to have, as well as to any special *prima facie* obligations or disobligations that may be involved; and only if it manifests sensitiveness to all these considerations in their right proportions. But if the agent is responsive to all the morally relevant considerations in their right proportions, he will in fact do the *right* act" (D:309). Such responsiveness assumes, however, that the "agent" is basically a morally good character; for "if a man is not morally good, it is only the merest accident that he ever does what he ought" (D:310).

## V

That the work of the deontologists should have far-reaching repercussions is only natural (5). The problem with which they were concerned is crucial to the whole field of ethics, and the thesis they set forth is, on the whole, clearly stated and well argued. But since we have already indicated various weaknesses in the over-all position of the deontologists, we can now be brief in our final evaluation.

According to all the deontologists, both ethics and science begin with subjective experience. There is, however, a crucial difference, which Ross points up most effectively. In science, the ultimate appeal is, and must be, to the facts of sense-perception; and this appeal provides a test of truth which is superior to any authority (D:3). In ethics, however, no such appeal is possible. Does this now mean that, in ethics, one man's opinion is as good (or as bad) as another's? The question is crucial. In attempting to answer it, Ross sets forth a partly intuitionist and a partly coherence theory criterion of truth. We "intuit," and, thus, know immediately and directly what is right and what is wrong; but, in the over-all view of our experience, ethical intuitions must also be harmonious and coherent.

However, as Ross develops this thesis, a shift in emphasis occurs in his position. What, in the end, is important is no longer a man's opinion, as such, but the content of that opinion —that about which the man has an opinion. In the realm of ethics this means that what really is important is the right and the good. To put it differently: The appeal is still made to observation; but the observation involved is of a particular nature. *"That which we mean to refer to,"* Ross states, "when we use the term 'right' or 'obligatory' " is "rightness" or "obligatoriness" (D:13. Italics added). The deontologists would admit, of course, that moral experience has its emotional overtones. But "the emotion of obligation," according to Ross, "is an intellectual emotion which arises only when we judge the act to have a certain character . . . and to be on that account obligatory" (D:26). Ross argues, in other words, that "moral emotions" presuppose an awareness of moral facts which, as such, are not a matter of emotions. And it is the special character of the "moral facts" in this sense which is of special concern to the deontologists. In this respect, at least, they have seen and emphasized a fundamental truth of our moral experience.

It is true, however, that any moral act has two distinct aspects. There is, on the one hand, its character of being obligatory. And there is, on the other hand, its productiveness of some good (however "good" may be defined). The question is, Can the obligatoriness of the act be explained in terms of its productiveness of some good? The deontologists deny that it can. For them, an act which is *right* would always be the right act to do and would thus be obligatory even if, under particular circumstances, it might not be productive of the maximum of good. The opponents of the deontologists argue, of course, that "the characteristic of being probably productive of at least as much good on balance as any possible alternative is both a necessary and sufficient property of all right acts. Any act to be right must have this characteristic, and if it does have this characteristic it is right" (F:252). "A thoughtful ideal utilitarianism," so the argument runs, "would agree almost completely with Ross as to which acts are right and which are wrong" (F:251). What this thesis overlooks is the fact that, according to Ross, the *rightness* of the act, rather than its productiveness of good, is of the essence of a *moral* act. Moreover, if the promotion of good consequences were really of the essence of every *prima facie* obligation, it should always enter into our consideration of what we ought to do. But it does not do this, or does so only indirectly.

After all has been said and done, the deontologists have clarified to a remarkable degree the actual procedures of moral judgment. They, rather than the teleologists, have pointed up the crucial role which obligation plays in our moral life; and they have clearly shown, I believe, that "right" cannot be defined exclusively in terms of "good." I am not sure, however, that the deontologists have given us a correct interpretation of the relationship of the "right" to the "good." This relationship is much more complicated than either the teleologists or the deontologists seem to realize, and can be untangled and properly defined only within the framework of a generalized theory of value—such as

I suggest in Chapter X. For the time being, however, we must examine further the position of the deontologists.

The central question to which we must find an answer is, Do the deontologists succeed in demonstrating that "conduciveness to maximum good is not what makes an act right?" (N:342) Or, what amounts to the same thing, are there aspects of our moral experience which escape this particular type of moral reductionism?

As Thomas E. Hill points out, "at least three lines of thought concur to show that immediate intuition cannot be the fundamental pathway to knowledge of right. First, it often happens . . . that an honest man who knows the situation in which he must act is bewildered concerning what is right in it and that further illumination concerning the probable consequences of the possible courses of action would resolve his problem. Second, one often comes to admit that he acted wrongly for the sole reason that he miscalculated the probable consequences of his action. . . . Third, the conceptions of right and wrong which have been and are held by various peoples in various times are far more divergent than an intuitive theory of right would permit to expect" (N:343). However, no matter what their negative force may be, we cannot accept these arguments as sufficient to swing back to a teleological conception of the moral.

The first argument, for example, loses much of its force when we realize that the "bewildered person" may also come to know what he ought to do when we clarify for him the various duties he has in the specific situation in which he finds himself now. And defining and pointing up duties is possible without recourse to consequences, good or bad. The second argument may even mean that, had the man analyzed his duties rather than contemplated consequences, he might have done the morally right act. Again the reference to "probable consequences" is misleading rather than helpful. In one sense, the third argument is entirely irrelevant here, for there are as many different conceptions of the "good" in the world as there are conceptions of the "right," and the conclusion drawn here to the disadvantage of the deontologists must be drawn to the disadvantage of all intuitionism.

But, admittedly, to the extent to which deontologists stand committed to an intuitionism, the argument is relevant and forceful. However, let us not forget even then that, in the theory of Ross at least, there is also an aspect of the coherence theory; and there is thus a corrective to simple intuitionism built into the deontologists' position. The harmonious integration of obligations is at least as essential as is our immediate intuition of them.

Moreover—and this also is crucial—in determining the rightness of an act, we must have before us the total situation within which a choice is to be made; and this situation includes values and valuations as well as facts. When the deontologists speak of the "rightness" of an action, they implicitly refer to valuations—whether they mean to do so or not. Without at least an implied reference to values, it would mean very little and would certainly be without moral significance to speak of "rightness" or "fittingness." A *moral* ought cannot be justified in terms of "fittingness" as such, unless it be understood that what is referred to here is *moral* "fittingness." But to maintain that this is the case leads us into a logical circle—a circle, from which we can escape only if we analyze the moral and the valuational aspects of any situation of choice more fully.

The deontologists are right, however, in maintaining that, if consideration of the maximum good is what makes an act a duty, then duty is reduced to a form of desire and is deprived of its distinctive compulsory character. And if it now be argued that the good does not always kindle our desire to do what is good, and that, therefore, we have a duty to do the maximum good, we can only point out that such an argument rests upon a confusion. It is, and remains, a fact that men desire whatever they are persuaded is good (either for themselves or for someone else whose interests they respect and cherish). If, under these circumstances, they prefer *what they regard as good* to what *is good objectively considered,* their error is one of ignorance, not of moral deficiency, and ought to be treated as such. That is to say, the remedy is a clarification of the true value relations, not an appeal to a moral ought. If it be argued that, at times, it may be necessary to persuade an individual even of the fact that he ought to do the act yielding the higher good rather than that which yields the lower, then a distinction must be drawn between the *prudential* and the *moral* meaning of "ought"; and it is only the prudential meaning which is directly related to value considerations and, therefore, to the ideal of "realizing the maximum good." That the distinction and, yet, interrelation of the prudential and the moral ought require most careful analysis is obvious. We shall return to it in Chapter X.

A more restricted criticism of the deontologists' position is indicated by Johnson, who maintains that the theory of putative rightness "runs . . . into insuperable difficulties" because of "the deontologists' assumption that our motives in acting can never form part of the content of our duty" (P:81). This criticism, it seems to me, misses the point.

Let us consider a simple illustration. If I promise you to have lunch with you to-morrow, then, when to-morrow comes, the promise I made logically entails an obligation. The obligatoriness derives, not from any specific content of the promise, but from the nature of the promise *as promise*. In this strict analytical sense my acting from a sense of obligation is not and never can be part of the *content* of the obligation. However, when I promised to have lunch with you to-morrow, value considerations (such as looking forward to a pleasant lunch hour, or finding the lunch hour to be a convenient time during which to transact some business) were the reasons for my promising to have lunch with you in the first place. This same value consideration—and, therefore, the very essence of the "content" which induced me to put myself under obligation—is still effective as a motive even to-morrow, but it is now supplemented by the explicit commitment I have made. And it is the latter which is the essence of the *moral* ought. The former involves the prudential ought only. But there is no reason whatsoever why both could not be motives (separately or together) for the same act. Since we commit ourselves on the basis of value considerations, it is beside the point to argue—as Johnson in effect does (P:92)—that, for Ross, it is inconsistent to hold that the goodness of motives is relevant to the rightness of actions. I am not saying that the deontologists (and Ross in particular) have adequately analyzed the interrelations of the right and the good; I am sure that they have not. But now I am merely pointing up the fact that there is no contradiction in accepting a conception of moral obligation which is akin to that of the deontologists, and to hold also that we make commitments which entail these obligations on the basis of value considerations.

Another criticism of deontology, frequently voiced, culminates in the assertion that the fact that a man has made a promise can no more explain why he keeps it than can any other fact (V:215). This criticism suffers from a basic confusion—the confusion, namely, of the nature of an obligation with the psychological attitude an individual may have towards an obligation. The first—the nature of the obligation as such—is clearly an analytic entailment of a promise or commitment; the second— the psychological attitude—is a fact of human experience and is not logically entailed. The obligation (as an entailment) may be there even though we fail to see it or, seeing it, refuse to accept it. No logic as such can or does account for the psychological facts—this is as true in mathematics as it is in moral matters.

Special problems arise because of the complexities of our human situation. If all our choices were but between obligations and desires, it might be a relatively simple matter to find appropriate solutions to situations of conflict; and it is true that "Ross has loaded the scales in favor of the sense of duty by presenting the only alternative as *impulses,* a word which suggests that they are sporadic, wayward, and capricious" (V:220). Still, even "sympathy, benevolence, patriotism, and ambition" are emotion-tinged and, in this respect, share in the nature of impulses. Although they may be pervasive and enduring, as other impulses are not, their real significance lies in the realm of values and not necessarily in that of morality. If not morally restrained, ambition and patriotism readily become disvalues. An age that has seen a Hitler rise to power should have no doubts on this point! And sympathy and benevolence, when not morally guided, are easily misdirected. Even the appeal to man's noblest emotions is, in itself, no guarantee of the moral value of the actions to which the emotions lead. The situation, in other words, is not as simple as Nowell-Smith makes it appear.

More important for our immediate purposes, however, is the fact that in our actual human situation one obligation often is in conflict with other obligations. Conflicts of this type are the truly moral conflicts; and they are crucial for any theory of ethics. Here, however, Ross is of little help to us; for he says: "In this region our knowledge is very limited. While we *know* certain types of action to be *prima facie* obligatory, we have only opinion about the degree of their obligatoriness. . . . While we can see with certainty that the claims exist, it becomes a matter of individual and fallible judgment to say which claim is in the circumstances the overriding one. . . . Each person must judge according to his individual sense of the comparative strength of various choices" (D:188-189). Here Ross is thoroughly mistaken in his analysis.

Although it is true that it is up to the individual to decide for himself the conflict of obligations in any concrete and actual situation, he need not do so without reference to objective and objectively discernible facts—the facts of his own prior commitments. Consider, first, an obvious and, therefore, a trivial example.

Let us suppose that I have promised you to have lunch with you but, after having made this commitment, I am asked to attend an important staff meeting during the lunch hour. Let us assume, furthermore, that I promised to have lunch with you simply because I enjoy your company, whereas the obligation to attend the staff meeting is entailed by my position on the faculty. It is now clear that, whereas my obligation towards you stems from a simple commitment directly made, my obligation to attend the staff meeting is part of a much broader and more encompassing duty which I assume by accepting the position I hold. As a reasonable and responsible person I can have no doubts as to what I ought to do in this case. I should certainly accept the principle that the more pervasive obligation must prevail. But this principle, of course, can be applied to innumerable situations of varying complexities and provides the first objective criterion to guide me.

But let us now consider an example which requires a somewhat different interpretation. Let us assume that, as a member of a certain society (as citizen of a state, for instance) I have certain fundamental duties (such as allegiance to the constitution of that state), and as member of some other group (as member of a certain church, for instance) I also have certain fundamental duties (such as to be loyal to the tenets of my church); and let us now assume that, in a given situation, my respective duties collide. What am I to do? There are those who will insist that I remain loyal to the secular state, and there are those who insist that I remain loyal to my church. In this situation I face two alternatives. The first is that I decide in favor of one or the other of the conflicting loyalties—in which case I do violence to the other and thus become guilty of a violation of my duty. The tragedy of our human existence lies essentially in this fact that in certain situations we must become guilty— morally guilty—of violating a basic obligation. It is in such cases that value considerations, i.e., considerations of the consequences of our actions, may mitigate our guilt to some extent. But, essentially, the conflict simply recurs at the value level.

The other alternative, however, is that, creatively, we rise to a new commitment which transcends and, therefore, integrates our conflicting obligations as partial truths within a new vision, a new all-encompassing commitment, a new humanity. The prophets of all times have taken this path. The principle underlying this course of action is a modification of the first principle stated above. It is a modification in the sense that the more pervasive obligation is not itself one of the alternatives in conflict but is the integrative surpassing of the conflict as such and the vision of a new and more comprehensive ideal—a new and more pervasive commitment. This modification of the first principle is a second objective criterion to guide us in our human-all-too-human situations of conflicts.

As Professor Kneale has shown (and at least some of the

deontologists would agree with him), there is a "close analogy" between the ways in which the lawyer and the moralist use such words as "right" (R:687). Both, for example, use the word "right" as equivalent to the phrase "in accordance with the law," and "A ought to do X" as meaning the same as "the law requires that A should do X" (R:685). But if this is so, then a distinction may be drawn between "obligatory," "indifferent," and "wrong" actions—actions being "indifferent" when they are "right but not obligatory." These distinctions correspond, on the one hand, to the distinctions between "necessary," "contingent," and "impossible" (at the level of cognition), and to the uses of "ought," "may," and "ought not" (at the level of common-sense proscriptions). The utilitarians, however,—and teleologists in general—must affirm or assume a complete and necessary coincidence between dutiful and good-producing acts; and this identification, since it does not allow for acts which are right but not obligatory, distorts the facts of man's moral existence. However, in so far as the deontologists adhere to a basic intuitionism, they, also, are unable to account for the facts. Only a specific, rationally supported interpretation of the ought will do justice to all the facts in the case and will enable us to preserve the distinctions between "obligatory," "indifferent" or "permissive," and "wrong."

## REFERENCES

1. Price, R., *A Review of the Principal Questions in Morals,* D. D. Raphael, editor, Oxford 1948. (Quoted as 'A'.)
2. Prichard, H. A., *Duty and Interest,* Oxford 1928; *Moral Obligation,* Oxford 1950. (Quoted as 'B'.)
3. Ross, Sir W. David, *The Right and the Good,* Oxford 1930; *Foundations of Ethics,* Oxford 1939. (Quoted as 'D'.)
4. Prichard, H. A., "Duty and Interest," in *Readings in Ethical Theory,* W. Sellars and J. Hospers, editors, New York 1952, 486. Also Falk, W. D., " 'Ought' and Motivation," *ibid.,* 495-496.
5. The references are here given in alphabetical order of their authors and are identified by capital letters.

    (E)    Baier, K. E. M., "S. Hamshire: Fallacies in Moral Philosophy; A Note," *Mind,* LIX (1950).

(F)    Baylis, Charles A., *Ethics: The Principles of Wise Choice,* New York 1958.

(G)    Broad, C. D., *"Moral Obligation:* Essays and Lectures by H. A. Prichard," *Mind,* LIX (1950).

(H)    Brown, St. M., Jr., "Duty and the Production of Good," *Philosophical Review,* LXI (1952).

(I)     Carritt, E. F., *The Theory of Morals; An Introduction to Ethical Philosophy,* Oxford 1928.

(J)     Garnett, A. Campbell, "Deontology and Self-Realization," *Ethics,* LI (1941).

(K)    Hall, E. W., "Practical Reason(s) and the Deadlock in Ethics," *Mind,* LXIV (1955).

(L)    Hamshire, S., "Fallacies in Moral Philosophy," *Mind,* LVIII (1949).

(M)    Hems, John M., "Subjective and Objective Rightness," *Philosophy and Phenomenological Research,* XV (1955).

(N)    Hill, Thomas E., *Ethics in Theory and Practice,* New York 1956.

(O)    Johnson, Oliver A., "Rightness, Moral Obligations, and Goodness," *Journal of Philosophy,* L (1953).

(P)    Johnson, Oliver A., *Rightness and Goodness: A Study in Contemporary Ethical Theory,* The Hague 1959.

(Q)    Joseph, H. W. B., *Some Problems in Ethics,* Oxford 1931.

(R)    Kneale, "Objectivity in Morals," in *Readings in Ethical Theory, op. cit.,* 681-697.

(S)    Maclagan, W. G., "How Important is Moral Goodness?," *Mind,* LXIV (1955).

(T)    Mandelbaum, Maurice, *The Phenomenology of Moral Experience,* Glencoe, Ill., 1955.

(U)    Mayo, Bernard, "Commitments and Reasons," *Mind,* LXIV (1955).

(V)    Nowell-Smith, P. H., *Ethics,* New York 1957.

(W)    Pickard, W. A., "Two Problems About Duty," *Mind,* XLI (1932).

(X)    Price, H. H., review of Ross, *The Right and the Good,* in *Mind,* XL (1931).

(Y)    Rees, W. J., "Moral Rules and the Analysis of 'Ought'," *Philosophical Review,* LXII (1953).

(Z)    Toulmin, S., "Knowledge of Right and Wrong," *Proceedings of the Aristotelian Society,* LI (1950-51).

*Conclusion*

# CHAPTER X

# Toward a Reorientation in Ethics

## I

The reader who compares the ethical theories of Moore, Ross, Stevenson and other modern writers with Aristotle's Nichomachean ethics, Bentham and Mill's Utilitarianism, or Nietzsche's transvaluation of values is forcefully impressed by the fact that, in our own days, philosophical ethics has undergone a radical transformation. Even the theories of Santayana, Perry, and Dewey reflect a philosophical approach which differs radically from that of our contemporary ethicists who are strongly influenced by ideas which originated in Vienna, Oxford, and Cambridge. The shift can perhaps be best understood when we keep in mind that actually there are three "levels" of investigation in ethics.

There is, first, the level of moral rules and imperatives as such, the level of laws and commandments by which men actually or presumably live. A study at this level may be anthropological in orientation—in which case it is the analysis of the moral patterns characteristic of particular cultures; or it may be primarily philosophical in orientation—in which case it is essentially an attempt to clarify accepted or implied rules and imperatives, or the discovery of new ones. We may call this the level of morality proper.

There is, however, a second level of philosophical inquiry—

the level of ethical theories. It is at this level that the various attempts are made to integrate the imperatives and rules of conduct into coherent systems of such a type that from a few basic definitions and broad principles the laws of conduct can be derived. Utilitarianism in all its forms, moral-sense theories, and the various doctrines of self-realization are classical examples of this level of investigation. This is the level of ethical theories as such. The aim is here to integrate moral codes much in the manner in which scientists integrate the laws of nature, deriving them from certain initial definitions and postulates.

But there is yet a third level of philosophical inquiry at which we are concerned with the meaning of ethical statements and with the clarification of the explicit or implicit presuppositions and justifications of ethical theories. This is the level of philosophical meta-ethics. Here the ethical theories themselves are critically evaluated, and the questions which must be answered before such theories can at all be constructed are raised and considered. It may be granted that at all times all three levels have been present in philosophical discussions—at least implicitly; but during the last fifty years or so the emphasis has definitely been shifted to the third level, and the interest of philosophers has been focused on meta-ethical problems.

Because of this peculiar orientation of modern ethical philosophy, it is not astonishing that the metaphysical problems inherent in ethics have generally been neglected by contemporary writers. "Nowhere," John Wild complains, "is moral analysis brought into any disciplined relation with a critical analysis of being" (44:463). As we shall see, however, a new trend may be emerging; for at least one major work published in 1960 culminates in suggestive metaphysical perspectives (2:201-226), pointing up the fact that our affective and conative experiences as such "are not only of or about reality but are also part of it" (2:226).

However, more important and of greater immediate urgency than the entailed metaphysical problems is the question of whether or not the recent shift towards meta-ethics makes any real difference at the level of moral codes and moral attitudes.

It may be (and has been) argued that differences in meta-ethical theories or even mistakes in analysis need not affect our actual use of moral concepts; that the meta-ethical level is so far removed from the level of morality proper and so dependent upon the latter that man's actions and attitudes remain unaltered by meta-ethical considerations. It can be shown, nevertheless, that "in at least one case, that of the emotive theory, the acceptance of a meta-ethical theory *does* affect our first order moral life" (*32*:160). "This effect is observable in a subtle modification of our procedures of moral judgment" and "occurs precisely because the theory is *not* merely an explication of our ordinary use of ethical words" (*32*:160) but an appeal to affect-accentuated conative decisions. It is, thus, an appeal to ultimately irrational factors in experience rather than to reason, an appeal to "emotive persuasion" rather than to rational analysis—an appeal which is bound to make a difference in our response to "moral imperatives." Why, for example, should I accept your conations as guide for my actions when what you intend or demand is counter to reason? Would you insist that right and good is but what you can persuade me to accept as right and good because of the emotive appeal or the conative force of the language you use? Such an attitude would clearly go counter to any common-sense interpretation of moral concepts and rules, and counter also to any conception of reasonableness in moral attitudes. Obviously, then, the goal of our inquiry must be the clarification and justification of the whole range of moral concepts. This means, however, the clarification and justification of the concepts and rules which directly govern man's actions and the goals and functioning of social institutions (*1*:571); but it also means the clarification and justification of ethical theories.

Now, "the primary evidence for the assertive character of the moral sentence [as distinguished from its emotive overtones] is the fact that common grammar so renders it" (*27*:241). The contention, therefore, that moral sentences are interjectional in character *and nothing else* (cf. Ayer) goes counter to this elementary fact. It cannot be denied, however, that, insofar as it is normative, the moral sentence also partakes of the nature of imperatives or commands. Indeed, we must admit that the moral sentence has all three characteristics: that of the assertive statement, that of an interjection, and that of a command. The ethical theories discussed in the preceding chapters are in themselves proof of this fact; for, be the key concept the "good" or be it the "right," each type of theory regards one aspect of moral statements as primary and makes it basic to the whole problem.

A possible solution of the difficulties which here arise has been suggested by Willis Moore who regards the hortatory sentence as the basic moral statement. "A hortatory sentence," he says, "is exactly like a simple assertion both in structure and . . . in first-stage semantic operation. . . . The hortatory or persuasive functioning of a sentence is . . . the second-stage semantic performance of what is structurally a simple assertion. The first stage is purely informative; the second stage is persuasively incitive" (27:243). It may be doubted, however, that this interpretation does full justice to such key concepts in morals as duty and obligation. Further analysis, at least, is required.

The counter-suggestion that all ethical statements serve either "to record a decision or to issue a command" (28:471) also reflects an incomplete analysis, for "the meaning of an ought-sentence [being normative] cannot be identified with or reduced to the meaning of a sentence expressing a decision" (28:475). It serves as a guide to making or evaluating a decision but does not express the decision (28:480). And so far as the "command theory" is concerned, it seems clear that (a) "we often make moral judgments in situations in which the assumption that we command the evaluated action is absurd or at least improbable," and that (b) "there is no reason to assume that the meaning of 'ought' changes in those cases in which a command is possible or even likely" (28:483). Moreover, a simple command-theory does not explain the difference between ethical and nonethical commands (28:483). That is, it does not explain why the moral "ought" derives its force from considerations of some rational ground, which is its justification, whereas the command proper is grounded only in the will of the commander. The difference is especially clear when we consider that a person can recognize and accept an "ought," but he cannot—except in a figurative sense—give himself a command.

A justification and evaluation of an "ought" is possible only if moral statements have cognitive meaning of some kind. In asserting this, however, we but return to the burden of the argument as developed throughout this book. But we can also appeal to the whole history of moral philosophy for support; for throughout that history the view has prevailed that moral judgments *are* cognitive. Noncognitive theories have come into prominence only during the last thirty years or so.[1]

Perhaps the dispute arises, as Glassen suggests, from the fact that moral judgments, though cognitive, are not descriptive in the ordinary sense (*11*:57-72). How, then, are they to be interpreted? Surely the ethicists of the past, who have adhered to various types of cognitive theories, have been fully aware of the fact that "ought"-statements and moral judgments have not been simply descriptive of empirical data. The normative character of such statements makes a purely descriptive empiricism impossible. But ethicists holding noncognitive views have, in general, rejected any recourse to synthetic a priori judgments and have recognized only two types of cognitive sentences: empirical and analytic propositions (*11*:59). The question is, Does this bifurcation cover the whole range of cognitive statements or are there statements which, being neither purely empirical (as that term is usually understood) nor analytic, are still cognitive?

To begin with, the bifurcation involved can itself be asserted only "a priori or on the basis of a survey" of all possible cognitive sentences (*11*:59). It is evident, however, that the assertion is not analytic. It can be justified, if at all, only on empirical grounds. And since this is the case, the question arises, Are there propositions, i.e., genuinely cognitive statements, which are

---

[1] See Carnap's thesis that "a value statement is nothing else than a command in a misleading grammatical form." Carnap, Rudolf, *Philosophy and Logical Syntax*, London, 1935, 24-25. An Ayer's assertion that "when I say that a certain type of action is right or wrong, and somebody else disagrees with me, 'there is plainly no sense in asking which of us is in the right. For neither of us is asserting a genuine proposition'." Ayer, A. J., *Language, Truth and Logic*, London, 1951, 108.

not descriptive of facts simple? An answer to this question can be given only when we take into account the intention of the speaker; when we understand what he means and what it is that he wishes to convey (*11*:60).

To be sure, even cognitive statements may contextually express that the speaker has certain feelings concerning the matter he speaks about *(31:passim)*, but this "emotive function" is incidental to their cognitive significance. At least it is evident from the characteristic features of moral discourse—in all languages and at all times—that moral judgments, like assertions, "seem to be intended to mean something" (*11*:62). That is to say, all moral judgments are presented in the indicative mood. Furthermore, as Glassen points out, there are the moral questions (e.g., Is it always wrong to lie?) which demand answers that apparently may be true or false, or that can (or do) have objective validity (*11*:63). There are the moral questions, in other words, which demand answers that have all the characteristics of cognitive statements. And, again following Glassen, there are certain complex statements (e.g., I know it was wrong, but. . . .) in which "moral judgments are indirectly referred to . . . as objects of cognition" (*11*:64). All of which is but evidence that, in ordinary discourse, people "intend to say something cognitive and are so understood" when they utter moral judgments. "On the imperative or emotive theory of moral judgments, such sentences as 'I know it's wrong to lie' . . . must either make no sense . . . , or be given a strained *ad hoc* interpretation" (*11*:64). In ordinary moral discourse we really mean that it is wrong to steal when we say "It is wrong to steal." In ordinary moral discourse, in other words, "it is quite appropriate to apply the terms 'true' or 'false' . . . to moral judgments" (*11*:65).

Moreover, in ordinary discourse "moral judgments have an impersonal character and objectivity is expected of those who make them" (*11*:66). Personal desires, emotions and prejudices are to be discounted in the case of moral judgments no less than in the case of factual assertions; and disagreement in moral judgment is not in all cases reducible to disagreement concerning empirical facts and/or disagreement merely in attitude. It may be a genuine disagreement concerning the truth or falsity of the moral judgment itself (*11*:71). Thus, one person may assert that lying is wrong under all circumstances, whereas someone else may hold that, under certain specifiable circumstances, it is not wrong. Both may agree in their attitude toward lying and both may agree on the facts in some concrete situation; but they could still disagree on the assertion that in this situation and under these circumstances lying is wrong, for they disagree with respect to the basic moral assertion.

This raises the question as to what, precisely, is the minimum requirement for a universally valid statement—be it in ethics or in any other field of cognition. The answer would seem to be "that it have the same meaning when uttered by different persons" (*32*:166). This requirement, however, is not fulfilled when moral assertions are interpreted in such a way as to make a reference to the person asserting them an essential part of the assertions themselves. The emotivists, as we have seen, do interpret them in just this way. We cannot expect, therefore, that the emotivists can provide a basis for universally valid moral statements.

The advocates of cognitive theories, on the other hand, maintain that moral principles are valid for everyone—even if, in actuality, some particular statement is not universally accepted (*32*:170). But if moral principles are universal in scope, by what reasoning can we permit exceptions to be made in special situations? (*13*:51-52). Patton has suggested that "we reason to a moral judgment from the facts of a situation, the moral principle(s) which the facts determine as relevant, and our knowledge of the classes of permissible exceptions which are associated with the moral principle(s)" (*33*:525). But this answer places the whole burden upon its last clause without suggesting a principle by means of which to determine possible exceptions. What is implied here is the necessity of including in the formulation of every moral principle a specification of every possible exception to it. This is a requirement impossible of fulfillment. Its fulfillment is impossible, not only because of practical considerations, but in principle. How, for example, should we decide in the case of a novel situation—and there arise situations which no one has faced before—whether or not an exception to an otherwise well-defined and relevant moral principle is permitted?

To this question an answer *in principle* is possible, and one which takes the problem out of the sphere of purely arbitrary decisions. But this answer assumes that, for the sake of human existence *as human,* certain principles of action are more basic and, therefore, more significant than are others. If, for the moment and for the sake of argument, such a "hierarchy" of principles be granted, if we may assume that some principles of action are more crucial than are others to a truly human existence, then our problem can readily be solved.

The solution is this: If in any concrete situation only one moral principle is involved, then decisions made in that situation must preserve the universality of the principle; for in such situations there is no reason whatsoever that would justify a violation or a limitation of the principle involved.

Unfortunately, however, human affairs, as a rule, are not that simple. In concrete situations two or more principles of action are usually involved, and our moral dilemmas arise because in any given situation we have obligations to pursue incompatible courses of action (*19*:811). We face here, not a problem of logical contradiction in principles, but one of the factual incompatibility of courses of action which, though each being good or right in itself, cannot all be pursued at the same time. The solution of the problem, derived from the standard indicated above, is that in such situations that course of action ought to prevail which best expresses, or most contributes to, a truly human existence. What is meant by "truly human existence" is, of course, a problem requiring further analysis, but one with which we shall not deal at this time.

## II

In our time, D. H. Monro has pointed out, the philosopher is faced, "in the first place, . . . by the logical objection to any form of naturalism: the impossibility of deriving 'ought' from 'is'; secondly, he is unlikely, in the prevailing climate of opinion, to feel satisfied with traditional forms of non-naturalism: with a transcendental world of values, for example, or with simple, unanalyzable, 'non-natural' qualities; thirdly, he is likely to feel that subjectivism, in any of its forms, fails to do justice to the way people actually think and behave. All the traditional answers, then, are unacceptable" (25:166). This raises the question, Where do we go from here?

One answer comes from a group of British philosophers (Hamshire, Hare, and Toulmin) who wish to safeguard "the place of reason in ethics" while, at the same time, they try to avoid all metaphysical commitments. Their concern is with concrete situations in which decisions must be made, and with the analysis of the meaning and the presuppositions of such decisions. More specifically, their basic question is, What is "a good reason" for making a certain decision? What is "a good reason" in ethics?

What complicates the matter is the fact that a decision is not just a logical inference from given descriptive propositions, but is also a declaration that "one ought to approve of, or pursue, or do something-or-other" (41:55), when the "ought" implies that the act is *worthy of* approval, or that the course of action is *worthy of* being pursued (41:71). The question, What is "a good reason" in ethics?, is therefore related to the question, What kinds of things or conditions make an action worthy of approval? That this question is akin to the question in science, What kinds of things or conditions make a conclusion worthy of belief?, is obvious. But the answer is not so clear. In the case of propositions of belief, recourse to facts in the case provides necessary and sufficient criteria. In the case of the propositions pertaining to the worth of an attitude or an action, however, recourse to the facts in the case or to purely descriptive propositions, while necessary, is not in itself sufficient.

Toulmin finds "the key to the logic of ethical arguments and sentences" in "the way in which we come to allow reasons to affect our choice of action" (41:131). At the basic level, so he reminds us, we are all members of some social group which, in the course of time, has evolved certain habitual or "standard" ways of doing things and, thus, has developed a "moral code." So long as one acts as a member of that group, i.e., "so long as one confines oneself to a particular moral code, no more general 'reason' can be given for an action than one which relates it to a practice (or principle) within that code" (*41*:148).

If one questions the rightness of a specific principle as part of a code, two answers may be possible: One is a "persuasive" appeal to the authority of tradition; the other is an attempt to show that the principle in dispute is a logical implicate of the basic conception of life which is central to that whole moral code. But let us suppose now that a skeptic challenges the authority of tradition and the very conception of life as reflected in the whole code as well. In all genuine "test cases" this is exactly what happens, either explicitly or by implication. And now the question returns with redoubled force: What are "good reasons" for accepting one moral code rather than another?

Toulmin suggests that the basis of all decisions in this matter is a "personal 'code'." In developing this "code" or "rule of life," we have "not only our own experience to guide us; we have the records which others have left of their attempts, failures and successes in the same quest, and the advice of friends and relatives" (*41*:157). "Given all this mass of experience, we can now 'reason' about proposed courses of action." The decision, however, "must be a personal one" (*41*:157).

This assertion—that, in the end, the decision must be a personal one—goes directly to the heart of the matter. It is here that the existentialists take their stand; and it is here that the crucial question arises, Why ought I do what is right? As far as Toulmin is concerned, this question can find no answer within the realm of ethics. "Ethical reasoning," he says, "may be able to show why we ought to do this action as opposed to that, . . . but it is no help where there is no choice" (*41*:162). Toulmin, therefore, restricts his discussions to questions more amenable to reason. That is to say, he restricts his discussions to problems within some given "code" or way of life. Even then, however, he finds that different people can agree in their ethical judgments only when they are fully informed *and* reasonable (*41*:165).

But let us assume now, with Toulmin, that moral reasoning has its place only within the framework of some established or generally accepted moral "code." Even then—and Toulmin admits this—"the moralist's task is not just to apply present principles to day-to-day problems. He must also be able to recognize when a principle or situation has outlived its usefulness" (*41*: 178) and what new practice or principle ought to replace it. This, obviously, requires criteria for the evaluation of moral practices or principles. And Toulmin suggests: "If the adoption of the practice would genuinely reduce conflicts of interest, it is a practice *worthy of adoption,* and if the way of life would genuinely lead to deeper and more consistent happiness, it is one *worthy of pursuit.* . . . If one asks me *why* they are 'good reasons,' I can only reply by asking in return, 'What better kinds of reason could you want?' " (*41*:224).

The significance of this argument must not be minimized. What better reasons indeed! Kurt Baier underscores the point when he says: "Our very purpose in 'playing the reasoning game' is to maximize satisfactions and minimize frustrations" (*3*:301). But it may be remembered that, earlier in this chapter, we distinguished three levels of analysis: that of moral propositions and judgments, that of ethics or ethical theories, and that of ethical philosophy. Toulmin never faces up to the problems of philosophical analysis in its ultimate sense (*cf.2*:123).

Baier presents a point of view which is similar in many respects to that of Toulmin. There is one aspect of the over-all problem, however, which Baier explicitly recognizes, whereas Toulmin deals with it only by implication. It is this: The "rules of reason" or "consideration-making beliefs" (as Baier calls them [*3*:95]) which serve as major premises of moral arguments "are not relative to particular situations or particular persons." "It is either true, or it is false, that the fact that some course of action is illegal is a good reason against entering on it. It cannot be true for me, false for you" (*3*:96). That is to say, "all consideration-making beliefs are person-neutral. They are simply true or false" (*3*:98). With the explicit recognition of this fact the basic thesis of emotivism in all its forms has been abandoned. And so we find that, for Toulmin as well as for Baier, "a good reason for an ethical judgment is a factual statement which in conjunction with an imperative premise logically entails the imperative of the conclusion" (*2*:126).

Still unsolved, however, is the problem of the basic imperative that can serve as the major premise of all moral reasoning. Toulmin holds that this imperative may simply be our obligation "to correlate our feelings and behavior in such a way as to make the fulfillment of everyone's aims and desires as far as possible compatible" (*41*:137). It is clear, however, that such an imperative, even if we were to accept it, is not logically derivable from the aims and desires in question. Nowell-Smith suggests that what is required is contextual rather than logical derivation (*31*:81). But contextual derivation implicitly assumes the crucial premises and so cannot serve as a special way of deriving the key imperative. Hare has seen this clearly. "If pressed to justify a decision completely," he says, "we have to give a complete specification of the way of life of which it is a part. . . . If the inquirer still goes on asking 'But why *should* I live like that?,' then there is no further answer to give him. . . . We can only ask him to make up his own mind which way he ought to live; for in the end everything rests upon such a decision of principle" (*13*:69). We are driven back to the thesis that "choices are . . . ultimately arbitrary, that is, non-rational" (*14*:688).

Actually, of course, every decision concerning some specific problem at hand is also a decision concerning the principle of action involved (*2*:154); for it is a decision as to whether we shall re-affirm the principle by conforming to it in our actions, or shall repudiate it by non-conforming. In this fact lies the freedom we have of which the existentialists make so much— the freedom to determine our future arbitrarily. But let us consider the whole problem from still another angle; for it is possible that the purely arbitrary aspect can be eliminated from our crucial decisions.

Emotivists and positivists maintain that "truth and falsity are terms not applicable to statements asserting the existence of moral values" (*14*:688); and if the reference is to an independent realm of values—such as that suggested by Nicolai Hartmann—then the emotivists and positivists have the better of the argument. But another approach is possible.[2] Frances Herring, for example, has argued that "primary value is a subjective quality of experience . . . possessing a *tone* . . . and differing . . . in degrees of *intensity* and . . . [in] *duration*" (*14*:689). And if this is so, then "propositions asserting something about primary values may be: (1) Simple or complex descriptions of the intuited or inferred quality of experience . . . [or] (2) Analyses of inter-relationships observed to hold among concrete instances of primary values" (*14*:689). In either case such propositions may be true or false and, therefore, are genuinely cognitive.

The question now is, How do "moral values" differ from the "primary values" just referred to? Herring's answer is that (1) moral value is not a value in its own right "but only by virtue of its capacity to affect primary values"; and that (2) "it is attributable exclusively to . . . human intensions and the choices and deeds resulting therefrom; and . . . to human characters having purposes" (*14*:690). More specifically, "the precise relation between primary values and the truth of propositions about moral values is this: proof that the primary values affected by a moral choice are, on balance, not positive furnishes the only *reason* for a choice being judged morally good or bad" (*14*:693). Herring is willing, therefore, to agree with the objectivists that "propositions about moral value are not relative to the viewpoint of the particular person asserting them"; but he is also ready to agree with the emotivists in holding that "the truth of propositions about primary values is relative to the

---

2 *Cf.* Werkmeister, W. H., "Problems of Value Theory," *Philosophy and Phenomenological Research,* XII (1950). Werkmeister, W. H., "Ethics and Value Theory," *Proceedings of the Eleventh International Congress of Philosophy,* Brussels, 1953, X. Werkmeister, W. H., "Prolegomena to Value Theory," *Philosophy and Phenomenological Research,* XIV (1954). Werkmeister, W. H., *Outlines of a Value Theory,* Istanbul, 1959. Werkmeister, W. H., "The Meaning and Being of Values Within the Framework of an Empirically Oriented Value Theory," in *Sinn und Sein,* Richard Wisser, Editor. Tübingen, 1960.

existence of the subjective states they assert to be occurring" (*14*:693). His problem, therefore, is to find some way of rising from the subjectivity of "primary" experience to the objectivity of moral judgments. As a solution of this problem he suggests that we take into consideration the possibility of predicting "primary" value experiences. When we do so, we find that reason is relevant to morality, for it is only on the basis of a rational interpretation of past experience, of the present situation, and of the means at our disposal that we can arrive at a reliable prediction that some particular course of action will be "most value-productive" (*14*:695).

But Herring goes a step farther. He also argues that "it is unreasonable to maintain that the *de facto* values of other persons affected by one's choices or deeds are irrelevant to the morality of one's acts" (*14*:696). "Occurrence in my subjective experience rather than in yours is not a dimension of *intrinsic* quality, but an external relation which admittedly can vary without altering the character of the experience as such" (*14*: 697). That is to say, according to Herring's argument, if "peace of mind" is a primary value, then it is irrelevant to its character *as value* whether I experience it or you do. Hence, "if *intrinsicness* is admitted as the ground for selecting primary values as determinative of the claim to moral value," then "the egoistic hedonist is inconsistent" (*14*:697).

There is much truth in Herring's arguments. His references to the implications of the "intrinsic quality" of primary values are especially important. There remains, however, as an unsolved problem the crucial question of the "ought." Even granted that the "intrinsic quality" of primary values entails the inconsistency of "the egoistic hedonist," why *ought* I to be just (for example), if in being just I enhance your primary value experience but deprive me of mine? Why *ought* I to be honest, if, by being dishonest, I can enhance your primary value experience as well as mine? Why *ought* I to keep a promise, if neither your nor my primary value experience is thereby affected one way or another?

Kant and the deontologists and, more recently, C. I. Lewis [3] and John Wild (44:471-473) all have argued that basic imperatives are involved in our very existence as human beings. The nature of this "involvement," however, requires further elucidation. What must be accounted for is the fact that moral imperatives have an "authority" which cannot be understood when the imperatives are assumed to have a merely *de facto* status within a consistent naturalism (2:166); and "any position which has to explain away [the authority of the imperatives] is to that extent unsatisfactory" (2:182-183). What must be realized is that "primary values" and basic approvals and disapprovals "are not simply the effect of certain causal conditions [as a consistent naturalism would have it], but are subject to being appraised as correct or incorrect" (2:187); that they are not completely interpretable by "the descriptive-explanatory method of modern science" (2:187) but entail a "value-requiredness" which is prior and foundational to any feelings of approval or disapproval. The experience of this "value-requiredness" is as basic for value theory as is perceptual experience for our descriptive sciences. In both cases the "primary" experience is already "cognitive," and our thoughts interpreting that experience assume the essentially rational nature of man—in the one case as in the other. As Hare puts it: "We cannot get out of being men; and therefore moral principles . . . cannot be accepted without having a potential bearing upon the way that we conduct ourselves" (13:162). Indeed, they cannot be accepted without having a bearing upon what we are as human beings.

As human beings, however, we have a nature which "prescriptively requires that we have good reasons for what we do" (2:198). In and through value-experience, therefore, we know a categorial feature of reality not otherwise open to inspection or analysis. Value theory and ethics thus open up metaphysical perspectives and raise questions of a complex and intricate kind. It cannot be said, however, that all questions arising at the non-metaphysical level have already been answered.

---

[3] Lewis, C. I., *The Ground and Nature of the Right,* New York, 1955, 85-86.

## III

It is implicit in Hare's thesis "that a way of life cannot be justified but only described" (25:176). Anthropologists, on the whole, would agree; and Toulmin specifically points out that, reason as we may about the ultimate meaning of "being human," "the final decision is personal" (41:153). But if this is so, then it follows at once that Hitler's Germany represented a "way of life" which cannot be challenged on moral grounds, all opposition being in the end but a "personal decision." But is there not also good sense to the thesis that, in some way, the meaning of "being human" transcends our arbitrary decisions, and that this meaning provides a necessary and sufficient basis for justifying and approving some of our decisions and for condemning others, not only as "imprudent," but as morally wrong? In other words, is there not also good sense to the thesis that a "way of life" may be challenged on moral grounds?

Perhaps an answer to this question can be found when we consider what it means to approve or disapprove something.

To begin with, it is evident that we can speak meaningfully of approval or disapproval only when the objects or conditions to be approved or disapproved are "completely subject to human control" (35:202). It makes no sense to speak of our approval or disapproval of the law of relativity or of cause and effect relationships. But it does make sense to speak of our approval or disapproval of human actions and decisions—at least so long as we can assume that man is free and, therefore, responsible for both. Common sense and societal practice imply as much.

However, as Pitcher has shown, at least one further condition is necessary: When we approve (disapprove) of something, we must have reasons for doing so. "Whereas one can like, want, or desire something without knowing why, one cannot approve of something without knowing why" (35:205). Approval (disapproval) depends on some kind of evaluation which claims objective validity. Not to have taken this fact into consideration was one of the deficiencies we found in the emotivists' theories.

If what we approve (disapprove) is some specific object,

action, or situation, the reason why we approve (disapprove) of it may simply be that it is a member of some particular class of objects, actions, or situations, and that we approve (disapprove) of this class. Because we approve (disapprove) of the class, therefore we ought to approve (disapprove) of the individual members. In referring thus to the class we have transcended our immediate liking (disliking) of the particular object, action, or situation which now confronts us, and our act implies that whosoever approves (disapproves) of the class *ought* to approve (disapprove) of its members. This, however, cannot be a terminal argument; for the question now is, Why do we approve (disapprove) of the class?

An appeal to "moral feelings" will here not do. The use of moral judgments to express our feelings is but one—and by no means the most important—function of "moral rhetoric" (*40*: 699-700). In fact, inherent in the common-sense function of moral language is a belief in "a fixed moral order in which it makes sense to claim universal validity for a moral principle" (*39*:25). Even with this fact as our starting-point, however, certain distinctions must be made. They are crucial to our whole problem.

In the first place, as Paul Edwards has pointed out, we must distinguish between "value-judgments" and "judgments of obligation." That is to say, we must distinguish between "judgments having as their predicate 'good,' 'desirable,' 'worthwhile,'" and "sentences containing 'ought,' 'oblige,' or 'duty'" (*9*:141). In the case of the value judgments, however, we must go beyond this classification and must distinguish further between statements of simple *valuation*—statements, that is, which contain the word "good" (or its equivalent) in the sense of "I like it," "I desire it"—statements of *evaluation*—statements, that is, which contain the word "good" (or its equivalent) in the sense of "worthy of being desired" or "ought to be pursued." And when this distinction is made, we are confronted with an ambiguity in the meaning of "ought." There is, on the one hand, the "ought" of morality, the "moral ought"—which we encounter in the form of duty; and there is, on the other hand, the "axiological ought" which we encounter in the pursuit of values. As is evident from the preceding chapters, each form of the "ought" has at one time or another been made the key concept of some theory of ethics. Our problem will be to show their interrelations.

Daya has suggested that the moral ought is "primarily concerned with the other persons among whom one finds oneself," whereas the axiological ought is "oriented to aspects, objects, and situations which have no direct relevance to persons other than oneself" (7:634). The reason which Daya gives for his distinction is that, in the case of the moral ought, "the interactive behavior of persons is always oriented to role-expectations which are defined in terms of patterned norms" whose fulfillment is "the *conditio sine qua non* of the functioning and, thus, the very existence of any social system," whereas, in the case of the axiological ought, the "obligatoriness" of the ought "has no such complementary character" (7:635). It must be admitted, however, that this argument is not convincing—and this for several reasons.

In the first place, there is patterned "interactive behavior"— such as considerations of politeness and "good form"—which finds no proper place in Daya's classification. More importantly, however, one may have obligations to oneself which cannot readily be interpreted in terms of patterned norms of interactive behavior of persons, but which yet must be regarded as moral. Thus, for example, our obligation to "authentic existence"—in the sense in which existentialists use this term—is a moral and not an axiological obligation. The argument of the existentialists are here convincing.

In the third place, Daya's emphasis upon "the very existence of any social system" as the *sine qua non* of moral obligation completely neglects the crucial case in which it may be our moral duty to rise above the established "norms" governing the "interactive behavior of persons" in order to create new patterns and a new society. This is the case wherever a new vision, a new ideal of humanity is at stake. The whole progress of human culture finds its moral roots in such transcending of the established patterns of "interactive behavior."

'Frankel has argued that "moral imperatives" are but imperatives of a certain kind: Whereas imperatives in general are
concerned with "the control or re-direction of particular bits of
behavior, *moral* imperatives are peculiarly concerned with the
control or re-direction of attitudes" (*10*:263). But this attempt
at a distinction also falls short of the mark, for the axiological
ought, no less than the moral, is concerned with "the control
or re-direction of attitudes." "I ought to pursue what is worthy
of pursuit in the arts and in literature" is an imperative concerned with the control or re-direction of my attitudes, but it
can hardly be said to be moral in the sense in which "I ought
to keep my promise" is a moral imperative. And it remains true
that "bits of behavior" may be but reflections of the attitudes
we take. The distinction which Frankel seems to have in mind,
and for which his arguments provide support, is that of commands ("Squads, right!") and moral imperatives. But to the
extent to which this distinction is intended, his whole discussion
misses the point with which we are here concerned.

A still different suggestion—that "non-moral imperatives are
always hypothetical" and may be divided into advices and demands—was made by John C. Harsanyi (*13a*:306). But if it
were true that "non-moral imperatives are always hypothetical,"
how could we justify the basic axiological imperative, "Always
pursue what is worthy to be pursued"? Here we are clearly
concerned with ends, not with means—unless we were to argue
that even here a suppressed conditional is assumed, to wit: "If
you want to be a rational human being. . . ." In this case, however,
the relationship involved is not a means-end relation, for the
pursuit of that which is worthy of pursuit is not a *means* to being
a rational human being, it is *being* such a being.

Harsanyi further maintains that "if we regard moral rules as
possible reasons (*i.e.* rational motives) for a person to perform
the acts enjoined by these rules," then the moral rules themselves
can be interpreted "only as hypothetical imperatives" (*13a*:
307). Thus, to use Harsanyi's own example, "If you want to
follow Christian ethics, do X." But this interpretation does not
account for the stringency of duty and moral obligation which

Kant and the deontologists have found to be characteristic of the moral ought. That Harsanyi himself is not satisfied with the interpretation of the moral ought in terms of hypothetical imperatives is evident from the fact that he supplements his thesis by combining it with Adam Smith's theory of "the impartially sympathetic observer" (*13a*:309). He then can give to moral rules the form: "If you want to do what an impartially sympathetic observer would recommend for general observance, do X (or refrain from Y)." But, as we have already seen, "[this] theory makes moral rules hypothetical imperatives of the non-causal type" (*13a*:311) and, in the opinion of its author, "comes very close to Kant's" (*13a*:310). In the process, however, we have lost the distinction between an axiological and a moral ought; and this distinction, it seems to me, is crucial for a clear understanding of value theory no less than of ethics, and of their specific interrelations.

But it may now be argued that the whole position which stresses the special character of normative or "ought" statements is wrong; that, indeed, we commit the "moralistic fallacy" when we maintain "that moral judgments are of a different order from factual judgments" (*26*:29). The argument rests upon the assertion that in ethics, as in science, we come ultimately up against "brute facts," which "simply are what they are" and cannot be explained (*26*:31). Such an argument, of course, does not in itself eliminate the problem of the "ought," for the "ought," in all its forms, may simply be a "brute fact" of human experience. Kant, for one, took it as such. Bernard Peach, on the other hand, does not take it in this sense. "Ethical knowledge," he says, ultimately advocates "certain *posits* as a basis for action" (*26*:34; italics added); and: "when we are faced with an ethical choice, the only problem is one of knowing what the consequences of the alternative courses of action will be" (*26*:39). But such a theory, it seems to me, is deficient in at least two respects. In the first place, in reducing all moral problems to problems of evaluating consequences, it eliminates the distinction between a moral ought and an axiological ought, and eliminates, therefore, the unique character of ethics as compared with a general value theory. In the second place, however, by reducing all ultimates to "posits," this theory provides no basis for dealing adequately with the problem of "ends sought." At best it reduces to a form of Hedonism and is therefore subject to all the criticisms advanced earlier against that position. Peach himself, however, holds that "the actual genesis of ethics is simply human ignorance of the consequences of action" (26:41), and thereby distorts completely the meaning and the basis of the moral ought, for the ought arises precisely because we know what is involved in a given situation and what the consequences of our actions will be. If we find that we are mistaken about the situation, the ought vanishes or is altered in some respects (17:495).

Does this mean that the "ought" is derived from the situational "is"? This question is not sufficiently precise to permit a univocal answer. If it means, Do we logically derive obligation-statements from descriptive-existential statements?, then the answer is an unequivocal No. This does not preclude the fact, however, that we assert obligation-statements on the basis of the existential conditions themselves (17:499). As Kattsoff puts it: "The obligation is somehow *in* the state of affairs; or it is some sort of trait which the situation exhibits," and "we 'derive' the obligation-statement from the existential situation by somehow recognizing in it the obligation trait" (17:500). But now the question is, Just what is the "obligation trait" in a given situation? However, before answering this question, let us examine more closely the nature of ought-statements.

Hare holds that all ought-statements entail an imperative (13:171). It would seem, however, that this is not a correct analysis. Ought-statements imply—as imperatives do not—that there are grounds or good reasons which support them (31:81-82). They have a "legitimacy-claim" (18:654) which, in some sense, corresponds to the truth-claim of purely descriptive statements. Moreover, ought-statements imply that anyone familiar with the situation to which they pertain will regard them worthy of assent (41:71ff). This means, however, that the grounds justifying an ought-statement must somehow be rooted in the "logic" of the situation and cannot be psychological only (18:

659). They must be discoverable by ethical reasoning. When obligations are in conflict in any given situation, there must be some rational ground for resolving the conflict (36:252), although, to be sure, not all conflicts can be resolved without our violating one or the other of our obligations. Nicolai Hartmann has pointed this out most emphatically and definitively. The ultimate appeal can in all cases be only to the general reasonableness of our decisions and actions, and to specifiable criteria of "more comprehensive" (or "higher") and "less comprehensive" (or "lower") obligations. What these criteria are can be determined only by further investigation.

## IV

Before coming to the conclusion of our argument, let me repeat that the distinction between the "axiological" and the "moral" ought is crucial to a true understanding of the whole range of problems encountered in the philosophy of ethics. The axiological ought pertains to value theory in its broadest aspects and implies the normative character of evaluative judgments wherever value preferences are expressed. It pertains, in other words, to the question, What values ought I to cherish or to pursue? What is worthy of being cherished or pursued?, and, in this sense, it is concerned with ends as well as with means. But the moral ought is of a different nature. It does not directly pertain to means or to ends. It simply points up an obligation which I have to do (or not to do) a certain act. A familiar example is the obligation to keep one's promise.

This obligation does not "derive" from the promise; it is the very heart of the promise itself. To make a promise is but to assume an obligation; and psychological considerations are beside the point. To be sure, whether or not I live up to my obligation may depend upon various conditions—psychological as well as situational; but the fact that making the promise creates the obligation is unaffected by such extrinsic considerations.

Another question, of course, is, Why should I promise something in the first place? It is here that value considerations come into play; for it is because I wish to preserve or bring about a situation which I value that I make the promise. The obligatoriness, however—the "I ought to do what I promised"—stems from the promise *as promise,* not from the value considerations which induced me to make the promise. The axiological ought, on the other hand, is thoroughly enmeshed in those value considerations and evaluations.

If it now be argued that "we do not create obligations except by doing something that is distinct from the obligation" itself (*24*:51), then this argument may well be accepted as valid, but it does not affect the position here outlined. After all, making a promise is an act which takes place here and now, but which binds us for a specified or indefinite future (*24*:54). So there is a distinction here in at least this respect of time. This difference in the time element, however, also makes possible misrepresentation and deceit (*24*:57); and so there appears to be at least one other distinction between promise and obligation. However, a "deceitful promise" it not a promise at all; it is simply a deceitful use of language. This means, however, that, in promising, I resolve to act in conformity with what I promise; that my promise is but an expression of my resolve; that I accept what I promise as an obligation. It is still true, therefore, that the assuming of an obligation in and through a promise is of the very essence of the promise itself.

If circumstances prevent me from performing the action which I promised, this does not in itself relieve me of my obligation. "A promise once made is made" (*24*:58); and with every promise I make I myself as a morally responsible agent am at stake (*24*:61). However, in consideration of "mitigating circumstances," I may be relieved of my obligation—especially if the person to whom I made the promise cancels it. To abrogate a promise arbitrarily is a "breach of promise" and, as such, a violation of a moral obligation.

Our Interpretation so far is incomplete in two essential respects. On the one hand, I have used promise-making as but an example of the kind of actions which entail moral obligations. On the other hand, we have considered only the simple case of a single obligation in a given situation. Human existence, unfortunately, is not as simple as this.

In order to make the first point clear, I should like to speak of commitments rather than of promises—implying a somewhat generalized conception of the act leading to moral obligations. Commitments may be made explicitly—as when we take the oath of allegiance on becoming citizens of a country not that of our birth; or they may be made implicitly—as when we assume citizenship simply by virtue of our birth in a certain country and by remaining in that country. And it is clear from the example of citizenship that our commitment may indeed be far-reaching, complex, and not evident in its full scope at any one time. In committing ourselves to uphold the Constitution of the United States, to be a bit more specific, we commit ourselves also to the observance of all laws now in existence or yet to be adopted under that constitution. Moreover, our example also shows in what sense moral obligation is basic to legal obligation, the latter arising from the established laws of the land.

However, as citizens we are also members of a highly complex social order, not merely of a politico-legal system; and diverse obligations arise because of our commitments to the various groups and subgroups of that order. As husband and wife we have our commitments; and we have them as scholars or merchants or day laborers. But, most important of all, we have them as human beings—as members, that is, of the human race, inheritors of a cultural tradition and sharers in human hopes and aspirations; and in our commitment to this society, actual and ideal, we assume obligations entailed by the commitment. Moreover, in each and every one of our commitments we ourselves are at stake as moral agents; and we are most at stake—at stake in our whole being as human—in our commitment to an enlightened humanity. Whether or not or why we should make such commitments is a problem for value theory and involves the axiological ought. But once we have made the commitments, our moral obligation is inescapable—or can be escaped only at the price of our own existence as a moral being.

These considerations lead us at once to our second and last

point. It is now evident why in any concrete situation not just one obligation is involved, and why there can be conflicts of obligations in such situations. To use an obvious example: My commitments to the ideal of a truly enlightened humanity— Kant's "Kingdom of Ends," Royce's "Beloved Community," or whatever other name we may give it—may entail obligations which are in sharp conflict with obligations entailed by my commitments to our actually existing social order. Because of this conflict I may not be able to live up to all my obligations. The sharper the conflict, the more difficult it may be to do so. Still, as a reasonable human being I may find it possible most of the time to remain true to the essentials of my obligations by helping to shape the actual so that it resembles ever more fully the envisioned ideal. In this process I am not merely at stake as a responsible moral agent; in it I also find the fulfillment of myself as a human being. That, despite my best efforts, I may not be able to eliminate all conflicts and may therefore become guilty of violating some of my moral obligations is part of the tragedy of human existence. But the hope lies in molding actuality ever more closely in harmony with the ideal.

## REFERENCES

1. Adams, E. M., "The Nature of Ethical Inquiry," *Journal of Philosophy*, XLVIII, 1951, 569-574.
2. Adams, E. M., *Ethical Naturalism and the Modern World-View*, Chapel Hill, 1960.
3. Baier, Kurt, *The Moral Point of View*, Ithaca, N. Y., 1958.
4. Beardsley, Elizabeth Lane, "Moral Worth and Moral Credit," *Philosophical Review*, LXVI, 1957, 304-328.
5. Blackstone, William Thomas, "Objective Emotivism," *Journal of Philosophy*, LV, 1958, 1054-1062.
6. Boughton, J. S., "Concerning Moral Absolutes," *Journal of Philosophy*, LV, 1958, 309-317.
7. Daya, "The Moral and the Axiological 'Ought'—An Attempt at a Distinction," *Journal of Philosophy*, LIII, 1956, 634-641.
8. Edel, Abraham, *Ethical Judgment*, Glencoe, Ill., 1955.
9. Edwards, Paul, *The Logic of Moral Discourse*, Glencoe, Ill., 1955.
10. Frankel, Charles, "Empiricism and Moral Imperatives," *Journal of Philosophy*, L, 1953, 257-269.

11. Glassen, P., "The Cognitivity of Moral Judgments," *Mind,* LXVIII, 1959, 57-72.
12. Grave, S. A., "Are the Analyses of Moral Concepts Morally Neutral?", *Journal of Philosophy,* LV, 1958, 455-460.
13. Hare, R. M., *The Language of Morals,* Oxford, 1952.
13a. Harsanyi, John C., "Ethics in Terms of Hypothetical Imperatives," *Mind,* LXVII, 1958, 305-316.
14. Herring, Frances W., "What Has Reason to do With Morality?," *Journal of Philosophy,* L, 1953, 688-698.
15. Jarvis, Judith, "In Defense of Moral Absolutes," *Journal of Philosophy,* LV, 1958, 1043-1053.
16. Kading, Daniel, "Re-defining Moral Judgments," *Journal of Philosophy,* LIII, 1956, 513-523.
17. Kattsoff, Louis O., "Obligation and Existence," *Philosophy and Phenomenological Research,* XVII, 1958, 489-502.
18. Ladd, John, "The Distinctive Features of Obligation-Statements," *Journal of Philosophy,* LIII, 1956, 653-662.
19. Ladd, John, "Remarks on the Conflict of Obligations," *Journal of Philosophy,* LV, 1958, 811-819.
20. Lafleur, Laurence, J., "The Transition to Ethics," *Journal of Philosophy,* LII, 1955, 571-580.
21. Mandelbaum, Maurice, *The Phenomenology of Moral Experience,* Glencoe, Ill., 1955.
22. Mandelbaum, Maurice, "On the Use of Moral Principles," *Journal of Philosophy,* LIII, 1956, 662-670.
23. Margolis, Joseph, "Some Famous Ghosts in Ethical Theory," *Journal of Philosophy,* LI, 1954, 549-559.
24. Melden, A. I., "On Promising," *Mind,* LXV, 1956, 49-66.
25. Monro, D. H., "Are Moral Problems Genuine?," *Mind,* LXV, 1956, 166-183.
26. Moore, Edward C., "The Moralistic Fallacy," *Journal of Philosophy,* LIV, 1957, 29-42.
27. Moore, Willis, "The Nature of the Moral Sentnce," *Journal of Philosophy,* LV, 1958, 240-248.
28. Moser, Shia, "Decisions, Commands, and Moral Judgments," *Philosophy and Phenomenological Research,* XVII, 1958, 471-488.
29. Mothersill, Mary, "The Use of Normative Language," *Journal of Philosophy,* LII, 1955, 401-411.
30. Mothersill, Mary, "Moral Knowledge," *Journal of Philosophy,* LVI, 1959, 755-763.
31. Nowell-Smith, P. H., *Ethics,* New York, 1957.
32. Olafson, Frederick A., "Meta-Ethics and the Moral Life," *Philosophical Review,* LXV, 1956, 159-178.
33. Patton, Thomas E., "Reasoning in Moral Matters," *Journal of Philosophy,* LIII, 1956, 523-531.
34. Peach, Bernard, "Analysis and Criteriology in Philosophy of Ethics," *Journal of Philosophy,* LII, 1955, 561-571.

35. Pitcher, George, "On Approval," *Philosophical Review,* LXVII, 1958, 195-211.
36. Rescher, Nicholas, "Reasoned Justification of Moral Judgments," *Journal of Philosophy,* LV, 1958, 248-255.
37. Rice, Philip Blair, "Ethical Empiricism and Its Critics," *Philosophical Review,* LXII, 1953, 355-373.
38. Sibley, W. M. "The Rational Versus the Reasonable," *Philosophical Review,* LXII, 1953, 554-560.
39. Taylor, Paul W., "The Normative Function of Metaethics," *Philosophical Review,* LXVII, 1958, 16-32.
40. Taylor, Paul W., "Moral Rhetoric, Moral Philosophy, and the Science of Morals," *Journal of Philosophy,* LVI, 1959, 689-704.
41. Toulmin, Stephen, *An Examination of the Place of Reason in Ethics,* Cambridge, 1950.
42. Walhout, Donald, "Is and Ought," *Journal of Philosophy,* LIV, 1957, 42-48.
43. Walsh, V. C., "Ascriptions and Appraisals," *Journal of Philosophy,* LV, 1958, 1062-1072.
44. Wild, John, "Tendency: The Ontological Ground of Ethics," *Journal of Philosophy,* XLIX, 1952, 461-475.

# Subject Matter

# Names

443